Love on the Racks

Love on the Racks

A History of American Romance Comics

MICHELLE NOLAN

McFarland & Company, Inc., Publishers
Jefferson, North Carolina, and London

LIBRARY OF CONGRESS CATALOGUING-IN-PUBLICATION DATA

Nolan, Michelle, 1948–
Love on the racks : a history of American romance comics / Michelle Nolan.
p.   cm.
Includes bibliographical references and index.

ISBN 978-0-7864-3519-7
illustrated case binding : 50# alkaline paper ∞

1. Romance comic books, strips, etc.—United States—History and criticism.   I. Title.
PN6725.N65   2008   741.5'3543—dc22   2008005116

British Library cataloguing data are available

Cover art ©2008 Shutterstock

Manufactured in the United States of America

McFarland & Company, Inc., Publishers
Box 611, Jefferson, North Carolina 28640
www.mcfarlandpub.com

For Bud Plant:
for four decades, the most trustworthy friend
anyone could wish for.

For Jim Vadeboncoeur, Jr., and Karen Lane:
always willing to share valuable insights
and to challenge me to be better.

For Dan Stevenson:
the ultimate comic collector, indexer
and all-around good guy.

For my son Ray Nolan, his wife Nikol
and their daughter Logan Grace:
with all my love and respect.

Table of Contents

Preface

This is the first book completely devoted to the obscure world of romance comics, which were produced by numerous American publishers, almost entirely from 1947 to 1977, and have vanished from the landscape. Nearly 6,000 issues with love themes appeared on the racks, yet little has been written about this significant aspect of Americana.

This volume is the result of the encouragement I received from dozens of collectors (you know who you are!) during the years I wrote 100 consecutive installments of the "Nolan's Notebook" column for *Comic Book Marketplace*, until the magazine expired in 2005. Encouragement continued from readers of my ensuing column in the monthly *Comics Buyer's Guide*. More than two dozen involved the romance genre and some of that research appears here, in modified form. "You should write an entire book on romance comics," numerous enthusiasts have told me. Here, then, is that book.

Romance comics were among the most commercially successful comics produced in the era before comic book specialty stores began to bloom in the 1970s. Aspects of fantasy and super heroics assumed almost total domination of the mainstream field, leaving behind other genres, including romance. There were times, however, in the 1950s when one in every four or five issues sold on the newsstands of America was a romance comic.

I have tried to cover the topic broadly, given more than 40 years of experience as a newspaper feature writer and more than 50 years as a collector. I seek to appeal not only to those with limited knowledge of the often arcane nature of romance comics, yet also to avid fans who already know much about them. With more than 25,000 romance stories to choose from, I have inevitably left out or given short shrift to someone's favorite story, title or artist.

I've included information about the types of stories and their creators, plus the history, numbers and publishing frequency of the titles, along with coverage of censorship, not a little sociological speculation, and how and why romance comics started and ended. I've included lots of numbers along with talk of themes, simply because I feel the numbers are important and the information is available nowhere else. I have, however, tried to avoid making all these numbers confusing.

A few leading collectors and historians—affable and knowledgeable people like Bud Plant, Jim Vadeboncoeur, Jr., John Benson, Dan Stevenson, Trina Robbins, Gary Watson and Stan Molson—have also long pursued romance comics, among others. They have all been of wonderful help in my research over the years. John Lustig of "Last Kiss" cartoon fame has provided welcome enthusiasm. Editors Maggie Thompson and Brent Frankenhoff of *Comic Buyer's Guide* and Roy Thomas of *Alter Ego*, along with Steve Borock and Bill Schelly, have been unfailingly supportive. I also thank Patty and Bob Lundquist for heartfelt encouragement.

How do I know so much firsthand information about romance comics? I have a collection of more than half of all issues published, plus I have received expert help. Since the 1980s, the unselfish Jim Vadeboncoeur, Jr., and Dan Stevenson have pooled information with me from our burgeoning collections. We made numerous amusing and amazing discoveries along the way, and were aided by a multitude of comic art enthusiasts. The result is the appendix in this book—the first complete list of the original generation of American romance comics ever published. We long ago learned to say "never say never"—and a discovery or two may remain to be made—but we believe our information to be as complete and accurate as humanly possible.

Readers may wonder why I can so confidently rattle off figures such as the total number of romance issues published in 1950 or the total number of romance comics to come from a given company, or how many even a given decade. The answer is simple: I could never have confidence in these numbers if Dan Stevenson and I had not been such exacting list-makers, with immense help from Jim Vadeboncoeur, Jr. Together, we have worked for more than two decades to verify the existence of every single issue of all genres, but especially romance comics. Dan, in fact, owns all but a handful of all romance comics.

In short, we have taken "trust but *verify*" to a different level. It's also true that when one has looked through untold thousands and thousands of boxes of secondhand comic books, as Dan, Jim and I have, one gets a pretty good feeling for what is rare and what isn't. It's highly unlikely that any mainstream American comic books would have eluded us by this time. And that's what this book covers. It does not cover foreign issues, underground comics, or fanzines and other privately published works.

In 2003, John Benson put his half-century as a comic book historian to effective use with the landmark volume *Romance Without Tears*, a book of reprints of excellent St. John stories by writer Dana Dutch and mostly by artist Matt Baker, perhaps the finest creators ever to work in romance comics. I especially recommend Benson's perceptive essay. John followed up in 2007 with a comprehensive companion volume, *Confessions, Romances, Secrets and Temptations: Archer St. John and the St. John Romance Comics*. These are must-reads for anyone interested in the field, especially since St. John produced many of the best romance comics. Because John's books cover St. John in far greater detail and with much greater expertise than I could have, I did not devote as much space to them as I might have. I would also be remiss if I did not mention Trina Robbins' entertaining and informative history of comics intended for female readers, *From Girls to Grrrlz*. The only other major book devoted to romance comics was the invaluable 1979 compilation of DC romance reprints, *Heart Throbs*, edited by Naomi Scott.

Bud Plant, in particular, has been a trusted and treasured friend for more than 40 years. Bud has operated Bud Plant Comic Art since 1970. His firm is located in Grass Valley, California, and is America's leading purveyor of new books dealing with comics and related aspects involving illustration and pop culture. He also sells out-of-print books. Words can't express how much I owe Bud for his support and friendship over the years. It's hard to believe it has been four decades since we were young partners in America's first true comic book store.

This book is my "payment" to all my friends in comics for their treasured support.

Introduction

Ask any woman of a certain age if she read romance comics, and you'll probably get a smile and maybe a sigh. Other than the occasional sub-teen and teen girls who weren't allowed to have comics, seemingly every female, including plenty of young adult women, read romance comics from the late 1940s to the early 1970s. For the better part of three decades, romance comics were an American institution. They were the first genre of comic books to deal with "real-life" situations instead of flying men and women, impossibly accurate gunfighters, glamorous gangsters, space explorers, jungle heroes and heroines, vampires and zombies, anthropomorphic animals, and the like.

"Real-life," of course, demands quotes, because the vast majority of the romance stories published in comics were contrived (and often banal) fantasies. They could have happened, but they almost never did. Or if they *did* develop—wounded soldier falls in love with gorgeous nurse, or rich girl marries poor boy—real-life love affairs would have been far more complex than most comic book stories could, or would, convey. Romance comics dealt with, at best, unlikely vignettes and circumstances. But that, of course, was part of what made them fun.

As author John Benson has detailed (see Preface), occasionally a writer such as Dana Dutch could turn in legitimate stories based on psychological reality. Most romance stories, however, reflected the times as well as wish fulfillment. Women were only occasionally shown to be the masters of their fate; they were seldom the equals of the men they pursued. Until the final decade of romance comics, story themes of daring, brassy women inevitably resulted in what kids used to call "mushy" endings. And, of course, even stories published in 1947–54 before the advent of the Comics Code Authority, a self-censorship body, could only vaguely hint of issues dealing with sexual activity, gender orientation and psychological pain and incompatibility. In some ways, most romance stories screamed "comic book" every bit as much *as did* the fantastic adventures of Superman, Wonder Woman and Flash Gordon.

Romance stories, however, dealt with an infinite variety of themes, conflicts and relationships and in an equally endless variety of settings. It wasn't difficult to write a romance story, but it was extremely challenging to write a good one, or at least a truly entertaining one. (I still get depressed thinking about having to read the often ludicrous but usually well-illustrated stories in Fawcett romance comics of 1948–53, in which the women almost invariably are portrayed as selfish, brainless, thoughtless or some other negative quality until shown the error of their ways by a man.)

Romance stories could only hint at some of the intense feelings and conflicts that their readers would endure or already had, just as most newspaper stories to this day touch only the surface of those truths. In fact, when privately produced "underground" comic books of the 1960s and '70s actually did deal honestly with many of these issues, they were either respected or reviled. There wasn't much in between! However, the undergrounds, self-published comics and fanzines are grist for a different mill.

The situations reflected in romance comics were similarly, if usually more complexly, portrayed in the thousands of pulp and confession magazines issued in the 1920s through the 1950s (and beyond, of course, with regard to confession magazines). Relatively few of pulp stories dealt with genuine human emotions in the raw, although romantic fiction in the "slick" magazines often did. Even today, many paperback romance novels are very much in essence "comic books" without art.

Beginning in the more liberated second half of the 1960s, the superficiality and artifice of romance comics began to suffer mightily in contrast to literature, film and eventually television. Much of this entertainment was available to the girls who once read comics. It's no wonder the love comics declined.

Were it not for collectors, romance comics would probably already be as largely ignored as are the thousands of dime novels of a century or more ago. Most of the attraction of romance comics to collectors is their art, since many of the best comic book artists worked at least briefly in the field—marvelous illustrators such as Matt Baker, Alex Toth, Everett Raymond Kinstler, Frank Frazetta, John Romita, Nick Cardy, John Buscema and so many others. Other collectors find appeal in the sheer Americana expressed, along with outrageous and funky aspects. Others, such as myself, seek out stories dealing with favorite themes; in my case, they include newspaper sagas and sports settings. Still other comic book hunters and gatherers simply like the challenge of pursuing obscure publications, or they seek to complete collections of entire companies. But it has only recently been thus with regard to romance.

For more than three decades, in the 1960s, '70s and '80s, the community of comic book collectors, historians and back-issue dealers pretty much ignored romance comics, even as the hobby grew. As comic-oriented fanzines began to pop up in earnest in the early 1960s and the first comic book conventions soon followed and as the increasingly "hip" Marvel Comics especially piqued public interest at the same time—the interest of comic historians also grew in genres other than super hero comics. The best (and often the worst) titles devoted to horror, science fiction, crime, western, teen humor and funny animals all gained well-deserved attention, along with their often underrated artists and writers. Several thousand magazines and fanzines devoted partly or entirely to the huge world of collectible comics have been published in the past half-century or so, as have hundreds of books. Hundreds of comic conventions have been held in the United States since the mid–1960s.

This lack of attention to four-color love is understandable, since romance comics were primarily marketed to and read by females, who are still a tiny minority in the world of collectors. Since fans of comics in the 1960s and '70s were mostly males, they tended to dismiss romance comics as repetitious, banal and generally less than interesting. To some degree, it must be admitted, they were correct. These guys wouldn't have been caught dead with a romance comic in the 1940s or '50s, so most fans continued to ignore them as adults. In addition, vintage romance comics were—and still are—much less valuable in general than other old funny books. In fact, many retailers and mail-order dealers ignored them for decades because they weren't profitable to carry to conventions, or to advertise. Why bother with *Girls' Love Stories* or *Love Romances* when there was so much more money to be made with *Batman* or *Spider-Man*?

However, as prices for collectible comics climbed in the 1990s, collectors' interest in romance comics significantly increased. Fans realized these marvelous period pieces could be had much less expensively than the vast majority of vintage comics. A collector with a $500 budget at a large convention in recent years might be able to buy a dozen or fewer collectible comics of merit. But such money could still bag dozens of romance comics. Fun! In the 1970s and 1980s, when the price of most old love issues ranged from 25 cents to $3 (which then seemed outrageous), I often could acquire a couple of boxes of love from the racks at conventions. In those days, the hard part wasn't paying for romance comics; it was finding them.

Now it's debatable how long non-iconic old comic books will retain their value—and which issues will still be worth big bucks. But there's no question that collectors still can acquire a dozen or more funky old romance comics for the price of one super hero or horror issue. In the current era—when copies of the vast majority of such 1940s or 1950s comics routinely run $100 to $200 and up in very good or better condition—romance comics usually cost $10 to $20, and often less, even in nice condition. Considering that most new comic books cost $3 or more today, vintage romance comics remain a bargain, as long as you're looking for a period piece and not necessarily excellent art or storytelling.

Thanks to online databases and a plethora of price guides now available, information on romance comics is also far easier to come by than it was not long ago. Even so, the occasional startling discovery continues to pop up, adding to the fun. The indefatigable comics historian Jim Vadeboncoeur, Jr., for example, learned in 2005 that *Love Experiences* from long-defunct Ace Publications has two issues labeled # 38—the real # 38, dated June 1956, and the real # 39, dated August 1956 but listed as # 38 by mistake in the indicia (the number was not listed on the cover at all). We also learned from the enthusiastic collector and historian Dr. Michael Vassallo that the contents intended for the long-sought *Love Tales* # 59 from Marvel/Atlas were actually published in *Lovers* # 42 (October *1952*) after *Love Tales* was discontinued with # 58 in 1952. *Love Tales* was resumed in 1955 with # 60, a number that resulted from a book-keeping error, since the stories intended for # 59 had been published and paid for. So # 59 does not exist.

In that spirit, I very much hope readers can enjoy this book with a sense of discovery. You may not care a whit whether *Diary Confessions* # 13 exists as part of a 1950s series (it probably doesn't!), but perhaps you will learn something to appreciate about what was once "Love on the Racks."

ONE

Pulp Love and True Confessions
What Came Before Romance Comics

In one form or another, pulp love has conquered all for more than a century.

Long before American comic books became smitten by their fling with the romance genre beginning in the late 1940s, love had been freely available in other forms on the racks of America's newsstands and drug stores.

There was much more love for sale, in fact, than any reader could possibly have handled. Just as nobody could possibly read all the paperback romance novels published today, nobody could have consumed the entirety of the pulp magazine oeuvre from the Roaring Twenties through the Fabulous Fifties.

How many love pulps were published? According to the comprehensive listings in *The Adventure House Guide to the Pulps* and *Bookery's Guide to the Pulps*, well over 7,000 issues! Considering each issue tended to average more than 100,000 words, that's more than 700 million words. The vast majority of these stories appeared during the "Golden Age" of the pulps—the 1930s and 1940s—before the expansion of commercial television along with newsstand competition from comic books and paperbacks. The pulps thrived during a period of depression, war and recovery, when most people could not afford hardcover books.

Many readers of the 1920–60 era, particularly upper-class and upper middle-class readers, subscribed to "the slicks"—*The Saturday Evening Post*, *McCall's*, *Coronet*, *Liberty* and others—in large part for generally higher-brow fiction by noted authors. It's likely, however, that even more readers turned for romance to the pulps, which vastly outnumbered the general-interest slicks. Pulps were the primary markets for writers of all types of fiction.

More than 40,000 pulps of all types

Catalogs and indexes list more than 40,000 issues of all pulp magazines published beginning with the transition of pioneering publisher Frank Munsey's *Argosy* to pulp format in 1896, though the pulp magazine industry didn't really get going in earnest until the 1920s. These were magazines devoted almost entirely to fiction and printed with wood-pulp paper. Some collectors and historians count more than 1,000 titles published from the 1920s to the 1960s, depending on how "title" is defined, since titles often made small changes.

Today, love pulps are at the bottom of both price lists and want lists for the vast majority of collectors. Enthusiasts avidly seek out tales involving mysteries (*Dime Detective*, *Black Mask*, *Thrilling Detective*); costume and super heroes (*The Shadow*, *The Spider*, *Doc Savage*); weird menace (*Horror Stories*, *Terror Tales*); science fiction (*Astounding*, *Amazing Stories*, *Thrilling Wonder Stories*); westerns (*Wild West Weekly*, *The Rio Kid*) and sports (*Baseball Stories*,

Thrilling Football). When love pulps are collected at all, it's more likely to be for cover art or compelling period piece imagery than for stories or specific authors.

Yet it's possible the love pulps outsold every other genre, though the nearly 10,000 issues with mainstream western themes may have corralled slightly more of the market than romance lassoed. It's no coincidence, though, that one of the most successful of all pulps, *Ranch Romances*, ran some 860 issues under three different publishers from 1924 to 1971. *Ranch Romances* successfully melded the two leading commercial genres during the magazine's long run. *Ranch Romances*, in fact, was the last of the original pulps still standing by the early 1960s.

The above commentary, by the way, does not include the infamous "girlie" pulps and bed-sheets (that's no pun; it refers to pulp magazines about the size of the ever-so-respectable *Life* and *Look*). These titles included *Saucy Stories, Spicy Adventure, Breezy Stories, Bedtime Stories* and the like. There were dozens of such titles. They are all well covered—or uncovered, as it were—by the only comprehensive book on the topic—*Uncovered: The Hidden Art of the Girlie Pulps* (2003) by leading pulp historian Douglas Ellis. These exotic, often under-the-counter publications were almost entirely the province of men. Perhaps, in fact, they were read by many of the same red-blooded males who sought more realistic thrills than could be provided vicariously chasing super villains with the Shadow and Doc Savage.

A multitude of love pulps

Women, on the other hand, purchased the vast majority of the love pulps, just as females purchase the overwhelming majority of romance novels today. And just as females from pre-teens to young women were the vast majority of the customers for romance comic books. Nor does the above pulp count include the numerous likes of *True Story* or Fawcett Publications' long-running *True Confessions*. Similar in slick-paper format to the multitude of love-oriented movie magazines such as *Photoplay*, magazines such as *True Confessions* sold in the untold millions.

In stark contrast to the romance comics, women were almost never shown in emotionally stressful positions, much less in compromising or endangered circumstances, on the covers of *Love Story Magazine, All Story Love Tales, Complete Love, Love Book, Exciting Love*, and the many other pulp romance titles. Instead of drama or danger, the covers invariably focused on idealized scenes either of lovers together or of fashionable young women dreaming of love, often with the latest hair and clothing styles. Even most of the western romance pulps focused on grins rather than gun smoke.

The first comprehensive compilation of all pulp titles ever attempted in a book, *The Adventure House Guide to the Pulps* (1998) by John Gunnison, John Locke and Doug Ellis, lists the titles, number of issues *printed* and dates of known pulps. Similar information is listed in *The Bookery's Guide to the Pulps* (second edition, 2005) by Tim Cottrill. There were at least 139 mainstream romance pulps published, ranging from 1912 to 1971. Many other pulp genres, of course, contain romantic themes, such as the love of the heroic Richard Wentworth (the Spider) for glamorous and valiant Nita Van Sloan in Popular Publications' 118-issue run of *The Spider* from 1933 to 1943. Later, comic books such as *Superman's Girl Friend Lois Lane* and *The Flash* made romance a staple along with fantastic heroics.

Considering the pulp love titles include more than 7,500 known issues (not counting the sex pulps "uncovered" by Ellis), there are surely at least a few more pulp romances waiting to be rediscovered, particularly since so few collectors have ever cared enough to research in depth the history of the romance pulp. Some of the pulp publishers—Street & Smith, Popular, Thrilling and Fiction House—have been well documented as to issue counts in all genres.

Others, not as popular with collectors and with no available official records, are still being researched, such as those from Ace and Columbia.

Love Story Magazine *led the romance field*

Street & Smith's *Love Story Magazine*, so popular it was published weekly during most of its existence, ran 1,158 issues from 1921 to 1947 and was by far the most successful of love pulps. It also may have had had the highest literary standards, or so some pulp fans proclaim. The innovative pulp publisher Frank Munsey's *All-Story Love Tales* published 582 issues from 1929 to 1955, including the years after the title was picked up by the prolific Popular Publications in 1943.

These were far from the only long-running romance successes, however. The fans of the most successful love pulps were intensely loyal for years. Many titles ran more than 100 issues—examples include *Complete Love* (100), *Cupid's Diary* (175), *I Confess* (209), *Gay Love Stories* (115), *Live Stories* (146), *Love Book Magazine* (196), *Love Fiction Monthly* (153), *Love Novels Magazine* (107), *Love Short Stories* (157), *New Love* (126), *Popular Love* (102), *Rangeland Romances* (217), *Romance* (115), *Romantic Range* (130), *Snappy Stories* (315), *Sweetheart Stories* (320), *Ten Story Love* (100), *Thrilling Love* (240) and *Thrilling Ranch Stories* (136). Those numbers in most cases are known to be exact. For a few titles, they are the best available estimates. Even so, they are all close enough totals to be statistically significant. Remember, too, that all this loyalty to love developed despite heavy competition on the racks with dozens of different titles in all genres each month in both pulp and slick categories. America, indeed, was a nation of readers, albeit sometimes low-brow readers, until the advent of television.

Compared to issues of *The Shadow*, *Weird Tales* or the detective classic *Black Mask*—many of which run to the hundreds of dollars in fine or better condition for collectors—old love is still cheap love. The vast majority of love pulps can be had for a few dollars—sometimes for less, in fact, than a new romance paperback. In fact, old romance comics—themselves often the cheapest genre pursued by enthusiasts—in recent years have come to sell for more than most of their generally older pulp counterparts.

Since collecting pulp magazines first became popular with the initial waves of nostalgia for them in the 1960s and 1970s, several dozen books have been published about pulp magazine history. Very little, however, has been written about the love pulps.

In 1937, the famed editor Harold Hersey produced *Pulpwood Editor*, the first book dealing with the popular influence of pulps. When Adventure House reprinted that rare old volume in 2002, a new generation of readers could learn what little Hersey had to say about romance pulps, as well as all the others. For the ill-fated Clayton Publications, Hersey created *Ranch Romances*, calling it his lone "home run" in the love field.

"Your sister and nobody's sister"

"There were only two kinds of women in the Western pulpwood," Hersey wrote in one of the great lines ever expressed about pulp epics, "Your sister and nobody's sister."

In talking about the "love story formula," Hersey pulled no punches in his often sardonic account of pulp publishing: "Purity and innocence and naivete are the watchwords of the publishers in this field," he wrote. "The heroines are legless, breastless and brainless. They adore the big, strong men. They are born housewives. They do have illegitimate children upon occasion, that is, a certain few; the majority [of the women] deal with the more serious problems of what to wear and whom to wear it with…. It is an eminently middle class, respectable public that devours the clean love story…. The combined sale of love story pulps exceeds three million copies a month!" In the 1930s, when Hersey wrote those lines, that meant it was likely an average of at least one woman in 10 read one or more love pulps each month in America.

The legendary Leo Margulies, one of the most accomplished of the pulp editors, labored from 1931 to 1950 for the Thrilling Group, produced by prolific publisher Ned Pines. Margulies wrote numerous articles in the 1930s and 1940s for trade publications, advising prospective writers of what his large line of magazines could use. He regularly covered all the pulp genres as the Thrilling line grew to dozens of pulps. Its modest Depression-era beginnings were three pulps on the racks of late 1931: *Thrilling Adventures*, *Thrilling Detective* and *Thrilling Love*, the latter likely a response to Street & Smith's rousing success.

In *Writer's Digest* for March 1935, Margulies offered the following advice for people seeking the formula for success with *Thrilling Love*, which was then his only mainstream romance pulp: "While most love magazines feed their readers the glamorous, sweet-young-thing overly sentimental type of story, we play up the more sophisticated variety of story with interesting dialogue, clever repartee and depictions of the 'modern girl.' And although we stay away from the risqué and the suggestive, we will permit the love scenes to be more emotional than heretofore. And the Cinderella theme, in this background, makes a swell story."

For *Writer's Digest* in December 1938, he provided further genre hints to would-be contributors, but this time advised strongly against the Cinderella plot: "We have a preference for the dramatic as opposed to the wishy washy, for gayety as opposed to drabness, and for vital characters as opposed to cloyingly sweet nincompoops. We have few taboos … but lately we've had a little too much of Hollywood, mistaken identity, unofficial wives and Cinderellas. Our pet hates are stories in which lovers are removed from active competition by being killed in auto accidents, and yarns in which 'she' [the protagonist] finds out she loves a man because he is sick in a hospital, etc. [and] sentimental devices which rob a story of its natural progression to a conclusion."

"Old-fashioned sentimental romance"

Margulies expanded on these thoughts in a long essay entitled "The Way to a Million Words" in *The Writer* for June 1943. He trenchantly observed:

> Old-fashioned sentimental romance, blended with sophisticated, smart present-day trends, will always make the pulse beat a little faster…. Our love stories are always told from the girl's point of view, and she must be neither a weak creature tossed hither and yon by Fate, nor a flirt, nor a too-forward or too-sophisticated hussy. Just a normal everyday girl like thousands of girls all over the country. In such girls lies romance, particularly if they are especially talented or beautiful.

Margulies went on to repeat the "romance no-nos" of the previous paragraph written five years earlier, then added, "Readers want vivacious, modern American girls who work out their problems with spirit and courage."

By 1950, his last year as Thrilling's editor, Margulies devoted only a few lines to the requirements for *Thrilling Love*, *Popular Love* and *Exciting Love*—among the needs for his many other magazines—at the bottom of an extensive article in *Writers' Journal* for April 1950. "All the stories [in those pulps] are stories of today's girl with today's problems. There is no place in these magazines for sordid sex stuff. Good, clean, wholesome stories are the type required."

Margulies was more specific when talking of characters for the long-running *Thrilling Ranch Stories* (1933–53): "These stories should show a nice balance between the masculine and feminine interest. They should show the western heroine as an aggressive sort of person who has plenty of pioneering blood in her veins and realized there were times when she had to stand shoulder to shoulder with him [the hero] in fighting the forces of nature and human greed."

The "modern" love story is often cited to have begun with Jane Austen's *Pride and Prejudice* in 1813. Austen, the Brontë sisters, and Louisa May Alcott are, of course, still being read and studied. But romance novels did not take off in the first 20 years of the modern paperback. These paperbacks, first popularized in 1939 by Pocket Books and imitated by dozens of other publishers who sold them for a quarter in the 1940s and 1950s, gradually helped doom all the pulps along with the post-war growth of television and comic books.

Paperback romance arrived late

Until the 1960s, however, the vast majority of paperbacks dealt not in the glories of love but the threat of death and danger. Mysteries, westerns, science fiction and literary fiction—much of it reprinted from hardcover books—dominated the paperback field. (There were 20th-century paperbacks before 1939, of course, but few are remembered or collected today, and even fewer were commercially successful.)

In an informative book on romance paperbacks, *The Look of Love: The Art of the Romance Novel* (2002) by Jennifer McKnight-Trontz, only 37 of the paperbacks pictured were published before 1960, compared to 80 produced since then. There was nothing included on the pulp magazines.

Canadian publisher Harlequin, so fabled for its fabulous line of thousands of romance titles since the 1960s, published only a relative handful of romance novels during its first decade (1949–59)—and most of those were nurse and doctor stories. Of the earliest major American paperback lines—Pocket, Avon, Dell, Popular Library, Bantam, Ballantine, Signet, Gold Medal/Crest and Ace—only Dell published more than a few romance novels. There was plenty of exploitation and cleavage, of course, on the covers of all genres. But until the 1960s, romance in print was largely left to the slicks, pulps, true confession magazines and comic books, along with a goodly number of hardcover books. Hardcovers, however, were bought largely by libraries during the pulp romance era.

Even Dell published relatively few romance novels in its early paperback years. Of the first 700 Dell paperbacks (1943–53), fewer than 10 percent were of the love genre—the books labeled with a heart symbol on the cover during much of the 1940s. Dell reprinted no less than 15 hardcover novels by a popular romance novelist, Faith Baldwin. It wasn't until the 1960s that another publisher, Bantam, did the same with a multitude of the clean-cut, classic romances by Emilie Loring and Grace Livingston Hill.

Nurses, doctors and gothic love

Ace, which became so profitable beginning in 1952 with its 35-cent "double novel" series of mysteries, westerns and science fiction, began to flood the market with nurse/doctor romance novels in 1961. Ace then hit the briefly popular gothic romance market hard later in the decade. At about the same time in the 1960–62 period, Harlequin quickly converted its polyglot line of many genres to exclusively romance titles, soon publishing an average of eight romances per month. In fact, from 1960 through 1979, Harlequin published an amazing 1,722 novels in its original numbered line alone, plus hundreds of others.

Thrilling Ranch Stories, Jan. 1948, copyright Standard Magazines, Inc. The heroine cuts the hero's bonds as he lets loose with both guns blazing.

Based on surveys by the authors of paperback price guides along with experience as a collector, it seems likely that the total number of romance paperbacks published since the 1960s is even greater than the total number of romance pulps produced from 1920 to 1960. The point is, love lingers on in print. Ironically, many used-book stores are loathe to buy large numbers of paperback romances, especially since they are so common they can easily be acquired in trades. Many stores carry only a small sample of paperback romances. Paperback exchanges, though, thrive on the little love books.

"True Love Triumphs" in pulp cover blurbs

The blurbs in the pulp romances attempted to attract readers just as they did in other genres. In an early issue of *Thrilling Love* for Oct. 1932, stories are introduced simply. The blurb for "Poor Man, Rich Man" by Harold Montanye is "a fascinating story of nightclub romance and a hat check girl's faith." For "Look in Your Own Heart" by Sarah Humbird, it's "true love triumphs over fear in this tense story of a girl's struggle with her own conscience."

Twenty years later, in *Thrilling Love* for June 1952, the blurbs hadn't changed much. For "Escape from Tomorrow" by Elizabeth MacArthur, the intro went, "Meg built a fortress around her heart, a fortress she hoped no man could tear down." In "I'll Wait for You, Darling" by Hazel Palmer, the editor's comment was "Everything was quite ready for the wedding ... everything, this is, except the bridegroom."

Stories covered the gamut of glamour, including career concerns in an era when most women weren't yet working. For example, in *Thrilling Love* for December 1937, "To Those Who Love" by Ethel Murphy was introduced with "People said that Zoe Marshall, career girl, was too cold-blooded to lose her heart, but...." And in "World's Fair Debutante" by Helen Ahern in *Thrilling Love* for August 1939, the blurb was the irresistible, "Vicky Hough, in the shadow of scandal, becomes a Girl Guide and faces the world—and loves—of tomorrow!" And so it went, on and on.

Descriptions in the western romance magazines were often considerably more pulse-pounding than in the mainstream love pulps. The western theme began with *Ranch Romances*, which was published by Clayton in 1924–33, Warner Publications in 1933–50 and Pines from 1950–71. *Ranch Romances* was the most successful of its kind, spawning more than two dozen imitations, including Pines's own highly successful *Thrilling Ranch Stories* beginning in 1933. Covers of the ranch love pulps lended themselves to blurbs. They tended to be either highly dramatic—a girl, a guy and a gun (or two)—or placid, moonlit images of lovers sitting (or hugging) around a campfire or a corral. This blurb for "Heart of the Range" by Paul Evan Lehman in *Thrilling Ranch Stories* for May 1949 pretty much says it all: "Aided by Faro Nell, owner of the Lonely Heart Saloon, Susan Perry and Barry Kirk battle for range justice against fearful odds—and hope for the fulfillment of their dream of romance!"

The blurbs were often drenched in drama, such as the entry for "Half My Kingdom" by Lily K. Scott in *Thrilling Ranch Stories* for December 1944: "Tacey O'Hare, the heiress of the Circle 0 Ranch, feuds with a tenderfoot—while dry-gulch terror stalks the range!" The cover of this issue features a grinning guy and gal going over a family photo album. All in all, the indexes show more than 1,800 western romance pulps were published among more than two dozen titles, led by *Ranch Romances*. That means nearly one in four love pulps featured a western theme.

It took more than pulps, however, to set the stage for romance comics. The lives and loves of popular comic book teen-agers "born" in the 1940s, led by Archie and Patsy Walker, along with other titles aimed largely at girls, provided the first hint of the onslaught of comic book romance.

Two

Twixt Teens and Tears

How Teen Humor and Girls' Comics
Provided a Bridge to Romance

Almost six years before the first real attempt at comic book love stories appeared on the racks, the company that was to become known as Archie Comics Publications unknowingly set the stage for four-color romance. Who could have guessed that Archie, which began as an obscure six-page backup strip in a well-established super hero comic, would become the most enduring American pop cultural image of teenage hi-jinks? Or that this constantly befuddled and bemused redhead would unleash many carloads of competitors?

The vast majority of comics were devoted either to super heroes or anthologies of newspaper comic strip reprints during 1941 and 1942, the period of Archie's earliest development. The never-ending pursuit of Archie by Betty Cooper and Veronica Lodge provided a comical beginning for comic book romance.

Archie and his coterie of Pals 'n Gals, as the *Archie* series famously called them for many years, emerged from MLJ Comics, as Archie's corporate creator was known. John Goldwater—whose name along with co-owners Maurice Coyne and Louis Silberkleit formed the firm's logo—worked with cartoonist Bob Montana to create Archie. "Old carrot-top" first appeared in the back pages of *Pep Comics*, a monthly anthology created during the height of the super hero boom, and *Jackpot Comics*, a quarterly anthology devoted to the best of the company's heroes. Archie debuted in *Pep* # 22 (Dec. 1941) and *Jackpot* # 4 (Winter 1941–42). *Jackpot* lasted only through # 9 (Summer 1943) but Archie never left the pages of *Pep* and took over as the title's primary feature with # 66 (March 1948).

In the most extensive history of Archie for the book market, Charles Phillips revealed Goldwater's creative efforts in *Archie: His First 50 Years* (1991). "According to John Goldwater," Phillips wrote, "he first got the idea for a 'normal' teenager from Andy Hardy [of the films] ... and decided to call the strip *Archie* after a high school chum. The story goes that Goldwater then turned to the MLJ bullpen and asked all the young artists and writers there to try their hand at working up the strip. It was Bob Montana who came up with the image of Archie, a younger version of today's familiar 17-year-old, who—wavy-haired, bucktoothed, and knickers-clad—does indeed resemble Mickey Rooney with a bit of Tom Sawyer thrown in."

Archie begins to take over

In one of the strangest of all Golden Age covers, two super heroes, the Shield and the Hangman, are shown carrying Archie—whom MLJ trumpeted as "The Mirth of a Nation"—

on the cover of *Pep* # 36 (Feb. 1943). Archie claimed exclusive cover rights in # 51 (Dec. 1944). Romance was very much a part of *Archie* stories that predated love comics. As *Archie* "biographer" Phillips wrote in perhaps the best explanation ever printed about the appeal of the love triangle, "The gleefully self-centered Veronica Lodge, America's premier high school rich girl, is a middle–American fantasy. Implied in her interest in Archie is at least a questioning of the ease and leisure provided by [her father] Mr. Lodge. Her money did not seem to have made her a snob, which for the average reader would be unforgivable, but it did produce a charming teaser, whose manipulations, appearing so natural, seem all but harmless in the long run. If her rivalry with Betty is an indulgence, it is a consuming one, making the wealthy sub-deb appear to be one of us, after all. In many ways, Betty Cooper—America's quintessential Girl Next Door—is defined by Veronica's jealousy as much as she is by her feelings for Archie. For it is their rivalry that elevates her schoolgirl crush to the level of myth. Betty's attraction to Archie is more visceral than Veronica's, and her methods for 'catching' him— as she would be the first to admit—are more direct, more physical, more honest. Betty is a down-to-earth girl, with a vulnerable and sensitive side that occasionally breaks through the boy-crazy facade. If Archie's male readers understand his attraction to Veronica, [Archie's] female readers understand Betty's attraction to him—and that makes the triangular formula work."

With most 10-cent comic books running to 68 pages (including covers) in the World War II era when *Archie* debuted, there was a constant need for back-up features. Enthusiasts over the years have delighted in spotting which of these initially unsung comic strips eventually emerged as icons among their hundreds of forgotten co-features.

Before Archie's appearance, MLJ actually created a far less memorable teenager named Wilbur. He debuted as a backup in the super hero-oriented *Zip Comics* # 18 (Sept. 1941)— three months earlier than Archie! Wilbur and Archie, however, operated in separate comic book universes. Wilbur, who gathered a group of friends in much the same fashion as *Archie* did, clicked well enough to be given his own comic book after *Zip* failed in 1944. Ace Comics also came up with a forgotten teen character who predated *Archie. Hap Hazard* debuted as a backup strip in 1940 and had his own title from 1944 to 1949 when, ironically, it became *Real Love* # 25 (April 1949)—Ace's first romance title.

Over the past half-century, Archie has appeared in so many thousands of comic books that baby boomers and their children and grandchildren might find it difficult to believe what a minor character he really was in the 1940s. World War II paper rationing and its aftermath led to only sporadic appearances of *Archie* in 1945 and 1946. In 1945, *Archie* appeared in only 10 comic books (*Pep* # 52–55 and *Archie* # 12–17) and in 1946 he frolicked in only 12 issues (*Pep* # 56–59, *Archie* # 18–23 and *Laugh Comics* # 20–21).

So the constant tension among Archie, Betty and Veronica had less to do with the creation of romance comics than many latter-day fans might think. What their love triangle did do, though, was to spark a flood of teen imitators as publishers sought other genres to replace the increasingly irrelevant Golden Age super heroes following the end of the war.

MLJ was still heavily committed to their heroes, however, when the company released *Archie Comics* # 1 (Winter 1942) only one year after his debut. That was the only non–super hero comic of the 48 issues the company published in 1942. *Archie* # 1 is generally recognized as the first true teen humor title, even though Dell released a *Harold Teen* one-shot of newspaper strip reprints earlier in 1942 and some purists claim that issue merits the honor. *Archie*, though, owed a lot more to the popularity of Henry Aldrich, the teenage sensation of *The Aldrich Family* radio show; along with the hugely popular Andy Hardy films with Mickey Rooney, than he did to any comic strip.

Archie shares his first issue with funny animals

Even at that, *Archie* # 1 was something of a hedge-your-bets polyglot, released in the darker days of the war under the inside front cover motto of "Keep 'Em Smiling," when everyone was trying to "Keep 'Em Flying." The historic issue contained four stories of the original funny animals, Cubby the Bear, Judge Owl, Squirmy the Worm and Bumbie the Bee-Tective, covering 27 pages and all pictured at the bottom of the front cover, along with five *Archie* tales occupying 28 pages. The issue also included a one-page biography of Bob Montana, complete with the erroneous information that he began *Archie* in 1940!

On a "Who's Who in Riverdale" page by Montana to open the issue, *Archie* is self-described in the *Riverdale High Brown & Gold*—Archie is listed as editor and publisher—as "all around athlete, honor student, best-dressed man, rug cutter extraordinary and man about town." Archie, cover featured as "The Mirth of a Nation" right from # 1, must have been a huge hit right from the start, since the title became bi-monthly with # 4 (Sept–Oct. 1943).

Archie began appearing on the radio in 1943 and ran for a decade, but radio historians have long maintained he was never more than a "second string" Henry Aldrich on the air. Oddly, the situation was dramatically reversed in comic books, where Henry's hilarious hi-jinks, which originally ran from 1939 to 1953 on the radio and were a pop cultural touchstone, were limited in the comics to a 22-issue run from Dell in 1950–54.

John Dunning, the eminent mystery novelist and old-time radio historian, described Archie's radio status well in his magnificent 1976 volume, *Tune in Yesterday: The Ultimate Encyclopedia of Old Time Radio, 1925–76*. "As developed on radio," Dunning wrote, "Archie was almost as zany as that other notorious teenager of the air, Henry Aldrich. But nobody could out–Henry Henry, and Archie at best was still second-string.... Although Betty, Veronica, Jughead, Reggie, and all the rest of Montana's cast made the transition, the radio show lost the flavor of the strip and reflected Archie as just another insane teenager."

Archie's 1940s comic books had a distinct feel of sensuality never again seen in the strip, especially after the Comics Code Authority was created (see Chapter Nine). The best explanation for this sensuality the author has seen was this observation by Charles Phillips in *Archie: His First 50 Years*: "An even greater appeal of the original *Archie* series was their repressed sensuality. 'Archie was pretty sexy stuff the way Bob Montana drew it' [an Archie observer named Brian Walker told Phillips]."

Phillips continues: "And, indeed, it is hard not to agree with him [Walker]. Betty Cooper's coy stance in the splash panel of the first Archie story [*Pep* # 22]; Veronica Lodge undressing in the back of a limousine on the way to pick up her father in *Pep* # 31; the shapely legs Archie photographs as an unknown woman lifts her skirt in the classic 'Camera Bugs'; Veronica taking a shower in the daily paper on Feb. 18, 1946 [in the *Archie* newspaper strip]; these and myriad other images led a generation of boys to romantic longings for Betty and (even more) Veronica—for the most part, secret longings."

What came before Archie

Teen humor in comic strips dates back at least to the long-running newspaper strips *Freckles and His Friends*, created in 1915 by Merrill Blosser, and *Harold Teen*, originated by Carl Edd in 1919. Metro-Goldwyn-Mayer's series of 15 Andy Hardy movies from 1937 to 1946, starring Mickey Rooney, may have made that befuddled teen character at least as much a household name in his decade-long teen heyday as Archie ever has been. And, of course, Paramount's nine Henry Aldrich films from 1939 to 1944, along with the immensely popular radio program of the same name, provided a huge boost to the teen humor movement. Ask any senior citizen and he or she still probably can remember the screeching of Henry's mother in the introduction: "Henreeeee ... Henreeeee Aldrich!" That unique call probably still rattles around in the dreams of many old-time radio fans.

The first all-teen humor comic book was *Dell Four Color* # 2 starring Harold Teen, published in the first half of 1942. *Harold Teen* newspaper reprints had been appearing in Dell's *Super Comics* right from # 1 (May 1938). Perhaps the first truly original comic book teen, however, was the hysterically funny Scribbly, who debuted in Dell's *The Funnies* # 2 (Nov. 1936). Scribbly was the creation of 19-year-old cartoonist Sheldon Mayer, a cartooning phenom who was destined to become one of the great creators and editors in comic book history, working for M.C. Gaines' All-American comic book firm and later National, which eventually absorbed All-American in the mid–1940s after the two had been business partners. Scribbly enjoyed his greatest glory in the pages of *All-American Comics* # 1–59 from 1939 to 1944.

Patsy Walker debuts in 1944

Outside of Archie's circle, light-hearted teen romance received its most significant boost in the comics with the creation of Patsy Walker for Marvel/Timely's *Miss America* title. Patsy, in fact, wound up being far more commercially super than the super-powered *Miss America*, a flying backup heroine in Timely's super hero anthology *Marvel Mystery Comics* from 1943 to 1948. Patsy Walker debuted in *Miss America* # 2 (Nov. 1944) with a seven-page story and soon became the lead feature when the eponymous heroine disappeared from the title after # 5. Like *Calling All Girls*—a squeaky-clean comic book begun in 1941 by the publishers of Parents' Magazine—*Miss America* quickly evolved from a super hero title into a comic book for sub-teen and teen girls. *Miss America* was complete with text stories and text features dealing with fashion, beauty, relationships and so on, plus perhaps consistently more advertising than any other comic book of the 1940s. Every issue of *Miss America* from # 2 (Nov. 1944) onward contained a story of Patsy Walker, who quickly graduated to her own title in 1945.

Patsy Walker was a Marvel mainstay for two decades, perhaps known to nearly as many readers in the 1950s as were Captain America, the Human Torch and Sub-Mariner in the 1940s. Early on, Patsy's multitude of adventures and misadventures—and her rivalry with the glamorous Hedy Wolfe—probably influenced the development of romance comics. Many of Patsy's covers had romantic themes, much more so than the wise-cracks on *Archie* series titles. In 1944, *Miss America* # 2 was a significant precursor to the romance titles. After a 14-page *Miss America* story, there were love-and-relationship text tales such as "Hear the Bluebells Ring," "Jane's Awakening," "A Wallflower Blooms," "Big Sister" and "Beauty Isn't Everything." There was also "Are You Having Date Problems" by Hollywood star Jane Withers "as told to May Mann." This preceded the multitude of advice texts in romance comics.

Patsy and Hedy: competitors for Archie

Patsy Walker, Timely's red-headed answer to blonde Betty Cooper, and Hedy, Timely's raven-haired counterpart for Veronica Lodge, were the first of a lengthy line of leggy lasses to emerge from publisher Martin Goodman's comic book factory to compete with the *Archie* titles in the next two decades. From 1947 through 1950, Marvel publisher Martin Goodman flooded the racks with no fewer than 232 issues devoted primarily to teen humor, covering 14 different titles. And this doesn't count Marvel's "working girl" comic books, such as *Millie the Model*, *Nellie the Nurse* and *Tessie the Typist*, who were slightly older "first cousins" to the teens.

According to a survey of historian Dan Stevenson's complete issue-by-issue data and Jim Vadeboncoeur, Jr.'s lists of his unsurpassed collection of Marvel/Atlas issues, no fewer than 1,047 issues appeared over a three-decade period from 1944 to 1973 devoted by title to the teenage and young adult likes of *Millie the Model*, *Patsy Walker*, *Hedy DeVine* and *My Girl Pearl*, to name only four. That count doesn't include boyfriend type titles like Georgie and Frankie, which also featured frantic females in their misadventures.

The long-unsinkable Millie Collins is by far the best remembered of the Marvel crowd, primarily because she lasted into the mid–1970s—nearly a decade beyond Patsy Walker, who last appeared in her original incarnation in *Patsy and Hedy* # 110 (Feb. 1967). But in her heyday, no females in comics but Archie's girls were a match for Patsy Walker, who appeared along with foil Hedy Wolfe in at least 331 comic books in the 1944–59 period alone—not to mention the last few years of the *Patsy Walker* and *Patsy and Hedy* titles, which continued to be published well into the Marvel Age of Comics in the 1960s.

Patsy Walker: a comic creation

Patsy Walker was strictly a character originated for comic books. She was designed solely to compete with the Archie gang and to appeal to female readers. Unlike Archie and some of his teen competition, Patsy Walker never appeared on television, radio or in books, comic strips or the movies, either in cartoon or life-action form. Probably no other 1940s or 1950s character appeared so many times in comic book format only.

In 1950, when Marvel cancelled many titles and reduced the frequency of others, *Patsy Walker* and *Miss America* remained bi-monthlies. Apparently, they were the company's best-selling comic books for a long time. The *Miss America* title had an odd, convoluted numbering system but collectors have determined that it ran 126 issues through # 93 (Nov. 1958), with Patsy Walker appearing in every issue but # 1.

Nor was any character more important to Marvel than Patsy Walker following the Atlas implosion in the summer of 1957. Forced by economic complications to circulate his comics in a decade-long agreement through DC's distributor, Independent News, Marvel publisher Martin Goodman was limited to printing eight comics per month in 1958 and 1959, with the number increasing incrementally through the 1960s.

How important were Patsy & Co.? *Patsy Walker*, *Patsy and Hedy*, and *Miss America* (featuring Patsy and Hedy, of course) were three of Marvel's 16 bi-monthly titles published through 1958. Few Marvel fans today realize that nearly 20 percent of Marvel's comic books in 1958 featured the same two teenage girls. In fact, the first true "Marvel Age" comic—the first issue minus the Atlas symbol in the upper-left corner—was *Patsy Walker* # 73 (Oct. 1957).

Patsy and Hedy appeared for four years in a fourth title, *Patsy and Her Pals*, for 29 issues before it was one of the dozens of victims of the 1957 implosion. Atlas also published a fifth Patsy Walker title, *Girls' Life*, for six issues in 1954. This unique project—subtitled, "Patsy Walker's Own Magazine for Girls!"—was supposedly edited by no less than Patsy herself! As Jim Vadeboncoeur, Jr., notes, "Patsy Walker was actually written and drawn for much of its run by artist Al Jaffee, who is famous for inventing/creating the popular MAD Magazine back cover fold-in."

For those who want a far more detailed description of Patsy & Co., Trina Robbins—the noted pop culture historian, author and artist—includes a comprehensive chapter covering Marvel's females in her groundbreaking book, *From Girls to Grrrlz* (1999). At least 17 other

Marvel comics of the 1940s and 1950s were titled after girls and women (not even counting the *Little Lulu* little kid knockoffs): *Cindy, Della Vision, Hedy DeVine, Jeannie, Junior Miss, Lana, Margie, Meet Miss Bliss, Mitzi, My Friend Irma, My Girl Pearl, Nellie the Nurse, Patty Powers, Rusty, Sherry the Showgirl* and *Showgirls, Tessie the Typist* and *Wendy Parker.*

Career-girl themes

It's interesting to note the presence of so many career-girl themes, with an emphasis on glamour. Even Nellie, Tessie and Betty Bliss, a teacher, were glamorous figures, albeit with humorous sub-texts. How many girls today even know what the word "typist" means?

My Friend Irma, usually drawn by the inimitable Dan DeCarlo before the popular artist joined *Archie* full time in the late 1950s, was taken from a wildly popular radio and television show. This was one of the few such Marvel titles. Irma Peterson was a wacky secretary who for a long time was the public's favorite "dumb blonde," appropriately played by the hilarious Marie Wilson. When the television show's original run ended in 1954, so did the comic book.

In a much more unorthodox nod to radio, Marvel converted its *Junior Miss* title from a comic book featuring teen heart-throb Cindy Smith into a radio adaptation for the last two issues, the highly scarce # 38 (May 1950) and # 39 (Aug. 1950). *Junior Miss* was a short-running CBS radio situation comedy, first appearing in 1948 and starring 20-year-old Shirley Temple as wacky bobbysoxer Judy Graves. The radio show was a knockoff of NBC's *A Date with Judy,* which debuted in 1943 and four years later became a long-running DC comic.

Breaking out of the super hero mold near the end of World War II, Marvel published a 36-page *Junior Miss* one-shot dated Winter 1944 (with a full-page house ad for *Miss America* # 5, dated Feb. 1945). "For the teen-age girl" was the cover blurb, and the strips included the life stories of Frank Sinatra and June Allyson, plus perhaps the only appearances of *Betty Lane,* a girl reporter strip, and *Peggy Brooks,* one of Marvel's first teen characters. This one-shot title is one of the toughest 1940s Marvel comics to find. *Junior Miss* didn't appear again until # 24 (April 1947) began a 16-issue run.

Marvel did another TV imitation with its four-issue run of *Meet Miss Bliss* in 1955, obviously inspired by the popular radio and TV show *Our Miss Brooks.* This title, written by Stan Lee and drawn by the ubiquitous Al Hartley, was an amusing, light-hearted look at an elementary school teacher's romantic complications. Miss Bliss deserved a longer run.

Meet Miss Bliss appeared during that confusing period when the creation of the Comics Code Authority forced publishers to try a variety of formats in the wake of the disappearance of most of the violent titles. Another such try-anything title was the unusual Lee-Hartley teamup effort *Della Vision,* a slapstick strip featuring the star of the Pringle Pretzel Hour. You must admit that sounds just like a 1950s show!

"Thru these pages you will enter the glamorous world of television," the cover blurb promised, giving no indication this was a wacky humor title. In the lead story in the last issue, # 3 (Aug. 1955), Mr. Pringle introduces his nephew, the homely Gormly Bristle, saying, "I'm sure that Gormly will one day take his place alongside the big names of show business!" to which Della's handsome co-worker replies, "Yeah ... like Rin-Tin-Tin, Lassie, and Trigger!"

Sherry the Showgirl

With lines like that, the *Della Vision* title was immediately replaced by the four-issue run of *Patty Powers* # 4–7, yet another Lee-Hartley glamor-girl effort, this one about a movie star.

Lee and Hartley weren't ready to give up, coming through with six issues of the classic *Sherry the Showgirl* in 1956–57 (# 1–3, 5–7) and three issues of *Showgirls* in 1957 (# 4, 1–2), on which Dan DeCarlo also worked. Both titles were victims of the Atlas implosion and deserved a much better fate, because they were genuinely funny, albeit often infused with the then not-so-politically-incorrect sexism of the day.

Most of these strips were pretty lightweight stuff, but occasionally one of them would make you think. A one-page gag strip in *Sherry the Showgirl* # 6 (June 1957) has Sherry Storm spending four panels receiving sophisticated fashion advice from a woman off-stage. In the final panel, she's revealed to be a homely scrubwoman as Sherry says, "Thanks so much for your advice, Amy ... I don't know what I'd do without you!" To which the scrubwoman, wielding mop and bucket, tells her, "That's OK, kid ... any time!"

One of the showgirls was Pearl Dimly, "America's Darling Dimwit," who also had her own short-lived title. Lee, DeCarlo and Hartley did some rollicking stuff with that strip, including numerous bad blonde jokes. The other showgirls were Sherry's rival Chili Seven, Sherry's roommate Hazel Hale, and, of course, Millie the Model, all of whom worked at the Silver Slipper nightclub. Millie's own title thankfully survived the Marvel implosion along with Patsy Walker's three titles.

An odd contest for girls in Miss America

In Patsy Walker's debut tale in *Miss America* # 2 in 1944, kid brother Mickey helps uncover the fact that crooning heart-throb Swoon Strong wears a toupee after rival Hedy Wolf (it wasn't yet spelled Wolfe) snags a date with him. Frank Sinatra, good old Swoon was not!

Timely followed up in *Miss America* # 2 with an absolutely astonishing offer of $500—that's right, $500!—for a 250-word essay on the subject of "tomorrow's world." That $500 would be the equivalent of $5,000 today for an essay that would run about 6 inches in a typical 12-pica newspaper column! The mind boggles.

There was one catch, though. Only teenagers were eligible for the prize. In fact, the cover blurb said, "$1,000 in Prizes for Teen-Agers." That means Timely apparently was willing to give away the price of 10,000 copies of the comic book, and the profits for many times that many. And this was in issue # 2.

The contest wording *was* an intriguing exercise in hype. "It has often been said that TEEN-AGERS are the FORGOTTEN PEOPLE! That's bad thinking because, truly, TEEN-AGERS are the most important people in the world; the reasons are too numerous and obvious to list here. MISS AMERICA wants to remedy this deplorable situation, but she cannot do it without your help! And because MISS AMERICA needs your cooperation to make TOMORROW'S WORLD a better place to live and develop—physically, morally, spiritually and mentally—she is offering the following in CASH PRIZES: $500 for first prize, $250 for second place and $25 for the next 10 prizes."

Thinking caps and the future of girls

"Put on your thinking caps! The subject is vital—concerns your future. Write 250 words on 'TOMORROW'S WORLD.' Give it all the serious thought and study and consideration you would to attain the highest mark in your class. Tell us how TOMORROW'S WORLD should be planned today; how, in your opinion, you, today's teen-agers, can become TOMORROW'S useful citizens. [Yes, that many commas were used.] What can, should and must be done to give today's teen-agers a place in TOMORROW'S scheme of life?"

Whew and double whew! One can only wonder how many replies Timely received. And how many of them really were from teenagers. It's also intriguing to note the appeal to teenagers. In those days, Timely apparently felt it could market to them even better than younger readers. The author's guess is that *Miss America* # 2 through # 5 didn't sell nearly as well as *Calling All Girls*, which was a huge commercial success for years for Parents' Magazine. But *Miss America* must have greatly improved its sales, because Timely never hesitated to keep it going. In fact, Timely's only other monthly title in 1945 was *Terry-Toons*, starring the ever-invulnerable Mighty Mouse.

Although the character of the flying Miss America herself was destined to last three more years as a backup strip in *Marvel Mystery Comics*, she oddly disappeared from her own *Miss America* title after # 5. Yet by 1946, Timely was boasting on the cover, "The largest selling teen-age magazine ... more than a million copies." Perhaps that was a stretch, but there's no doubt that *Miss America* was a top seller, or at least advertisers thought so. *Miss America* remained at least 68 pages through the middle of 1947. At least one issue—Vol. 4 # 5, Sept. 1946—was a whopping 92 pages for a dime!

Miss America # 2 began a run of about seven years of photographic covers. Issue # 2 featured a 15-year-old beauty, identified as Dolores Conlon, in nothing less than a striking red and purple *Miss America* costume, complete with cape and cap. As far as the author knows, issue # 2 is unique in Golden Age history—the only super hero cover featuring a real person.

Collectors also prize highly *Miss America* Vol. 4 # 3 (July 1946), featuring a striking 14-year-old Elizabeth Taylor, coming off her huge success in the film *National Velvet* and looking several years older and surely more glamorous than any 14-year-old who might have picked up the comic book. That, however, was one of the few issues of *Miss America* with an identifiable teen movie star on the cover—Timely may not have wanted to pay the photo fees.

National's "town's top teens"

National, a rock of publishing stability in the 1940s, got a late start on teen humor but soon seemed to compete well with *Archie & Co.* National's answer to *Archie*, *Buzzy*, in 1944 became the firm's first teen title, followed by *A Date with Judy* (1947), *Leave It to Binky* (1948) and Sheldon Mayer's brilliant but ill-fated *Scribbly* (1948).

Judy, Binky and Buzzy were popular for a decade or more. But after 1950, Marvel's teen humor comics were devoted primarily to Patsy Walker and her retinue. Patsy and her pals appeared in at least 210 comics from 1951 to 1959, more than any teen character except the *Archie* gang. It's no wonder many middle-aged women often remember Patsy & Hedy almost as well as they do their zits and Betty & Veronica.

Beginning with the historic *Archie* # 1, a count based on Dan Stevenson's lists shows no fewer than 1,883 comics covering 116 titles devoted primarily to teen humor over the next 17 years through 1959. This includes 562 from Archie (not counting *Pep* # 21–65, with but a single *Archie* story in each issue), 518 from Marvel, 232 from National and 571 from others.

Other significant teen characters were ACG's long-running *Cookie and The Kilroys*, Four Star/Superior's *Aggie Mack* and Dell's single appearance of Betty Betz's *Dollface and Her Gang* in 1951. Then there were Fox's sleazy *Junior Comics*, *Sunny Comics* and *Meet Corliss Archer*, Eastern's *Juke Box* and *Sugar Bowl Comics*; four issues of *Susie Q Smith* from Dell; and three-issue runs of Hilda Terry's classic newspaper strip, *Teena*, licensed by both Magazine Enterprises and Standard.

A teen-humor one-shot, Ace's *Four Teeners* # 34 in 1948, epitomized the turmoil the industry endured in the early days of romance comics, near the end of the Golden Age. This title went from *Four Favorites* # 32 (a title once filled with World War II super heroes) to *Penalty* # 33 to *Four Teeners* # 34 to *Dotty* (a teen humor title) # 35 to *Glamorous Romances* # 41—five different titles in a 10-issue span!

Another bridge to romance: early comics for girls

Considering the times, a number of mainstream comic books were remarkably liberated with regard to the interests of schoolgirls of the 1940s. For example, the corporate umbrella Parents' Magazine took a financial gamble with the publication of the ground-breaking *Calling All Girls* # 1 (Sept. 1941). The newsstand comic book as we know it was only seven years old in 1941. And in that fateful year, at the end of which the United States was plunged into World War II, nearly all comics were devoted either to fantastic heroics, super or otherwise, or to newspaper reprints, most of which also stressed adventure themes. Of the 832 newsstand comic books with 1941 dates, fewer than 50 issues involved themes other than sheer adventure, fantastic or otherwise. *Calling All Girls* was the first comic book designed specifically for female readers. The historic title was so successful it took only three years to surpass half a million in circulation per issue, if cover boasts could be believed. *Calling All Girls* needed only four issues to become primarily a monthly early in 1942, and it ran 44 issues through 1945. Going monthly was the exception for all publishers rather than the rule in 1942: there were fewer than three dozen such titles. Girls flocked to read *Calling All Girls*, since there had been nothing like it, as indicated by the letter from the publishers on the inside front cover.

The cover girl on # 1 was a 13-year-old actress who was born Gloria Jean Schoonover but who went by Gloria Jean in movies that consistently appealed to teen girls. (Some film references list her as born in 1928, others in 1926). Gloria Jean was, according to David Quinlan's *Illustrated Directory of Film Stars*, "a kind of teenybopper's Diana Lynn. Kept at Universal as a minor-league rival to Deanna Durbin, Gloria was pretty as paint and as cute as a button. Her youthful face enlivened many a penny-pinching swing session, and she deserved better than her relatively brief career."

The 68-page first issue of *Calling All Girls* contained four comic stories—an 8-pager on Queen Elizabeth (the mother of the current queen); a 9-pager on famed author Osa Johnson, "the famed jungle adventuress," as the story so quaintly dubbed her; a fictional 7-pager on Judy Wing, Air Hostess No. 1 (aviation themes were huge in the early years of comics, just as they were in all of popular culture); and a fictional 8-pager on the teenage adventures of the Yorktown Younger Set, which "lives in a town like yours."

Calling All Girls *offered variety*

The other half of the first issue contained text stories of a wide variety, with an astonishing amount of reading material for the teen girl's dime. There was a 4-page story devoted to Connie Martin, a Nancy Drew knockoff; a 4-pager devoted to circus girls; a 3-pager on Gloria Jean herself; a 3-pager by publisher George Hecht on "13 ways girls can help in the national defense"; a 2-pager on manners; a 3-pager by best-selling sports novelist John R. Tunis on women in sports; a 2-pager on grooming; a 4-pager on a fictional female boater; a 2-pager on films; a 2-pager on fashion, with delightful drawings; a page on fashion accessories; and a 2-pager on cooking, by the famed food writer Cecily Brownstone. This issue gave girls an awful lot of reading, some of it inspirational and showing they could be more than "just a girl," as the boys in Tubby's clubhouse used to call Little Lulu and her friends a decade later in their Dell Comics adventures.

Calling All Girls # 1, Sept. 1941, copyright The Parents' Magazine Press. The first comic book expressly for girls appeared six years before the first romance comic.

The most intriguing aspect of *Calling All Girls* is that it approached schoolgirls not as boy-crazy or male-dependent, but as interesting individuals in their own right. The ensuing issues of *Calling All Girls* expanded on this theme. This was definitely a mini "feminist manifesto" for teens! With the December 1945 issue (# 44), *Calling All Girls* eliminated the comic strips. Its two 1945 strips, *Judy Wing* and *The Victory Club*, became text stories, with an explanation from the editor involving the different types of paper needed to print comics.

Younger girls get a sister comic

The real reason seems to have been two-fold. First, *Calling All Girls* had become so popular that there were dozens of advertisements for girls (there were none in the first issue). Second, Parents' Magazine was about to embark on publishing its second magazine for girls—*Polly Pigtails*. Polly was targeted for grammar-school girls and debuted with # 1 in January of 1946. Parents' Magazine by this time may have felt comic strips lacked interest for older girls, for they confined them to *Polly Pigtails*, which was advertised as "of interest to girls 7–12." *Polly Pigtails* also quickly became a monthly, with the third issue, and remained so through the first half of 1949, the year Parents' Magazine stopped publishing comic books. In 1950, *Calling All Girls* changed its name to *Senior Prom* with # 90 and at the same time *Polly Pigtails* became *Girls' Fun and Fashion Magazine* with # 44, reflecting the increasing sophistication of the postwar era. *Girls' Fun and Fashion Magazine* lasted only four issues, although it continued to publish the same comic strips that ran in *Polly Pigtails*. *Senior Prom* eventually reverted back to a digest form of *Calling All Girls*.

Parents' Magazine's two monthly publications for girls became so popular that the company tried a third title, *Sweet Sixteen*, which ran 13 issues from # 1 (Aug.–Sept. 1946) through # 13 (Jan. 1948), with a mixture of fictional and factual comic strips designed for teen girls. The last nine issues of *Sweet Sixteen* ran monthly, meaning that in 1947 Parents' Magazine was publishing three monthly comic books for girls. Such a market boded well for the success of romance comics late that year.

Martin Goodman's *Miss America* title quickly tried to take advantage of the popularity of *Calling All Girls*. For example, the issue of *Miss America* for Oct. 1945 (Vol. 3, # 1) was 76 pages long for a dime. It contained no less than 28 major display advertisements, showing just how strong the market for female readers was. There were only 13 pages of comic strips—a 7-page *Patsy Walker* strip and a 6-page *Betty Blair* story. The rest of the issue was packed with text features on film, health, records, hair, fashion, pets and recipes. There was also a marvelous text feature urging tolerance for diversity entitled, "Are You a Hater?" by the famed singer Kate Smith (or, perhaps, ghost written for her).

By the middle of 1947, thanks to its healthy advertising base, *Miss America* was still a full 68 pages—which had been the standard size for comic books in the first decade of their existence but was largely abandoned by the end of 1943. But in the second half of 1947, *Miss America* dwindled to the standard 52-page size. And as time went by, there were fewer and fewer text features and more and more comics, until *Miss America* had become pretty much a standard teenage comic.

It's interesting to note that by the issue for April 1950, *Miss America* contained only nine advertisements (typical for the period) in a 52-page issue, along with two 7-page *Patsy Walker* stories, two 6-page serious romance stories and a 5-page romance text story entitled, "Roadside Romance." The romance story plugged on the cover was entitled, "Happiness Is a Lad Named Larry"—which just happened to be the name of editor Stan Lee's brother, Larry Lieber.

Comics for girls give way

Gone was any sort of inspiration for girls to become much more than love objects, unlike comics for girls in the pre–1947 period. There were a few text features, but the feel of the comic was definitely different. This, of course, was due in part to the success of teen humor comics along with the new romance comic genre, which became a newsstand flood in 1949 and 1950 after the first tentative flings in 1947 and 1948.

It was also due, in all likelihood, to the fact that beginning in the late 1940s, women were increasingly urged to follow domestic lives and typically female pursuits and to let the men resume the education and the power careers that had been interrupted by the war. Women were needed to do so-called men's jobs on the homefront during much of the 1940s, but that time had passed—at least in the minds of many people. That's one big reason there were no comics like *Calling All Girls* or the original *Miss America* in the 1950s. A typical 1943 issue of *Calling All Girls* would have seemed out-of-place, indeed, on the 1950s comic book scene, despite the popularity of romance comics.

Other than the teen humor, movie and romance titles, there was one other genuine attempt at a comic aimed at girls—six issues of *Keen Teens* from Magazine Enterprises in 1945–47. *Young Life* # 1–3 and its successor *Teen Life* # 4–5, were published by New Age Publishers, but these were general-interest teen titles. *Keen Teens* featured articles like, "Are You on the Boys' Hate Parade?" (# 4, April–May 1947). Issues # 2–5 featured male heart-throb singers on the covers. The last issue, # 6 (Aug.–Sept. 1947), featured actress-ballerina Bambi Linn. These period pieces, however, contain little of real inspiration to girls in the manner of *Calling All Girls* and the early issues of *Miss America*.

Politically incorrect Moronica and Starlet O'Hara

Can you imagine a comic strip succeeding today with the title, *Moronica—Miss Nitwit of 2008*? Of course you can't. Dumb blonde jokes may survive on the late-night circuit, but politically incorrect popular culture is largely confined to word of mouth in these supposedly more enlightened times.

More than a half-century ago, though, Moronica, Miss Nitwit of 1953 was one of the stars of the six-issue run of *Dizzy Dames* from the American Comics Group, one of the leading second-tier publishers of the period. Issues of *Dizzy Dames* are hotly sought after by a small but avid group of collectors who enjoy gathering up the politically incorrect relics of our culture, produced before the movement toward a wide variety of human rights began in earnest during the 1960s. These artifacts provide a fascinating insight into our not-so-long-ago culture, not to mention attitudes that continue to linger.

Politically incorrect humor, much of it quite outrageous by today's standards, was often found in early teen humor comic books. Teen humor, though, has been refined and cleaned up to an astonishing degree ever since by the Archie folks, beginning in the 1960s, since they have had a virtual monopoly on the market since then. Yet a handful of pre–Comics Code humor titles went completely over the top. This was in much the same comic book spirit that America's World War II and Korean War opponents—even as genuinely nasty as their military leaders proved to be—were malevolently caricatured in comic books of the era, thus greatly enhancing the collectibility of those comics.

Two such humor titles were *Starlet O'Hara in Hollywood*, a four-issue run from Standard in 1948–49, and *Dizzy Dames* in 1952–53. The material in both was provided by the B. W. Sangor Shop, a leading producer of comic book stories. The Sangor Shop was especially

Starlet O'Hara # 1, Dec. 1948, copyright Visual Editions, Inc. Here is the height of political incorrectness: Moronica, "Miss Nitwit of 1948."

important for both the comic book arm of Ned Pines's Standard publishing empire and for ACG, whose origins date to 1943 with several sub-publishers and which morphed into a company with a familiar little logo that began appearing in the late 1940s.

"Miss Nitwit" of every year

Moronica may have debuted with three backup stories in Standard's *Starlet O'Hara* # 1 (Dec. 1948). Moronica tales continued through *Starlet O'Hara* # 4 (Sept. 1949), although Standard reduced its titles to 36 pages in 1949, so she was limited to one story per issue.

The cover of the first issue of *Starlet O'Hara*—a star-struck Hollywood wanna-be who was drawn by Owen Fitzgerald—featured a plug for "Moronica, Miss Nitwit of 1948" at the bottom and "The Terrific Teen-Age Comic" in a star at the top right. Moronica wasn't plugged again until # 4—by which time she had graduated to "Miss Nitwit of 1949"—and beginning with # 2, that top blurb was accurately changed to "Her Romantic Adventures *in* Movieland," referring to Miss Starlet.

Although the *Starlet O'Hara* title doubtless was at least partly aimed at teen readers, it more properly was categorized as a comic book of "working girl" stories in the classic tradition, long since a part of the comic strips and made famous in comic books by the likes of Marvel's *Millie the Model* and *Nellie the Nurse*.

Moronica, though, found her primary home in *Dizzy Dames*, with each issue cover-bannered, "Screwballs in Skirts!" She was accompanied by the looney-bin likes of Man-Huntin' Minnie of Delta Pu, Dee Licious, Knothead Nellie and Knothead Nancy (must have been sisters!), Broadway Babes, Looney Lucy, Screwball Sal, Daffy Damsels ... absolutely the height of politically incorrect female characters!

Moronica starts a riot

Moronica started a riot in *Dizzy Dames* # 1, over her appearance on television in a "man on the street" program, causing the announcer to say, "Radio may be dead, but believe me, Buster, I'm going back to it!" The question was, "What do you think of America's tax structure?" to which Moronica replied, "I think it's beautiful ... I think America's tax structure is one of the prettiest buildings in Washington!"

By the time Moronica graduated to "Miss Nitwit of 1953" in *Dizzy Dames* # 3, she's sitting on a park bench looking for a job, causing two squirrels to look at her with dismay. "I'm not giving her any more of my nuts, because she never plays with us like the other squirrels do!" And when the employment agency finally sends her out on a job as a gardener, the woman at the door asks, "Are you a horticulturist?" to which Moronica amazingly replies, "No, ma'am, I'm a Republican!"

That elicits the response, "Please, Miss! Don't show your ignorance!" to which Moronica responds, "That's not ignorance, that's a vaccination scar!" When she puts pillows and sheets in the flower beds and is asked what kind of gardener she is, she replies, "A girl gardener!" Then she proceeds to pluck out all the daffodils, explaining, "Who wants crazy flowers growing around their house? If you want dils, I'll plant sane dils, not these daffy ones!"

Hillman's My Date: Simon and Kirby's bridge to romance

For years, many comic book collectors considered Hillman's *My Date* the first romance comic, probably because of the title and its creators, Joe Simon and Jack Kirby, along with

"My" in the title. *My Date*, however, is more properly categorized as one of the teen humor titles that served as a bridge to mainstream romance. *My Date* ran from # 1 (July 1947) through # 4 (Jan. 1948). *My Date* featured covers and artwork by Simon and Kirby in each issue, during the same period they were creating and publishing the early issues of *Young Romance*, the first true romance comic.

My Date's feature, "My Date with Swifty Chase" featured the amorous adventures of teen hero Swifty in his fevered chase of Sunny Daye, who resembled sweet Betty Cooper from the *Archie* Series. Swifty constantly battled wealthy Snubby Skeemer III, a knockoff of Reggie in the *Archie* titles. In Swifty's first madcap adventure, a 14-pager in which he is Hillsdale High's basketball star, Swifty finds a way to help Sunny's Hollywood heart-throb, Humphrey Hogart (a parody of Warner Brothers star Humphrey Bogart), claim the heart of young Chandra Blake, who just happens to live in Hillsdale.

My Date # 1 featured three other teen humor characters: Ginny, Ultra Violet, and teenage aviatrix Kitty Hawk, plus the bizarre and humorous "My Date: Unusual Dates as told to Jean Anne Marten, *My Date's* Young People's Counselor." In the amusing and unique *Ultra Violet* strip, a teen named Violet Ray's overpowering daydreams turned her into an ultra female adult.

My Date also featured a genuine romance story in later issues, in much the same 1949–50 manner as National's *Sensation Comics* and Marvel titles *Junior Miss* and *Miss America*. In *My Date* # 2 (Sept. 1947), Simon and Kirby created a nicely portrayed comical moocher named House-Date Harry in the Swifty Chase stories.

At the same time, Simon and Kirby rocked the comic book world when they introduced true love to the comics with *Young Romance* # 1.

THREE

Young Romance in Bloom
How Love Came to the Comic Books

In hindsight, it seems romance comics were inevitable in the post–World War II market. Love had been a pulp magazine staple for more than two decades, along with being the primary focus of "slick" confession magazines and movie star publications. No one was surprised when Joe Simon explained in his memoir, *The Comic Book Makers* (1990), what gave him the idea to create the first romance comic: "I wondered how they [female readers] would accept a comic book version of the popular *True Story Magazine*, with youthful, emotional yet wholesome stories supposedly told in the first person by love-smitten teenagers. Visually, the magazine love stories seemed a natural conversion for comic books."

When the always entrepreneurial Simon, a co-creator of the iconic Captain America in 1941, wrote his memoirs, he devoted a mere four pages of the 208-page volume to his work with Jack Kirby in creating the first true romance title, *Young Romance* from Crestwood Publications in 1947. Nearly two decades later, the prolific Simon seems to have short-changed himself in retrospect. *Young Romance* # 1 (Sept.–Oct. 1947) has become an icon of Americana in its own right, a much sought-after collectors' item, though not in a league with Captain America # 1. DC Comics (formerly National), in fact, considered *Young Romance* # 1 to be so historically significant that the company reprinted it as part of its DC Millennium Series of 2000–2001. That reprint exposed many more collectors to the historical significance of the first romance comic. DC was able to reprint the issue because it bought out Crestwood in 1963. DC published *Young Romance* until 1975 and its companion, *Young Love*, until 1977, and they were the venerable company's final love comics.

Simon finds a successful formula

Simon could not have been more correct, both in 1947 and 1990, although by the latter date his pioneering title, *Young Romance*, had been dead for 15 years. He exaggerated a bit when he said, "The magazines prospered and endured with the same format for three generations"— unless you consider three decades to be three generations. He was 100 percent correct, however, when he claimed *Young Romance* "shook up the industry" in a caption underneath a reprint of the cover of # 1. To say *Young Romance* had "600 imitations," as he claimed, wasn't quite correct, unless he was talking about the total number of romance issues published through 1950. The aggregate number of romance titles was only about 300 their entire history.

He must have used "wholesome stories" with regard to the moral lessons they taught, because few of the stories were anything but hearts and flowers. Simon's real genius came in recognizing the need for a fresh genre in comic books, with stories driven by plots and not continuing heroics such as in *Captain America* and *Boy Commandos*. Those worthies were two of the most popular among the multitude of heroic strips Simon and Kirby produced before they turned to romance. Comic book love, however, enabled them to make a good living for about a decade when all of their heroes were discontinued by the end of the Golden Age.

In the world of comic book collectors, it took a while for *Young Romance* to be recognized as the first romance title. Some fans formerly felt Simon and Kirby's own *My Date*, a teen humor title from second-tier publisher Hillman with romantic overtones, deserved the distinction earlier in 1947. Still others cited the one-shot *Romantic Picture Novelettes* from then-tiny Magazine Enterprises in 1946, but that issue was nothing more than a romantic cover and a book full of Mary Worth newspaper strip reprints. To be sure, the love-themed cover of *Romantic Picture Novelettes* was a comic book "first."

Simon recalled in his memoir that *Young Romance* # 1 was "a complete sellout." He noted both how *Young Romance* and its sister title created in 1949, *Young Love*, eventually sold more than a million copies per issue for Crestwood, a small publisher that had never enjoyed any title even remotely that successful. Regardless of the real numbers—many publishers claimed sales in the millions, when in reality they were often referring to pass-around readership totals—there's no doubt these two titles were rousing commercial successes. In 1950, when nearly 80 percent of all romance titles failed (see Chapter Five), *Young Romance* sailed along on a monthly basis and *Young Love* also went monthly in March of 1950.

Crestwood, also known as Feature Publications and Prize (for its cover logo), might have seemed an unlikely candidate to debut such a momentous comic book. Even so, as Simon explained in his memoirs, he didn't feel it would be wise for the Simon and Kirby team to self-publish (they would try that unsuccessfully and briefly with *Mainline* in 1954–55). Simon said Crestwood accepted the duo's proposal that they and the company would split the profits, since it was up to the longtime team to provide the stories and art, some from other artists. Crestwood published only 20 other comic books in 1947 in addition to the first two issues of *Young Romance*.

One of the top 100 comic books

Young Romance # 1 was paid a historic tribute in 2004 in *The 100 Greatest Comic Books*, a book by longtime comics fan Jerry Weist that resulted from a vote by 44 people prominent in the world of comics. The committee, including the author of this book, voted *Young Romance* # 1 as No. 28 in terms of votes compiled. It was the only romance comic to make the list. But it was also the only one really necessary, especially given how many iconic American comics have been published over more than 70 years.

Indeed, the comic book world would be all shook up by romance, but it took a lot longer than might have been reasonably expected—almost a full year. *Young Romance* appeared only bi-monthly for its first eight issues, through 1948. Timely/Marvel, always keen to jump on any trend, hit the racks with the second romance title, *My Romance* # 1 (Aug. 1948). The style of the large logo, blatantly imitating *Young Romance*, seems to have been designed especially to tell readers that they had another option for four-color love.

The sleazy publisher Victor Fox, another guy always on the lookout for the latest themes that would sell, was third in the romance stakes with *My Life* # 4 (Sept.1948), which was a numerical if not thematic extension of *Meet Corliss Archer*, a sexy teen humor title based on a decidedly non-sexy novel and radio show. Then followed one of the industry's titans, Fawcett Publications, with *Sweethearts* # 68 (Oct. 1948). Since *Sweethearts* was a numerical continuation of *Captain Midnight* # 67 (which was dated both Sept. and Fall 1948), one can only speculate how young subscribers might been have been shocked to receive *Sweethearts* # 68 in the mail! (If that, indeed, is the way it happened. Companies handled title changes differently with regard to subscriptions.)

No plugs for Sweethearts

Fawcett apparently didn't want most of its readers to know about *Sweethearts*. Fawcett did not list *Sweethearts* (or any of its many ensuing romance titles) along with the comic books regularly plugged in lists on the first page of the company's numerous titles. The best-selling *Captain Marvel* and *Whiz Comics*, Fawcett's flagship titles, neither advertised *Sweethearts* nor listed it among the company's titles, even though "A Fawcett Publication" clearly appeared on the cover of *Sweethearts* from its inception. Clearly, *Sweethearts* was not being marketed to the fans of *Captain Marvel* or fellow Fawcett best-seller *Hopalong Cassidy*!

The first five issues of *Young Romance* had no competition in the realm of romance comics in 1947 and 1948, and purportedly sold very well, yet they remain difficult to find for many collectors. Many comic books that ostensibly did not sell as well are easier to find. Why this situation seems to be the case remains something of a mystery. It should be noted, though, that *Young Romance* # 1 (Sept.–Oct. 1947) through # 3 (Jan.–Feb. 1948) carried a large banner beneath huge logo: "Designed for the more ADULT readers of COMICS." That, however, may not have prevented their sale to younger girls, though it seems unlikely boys of any age would have been attracted to them.

The first four issues of *Young Romance* were all distinctly different, with story themes that did not duplicate each other in the least. They contained a polyglot of stories ranging from pure romance to crime to contrived heroics and unlikely coincidences. Virtually all of the stories in these early issues of *Young Romance* were destined to be told many times over by dozens of publishers, though the occasional early romance comic themes involving crime and violence were drastically toned down when the Comics Code Authority symbol began appearing in 1955 (see Chapter Nine).

"I Was a Pick-Up!"

The first page in the first romance comic must, indeed, have been a shocker to the parents of any 12-year-old girl who might have found the issue in her bedroom. "I Was a Pick-Up!" was the title, in large letters, of the opening story in *Young Romance* # 1. The first balloon shows a young man in a suit and tie telling a fully dressed girl who is half out of a car, "Don't put on that act with me, Toni! After all, I did pick you up! Now, how about a kiss?" Nothing like starting a new genre with a bang! Nothing like that title had ever appeared in the slightly more than a decade comic magazines had been on the racks.

In many ways, this first story—a 13-pager—is an archetype of the "sheltered girl goes wrong but still finds love." Toni Benson, a 17-year-old high school student, lives a sheltered existence with her protective grandmother after being abandoned as a baby by her mother, who is described as "bad." Indeed! When Toni finds a trunk with her mother's clothing, she sets out to create a "dream dress ... Granny will never know!" The low-cut, red gown inspires her to take a walk: "How can I explain what I felt? Was it the dress or was I growing up? This day seemed to be different from any other ... it was spring, 1945 ... and the breeze seemed to whisper a strange temptation through my very being." That was pretty racy writing for the comic books of 1947, albeit the type of purple prose that had been appearing since 1942 in Lev Gleason's ground-breaking *Crime Does Not Pay*, the first crime comic book.

(Just as *Sweethearts* succeeded *Captain Midnight*, *Crime Does Not Pay* picked up for *Silver Streak*.)

During Toni's walk, a fellow in a convertible—one that seemed surprisingly modern and snazzy for the ration-influenced World War II year of 1945!—picks her up with the usual line: "Pardon the greeting, lady ... but it's not often I see a dream floating by." Toni finds out his name is Bob Scott. Young Mr. Scott then declares, "Why, Dad runs this town—almost, anyway!" Several dates later, or so it seems, Bob takes Toni to a roadhouse, complete with roulette wheel. In thoroughly cowardly fashion, he leaves her stranded when the place is raided by the cops. Gambler Stanley Budko, described as "one of the town's black sheep," rescues her, kicks a table into a police officer so they can escape, and gets her home to grandmother (Stanley apparently never does have to answer for assaulting the officer!). Her grandmother refuses to have anything to do with "that gangster," but she and he take up with each other, until he leaves her in pain with this letter: "You're a sweet kid ... and I'm just a guy who's been around too much—so I thought it best I leave before you're hurt ... Stan."

And thus were shed the first tears in a romance comic book panel!

The first contrived happy ending

The first of untold thousands of contrived happy endings occurs two pages later, after Toni has fled the octopus-like fellow portrayed on the splash page. She walks into a gas station and sees her lost love: "Stanley Budko! Oh, Stan! You turn up in the darndest places!" In the final three panels, he explains he has gone straight, is doing well as owner of the gas station, proposes to Toni, is accepted, and carries her off. And, surely, they must have lived happily ever after.

The second story in *Young Romance* # 1, "The Farmer's Wife," was an 8-page piffle about the adjustment of a 21-year-old bride and her 36-year-old husband, a fellow named Bill Toomey (a few years later, there would be a famous track and field athlete by that name). The third tale, "Misguided Heart," packs a wallop for an unpredictable 7-pager. A factory worker, June Collins, realizes the man for her is not the factor owner's snobby son, but one of her co-workers who punches the prima donna offspring, much to the approval of the down-to-earth factory owner himself.

The bizarre 7-page fourth story, "The Plight of the Suspicious Bridegroom," reveals how said bridegroom foils the "hobby" of a perverted bellhop who took joy in breaking up engagements by writing false accusations to engaged people. The pervert, however, doesn't realize he is talking to the suspicious bridegroom, from whose perspective the story is told. After the twisted fellow receives a beating, he takes up stamp collecting! Surely one of the strangest stories ever to appear in a romance comic, this was not drawn by S&K. The final little epic, an 8-pager entitled, "Summer Song," is an archetypical girl-realizes-which-boy-she-belongs-with story in a conflict of social classes. Simon and Kirby would go on to write and draw far better material than appeared in this first book. Yet their writing, drawing and editing efforts represented an adequate beginning, considering the mediocre quality of much of their contemporary non-romance competition on the racks. Contrary to the cover blurb, only the first story in *Young Romance* # 1 provided a hint of adult themes.

"Boy Crazy" and then some

Young Romance # 2 (Nov.–Dec. 1947) offered the first downbeat ending in romance comics history with the lead story, the 14-page "Boy Crazy." When Suzi Burnette tries to steal the man her aunt loves, she learns the hard way about unethical behavior. "Well, that's the story of my foolish campaign against my aunt—I never thought my victory would turn into a life-long defeat—I'll always miss Clint—always." This naturalistic opus isn't bad.

"My Broken Heart Was Page-One News" is an amusing story of how a reporter and photographer realize they are meant to be, despite the catty efforts of the "debutante society editor." "Dangerous Romance" was an out-and-out crime story in which the heroine realizes she is dating a killer. Opposite the final page, ironically (or perhaps purposefully) is a full-page advertisement for the first issue of Simon and Kirby's *Justice Traps the Guilty*, a Crestwood crime comic. Also in *Young Romance* # 2, "The Poorest Girl in the World" is a crime tale in which a kidnapped girl's upper-class father accepts her lower-class heart-throb after he rescues her. "Her Tragic Love" tells the grisly story of a girl who commits suicide with a leap out of a tall building at midnight because she thinks her man has been wrongfully executed for a crime he didn't commit. She doesn't know he has been saved by new evidence at the last minute and the story ends with the dead girl's sister, who loves the same man, hoping to somehow salvage his broken spirit. *Young Romance* # 2, in short, is a crime comic in everything but name and provides an astonishing contrast to the stories in # 1. The cover of # 2, by the way, has nothing to do with any of the stories inside, but that is also true of the other early issues.

The lead story in *Young Romance* # 3 (Jan.–Feb. 1948), "Marriage Contract," is the best story in the first three issues of the title, though it is an obvious takeoff on all the Warner Brothers films that dealt with juvenile delinquency and the responsibilities of society. A young lawyer wins his lady love after saving her younger brother from a jail sentence. Part of the lawyer's winning argument in court: "Society never asks why! It condemns the young delinquent but tolerates the slum which molds him! Johnny Burke is guilty of his crime—but we must share that guilt and bear its shame! I ask another chance not only for Johnny, but for all the underprivileged kids like him! We owe it to them!"

In "Campus Outcast," a department store clerk ultimately realizes the man who really loves her—who is about to enter college on the G.I. Bill—is better than the snobby college kids she admires. "His Best Friend's Sweetheart" is another foolish-girl-finally-gone-right archetype, when the best friend of the man she loves turns out to be a heel. "Love Or a Career?" offers the first humorous ending in a romance comic, when a career-driven radio commentator and a jealous career-driven female writer find love with each other—after much turmoil by doing a radio show together as newlyweds. "Man-Hater!" is another archetype, that of the stubbornly independent female athlete who learns that men aren't so bad, after all—especially the man she almost kills with weariness after she challenges him to climb a mountain with her.

Taking out the ADULT in COMICS

All in all, *Young Romance* # 3 is by far the best of the first three. Crestwood, however, must have felt that the cover banner, "For the more ADULT readers of COMICS" was hurting circulation, for it was removed for good with # 4 (March–April 1948). In the 1940s and '50s, publishers often preferred not to make it obvious to readers—or newsstand dealers—when their titles were new. That probably explains why Crestwood did not print numbers on the covers of the first four issues of *Young Romance*.

Young Romance # 4 (March–April 1948) also represented significant improvement on # 1 and # 2. This issue, the fourth romance comic, featured a cover theme that would be duplicated countless times in the next three decades: A campus hero talks with a girl in a soda shop while another girl tells her friend, "Don't count me out yet, Babs! No homespun, little snip is going to steal any marches on me! I always get what I go after—and I'll get Bob!"

The first story, "Blind Date," is yet another archetype, dealing with friends of the opposite sex who took 11 pages to examine themselves and realize they were really meant for each other—when neither suspects such is the case at the beginning of this predictable story. Unlike so many of the stories in the first three issues, this was pure, relationship-driven romance, with no exotic plot complications.

The second story in # 4, an illogical 8-pager entitled, "Guilty," involves a romance between a conscience-stricken cop's daughter and a crook whom she loves but refuses to alibi for. "There can't be anyone else but Johnny," she says after the crook, portrayed as an unsavory no-goodnik, goes off to serve a five-year jail term. "I didn't betray him out of malice—I just want him to clear his name with society." The penultimate panel shows her on the day of his release: "I know he'll come to see me—will it be for vengeance or for love? I can only sit here waiting and hoping." As she opens the door, he greets her with flowers and "Dotty darling!" This is the kind of poor story that gave comics a bad name for treating even real-life possibilities in less-than-logical terms. Fortunately, even as banal as some romance stories were in the 1950s, most of them made more sense than this, especially from publishers with competent writers such as National and St. John.

The next two stories in *Young Romance* # 4 also were told many times over in coming years: "I Love You, Frank Gerard" reveals how an ostensibly hard-driving, controversial career woman named Randy has set her sights for a man she loves and lands him by convincing him that a woman really can combine brains and beauty. "Her Rival!" ends with the loser of a "national beauty contest" working as a carhop, waiting for a devoted test pilot to realize he loves her as much has he cares for air speed. This one hit the racks a few months after Chuck Yaeger became the first man to break the sound barrier and may have been inspired by that event.

"Frauline Sweetheart"

The 9-page "Frauline Sweetheart" in # 4 is outstanding (despite the misspelling of "Fraulein"). This one foreshadows the many strong stories about contemporary issues and events that Simon and Kirby produced for *Young Romance*. A former Hitler youth leader falls in love with an American soldier during the post-war occupation of Nazi Germany, but she can't forego her true feelings or her background, devoted to the Nazis. Even so, she can't let the American be blown up in a bomb plot, even though he has renounced her—despite his love for her—and ultimately leaves her. The last panel is highly unusual for the comics of 1948: "My American was but a tender memory now.... He had opened the door of my heart so I could see a little more of the truth.... I knew now what Jack had been trying to tell me: that one cannot harbor love and hate in the same heart ... that one must love everybody in order to love at all.... The sun suddenly splashed the shadowed streets with warm light.... Was it an omen?"

It wasn't atypical of romance comics to leave the reader hanging with regard to the future of the protagonists, but there seldom was such a possibility of realistic psychological and character change leading to happiness. One can't help but want Annaliese to win back her love in the glowing promise of post-war America.

Timely love and romance

When prolific publisher Martin Goodman decided to take a leap into love in 1948, Crestwood's pioneering *Young Romance* had been on the stands nearly a year. Since Simon and Kirby had played such a key role while working for Goodman's *Timely Comics* in the early 1940s, there's no doubt he heard about the sales figures for the first three issues or so, and leaped into comic book love. His classic super heroes—Captain America, the Human Torch, Sub-Mariner—were on the way out and he and editor Stan Lee, then in his mid–20s, had already begun experimenting with several genres new to the company.

In 1947, Timely—also referred to both earlier and later as Marvel—produced only 128 issues, about only one-third of the immense output the publisher pumped out under the Atlas cover logo in the 1952–56 period. In 1948, though, all this genre experimentation resulted in 212 issues, second only to National's 224. The full flowering of the romance genre in the second half of 1949 enabled Marvel to lead the industry that year with 272 issues, despite the demise of the costume heroes.

Timely didn't boast about its circulation figures the way several other publishers sometimes did. *My Romance*, though, seems likely to have sold well indeed, or else the publisher would not have soon flooded the market with four-color love (see Chapters Four and Five). But then, the title should have sold well, with "Romance" in the same large letters across the top of the cover that helped *Young Romance* receive instant notice.

At a time when Timely/Marvel had shrunk many of its comics to 36 pages (including covers), the firm unleashed the first four issues of *My Romance* at 52 pages, perhaps because the editors wanted to compete with the 52-page *Young Romance*. The title became *My Own Romance* with # 4 (March 1949).

The only fanfare that Timely gave *My Romance* # 1 (Sept. 1948) was a deep-red heart on the cover, centered among pictures featuring four stories. Inside the heart it read: "All the world loves a lover, and here is a magazine designed especially for anyone who ever dreamed of romance, and orchids and moonlight! Here is laughter and tears, hope and heartbreak, all told by those in love! In short, here is *My Romance!*"

The first Timely romance story, the 10-page "Love for a Crooner!" is one of those marvelous period pieces that collectors drool over (it was "Crush on a Crooner" on the cover). The story is right out of "American Idol": small-town boy makes good on his chance to sing, small-town girl follows him but misunderstands his popularity with women, and love finally prevails. While the ending is happy, it's also logical.

Routine roads to romantic happiness

The other four stories are all routine roads to romantic happiness: A girl learns who really loves her and why he's best for her in "The Ring." A girl learns why an older man isn't really a good fit in her world and returns to a boy her own age in "Too Young for Romance." A girl gets back her boyfriend in "The One Who Waited!" A girl convinces a football hero to give up the game for both her sake and the academics he loves in "Love and Football Don't Mix!"

Like the five stories in # 1, the five stories in *My Romance* # 2 (Nov. 1948) and the five in # 3 (Jan. 1949) all feature happy endings for the girls and good guys involved. The first story in # 2, "With This Ring, I Thee Wed," is a truly ludicrous piece about a hyper-competitive female sports star who can't, or won't, give any guys a break on the tennis court or in the pool—until she falls in love. "Sports! Games! Who cares about them? I'm in love!" she says. In contrast, "Plain Jane!" is a nifty little tale of how a daughter learns her mother overcame an inferiority complex—and how her daughter is also likely to do so. But the only really solid story among the 10 in the first two issues is "The Outsider!" in # 3, in which an American reporter offers bigots a two-fisted lesson in tolerance—and wins the love of a European girl who was the outsider in her town. It's not profound, and it's told tongue-in-cheek, but it wasn't bad reading for the period.

The first three issues of *My Romance* could not have been much more different from the first three of *Young Romance* if the publishers had deliberately set out to produce entirely different story styles in the same genre. But that's what makes old romance comics fun, because they provide surprising variety. There's an innocent feeling to *My Romance*, in contrast to the often grim themes in early issues of *Young Romance*, but that's probably because Marvel seems to have aimed the stories at younger readers.

In contrast to the feeling of the stories, the covers of both # 2 and # 3 present dramatic scenes—unrelated to any stories—of women being victimized by men. Marvel went on to use this theme much more often than not on most of its 1949–50 romance issues, including its first photo cover, on *My Own Romance* # 4. But there are five more stories with happy endings, making Marvel 20 for 20 in positive outcomes in its first venture into romance.

Marvel defends comic books

Interestingly, *My Romance* # 3 carries a letter from the editors concerning criticism about comic books in 1948 issues of the *Saturday Review of Literature* by a "Dr. Wertham." This letter, which appeared in all the publisher's titles, was apparently the first reference in comics to Dr. Fredric Wertham, whose screed, *Seduction of the Innocent* six years later would help lead to wholesale changes in how comic books were presented (see Chapter Nine).

It is especially interesting how Marvel's letter nails a primary flaw in Wertham's cause-and-effect theories about comic book reading: "Ninety-three percent of all young people (from 8 to 16 years of age) read comics. Naturally a few young people get into some kind of trouble ... so do a lot of older ones ... and of course many of the kids who get into trouble do read comics. But that the article does not state is the fact that 93 percent of the boys and girls who get into *no trouble at all* also read comics." The logic was irrefutable.

Marvel listed all its 50 comic book titles on this page, including *My Romance*. Only seven were crime titles; there were no horror titles yet, and no other romance titles. When the title became *My Own Romance* with # 4, the editors published a different, less logical pro-comics letter, reminding readers of when some of the earliest novels, such as *Robinson Crusoe* and *Gulliver's Travels*, were once called "slop" in eighteenth-century England. The letter in # 3 made a lot more sense.

The Goddess of Love gets involved

Any discussion about the earliest romance comics should include the fantasy title *Venus* from Marvel in 1948–52. *Venus* is one of the strangest of all comics. After all, how many comic books ran only 19 issues, yet evolved into five distinct genre titles?

Venus can be included with any list of comics with ultra-powered heroines. Early issues of *Venus* also have a girlish/teen humor feeling. Romance titles? There are at least three issues of *Venus* that no romance collection would be complete without. Several mid-range issues of *Venus* also involve science fiction with the constant fantasy. The final five issues of *Venus* are among some of the grisliest horror comics ever produced. As for artists of note, Bill Everett drew some of the most intriguing art in all of comics for the last six issues.

All that and more is to be discovered in the 19 issues of *Venus*, which was a comic book phenomenon unique in the industry. *Venus* represents Marvel's attempt to take a character and match her to whatever trend she seemed to fit best at the time. Unfortunately, each of her appearances in the different genres was so brief that the character never really had a chance for development, and so remains a largely forgotten oddity except by enthusiasts. But *Venus* should not be forgotten; it among the wildest of esoteric comics (titles outside the mainstream).

The first half of the run deals primarily with Venus's love for Whitney Hammond, the handsome publisher of *Beauty Magazine*. Venus works as an editor/reporter for Hammond, who refuses to believe Venus really is the Goddess of Love but marvels (no pun intended) how she deals with human emotions—as does Whitney's secretary Della, Venus's scheming rival. *Venus* was the lone survivor of Marvel's failed experiment in super heroine titles at the close of the Golden Age. Yet she may be the least known of its heroines, since she appeared only in her own title and did not connect with the rest of the "Marvel Universe."

The first issues of *Venus*, along with heroines *Sun Girl* and *Namora*, were dated August 1948 as companions for Timely's established *Blonde Phantom* title. The other three were soon discontinued but *Venus* survived. However, as if to debate the wisdom of comics featuring the females of fantasy, Marvel skipped an issue date and did not come back with *Venus* # 4 until April 1949. The *Venus* epic in # 5, however, is a "serious" three-part, 19-page tale of gods and goddesses, good and evil, and love conquering all. It didn't match the humorous cover at all, but that was just another oddity in the odd history of *Venus*.

The fifth issue also began the practice of running filler romance stories, which ran through issue # 9. These issues of *Venus* are thus a must for romance completists. With issue # 6 (Aug. 1949), the integration of covers, themes and stories becomes complete for the first time. The blurb atop the logo is "Romantic Tales of Fantasy," which lasts three issues and was obviously an attempt to tie in with the romance comic craze. The cover blurb is "The Wrath of a Goddess," which is also the title of the third chapter of an epic 19-page tale. Roman and Greek gods and goddesses, along with other Satanic figures of evil including Satan himself, were freely used in the pages of *Venus*, along with references to numerous famous females, legendary and/or historic. It was far, far too much of a mishmash, though readers educated in mythology find the juxtapositions both funny and fascinating.

Issues # 7 (Nov. 1949) and # 8 (Feb. 1950) featured beautiful painted covers that would lead readers to believe they were romance comics. And, were it not for the fantasy elements in the stories, they could indeed be classified as such. Romance, though, was soon de-emphasized and in its place came heavy duty mythology with the publication of the landmark # 9 (May 1950), which once again used the ever-generic Marvel title, "Whom the Gods Destroy!" on the cover. That title was nowhere to be found in either of the two stories in the comic book, which was the first of the only two 52-page issues of *Venus*.

Venus # 9 is of particular sentimental value to the author, who was 10 years old in 1958 when stumbling upon this issue in a second-hand book store. I was enchanted with this comic, since nothing like it was on the racks at the time. In fact, I must have read this issue 10 times over; the childhood copy became so tattered that many years later a replacement copy was obtained. It's uncertain who drew this sentimental favorite, but # 9 is filled with marvelous images of fantasy. The two *Venus* stories, "The Man She Dared Not Love" and "Beauty for Everyone," make this the most enchanting issue of the entire run.

Venus # 10 is also an excellent issue, the only one with three separate, full-length stories. The contrast in themes is interesting: Separate battles with Satan, Venus's rival Della and a mad scientist. If a collector can't find # 9, *Venus* # 10 also works nicely as an example of the wonderful hokum this series represents.

With # 11 (Nov. 1950), Venus morphs into a hard-nosed character concerned only with investigations into elements of the weird/science fantasy/horror in her role as a reporter for *Beauty Magazine*. (Who knows what a reporter for *Beauty Magazine* was doing investigating

Venus # 9, May 1950, copyright Leading Comic Corp. This unique title, a melding of fantasy and romance, was one of the author's favorite comic books to be found in the second-hand stores of the 1950s.

the supernatural!) The fillers were science fiction in # 11–13 and horror in # 14–19. Once again, this was in line with Marvel's policy of following the hot trend of the moment, and horror became all the rage beginning in 1950–51 (after horror's earlier appearances in a few comics of the 1947–49 period, which were nowhere near as gruesome as the horror comics of the 1951–54 era).

Most of those *Venus* stories are grim indeed. She becomes much more hard-bitten and her romance with Whitney Hammond is less and less a focus, until it virtually disappears in most of the later tales. Marvel picked the perfect artist to illustrate the *Venus* horror stories: Bill Everett (covers # 13, 15–19; interiors # 14–19). He frequently used stories dealing with water, his artistic specialty, and he perfectly melded the beauty of Venus with the horror of her opponents.

Whitney Hammond appeared until the end, but Della vanished much sooner. Della doesn't appear at all after her role in a story in # 16 (Oct. 1951) entitled, "The Ashes of Death." It's no wonder—in a twist that must have made editor Stan Lee laugh out loud, Venus has Della play a decoy while trying to foil a madman intent on cremating beautiful women! Della survives, but she retires for good. In addition to being one of the grimmest stories in the history of comics—the madman apparently was the devil himself—this is one of the least logical tales with regard to the admittedly loose continuity of the series.

Fawcett produces the first monthly romance title

A little more than two decades before Fawcett became one of the most noteworthy comic book publishers in the early days of the Golden Age, the family firm produced the naughty *Captain Billy's Whiz Bang* magazine, beginning in 1919. Many of the "naughtiest" covers—pin-up styles that seem charmingly innocent today—earned the sort of reputation that gave the magazine a mention for its racy nature in *The Music Man*. Fawcett followed with "true story" romance and confession magazines, such as *True Confessions* (its perennial best-seller), *Life Story* and *Romantic Story*, which were especially popular in the 1940s before the advent of television.

It was hardly a surprise, then, when Fawcett became the fourth publisher to jump into the romance market, following Marvel and Fox by one month in the wake of the sizzling sales of Crestwood's *Young Romance*. What was a surprise was Fawcett's decision to launch *Sweethearts*, its flagship title, as a monthly beginning with # 68 (Oct. 1948). From 1947 through the 1950s, several companies eventually published romance titles on a monthly basis, but Fawcett was the only comic book publisher to begin any of the 147 titles on the stands in 1949 and 1950 as monthlies. Fawcett obviously figured there was big money to be made in romance. *Sweethearts* purportedly was a rousing success, so the company also began *Life Story* as a monthly with # 1 (April 1949). The first eight issues of *Cowboy Love* in 1949–50 also were monthly before that title faltered. *Romantic Secrets* also became a monthly with # 3 (Feb. 1950), making Fawcett the only company in 1950 with three uninterrupted monthly romance titles.

Fawcett became best known in the 1950s for *Popular Science*, *Popular Mechanics*, *True Magazine* and the company's Gold Medal line of paperback novel originals, which started in 1950 and achieved phenomenal success. But in the 1940s, the company made immense profits in comic books, led by its *Captain Marvel* franchise, well before the Fawcett brothers began their profitable line of romance and western comics. Ironically, *Captain Marvel* led to the company's comic book undoing in 1953, when Fawcett quit the comics field after engaging National Comics in a drawn-out lawsuit over *Superman/Captain Marvel*. But at the time the first issue of *Sweethearts* appeared in 1948, Fawcett was heavily promoting monthly publication of

Captain Marvel, Captain Marvel Junior, The Marvel Family, Whiz Comics (with Captain Marvel) and *Master Comics* (with Captain Marvel Junior). (*Mary Marvel Comics*, along with the title in which she also once starred, *Wow Comics*, had already been discontinued.)

Mary Marvel's own title, which ended with # 28 (Sept. 1948), appealed primarily to girls, just as National's *Wonder Woman* did. Even though Fawcett technically succeeded *Mary Marvel* with *Monte Hale Western* # 29, and even though the firm followed *Captain Midnight* # 67 with *Sweethearts* # 68, it was *Sweethearts* that really took *Mary Marvel*'s place on the publishing schedule. *Mary Marvel*, in fact, was one of the few eponymous 1940s super hero comics that was published monthly in its last year of existence. Perhaps Fawcett decided that *Sweethearts* would simply provide a new publication of obvious monthly interest to girls. Whatever the commercial motivation was, *Sweethearts* was successful enough to continue monthly publication all the way through the industry turmoil of 1950 and, in fact, until # 119 (Jan. 1953). *Sweethearts* # 120 and # 121, the last two Fawcett issues, appeared bimonthly. That stamps *Sweethearts* as one of the most commercially successful romance titles of all time, albeit for only a little more than four years.

Sweethearts set the tone for all of Fawcett's 235 romance issues from 1948 to 1953, consistently using upbeat, pleasant photo covers of models—both individual girls and couples, though never men alone. The back covers of early issues of *Sweethearts*, though, were reserved for large photos of raffish-looking male movie stars. The first, Robert Mitchum in # 68, was labeled as "My romance of the month" but the phrase became "dream beau of the month" with the next issue. That may have been because Marvel had started publishing *My Romance*.

While *Sweethearts* invariably offered happy photo-cover scenes, cover-featured story titles hinted of conflict: "Beauty Was My Snare" in # 68, "Betrayed By My Temper" and "I Led Him On" in # 71 (Feb. 1949). The introductory blurb on the cover of # 68 read as though it came from a confession-magazine publisher (which, indeed, Fawcett was) rather than a comic book outfit: "Thrilling Romances! Exciting! Pulse Quickening! Real Love Stories of Real People Told in Dramatic Picture Stories. Revelations You Will Never Forget!"

Many, if not most, of Fawcett's romance stories, plenty of which were nicely drawn by the skillful Marc Swayze of *Mary Marvel* fame, had a familiar theme: girl finds love through boy's wisdom after girl makes serious mistake and nearly loses boy. That was the essence of the first story in Fawcett's first romance comic. *Sweethearts* # 68 opens with "My Jealous Sin," in which a photographer's fiancé is irrationally jealous of his models. She ruins pictures he makes, gets him fired, and, remorseful, shows the boss engagement pictures her fiancé took of her, so the boss can see his skill and he can get his job back. "I went home, and for the first time in what seemed ages, I slept that night. Yes, my heart still ached for Bill, but I felt relieved for my confession of truth!" Three panels later, he has taken the contrite woman back and they are heading for their wedding. Says she: "Let's go, darling—there's a wonderful life waiting for us!"

Likewise, in "I Was a Snob," it takes a man to teach a girl the error of her ways before he can fall in love with her. "False Love" teaches a girl about the evils of insincere flirtation. In "Reckless," a girl learns that taking chances to show off, such as speeding on the highway, are no way to win the heart of a wiser man. "Beauty Was My Snare" sends a gorgeous but conceited girl into a tailspin of danger until both her father and her boyfriend teach her about the perils of vanity. That is five happy endings ... after five females absorbed lessons from wiser men!

When *Sweethearts* reappeared with # 69 (Nov. 1948), movie star Glenn Ford was "dream-beau of the month" but otherwise the formula was exactly the same: four erring females in as many stories learn about life from the men they happily wind up with. So many of Fawcett's stories turned out this way that "And They Lived Happily Ever After—After She Had to

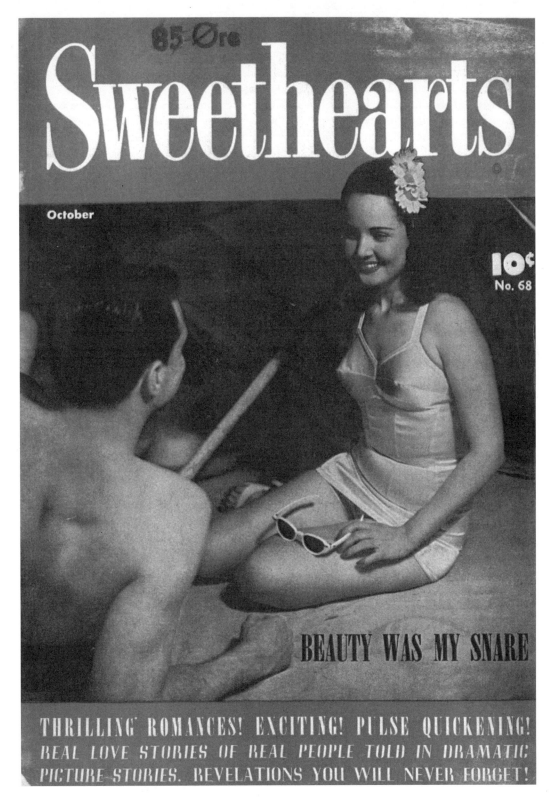

Sweethearts #68, Oct. 1948, copyright Fawcett Publications, Inc. Idyllic photograph covers—but tension-riddled stories of remorse—were typical right from this first Fawcett Romance issue, converted from *Captain Midnight* #67.

Become Miserable Before" might as well have been a standing title at Fawcett. Since so many of Fawcett's confession magazines had stories with similar themes, this may account for the firm's penchant for monotony, misogyny and/or misery.

Notwithstanding the repetitious themes of Fawcett's romance stories, there were a good many moral principles involved along with the tears. It just would have been nice if more of the Fawcett females had been less grasping and selfish to begin with. For example, "Heartless" in *Sweethearts* # 69 tells a meaningful tale of teenage peer cruelty, and how a girl realizes that it could have cost her the love of a boy whom she learns is not such a nerd, after all. (The word "nerd," of course, probably never appeared in a romance comic story through the original run of the genre from 1947 to 1977.)

In contrast to Fawcett, the romance comics from Fox—a second-tier publisher whose most successful comic creation in its dozen wildly inconsistent years of existence was *The Blue Beetle*—were an almost unreadable combination of the crass and the sleazy. Both the art and stories were usually poor—pretty much, in fact, the worst in the entire field. The brutal cover on Fox's first romance comic, *My Life* # 4 (Sept. 1948), pretty much set the stage for all 105 cruelty- and cliché-filled romance issues to follow over the next couple of years. A man takes a violent swipe, knocking over a table, while blurting, "This marriage is all washed up, baby! We're finished!" To which a scantily clad woman responds (while looking into a mirror!), "Run along, Junior, you bore me!" The romance comics from Fox must have bored almost everybody, but collectors seek them out for the same reason some people pursue videos of so-bad-it's-good movies such as *Plan Nine from Outer Space*.

Some comic book historians have tried to stress the effects of the growing emphasis with post-war domesticity for the growth of romance comics. Post-war conditions, in which peace and costume heroes didn't seem to go especially well together, did leave more room on the racks for romance. Even so, it should be remembered that the girls who read romance comics in the early years of the genre were not the baby boomers who began coming along in 1946. Those girls didn't start reading romance comics until well after the Comics Code came into effect in 1955.

Assuming the vast majority of the romance comic readers in 1947–50 were 12 to 20 years old—it's difficult to imagine younger girls enjoying and/or really comprehending these comics, although many adult women probably did—these were females who grew up with the hardships of the Great Depression and World War II. Who could blame the females of the Greatest Generation for doing a little romantic dreaming in the first few years after the war?

In contrast, many of the parents of the teens and twenty-somethings who read romance comics in the late 1940s and early 1950s hardly knew what a comic book was. Most of these parents grew up before the advent of the 10-cent newsstand comic book in the mid–1930s. Instead, woman who were in their 30s or 40s in 1950 had fulfilled their printed romantic fantasies not with comics, but with the combination of pulps, movie star and confession magazines, lending-library novels and some of the "slick" fiction in magazines such as *The Saturday Evening Post*. For them, "comics" meant newspaper strips.

In all, only 15 romance comics with 1947–48 dates appeared from the above four publishers. The pace picked up only slightly during the first six months of 1949, with 42 love comics dated January through June. Then came the comic book version of an earthquake.

FOUR

Love Conquers All

The Record Growth of Romance Comics in 1949

One of the enduring American pop cultural myths is that Superman and Batman created the greatest explosion of comic book success in the industry's history. That's not quite true. In 1949, comic book publishers learned there was nothing more super than a kiss.

The modern comic book industry, in the form of regularly appearing titles, was only four years old when Superman debuted in *Action Comics* # 1 (June 1938). Batman, the next enduring costumed character created originally for comic books, followed in *Detective* # 27 (May 1939). In 1940, the total number of issues more than doubled to 698, from a total of 322 in 1939. Publishers may have been surprised, but they could hardly have been shocked. The industry was still in its infancy in 1939. The same could hardly be said for comic book publishers in 1949, however. The industry had matured to the point that more than 13,000 issues were published during the 1940s, commonly referred to as the Golden Age of Comics.

Until the second half of 1949, exactly 57 among those 13,000-plus issues could be called romance comics. Love on the racks took a long time to bloom. Then the comic book creators, editors and publishers, the vast majority of them male, and the romance readers of America, the vast majority female, went love crazy. Stark, raving crazy. The numbers between July and December in 1949 were not to be believed. The first 57 issues were published over a period of 21 months since the first two romance comics, *Young Romance* # 1 and 2, appeared in the last three months of 1947. In the second half of 1949, however, 256 romance issues were published by 22 companies who dreamed up 118 titles. Those 256 issues contained well over 1,000 stories.

Love was on the racks everywhere. Never before, and never again, did a single genre of the comic book—an original American commercial concept—explode in such an orgy of financial opportunism. There were even more romance issues in the first half of 1950 (see Chapter 5), but that was a hangover from 1949.

Some historians have theorized that the demise of the pulp magazines had something to do with this unprecedented frenzy for love, but that is true only on a marginal basis, if it all. There were still plenty of love pulps along with 25-cent paperback books in 1949—probably more, in fact, than any one person had time to read.

No, the answer—if there is a rational answer—is that it was just time for love. Teenage American girls—for it was they who read the majority of romance comics—were ready for romance. No young miss could possibly avoid spotting love on the racks when it was that freely available. And more love begat even more love. In fact, just about the only romance title that was not eventually taken was *More Love*!

Satirists, past and present, have had a field day talking about titles that never existed in 1949: *True Love*, *True Blue Love* and *Blue True Love*. Jim Vadeboncoeur, Jr., notes that in cartoonist Mel Lazarus's 1964 novel, *The Boss Is Crazy, Too*, love titles included "Communist Love Tales," "Muriel Train, Girl Borax Miner," "True Doctor Rape Tales," "Trial Marriage Comics," "Overage Romances," "Rex Oedipus, Boy Lover" and "Poverty Stricken Comics."

There was money to be made in comic book romance, and nearly everyone who was anyone in the industry—with the noteworthy exception of chaste Dell Publishing—plunged into the romance game. Ironically, Western Publishing—which produced Dell product—was primarily responsible for what few purely romance paperback were available in the 1940s (see Chapter One).

The tsunami of four-color love began slowly in 1949. In fact, more romance comics were dated December, 1949—at least 64!—than appeared in the entire first seven months of the year (63). Only 11 romance issues appeared in the first three months of the year, and they were all continuations of the four titles in existence at the end of 1948 (see Chapter Three) except two issues. The fifth love title on the racks was *Teen-Age Romances* # 1 (Jan. 1949) from St. John, which was soon destined to publish many of the issues collectors eventually would most cherish from a remove of more than half of century. The sixth new title was Harvey's first love comic, the fittingly named *First Love* # 1 (Feb. 1949).

In April, five new titles appeared—Ace's *Real Love* # 25 (converted from a teen humor title), ACG's *Romantic Adventures* # 1, Timely/Marvel's *Ideal Love Romances* # 5 (immediately converted to *Love Romances*), Fawcett's *Life Story* # 1 and the first issue of St. John's *Teen Age Diary Secrets* (technically *Blue Ribbon Comics* # 2).

An avalanche of love and romance soon followed. It wasn't enough to bury the entire comic book field, but, as historian Dan Stevenson notes, it was enough to ensure that more than one of every five comics in the second half of 1949 was devoted to hearts and flowers, love and romance ... and cold, hard cash. Anyone who could draw pretty girls and handsome guys—and lots of hacks who really couldn't—could find work in comics for a while.

There were so many romance comics that sometimes they fooled the so-called experts, such as Dr. Fredric Wertham, the notorious anti-comic book crusader whose *Seduction of the Innocent* in 1954 soon led to the creation of the Comics Code Authority (see Chapter Nine). In his chapter, "I Want to Be a Sex Maniac!" he refers to a number of comics, including one that did not exist but probably should have—*True Love*. (He undoubtedly meant one of the comics with a variation on that title.)

Of the 22 romance publishers in 1949, eight jumped on the bandwagon especially hard, ranging from sleazy Fox (52 issues, 18 titles) and knock-off kingpin Marvel (47 issues, 27 titles) to slickly produced Quality (14 issues, 10 titles). Interestingly, the two primary romance comics publishers in the 1960s and '70s during the second half of the genre's commercially viable existence, National and Charlton, began very cautiously.

Charlton, which ultimately published more than 1,400 romance comics, had only one short-lived romance title in 1949–50, *Pictorial Love Stories* # 22–26, a continuation of *Tim McCoy Western*! National, destined to be No. 2 in quantity in the romance stakes with more than 900 issues, came in a little late in 1949, with three titles and seven issues, including the western hybrid *Romance Trail*.

Romance came along at the right time, or so it seemed, for financially shaky Fox (see more in Chapter Five), which gave up on most of its costume heroes and jungle men and women in favor of love. In the wake of the first four issues of *My Life* (# 4–7), Fox flooded the market with 17 new romance titles in the last seven months of 1949. Of those 17, fully a dozen were continued from titles in other genres, with Fox hoping to save on the cost of new postal permits. Fox was far from the only publisher that did this, but was consistently one of the worst offenders until the company went out of business in 1950 (except for a handful of mysterious issues dated August and September 1951 during an abortive comeback).

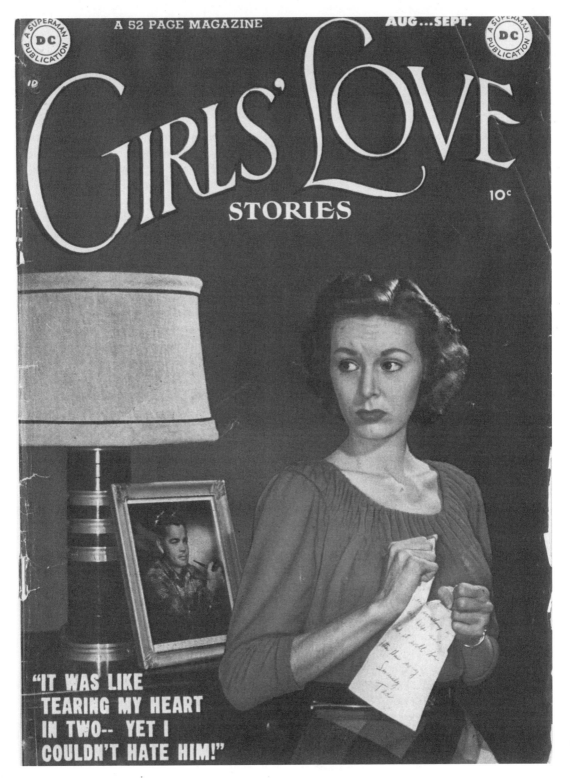

Girls' Love Stories # 1, Aug.-Sept. 1949, copyright National Comics Publications, Inc. The first DC romance issue (other than *Romance Trail*) features an intense photograph cover.

Only two of Fox's 18 romance titles in 1949—not counting rebound/reprint 25-cent giants, with which the publisher also flooded the market—did not begin with "My." Although other publishers tried "My" occasionally, this was definitely a Fox phenomenon. (The other two from Fox were *I Loved* and *Women in Love*.) When Fox introduced three more titles in the first three months of 1950, they all started with "My."

Fox was a key factor in an intriguing development in comic collecting beginning in 1989–90 with the publication of the two volumes of the monumental *Photo-Journal Guide to Comic Books* by Ernst and Mary Gerber. These two coffee-table-size volumes were the first books of their kind. In addition to essays about various aspects of collecting and preserving comics, they came with the authors' "scarcity indexes" based on perceived scarcity (this has provided much material for debate up to the present day). Their main objective, though, was the presentation of more than 21,000 cover images from the 1930s to the early 1960s.

The groundbreaking two volumes were nowhere near complete—less than half the total American comics published from 1933 to 1963 were pictured—but the authors were especially careful to include virtually all of the most colorful, most valuable and most sought after issues, with a heavy emphasis on "colorful." Romance comics were given short shrift, since they were still not of great interest to most collectors in the late 1980s, although the authors did include most of the best or most bizarre covers. Under the category of "best" came Matt Baker's lush work for St. John and many of the prettiest covers from National. Under the label of "bizarre" came the sleazy likes of Fox—not just in romance, but in crime, teen humor, western and the like.

The Gerber volumes gave a huge "bump" to comic collecting, more than half a decade before the advent of eBay and Internet shopping. Many fans began to seek out issues they had never heard of, but which looked intriguing. Many other enthusiasts realized they wanted complete sets. Fox romance issues, merely a low-grade curiosity until about 1990, suddenly became sought-after collectibles in the "so bad, they're good" category, along with other genres from Fox. Since Fox published only 106 non-reprint romance issues, some collectors began looking for all of them, even though the vast majority had what could most charitably be called rough art and even rougher stories. It was no coincidence that Dr. Wertham frequently cited examples from Fox as among the worst offenders in the way of crudity and cruelty in comics.

Fox stories tended to portray human nature in a poor light. The authors picked on members of both sexes. Many of the stories were downbeat; others were upbeat, but with lots of bad behavior along the way. It's safe to say that few, if any, Fox stories could have come close to passing the Comics Code Authority in 1955, if Fox had still been in business. Indeed, Fox did not join the first attempt at self-censorship, the Comics Code established in 1948 by the Association of Comics Magazine Publishers. That, in and of itself, is not to condemn Fox, since such wholesome publishers as National, Fawcett and Dell did not join in 1948, either. The difference, though, is one of degree; most Fox stories couldn't have passed any form of censorship, while the likes of National, Fawcett and Dell produced stories that often required no censorship to stay within the bounds of good taste.

Fox stories were virtually all a hard slog of depressing activity, with titles such as "My Dreadful Secret" and "They Said I Was Guilty" in *My Love Affair* # 2 (Sept. 1949); "I Slaved for Him" and "He Knew My Secret" in the first issue of *My Private Life* # 16 (Feb. 1950); and "I Loved a Weakling" and "My Past Followed Me" in *My Secret Affair* # 2 (Feb. 1950). It's not surprising that issues from Fawcett, Quality, Timely/Marvel and Crestwood are much more common than those from Fox; they must have sold better.

Fox romance covers were generally the most "noirish" in the industry, with numerous scenes from night clubs and boudoirs. Women were generally drawn in a style that might best be called "glamorous cheesecake." Men were portrayed as violent, sleazy or desperate. Even

Fox realized this formula was far from a winner, since the company converted 18 of its 21 romance titles to other genres in the second half of 1950 and discontinued the other three titles, all shortly before Fox went out of business (see Chapter Five).

Ironically, Fox romance comics—and many others from the firm—seem to resemble the worst of the most sensationalistic pulps of the 1930s, a decade in which many of the pulps did not present a clean-cut image, to say the least. By the 1949–50 period, however, the remaining pulps—most of them from Popular, Thrilling and Columbia—had largely toned down their act and the covers tended to be significantly tamer from the standpoint of potential controversy. Fox's romance comics must have looked far more lurid on the racks than any of the love pulps did. Horror comics were just beginning to come into vogue when Fox went out of business; collectors often have enjoyed speculating on what Fox might have done with the zombie and vampire genre. The romance issues provide a garish hint.

For a short time in the second half of 1949, Marvel overwhelmed the racks not only with straight romance titles, but with the western romance hybrids (see Chapter Six). Like Fox, Marvel had only one romance title, *My Romance*, for four issues until it converted *Ideal—A Classical Comic* into *Ideal Love and Romance* with # 5 (March 1949). With issue # 6 (May 1949), the title was changed to *Love Romances*—one of 26 new titles Marvel unleashed on the unsuspected reading public within a seven-month period. Marvel's romance comics, however, were nowhere near as unsavory as those from Fox, and most of the stories had happy or at least moral endings (see Chapter Three).

An early creative approach

In contrast to Fox and Marvel, another early major publisher, Quality Comics, seems to have put much thought into its romance line. Or at least a lot more thought than most publishers who tried to take advantage of the exponential growth of love comics in the second half of 1949. Quality, the home of numerous highly imaginative Golden Age super heroes, was phasing out most of them by the time publisher Everett "Busy" Arnold's respected line published its first romance issue, the nicely named *Heart Throbs* # 1 (Aug. 1949). By the end of the year, Quality had published 14 issues across 10 titles, most with distinctive names and themes, even though the firm tended toward the same format. There were four stories in every issue, and lovers in arms in the final panel of almost every tale. Of the 56 stories in those first 14 issues, only two tales did not have happy endings!

Unlike the variable and volatile mixture of stories from pioneering Crestwood in *Young Romance*, Quality apparently was insecure without "and they lived happily ever after" endings. Yet Quality didn't seem at all nervous about presenting stories in widely varied, often exotic locales. In addition, Quality used a lot of sexy, stylized art by Bill Ward, who went on to achieve great success as a girlie cartoonist and pinup artist. He is known in the comics for his artistic success with Torchy, a lace-and-lingerie "girlie girl" comedic backup strip in *Modern Comics*. Torchy ran through *Modern* # 102 (Oct. 1950), the last issue. She also appeared in six issues of her own title in 1949–50, then disappeared.

Like all the publishers who flooded the market in 1949 with romance comics, Quality encountered rocky times during the "Love Glut" of 1950 (see Chapter Five). All 14 Quality romance titles were cancelled after a total of 80 issues, although the classy company came back strong in 1951 (see Chapter Seven). Quality, in fact, remained a major player in the romance field until the firm left comics in 1956, selling out to National. But the "quality of Quality," so to speak, was not the cause of its troubles. It's hard to pinpoint cause-and-effect, but Quality cancelled 22 of its 30 titles in 1950.

Readers may have been sorely disappointed to see Quality's romance titles disappear (although three returned in 1951 and a fourth in 1952). Quality displayed polish and production values seldom seen throughout the industry. Quality's high-toned style made it the M-G-M of romance publishers, all glitter, glamour and variety. *Campus Loves* # 1 (Dec. 1949), one of the first comics devoted to the campus scene, is a fine example. *Campus Loves* more than lived up to its cover blurb: "Alluring coeds reveal their loves and heartbreaks."

The first story, "Love's Victory," drawn in bravura style by Ward, was an wonderfully hokey example of how Quality's writers went to great lengths to contrive original, albeit often highly unlikely, scenarios for romance. The daughter of a graduate of all-male Cargill College sees her dreams of attending the beautiful school come true when the college decides to admit women, but she notices her father seems sad over her choice. She learns why when she falls for a fellow: a school official informs her that her beau's dad had framed her father for a campus fire! The girl's father had been expelled and had been bitter about it ever since. The couple still finds love when the young man's father acknowledges his guilt. The story ends when the two fathers see the couple kiss and one tells the other, "Jupiter, Fabian, we didn't see things like this on Cargill Campus in our day!" to which the other replies, "Maybe we missed something, Greg!"

The next two stories in *Campus Loves* # 1 carry stereotypical titles: "I Stole My Roommate's Man" and "Campus Cheat." In the first story, the weakest in the issue, two roommates predictably wind up falling for each other's fellow after wallowing in guilt. The second story tells the tale of a spoiled, dishonest rich girl who, when forced to attend a state college, tries to buy her way to friendship and success. One of her lies results in an injury to one of her rivals and threatens her relationship with a campus heart throb, but she learns that not everyone is grasping and greedy like her. She winds up with her man the hard way. This one contains a description that wouldn't have made it years later in Comics Code-approved stories: our spoiled rich girl calls her roommate "a fat, giggling creature." It was that overweight roommate, "Squeals" Conner, who eventually teaches her the meaning of humility.

Humor enters the picture

The last story, "Undesirable Male," was told from the unusual viewpoint of a psychology teacher who has no use for frivolous, spendthrift men and emphatically tells her female students so. The students disagree, saying human faults don't doom a relationship. One student introduces the teacher to her older brother, a playful sort. He teaches the teacher to come down off her high horse, making for a humorous story not often in evidence in early romance comics.

Love Diary # 1 (Sept. 1949), cover billed as "Glimpses into the intimate secrets of girls in love," also provided a good example of how Quality's writers often tried to shift viewpoints. In three of the stories, it is the girls who write "Dear Diary" at the conclusions. But in the other story, "Reckless Romance," it is the man who pens the conclusion—in the girl's diary! In this story, an airline stewardess feels her pilot is too stodgy for her because of his emphasis on by-the-book safety, so she spurns his affections for one of his devil-may-care wartime buddies. The buddy's recklessness, however, leads to a crash when he takes off with a damaged plane. And who should come to their risky rescue but Mr. Stodgy, otherwise once known in battle—although not to the stewardess—as "Wildcat Jeff Foster the most daring pilot I ever knew!" according to a passenger. Foster ends the story with this bold entry in her diary after he reads her writing to find out her true feelings: "Thanks, Diary, for straightening things out for us! You can say Jean kissed me—and then go back in your drawer and relax! I'm handling things from now on!" So much for personal ethics! The sense of humor displayed in

"Undesirable Male" and "Reckless Romance" was not common in early romance comics, so it's much to Quality's credit.

One of the seemingly inevitable results of the six-month chaos when more than 100 romance titles were introduced in the second half of 1949 was a quick Quality title change: *Love Diary* became *Diary Loves* with # 2 (Nov. 1949), surely because tiny Our Publishing Company got there first with its *Love Diary* # 1 (Aug. 1949). Well after both titles were defunct, Charlton Comics began its *Love Diary* with # 1 (July 1958).

Tyranny and trysts

During the early stages of the Cold War, probably no comic book company consistently used communists as villains more often than Quality, most notably in grim, heroic titles such as *Blackhawk* and *T-Man*. But communist types also popped up occasionally in Quality's romance titles, such as the unintentionally hysterical period piece, "Tyranny Broke My Heart" in *Flaming Love* # 1 (Dec. 1949). *Flaming Love* had one of the best of the love logos, with "Flaming" in (what else?) flames at the top.

When an American journalist, Gail Manners, visits a ruritanian communist country that she "cannot call by its real name"—she dubs it Messalia—she falls for her guide, Will Nekaro, the son of an American mother and a European father. When secret policeman Virlo also falls for her and makes a suggestive comment, Will protests, and Virlo responds, "Ah! So she has already infected you with the so-called chivalry of the democracies! Fool! These American women are free with their kisses, especially when they want to make a man talk, perhaps make him slander his own land!"

Like any red-blooded man with American blood would do, Will lands a hard left on Virlo's jaw, then accepts his arrest. The communists tempt Will with the exotic Marva but Gail isn't fooled when she finds Marva slithering into Will's lap. She screams her love to Will, and, in a disappointing and contrived denouement, he is released when it's determined that his father had become an American citizen before Will's birth. And they lived happily ever after, in America of course. Stories like this, accompanied by the allure of intriguing art, have long made Quality a favorite of collectors. Quality seldom named actual communist nations, however.

Ward drew the first Quality romance cover, for *Heart Throbs* # 1, with a huge moon lighting an embrace on a ship between a deckhand type and a blonde with beautiful tresses, complete with purple flower in her hair to match long, purple gloves. Ward's story, "Spoiled Brat," is a simple class-struggle conflict between a seaman and the eponymous brat. When he rescues her from a storm, finds out she has courage he never suspected, and falls into her arms in the final panel, he tells her, "Of course, you'll have to live on a seaman's pay, Mona!" To which she responds, "Who cares? With you, darling, I'd live happily on bread and water!" Somehow, though, we can't help but suspect that she will find a way to raise his economic expectations.

The stories in *Heart Throbs* were likely to be told in any locale, such as "Siren of the Tropics" in # 2 (Oct. 1949). Quality loved to throw out-and-out villains into its early romance titles, such as Tari, the scheming siren who cheated on "rising young industrial engineer" Kent Rawlings while scheming to defraud his company. Rawlings breaks up the scheme after learning the hard way that the woman for him is a seriously dedicated secretary back home.

In the early days of romance comics, becoming a sob-sister on a newspaper was one of the few quasi-professional jobs women could aspire to outside the realms of education and medicine. "Heartbreak Headline" in *Heart Throbs* # 2 provided a wild example. Sob-sister Mona tricks herself into the life of handsome millionaire socialite Don Hampden, hoping to get the scoop on his love life, then gets the scoop all wrong before he ultimately forgives her instead of launching a libel suit that would have been worth many millions. Before realizing the *error* of her ways, the sob-sister says she has "a bulletproof heart," then later realizes, "I'm so in love with him I'd cook his meals and darn his socks—and I've ruined everything!" The story ends with the embattled city editor shouting in the best newspaper movie tradition, "Get those presses rolling! We've got the story of the year—Don Hampden to marry reporter who tricked him!"

There was no limit to the unlikely but entertaining themes and locales Quality could use. In *Heart Throbs* # 3 (Dec. 1949), the titles tell all: "Swamp Flame" and "Hijacked Heart." The latter story reads like something out of a Warner Brothers movie, with the heroine improbably rescuing the hero during one of a series of highway hijacks plaguing a trucking firm. In those days, "hijacked" was more likely to refer to a land vehicle than a commercial airplane.

Lingerie and love

Like many early Quality romance stories, "Hijacked Heart" contained lingerie scenes along with love, although seldom in the sleazy Fox manner. There were dozens of panels of girls in various stages of undress—though never of men except in likely locales such as the beach—and one gets the feeling they were there in large part because the artists liked to draw girls. Or perhaps the writers, editors and artists were seeking to appeal to what they perceived as teen readers' dreams of becoming alluring. Even though the overwhelming majority of romance readers were female, it's also possible that Quality and other lingerie-oriented companies were trying to appeal to male readers, too, with what collectors came to call "lingerie panels."

Girls who sought careers could not have been too encouraged by stories like "Back Door Romance" in *Love Confessions* # 2 (Dec. 1949). In this little epic, Vicki Carter, determined to break into television through the back door, worms her way into a job as a secretary to a television star who turns out to be a "philanderer," as his wife accurately calls him. When said philanderer continues to put the moves on Vicki, the clean-cut newspaper reporter who cares about her, Tim, punches out the wolf, only to see Vicki reject the good guy of the piece. When Vicki finally realizes she has thrown away a chance at real love, she rushes home "to bury myself in shame!" only to see him waiting inside her apartment. "There won't be another back door romance for me!" she tells the reader in the final explanatory panel. "If I get a job in television, it'll be through the front door! And if I don't ... well, Tim won't care! He doesn't want his wife to work anyway."

That ending was typical of most romance comics of the early period, when the woman almost always surrenders her career for love, or at least sublimates her occupational goals in favor of the man's plans. The not-so-subtle message was clear: love means everything. The idea that a woman could have both a professional life and love is only occasionally presented in the early romance comics from most companies, including Quality. Such approaches, though, slowly changed toward the end of the three-decade run of corporate romance comics (see Chapters Eleven and Twelve).

Quirky variety from tiny ACG

The solid second-tier American Comics Group (ACG) never published more than a handful of titles at a time, but it must have made a tidy profit on its two long-running romance titles. *Romantic Adventures* and *Lovelorn* both started in 1949; a decade later, they were successful enough to make ACG the only company with two romance titles that had reached 100 issues. Most ACG titles, edited by the legendary Richard Hughes, enjoyed only moderate success at best, if their short to moderate runs are any indication. The firm's only titles that could compare with the success of the romance comics were *Adventures into the Unknown* and *Forbidden Worlds*, which started out as horror comics and became a mixture of science fiction and fantasy following the imposition of the Comics Code. Those titles, however, were apparently enough to keep ACG profitable in the 1950s and early 1960s, or else the firm would have gone the way of so many other small companies.

Right from the start, ACG used line-drawn covers, usually in a less glamorous, more cartoony style than most other romance publishers. The covers occasionally featured mild conflict, sometimes hearts and flowers, and occasionally humorous themes. What the covers seldom were, except for a brief period in 1954, was either sleazy or exotic. The covers were, if nothing else, usually down to earth, often stressing personalities or plots over glamour girl art.

Indeed, the often highly unlikely, plot-driven stories were often far more quirky and complicated than the covers could even hint at. The 13-page first story in ACG's first romance comic, *Romantic Adventures* # 1 (March–April 1949), set the tone for many of the hundreds of ACG stories that followed. In "Second-Hand Love," the mother of a college co-ed tells her daughter a story she had never heard, hoping her daughter would reconsider her plans to attend the prom with a flirtatious football star instead of the "steady Eddie" type who really loves her. The mother tells her daughter a tale of football gambling, an unintentional shooting, cat fights and fistfights and eventual redemption through marriage to a professor of Latin who really loves her. In the last panel, the steady Eddie gets a phone call and tells his roommate: "She just phoned me to tell me our date for the junior prom is on again—and that she's my girlfriend for good! Says she prefers me to any brawny football player going! You know—sometimes I just can't figure women out!"

Neither could the largely male writers in early romance comics, considering how untrue to life some of their stories were. What the writers quickly discovered, though, was an unlimited number of story plots, settings and characters, even if the many stereotypical endings were generally either happy (the vast majority) or unhappy. That must have made writing the stories more fun than composing endless epics of super heroes, cowboys or gangsters. And no company seemed to have more fun than ACG with its stories, many written by Hughes himself.

The rest of the stories in *Romantic Adventures* # 1 were filled with variety: "You Can't Learn Romance," about a school teacher learning about love from a country bumpkin; "Hollywood Heartbreak," dealing with how a would-be star learns there are no shortcuts to either success or love; "I Was a Fugitive from Love," in which a mother is reunited with her husband after 17 years apart, thanks to their daughter; and "Woman in White," a nurse story with an unhappy ending but a moral that leaves the nurse hoping for better things after learning a bitter lesson about love.

There was more of the same in *Romantic Adventures* # 2 (May-June 1949), including stories about a reporter, a hard-driving business woman, a department store clerk, a telephone operator and a secretary, all of whom learn their lessons. All five stories ended with lovers in arms after numerous trials and travails. If nothing else, ACG's romance comics were certainly a pleasant diversion. Even though most of the stories pose an unlikely combination of circumstances, they hold up better today because their themes tend to be universal.

During the beginning of the brief western romance craze (see Chapter Six), ACG declined to hop in the saddle with a western love title. But the company did try a typically clever story that begins on a present-day dude ranch in *Romantic Adventures* # 3 (July–Aug. 1949). In "Romance on Valentine Ranch," the kindly middle-aged mother who runs the ranch tells a

Romantic Adventures # 1, March-April 1949, copyright B&I Publishing Co., Inc. The tiny American Comics Group (ACG) quickly plunged into the market for romance with this first of 254 romance issues over a 15-year period.

confused girl how the ranch got its name, when she was a spoiled, youthful spitfire who used six-guns and her wits to rescue the man she loved from a gang of rustlers. Naturally, the young girl who hears this story relents and falls into the arms of the man she has rejected for fear they came "from different worlds."

Romantic Adventures must have been judged a success, because ACG quickly followed with *Lovelorn* # 1 (Aug.–Sept. 1949). The first issue, a full-size 52-pager like most ACG comics until midway through 1952, contained only one page of interior advertising, possibly indicating a quick decision to put together a second romance book. There was no discernable difference in either title, though *Lovelorn* # 1 also featured a western romance story, "Romeo of the Ranch." More than most companies, ACG's allegiance was allied to alliteration.

In *Lovelorn* # 2 (Oct.–Nov. 1949), the story "Lure of Latin Love" dealt with the complications of an actress, her American suitor—and a Frenchman! This oddity was a good example of how romance writers often trafficked in stereotypes: On the cover, Andre holds a smiling French lass while spouting off, "What do you Americans know about love? We French are born to it! It's in our hearts—in our blood—part of our life!" There were no interior ads in this issue—a far cry from the heavy load of advertising ACG carried in many future issues.

From pulp romance to comic book love

Ace Magazines, owned by A. A. Wyn, was the only dual publisher in 1949 to discontinue most of its pulps in favor of publishing more comics, primarily romance titles. It was no coincidence that Ace also continued several pulp romance titles until the mid–1950s, when it kissed off those in favor of focusing on its increasingly profitable line of paperbacks. In contrast, when Street & Smith discontinued comic books in 1949, the venerable firm's pulps also got the boot.

Ace introduced nine romance titles in 1949. It's easy to trace Ace's business decision: the first three issues, *Real Love* # 25 (April), *Glamorous Romances/Dotty* # 40 (May) and *All Love* # 26 (May) were continued from the teen humor titles *Hap Hazard*, *Dotty* and *Ernie*, respectively. It's intriguing to note how Ace decided teen humor was a financial loser, whereas National kept all of its four teen humor titles in 1949 when it began three romance titles. Even so, Ace's teen characters were nowhere near as well known as those from National, Marvel and Archie.

As publishers joined the frantic race to throw more and more love on the racks, ownership statements were revealing. For example, *Real Love* # 25 contained a statement attesting to the legal status of *Hap Hazard Comics*! It was the last mention of poor old Hap. The titles of Ace's first four efforts at romance in *Real Love* # 25 pretty much indicated the nature of the company's constant themes of risk vs. relationships: "Whispered About," "Heartbreak Infatuation," "Save My Reputation" and "Dangerous Dates!" All eight stories in *Real Love* # 25 and # 26 ended with lovers embracing or smiling. Although women sometimes "learned their lessons" in Ace stories the way they did so often in Fawcett's titles (see Chapter 3), most endings had to be happy to assure commercial satisfaction. Any title that consistently ended stories with most of the female protagonists in misery may not have sold well.

Ace played up its romance titles in a big way; the company loved to run full-page house ads with all the current covers. The ad in *Real-Life Secrets* # 1 (Sept. 1949) said, "Watch for these love comics—Exciting! Fascinating! Different!" While the stories and art were far superior to the schlock from Fox and several other companies, it's a stretch to call them different. For seven years, Ace essentially produced competent generic romance. The four stories in *Real-Life Secrets* all ended happily, unlike the odds against any given four real-life stories. The title changed to *Real Secrets* with # 2 (Nov. 1949), probably because of another title snafu.

Standard's long running *Real Life Comics*, itself a knockoff of *True Comics*, had long since gotten there first. *Glamorous Romances* # 40 was entitled *Dotty* in the indicia and on the cover with the large overline, "Glamorous Romances," but it was really a romance comic through and through. Young Dotty Draper was the glamorous star of humor stories in *Dotty* # 35–39 in 1948–49, but she became the object of romance in # 40 in an odd hybrid title, with two romantic Dotty stories and two romance tales. In the final five panels of the first Dotty story in the issue, "Take a Chance on Love," the ending was uncharacteristic for Ace. Dotty saves a boy who has fallen off a cruise ship while the fellow she is dating refuses to dive into the water. "It would be better if we didn't see each other any more, Del! I'm sorry!" she tells him. Then, turning to the reader, she confides, "He had so much ... yet he lacked the one thing a man should really have ... physical courage! I'm glad I found out in time!" And in "Three-Cornered Romance," Dotty ends the story on the arms of two bachelors, having found friendship in both but love with neither.

In # 41 (July 1949), the title is *Glamorous Romances* with "formerly Dotty" in smaller type on the cover—something seldom seen from any publisher. Said the ever-elusive Dotty at the end of her only story in this issue: "All right, Henry! I'll be your friend but not your wife! Take me home now, please!" And that was the last ever seen of Dotty in the comics.

Ace's *Love at First Sight* # 1 (Oct. 1949) had a nifty title and stories with similar themes. Yet *Love Experiences* # 1 (Oct. 1949) had one of the more generic of all titles, along with *Revealing Romances* # 1 (Sept. 1949) and *All Romances* # 1 (Aug. 1949).

From The Green Hornet *to the green-eyed monster*

Like Ace, Harvey emerged in the early days of the Golden Age as a publisher of numerous costume heroes. Until Harvey's licensed version of newspaper comic strip hero Joe Palooka came along, two of the firm's most notable titles was its adaptation of radio's *The Green Hornet* along with Harvey's original creation, *The Black Cat*, whose primary power seemed to be the ability to fight crime and perform judo tricks in stiletto heels. Like Ace, Harvey took a major leap into the love pool, quickly pumping out seven romance titles in 1949, all with the almost inevitable happy endings.

Harvey's early romance stories, such as "Should a Career Girl Fall in Love?" and "I Tried to Lasso My Love" in *First Love* # 2 (April 1949), tended to be short and not nearly as sensational as they became a couple of years later. On the cover of *First Love* # 5 (Oct. 1949), Harvey became one of the first publishers to feature a cover with the heroine's tears, but the cover had nothing to do with any of the three stories. Jealousy, the green-eyed monster, had replaced the *buzz* of *The Green Hornet*!

Early Harvey romance comics, in fact, could be frustrating because the covers usually had little to do with the stories. However, unlike the generic photo and painted covers of several other early publishers, Harvey's covers presented dramatic situations. For example, the cover of *First Love* # 6 (Dec. 1949) showed a battered but triumphant football player holding hands with a female fan while a sad-faced girl a couple of rows behind in the stands laments, "Has he forgotten! [*sic*] He promised to take me to the victory dance!" No players gave the boot to any girls inside, however. Collectors of "themed" stories—such as sports and love—need patience.

Harvey was in such a hurry to tumble into the romance market that it turned out *Love Stories of Mary Worth* # 1 (Sept. 1949) with a combination of romance shorts and *Mary Worth* strip reprints from Publishers Syndicate "based on the true case histories of the famous newspaper love advisor." The title bombed, running only five issues.

Harvey had an unusual solution for yet another of the 1949 title mix-ups by several publishers. Harvey was all set to publish *Love Letters* # 1, but apparently discovered that Quality had the same plans. Indeed, Quality did release the first issue of its long-running *Love Letters* in November. The Harvey issue has *Love Letters*, October 1949, # 1 in the indicia, but a unique silver metallic logo strip says, "Love Lessons" on the cover. Read the inside front cover, though, and you can see "Love Letters" in the logo. The metallic overlay changed the title! Alas, this title, which also featured a girl in tears on the cover of # 1, also bombed after five issues, the sad fate met by *Sweet Love*. *Love Lessons* also had a gimmick: the early stories were narrated by "Doris Bigelow, famous social consultant." The publishers even had a message on the first page of # 1, inviting readers to write to Doris: "The sooner you tell Doris your personal love problem, the quicker you will benefit from her vast experience." The result, "Doris Bigelow's Mailbag," was typical of several such advice columns.

A Dutch treat from St. John

The eminent comics historian John Benson, the foremost expert on the highly collectible St. John romance line, wrote a perceptive essay about the company's primary romance writer, an otherwise little-known man named Dana Dutch, in *Romance Without Tears* (2003). This volume of 20 reprints, all more than 50 years old, was the first exposure to the general modern-day public of Dutch's classy and classic romance stories, mostly illustrated by the remarkable and highly prolific artist Matt Baker. Benson since has produced an entire book on St. John, *Confessions, Romances, Secrets and Temptations: Archer St. John and the St. John Romance Comics* (2007). The author highly recommends this volume.

St. John, a solid second-tier publisher for more than a decade in the 1940s and 1950s, was the fifth firm to hit the racks with a romance comic, following Crestwood, Marvel, Fox and Fawcett. *Teen-Age Romances* # 1 (Jan. 1949) was the first of 168 St. John romance issues covering several titles through 1955, also including a final three issues in 1957–58. There were also seven reprint giants, some with original Baker covers. (Benson noted that Baker produced every line-drawn St. John romance cover—other than one rebound giant—some 139 in all.) St. John later reprinted many of Dutch's original stories. St. John also used many non–Dutch stories, plus tales from Ziff-Davis inventory when St. John bought out most of the pulp publisher's comic book line in 1953.

In his essay, one of the most perceptive pieces of writing ever done dealing with romance comics, Benson reveals what publisher Archer St. John sought in the new field: "And in his romance comics, St. John did want to make a statement. One of his editors, Irwin Stein, said that he had 'a very strong editorial conception' for them, which Stein saw a 'reality as opposed to the glamour nonsense. Other publishers had the ladies become Hollywood stars, and all sorts of nonsense. It was either glamour or pain and suffering. Or pain and suffering in a glamourous setting.'"

Dutch carried out this concept with his thoroughly no-nonsense, realistic stories. Benson pointed out that Dutch toiled in self-chosen anonymity, since he did not even want to sign his nicely crafted text stories. (It was not common in that period for comic book writers to receive bylines on illustrated stories, though artists were sometimes allowed to sign their work.) In fact, since Benson said records are not available for St. John, "not even one story can positively be attributed to Dutch. But there was clearly a single outstanding writer who produced a unified body of unusual stories with many distinctive qualities and stylistic similarities, and I'd very surprised if any of the tales [in *Romance Without Tears*] were not by Dutch."

Benson compares Dutch to other romance writers this way:

> Romance comics were inherently didactic. Many were remarkably explicit, their lessons stated in great blocks of text at the start or the end of the story.... Dutch's apparently innocuous stories about teenagers seemed to avoid the didactic, but were actually filled with hidden messages that worked together to unfold a natural, healthy attitude toward young romance that rejected the standard myths and clichés.... Dutch's protagonists were lively, active young women who, though often naive and inexperienced, had character, a sense of self-worth, and a great deal of common sense. They might make mistakes, but were quite capable of thinking things through with no help from anyone. And they had the strength of will to go after what they wanted, and to do what's right, despite what others might think.

Thus, the conception of the title of Benson's volume of reprints: *Romance Without Tears*. In short, unlike the teary-eyed protagonists of many romance comics, especially after the Comics Code Authority was established, Dutch's characters didn't need tears to tell their tales, and tears were not seen on St. John romance covers.

The first story in *Teen-Age Romances* # 1, an 8-pager entitled, "They Called Me a Wayward Girl," set the tone for dozens of Dutch treats to follow. After being unfairly fired from her job as a car hop who unwittingly attracts one of the town wolves, Dotty Jenkins allows her head to be turned by both the wolf and another fellow of his ilk. Meanwhile, she pays no attention to a clean-cut soda jerk, who eventually wins her heart after she learns how painful it can be to become the object of gossip and her parents' scorn. This tale is typical of Dutch's penchant for realism; there are no improbable occurrences.

"Too Many Dates Were My Downfall," "Was I Too Young for Love?" and "I Spelled Ki$$es the Wrong Way" rounded out the issue, all with upbeat, albeit realistic, endings. Benson, pointing out how a first romance ends in disappointment in "Was I Too Young for Love?" makes a good point: "I love the last line of that story: 'In spite of the tears and heartbreaks, it had been fun!' That's the essence of Dutch!"

Most of Dutch's stories stressed the ultimate effects of learning about ethics, decency and being true to oneself. Benson, though, points out this about the "subversive" nature of writing by Dutch: "Of course, most parents [like Wertham and the do-gooders of the era] only looked at the pictures and didn't look at the text, and St. John's comics weren't pictorially vulgar, and the subversive stuff was in the plots and the text, not in the pictures."

St. John produced 20 romance comics in 1949 as one of the eight leading early publishers in the romance field. Several of these issues were a half-inch oversized in the manner of publications such as *True Comics* from Parents' Magazine, and thus are seldom found in fine or better condition. In fact, Archer St. John briefly tried to convert both *Teen-Age Romances* and *Teen-Age Diary Secrets* into a hybrid format similar to the earlier versions of *Calling All Girls* from Parents' Magazine and *Miss America* from Marvel, both of which for a while featured a mixture of comic stories, illustrated text stories and female-oriented advertising.

Teen-Age Romances # 1–3 were standard 36-pagers (though many publishers still produced 52-page issues). Issue # 4 (Aug. 1949), however, became an odd 68-pager containing only 18 pages of comics—a startling transition. With a mix of slick paper and newsprint, there were dozens of ads, mostly for fashions, along with text stories and features such as "Does Necking Increase a Girl's Popularity?" St. John soon returned to the traditional format.

On the title page of *Teen-Age Romances* # 4 is a surprising house advertisement, showing the covers of both that issue and *Teen-Age Diary Secrets* # 4 (Sept. 1949), which is a 52-page oversized issue with 32 pages of comics (including a one-page ad) in the center of the comic. The first three issues of *Teen-Age Diary Secrets* (published as part of the six-issue *Blue Ribbon* series) were regular comics. It also looks as though # 4 originally was intended to be also, especially because *Teen-Age Diary Secrets* # 5 (which is not numbered but is also Sept. 1949) and # 6 (Oct. 1949) are regular comic books. But *Teen-Age Diary Secrets* # 7 (Nov. 1949) is a digest-sized issue, which was reprinted as a digest in # 9 (Sept. 1950) with a different cover.

"Five Million Girls Are Reading Them," proclaimed the astonishing house ad in *Teen-Age Romances* # 4, apparently counting the "pass-along" factor among young readers, since their newsstand circulation could hardly have been so high. The ad promised, "True life confessions of real girls who have strayed from the 'straight and narrow.'" What makes this blustering ad so over-the-top is that, when it was prepared, only the circulation figures of *Teen-Age Romances* # 1 and # 2 (April 1949) might have been available for analysis!

Teen-Age Romances # 5 (Sept. 1949) and # 6 (Oct. 1949) were 52-page issues with a full-sized 32-page comic section in the middle, so the experiment with rotogravure, text and numerous ads didn't last long. *Teen-Age Romances* # 7 (Nov. 1949) was a regular comic book, as were succeeding issues, albeit many of them oversized.

Teen-Age Diary Secrets # 5, the issue without either a number on the cover or an indicia, is labeled, "September Fashions Issue" on the cover, which featured an alluring photo and the story title, "I Gave Boys the Green Light." The story was nowhere near as sensational as the title seems to indicate, especially in view of today's "hook-up" culture among young people. It's a tale, almost surely by Dana Dutch, about how a girl shares her feelings and experiences with other girls after she learns that necking without real affection leads to a negative outcome.

St. John also tried an intriguing mixed-genre experiment with *Adventures in Romance* # 1 (Nov. 1949), which is sometimes listed as *Adventures* even though the indicia and cover both have the full title. It's an oversized issue with four stories—one dealing with Elizabethan intrigue, one with a sea storm setting, one in the Old West and one in college football edited by Warren King and Leonard Starr. They also drew the issue, except for the football story by Frank Bolle. Issue # 2 (Feb. 1950), titled *Spectacular Adventures* on the cover and merely *Adventures* in the indicia, is not considered a romance comic by some enthusiasts.

In 1949, St. John also came out with three 25-cent giants filled with remaindered romance comics: *Giant Comics Edition* # 7 and # 9 (part of a series) and *Romance and Confession Stories* # 1. Of all the publishers in 1949, no one was even close to St. John in the way the firm experimented with different and unusual formats. These drove collectors batty for years until a few tireless comic book hunter-gatherers figured everything out.

The memorable Matt Baker

Matt Baker (1921–59), the most accomplished African American artist in all of comic books during the 1940s and 1950s—and one of few—was the subject of a book-length tribute from several historians in the comics-oriented magazine *Alter Ego* # 47 (April 2005), edited by Roy Thomas. This issue remains one of the finest pieces of scholarship ever produced in the comics field and is highly recommended.

Baker produced thousands of comic book pages and hundreds of covers, working for numerous companies, especially St. John, where he also served as art director from 1952 to 1954. Few artists are as avidly collected as Baker, whose style was at once evocative yet highly realistic. Those who appreciate the bravura realism of such as Alex Raymond, Al Williamson and Murphy Anderson—all of whom focused heavily on science fiction—can find their equal in the romance field in Baker (although Baker worked in many other genres).

Baker was seldom, if ever, at a loss to illustrate glamorous yet "real" women in appropriate fashions. A comprehensive collection of Baker art would reflect American life as few other artists could during his 15-year career. Not all of his inkers—and he had many—were capable of bringing out the best in his work, however. At St. John, though, his work almost always shines.

In his appreciation of Baker in *Alter Ego* # 47, John Benson perceptively explains Baker's appeal to readers and collectors alike:

> Until Baker began doing romance comics [in 1949], his successes in comics were largely in drawing enticing pictures that were attached to primitive narratives. The pictures had only to be dynamic and eye-catching, and to make the action of the story reasonably clear. Romance comics, particularly the St. John romance comics, deal with ordinary people in realistic settings, which called for an entirely different kind of comics art. At first, Baker's romance work was somewhat hesitant. Sometimes the figures were surprisingly stiff, standing rigidly upright as though Baker had used a ruler, or in stock poses.... But it didn't take long for him to develop an interest in this different sort of comics narrative, one where facial expression and body posture were the most significant storytelling tools.
>
> In these stories it was essential for the artist to understand what the characters were thinking and feeling and to become a partner with the writer in communicating not action but rather attitudes and emotions. Instead of pin-up style beauty, he had to draw realistic, attractive young women who would appeal to female readers. The St. John heroines were lively and purposeful, yet still a little naive. Their fellows were handsome, but often quiet and a bit reticent. Baker's total understanding of these small-town teenage characters and his ability to render them in an appealing way is the key to the success of his work in the genre. The girls may be beautiful and the guys handsome, but they have *personality*, which is the essential ingredient needed to bring the scripts to life.

Benson also pointed out what made Baker's St. John romance covers "the most extraordinary part of his work.... Every cover is different, original. Over the course of the run, Baker did montage scenes, iconic close-ups and simple scenes of couples in embrace, occasionally even using a grease pencil effect. But, mostly, the covers were detailed scenes that told a dramatic incident, usually suggesting a longer narrative that might come before an after. The variety of events depicted on these covers is incredible. Virtually no cover repeated any other cover, even slightly, not only in the events depicted but in the composition.... Taken as a whole, these covers have to be considered a high point for four-color comics."

National's odd experiment with Sensation Romance Comics

National's *Sensation Comics* # 94–106, the last 13 issues before a radical format change, seem not to have sold well, or else why would the company have changed the format to fantasy/horror with # 107 (Jan–Feb. 1952)? In fact, the title became *Sensation Mystery* with # 110 (July–Aug. 1952) for its final seven issues. The 13 issues of *Sensation Romance Comics*, which seems like a good title for them even though the official title did not change, suffered because super heroines were as passé as super heroes in 1950–51, and romance comics endured the "Love Glut" of 1950 (see Chapter Five).

These often hard-to-find issues of *Sensation* have unusual crossover appeal, to collectors of super heroes (*Wonder Woman*), science fiction comics (*Astra, Girl of the Future*, which began in # 99) and romance titles (*Romance, Inc.*). The other strip was the unusual *Dr. Pat*, about a stubbornly independent female physician. Some fans of National romance feel their collections are incomplete without the 12 issues through # 105, which include *Romance, Inc. Sensation* not only became an unusual "all-girl" comic (in those days, "girl" and "woman" were virtually synonymous), but *Sensation* tried melding a variety of female features in an apparent attempt to lure the market of girls who had recently been captured by the creation of the romance genre. These females in *Sensation Comics*, however, were not the helpless, scheming and/or dreamy-eyed "girls" that many of the romance comics portrayed. These were women of strength and courage uncommon in comics of the period.

In this curious experiment, Wonder Woman resumed battling her usual blend of fantastic villains beginning with # 99. But her stories in # 94–98 were, pure and simple, tales of romantic adventure. In fact, the cover of *Sensation* # 94 (Nov.–Dec. 1949)—drawn by Bob Oksner, who did so much gorgeous work on National's teen humor titles and drew all 13 "all-girl" *Sensation* covers—is a radical departure from the previous 93 issues. Wonder Woman's sweetheart, Steve Trevor, is shown carrying her across a stream as she sweetly smiles in a classic "my hero" pose. When the author first saw this cover many years ago, her first reaction was something like, "Huh? She could leap that stream without even trying! She must be trying to make Steve feel useful!"

A drastic change for Wonder Woman

Seldom, if ever, had any long-running comic made such a drastic shift in cover style with the same fantastic character. In all of the previous 93 issues of *Sensation*, Wonder Woman is portrayed as the indomitable Amazon she was, drawn in a unique rococo style by the veteran H. G. Peter (who continued the interior art for # 94 to # 106 during 1950–51, accounting for some of the differences between the covers and the stories). Nor was Wonder Woman ever portrayed in such a position on the cover of her own title, even during this period. But now, suddenly, she needs to be carried across a stream! As the Amazon herself might have said, "Suffering Sappho!" The scene does not appear in the story, a romantic tale in which Steve's heroics still can't convince Wonder Woman to marry him.

On the cover of *Sensation* # 95, Steve removes the glasses from Diana Prince and accuses her of being Wonder Woman—with a portrait of Wonder Woman on the wall above the pair. Once again, this cover is unique in the series. In the romantic story inside, Wonder Woman finds a way to convince Steve she is not Diana.

The cover of # 96 is the most unusual of all. Wonder Woman wears five different costumes, including her own; the other four outfits would appeal to teen girls. It's another romantic tale, about how Steve is forced to choose between kissing Diana and Wonder Woman, who, of course, is playing both roles at hyper speed at a charity bazaar. Steve kisses Diana, but only to spare her the humiliation of not being his real choice! It's a frustrating situation for Wonder Woman, because she knows that Steve must fall in love with her as Diana, since by Amazon law she would have to become the mortal Diana if she married, rather than remain the immortal Amazon Wonder Woman.

"Wonder Woman, Romance Editor"

The cover of *Sensation* # 97 is the most romantic of all, with Steve coyly offering a bouquet of roses as Wonder Woman begins to type her answer to his plea to wed. On the wall is her new title: "Wonder Woman, Romance Editor." She takes over—for a long series of frazzled men who couldn't do the job!—as editor of the "Hopeless Hearts Department" of the *Daily Globe*. Eventually, she realizes anew the world needs a Wonder Woman even more than Steve does.

One can picture teen girls reading this story with total empathy, and teen boys absolutely refusing to buy this issue. It's not hard to imagine the ribbing a boy of 1950 would have received with a copy of *Sensation* # 97 rolled up in his back pocket! The author contends, incidentally, this is one of the scarcest comics from the early 1950s.

The feature in # 98 is another romantic opus, but the cover returns Wonder Woman to a more typically action-filled role, saving three circus acrobats along with Steve Trevor. Oddly, she is referred to as "Romance Editor," as if that was the job she had held for many years instead

Sensation Comics # 97, May-June 1950, copyright National Comics Publications, Inc. For a short time, Wonder Woman's love life with Steve Trevor took precedence over her super heroics as Bob Oksner turned in compelling covers.

of only in the previous issue. This is the last of the truly "romantic" Wonder Woman stories, for in her remaining appearances in *Sensation* # 99–106, she goes back to spending most of her time battling unusual menaces.

The *Romance, Inc.*, stories, with kindly middle-aged counselor Ann Martin serving as hostess, were good examples of the genre. *Romance, Inc.*, which later made a few appearances in mainstream DC romance titles, featured considerably more complicated romantic epics than the average love comic. Ann Martin predates newspaper advice columnist Ann Landers (a pen name) by several years! Perhaps "Ann" just sounded like someone a girl would want to tell her troubles to.

In 1950, publishers of romance comics had a lot of their own troubles to talk about. The "Love Glut" was about to threaten the stability of the field.

FIVE

The Love Glut

The Romance Boom and Bust of 1950

As 1950 arrived and the Golden Age of Comics steadily continued to fade, most of the comic book industry's more than two dozen significant publishers surely must have figured an emphasis on romance was the new financial formula they needed to thrive. Most of the four-color moguls would have vividly remembered 1940, the frantic year the Golden Age got going in earnest with dozens of new super heroes and costumed characters. Thanks to this breathless new form of pop culture, the total number of issues more than doubled that year and captured new readers' attention as comics never have again in such a short span. Or so publishers surely must have lamented when sales of the multitude of super guys and ultra gals began to slip in the immediate post-war period and accelerated in the late 1940s. Then came the super financial jolt of romance comics.

By 1950, of course, love and lust had been pulse-pounding pulp magazine staples for more than 20 years (see Chapter One). But the pulps were on the way out, doomed by the ever-increasing popularity of 25-cent paperbacks and television, not to mention the ever-burgeoning comic book industry with all its variety and the rack space its product required. Only a handful of pulp titles survived past the mid–1950s; many did not even make it into the decade.

So the beginning of the new decade was a prime time for comic book romance, or so publishers obviously felt. The publishers were proven correct when the full decade of the 1950s is considered in distant hindsight, but they couldn't have been more wrong during 1950. The author some years ago coined a term for the industry's publishing disaster: the Love Glut. In 1950, publishers kissed off no fewer than 117 of 147 romance titles! Most were never seen again, but the breakup turned out to be temporary for 33 titles that resumed publication in 1951.

Confounding and intriguing numbers

In retrospect, the numbers are confounding and intriguing. The stunning total of 256 original romance comics dated for the final six months of 1949—after only 42 love comics appeared in the first half of the year—should have been considered a portent of publishing distress. But while it must have been obvious that something radically different was happening that year, it's doubtful if the publishers fully realized just how many romance comics would be waiting to be picked up on the racks early the next year.

The total of comics with dates ranging from January to June 1950 was a staggering 332 issues! That was an average of nearly two new romance issues every day. No new genre in the history of comics from the 1930s through the 1970s ever so dominated the racks over a six-month period. In the entire year of 1939—when the first rivals of National Comics' *Superman* appeared, including National's icon-to-be *Batman*—only 322 issues were produced of all types of comics.

Even the super hero boom of 1940 couldn't begin to compare with the Love Glut. The total of all comic books more than doubled in 1940—to nearly 700 issues—but newsstand competition in that year was nowhere near what it became in 1950. For unsuspecting publishers, that was a huge part of the problem romance comics faced. In 1949, newsstand comic books had broken the 2,000 barrier for the first time, with 2,251 issues. If we assume that roughly half these issues appeared in the second half of the year, it's clear that more than one in five of all comics published during that span was a romance comic. However, only slightly more issues were produced in 1950—2,280. That means more than one of four comic books published in the first six months that year was a romance comic.

Such a torrid pace was not sustainable. Indeed, when famed horror comics publisher EC Comics bowed out of the love stakes in 1950 with *Modern Love* # 8 (Sept.), the small but influential firm produced a brilliant eight-page parody of the industry's woes, entitled, "The Love Story to End All Love Stories" (more on this at the end of this chapter). This tale presaged the fabulous success EC would have beginning two years later with *Mad*, the first and best of the parody comics.

By the time *Modern Love* # 8—an issue that must not have sold well, or it wouldn't be so scarce—hit the stands, torrid affairs were temporarily toast in 1950 comic books. It was, indeed, a long, long way from May to December! Only 150 issues were dated July through December, in steadily declining numbers—from 34 for July to only 18 for December.

Looking at it another way, in the final three months of 1949, there were 164 romance issues. In 1950, there were 61 total from October through December. In one year, that represented a decline like nothing ever seen in comics until the industry's self-censorship of the Comics Code Authority first manifested itself in 1955.

Marvel and Fox suffered the most

The two publishers best known for extensive knockoffs in a variety of genres—Martin Goodman's *Marvel Comics* and Victor Fox's often unsavory *Fox Feature Publications*—suffered the most. How much the Love Glut contributed to their financial woes is uncertain, but there is no doubt they were the publishers who attempted to take the greatest advantage of the young females who were willing to plunk down dimes for four-color love.

Marvel saw fully 25 of its 30 romance titles cancelled or suspended in 1950, a year the company endured a general financial slump. The vast majority of Marvel's romance titles did not make it beyond a second or third issue. The market forces proved even more fickle for Fox—all 21 romance titles died in 1950, along with the entire company. Fox attempted a brief comeback midway through 1951 with a handful of one-shots, then disappeared forever.

The other two major purveyors of romance comics, Fawcett and Quality, suffered similar fates, though both eventually rebounded nicely. Those two companies, which were among the primary movers of the Golden Age with the best-selling likes of Fawcett's *Captain Marvel* and *Captain Marvel Junior* and Quality's *Blackhawk* and *Plastic Man*, came close to a romance wipeout in 1950. Fawcett cancelled or suspended 13 of 17 romance titles and Quality did the same with all 14 of its love comics. Both prolific companies were destined to be comic book short-timers—Fawcett's final issues were dated January 1954 and Quality's last comics were dated December 1956—but *both firms* survived the Love Glut to emerge as industry leaders.

Of the eight corporate publishers that produced more than 100 issues in all genres in 1950, only Dell (Western Printing and Lithographing Co.) did not publish romance comics. That was a blessing in disguise for Dell, which concentrated on humorous titles and westerns. Indeed, the only readily identifiable romance comic Dell produced through the 1950s was a 1951 one-shot in the *Four Color* series, entitled, "I Met a Handsome Cowboy." That issue apparently was produced to take advantage of a short-lived western romance craze (see Chapter Six).

Of the remaining three leading publishers in 1950, National (later DC) discontinued two of four romance titles and Harvey cancelled or suspended all seven. Standard, which ranked eighth in 1950 with 110 issues published in all categories, was the only publisher to continue every romance title into 1951, albeit continuing its five titles bi-monthly or quarterly.

Among the second-tier publishers in 1950—the 17 firms that produced fewer than 100 issues but at least 20 issues—all but two publishers also were part of the Love Glut. United Feature Syndicate, best known for *Nancy and Sluggo* among its newspaper reprint titles, never published romance titles. Magazine Enterprises, by 1950 one of the industry leaders in well-done western titles, did not experiment with romance until 1954.

Only five firms were untouched

Along with Standard, only four other firms did not cancel or suspend at least one romance title in 1950. All four published only a handful of titles in various genres that year, averaging fewer than half a dozen comics on the racks each month. Lev Gleason, the notorious crew that continued to publish *Crime Does Not Pay*, kept both its romance titles, *Boy Meets Girl* and *Lovers' Lane*, perhaps because the two were among the best-named love comics in the industry. Eastern, best known for making *Famous Funnies* the first regularly published modern comic book in 1934, maintained *Movie Love* and *Personal Love*. Jungle girl kingpin Fiction House had its quarterly *Cowgirl Romances*, and tiny Our Publishing Co. produced the often intriguing *Love Diary*, which specialized in unusual cover teases. In all, 25 companies participated in the Love Glut of 1950. Twenty companies felt compelled to cancel or suspend at least one romance title.

It's also interesting to note that of the 147 romance titles published at some point in 1950, only two were monthly that year. They were Fawcett's attractive photo-covered flagship titles, *Sweethearts* and *Life Story* (also the name of a "true confession" magazine from the same company). *Sweethearts*, in fact, enjoyed the unique romance comic distinction of monthly publication from its inception with # 68 (Oct. 1948) through # 119 (Jan. 1953). The appearance of Marilyn Monroe on the cover of # 119—nearly a year before she was to cause an uncovered sensation in the first issue of *Playboy*—could not prevent *Sweethearts* from going bi-monthly for its final two Fawcett issues.

Comic book publishers of the 1940s and 1950s often tried to avoid paying for new second-class postal permits by continuing the number of a comic book even when it changed title and/or genre. That would not have mattered if Fawcett had continued *Sweethearts* from a title named, for example, *Sweetheart Love Stories*, rather than *Captain Midnight* # 67. In those days, moreover, many publishers preferred a higher number on a new title, giving the impression it had been around for a while and was thus commercially tested. Fawcett got away with starting *Sweethearts* that way—publishers such as Fox were forced to go from something like # 70 to # 2—but all of Fawcett's 16 ensuing romance titles began with # 1.

During the prehistoric era of comic collecting—the early and mid 1960s, before the onslaught of price guides and indexes—fans delighted in connecting the likes of *Captain Midnight* with *Sweethearts*, though they knew little or nothing about the Love Glut. For one thing, it assured the collector of the identity of both last and first issues. Fanzine writers, such as this author, would breathlessly announce every new discovery, as if they were latter-day

Columbuses and Balboas of the four-color oceans. Not all the connections were accurate, especially in the romance field, since 40-plus years ago, few collectors would even look at love comics, much less pay a dollar or more for them!

More money in romance comics

Now, though, romance comics of the 1940s, '50s and '60s can sell for more than $10 to $20 or more, especially if they are in nice condition or contain art by a collectible illustrator. As recently as the 1980s, though, most moldering and smoldering romance comics cost no more than a dollar or two, and often less. They were clearly the least collected of vintage issues.

Beginning in the 1990s, however, collecting interest began to pick up incrementally following the appearance of the two-volume *Gerber Photo Journal*. In part, interest increased because fans discovered the funky period-piece nature of romance comics. And with most other genre titles skyrocketing in value—it's difficult to find pre–Comics Code titles in many of the most popular genres for less than $25 to $100 even in worn condition—romance comics began to be perceived as a bargain.

Collectors also began to notice intriguing differences in early romance comics. These differences were especially pronounced during the Love Glut, when every publisher seemed to offer a distinct approach. As a result, today some collectors pursue early Quality titles for their art and exotic nature, or Fox issues for their overtly uncouth approach, or National titles for their polished style. Collectors often get a kick out of speculating how some parents' eyes must have popped out when their 10- or 12-year-old darling brought home a suggestive issue.

Following the imposition of the Comics Code Authority with early 1955 issues, romance titles began to seem far more homogeneous, if only because there were distinct limits to art and story content (see Chapter Five). Not only were editors proscribed from slapping on titles like "I Was a Man Trap!" but artists were not even allowed to show cleavage, much less nightgowns.

But all that was five years in the future during the Love Glut of 1950. Experienced romance collectors can instantly spot the different styles of all 25 companies that played the romance field in that fateful year. No doubt readers of more than half a century ago also could differentiate their favorites on the racks.

Fox Feature Publications: Sleaze, Inc.

Fox Feature Publications, operated by the notorious Victor Fox, continued to produce many of the titles that were most heavily criticized by librarians, educators and parents, not to mention Dr. Fredric Wertham in his late 1940s Parents' Magazine articles lambasting the effects of comics on children. Fox's short but highly controversial run of *Phantom Lady* (# 13–23 in 1947–49)—a female version of Batman—and numerous crime and jungle titles were among the most heavily criticized comics of the period. The romance titles were invariably just as sleazy— if not more so—but weren't nearly as well known.

Fox issues may well have been marketed primarily for older readers. Although several publishers occasionally overstepped the bounds of propriety for pre–teen readers of romance, Fox did it far more often and often far more egregiously than any other publisher. To what degree the Love Glut contributed to Fox's financial woes is pure speculation, but it seems likely the publisher's wholesale plunge into the overcrowded romance market was a significant factor in the demise of the entire Fox line late in 1950.

Fox was often criticized for its pay scales—or for lack of payment at all—by artists who sometimes went on to better things, so it's no surprise the publisher usually tried to avoid paying for new second-class mailing permits by changing genres but not numbers on a series. This led to several unintentionally comical title juxtapositions, such as when *Murder Inc.* # 15 morphed into *My Private Life* # 16. Likewise, when the star-crossed company tried to bring back *Murder Inc.* late in 1950, *My Desire* # 4 became *Murder Incorporated* # 5!

Odd title changes

Three other amusing examples of this trend: *My Love Affair* # 6 became *March of Crime* # 7; *My Past Confessions* # 11 became *Crime, Inc.* # 12; and *My Intimate Affair* # 2 emerged as *Inside Crime* # 3, which quite unintentionally summed up the publisher's approach to comic books. In all, when Fox dropped its 21 romance titles, the publisher used 18 of them to start other titles without paying for the postal permits.

Fox committed similar sins when it became one of the first companies to follow pioneering Crestwood (Prize) into the romance market. *Western Killers* # 64 became *My True Love* # 65 and *Western Outlaws* # 8 became *My Love Memoirs* # 9! It took years for a small band of Fox completists to connect all these Fox dots, especially since many issues from the publisher can be hard to find.

When the two-volume set of *Gerber Photo Journals* appeared in the late 1980s, with an unprecedented 21,000-plus cover images of comics from the 1930s to the early 1960s, collectors began to search out Fox romance comics with a vengeance. They couldn't quite believe their eyes, so cheesy were the covers of most of the 106 romance comics Fox published. They were unlike anything else on the market ... but then, so was *Phantom Lady*.

The cover of *My Desire* # 31 (Oct. 1949) is particularly instructive, showing a blonde smiling over dinner with a man while her hand reaches out to a mysterious hand on the opposite side of the table. The hand offers a card with "Call Me ..." written on it (but no phone number). One can only speculate that two-timing on a significant scale was afoot. This may explain why Fox's heavy flirtation with romance titles lasted little more than a year. Women were routinely physically and mentally abused on Fox covers and in the stories.

Marvel: Romance in volume

Marvel made an even stronger attempt than Fox to dominate the market, producing no less than 31 romance titles in 1949–50. Even though all but five were discontinued or suspended early in 1950, the company survived into 1951 to rival Quality and Fawcett as the leading purveyors of early comic book love. Marvel, which generally became known as Atlas in recognition of the distribution company's imprint in the upper left corner of each title, imploded midway through 1957 in a distribution fiasco. Even so, the firm published an industry-leading 446 romance comics through 1959.

In 1949 and 1950, Marvel distinguished itself with a long series of photo covers involving astonishingly hokey and obviously staged situations. These are now among the most dated of all romance comics, but some collectors love them for their unparalleled funkiness. Most publishers who relied heavily on photo covers used photos of movie stars or models, but such glamour was not good enough for mighty Marvel. When the story called for an image of cheating, Marvel was happy to comply with the photo of a shocked woman screaming (inwardly, anyway) when she spots her boyfriend kissing another woman. Some of these have to be seen to be believed, and they were certainly unique in their day.

Marvel, always among the first to spot a trend, actually deserves credit for being out in front when it came to romance. Crestwood's *Young Romance*, the first love comic, had published only six issues when Marvel hit the stands with *My Romance* # 1 (Sept. 1948), which tied with Fox's *My Life* as the second genuine romance release. The title became *My Own Romance* with # 4 (March 1949). Twenty-six more titles followed by the end of 1949, almost all of them doomed by the Love Glut.

One of those titles, the western romance *Love Trails* # 1 (Dec. 1949) lasted only one issue, although for many years collectors searched in vain for a reported # 2. Why? Ace had already corralled the rights to the *Love Trails* title when Ace converted *Western Adventures* # 6 into *Western Love Trails* # 7 (Nov. 1949), so it's possible that Ace protested to Marvel, or Marvel anticipated a protest, and killed *Love Trails* after only one issue.

Marvel even experimented with turning the teen humor title *Junior Miss* into a romance comic. Issues # 35 and 36 were a mixture of teen humor and romance stories, with romance covers, and # 37 (Dec. 1949) was almost all romance. The covers of all three, however, were humorous Norman Rockwell-like paintings of boy and girl. The last two issues (# 38 and 39) returned to the not-so-serious antics of infatuation-addled teens, based on a highly popular radio show toward the end of the radio drama era.

Marvel becomes racier

Marvel, though, soon became racier. Witness the photo cover of *My Own Romance* # 5 (June 1949): "Sure, sure—you can have these letters back—for ten grand!" a smiling women tells a worried man, who responds, "Ten thousand dollars! I—I haven't got it—but I'll get it somehow! Please, Betty, my wife must never know!" On the right side of an open door, a distraught woman enters with "Oh ... oh, Frank!"

Apparently going for the dramatic jugular, Marvel soon tried to enhance the drama with a touch unique to this company: using names in story titles. In *My Own Romance* # 14 (Jan. 1951), the cover blurb "The Vengeance of Cathy Howard!" became just "Vengeance!" inside. There were many such titles: "The Deception of Sylvia Thompson!"; "The Courtship of Carol Sawyer!"; "The Heartbreak of Ellen Chase!"; "The Heartbreak of Jennifer Gray!"; and "The Heartbreak of Janice Tildon!" (Somewhere, there must have been a story entitled, "Heartbreak Hotel!" several years before Elvis.)

Then there were "The Secret of Janet Tilden!" (apparently no relation to Janice Tildon); "The Man for Phyllis Storm!"; "The Horrible Secret of Harriet Arnold!"; "The Tragic Decision of Kathryn Summers!"; "The Strange Love of Carol Ames!" "The Miracle of Millie Malloy!"; "Jean Vail's Search for Lover"; "The Downfall of Lizbeth Webster!"; "The Decision of Ann Tressley!"; and "Cora Dodd's Amazing Decision!" *Marvel* even tried this name gimmick in a comic book title, using *Molly Manton* in the title for two issues of a comic in 1949 before the series ended with the one-shot *Romantic Affairs* # 3 (March 1950).

Marvel tried a noteworthy experiment with 12 issues of *Girl Comics* in 1949–52 (see Chapter Seven). Issues # 1 (Oct. 1949) through # 4 (June 1950) were typical romance issues. With # 5 (Oct. 1950), the title plugged, "Mystery, Adventure, Suspense" at the top and "Real Adventures of Real Girls!" below the title for the remaining eight issues. These featured grown-up versions of Nancy Drew and other girl sleuths and adventurers.

Every now and then Marvel would pop up with a surprise, such as in *Love Classics* # 2 (Feb. 1950). The cover alone—a gorgeous photo of Virginia Mayo from *White Heat*—makes this issue highly collectible. The title blurb—"I Was a Small-Town Flirt!"—led the reader to an uninterrupted 30-page epic. This may have been the longest single-issue story ever to appear in a 1950s romance comic. It is discoveries like these that especially appeal to collectors of romance comics, which have been indexed less than any other primary genre.

Lev Gleason: Two titles to tango

Lev Gleason was best known in comic book annals for introducing the first crime comic—*Crime Does Not Pay*—in 1942 and followed up with *Crime and Punishment* (!) in 1948. Both titles were making lots of loot during the Love Glut, along with the long-running *Daredevil* and *Boy* titles, devoted to the heroics of the unique costumed adventurers Daredevil and Crime-buster, respectively. Apparently, though, the over-exposure of love on the racks of 1950 did not seriously affect Gleason's two new titles, *Lovers' Lane* and *Boy Meets Girl*.

Gleason's titles, edited by Charles Biro and Bob Wood until almost the point where the company abandoned comics in 1956, were known for the wordiest captions and balloons in the industry. The Biro-led storytellers wrote genuine short stories with illustrations, presaging the graphic novel of three decades later. Gleason's two romance comics were no different.

When *Lovers' Lane* # 1 (Oct. 1949) and *Boy Meets Girl* # 1 (Feb. 1950) hit the stands, a small cover emblem with a star informed readers that each title was "Authorized A.C.M.P.—Conforms to the Comics Code." This was hardly a genuine attempt at good taste and censorship, as the crime, horror and romance titles of the period often vividly attest. Even so, several entrepreneurs from the Association of Comics Magazine Publishers (ACMP) slapped this symbol on their covers beginning in the late 1940s. Some abandoned what in retrospect seems something of a sham sooner than others. Gleason used it until the real Comics Code Authority was established in September, 1954, with a much larger CCA symbol that began to appear on the upper right-hand corner of covers early in 1955.

Amy Kiste Nyberg, in *Seal of Approval: The History of the Comics Code* (1998) detailed why the ACMP formed the earliest Comics Code:

> On July 1, 1948, the association announced the adoption of a code to regulate the content of comics. The six-point code forbade depiction of sex or sadistic torture, the use of vulgar or obscene language, the ridicule of religious and racial groups, and the humorous treatment of divorce.... The ACMP hired a staff of reviewers who read the comics before they were published, and approved comics were allowed to carry the association's seal of approval on the cover. The president of the association, Phil Keenan of Hillman Periodicals, warned the public not to expect overnight miracles, because the improvements would be made to comic books currently in production, and those books would not be put into circulation for several months.... Almost immediately, the industry ran into trouble trying to enforce its code. While there had been strong support initially for a trade association, many of the largest publishers broke ranks. Some left the organization because they did not want their companies associated with those publishing what they felt were inferior comics, some because of objections to the code, some because of the time and expense involved in supporting pre-publication review, and some because of what ACMP executive director Henry Schultz characterized as "internecine warfare within the industry." As a result, only about a third of the publishers actually supported the new code, and that number dwindled until, by 1954, there were there were only three publishers left in the organization and the prepublication review process had been abandoned.

Of the large publishers, Dell, National, Fawcett, Quality and Fiction House all declined to undergo prepublication reviews in the late 1940s and never displayed the ACMP symbol, although Marvel did for several years. Dell, of course, never did participate in a Comics Code, and Fawcett and Fiction House were both gone by the time the Comics Code Authority was created, with Quality soon to follow.

"Not Intended for Children"

Lev Gleason's two romance titles, both bi-monthlies in 1950, were among 30 that continued unabated through the Love Glut. *Lovers' Lane* skipped two months, not one, between # 6 and 7, so there were 11 Gleasons published in 1950, representing about one-sixth of the small but successful company's output. That was a significant financial gamble for such a small company, which published fewer comics all year than Fawcett or DC did in three months.

Gleason did something unique on the newsstands of 1950: In the prominent strip crediting Gleason, Biro and Wood below the title, were the words, "Not Intended for Children." Granted, they were in tiny type, but they were clearly visible. In this case, "children" surely must have meant pre-teens, since no publisher wanted to ignore the lucrative "bobbysox" market of teen girls. Besides, what *teen* girl would consider herself a child? This was a comic book example of "cover your ass," much as Crestwood's slogan "for the more ADULT readers of COMICS" on its first three issues of *Young Romance*.

It's interesting to note how Gleason targeted advertisers who appealed to the insecurities of teen girls (maybe it should be how advertisers targeted romance titles). Full-page ads read, "I Was Ashamed of My Face" (pimples); "The Wonderful New Beauty Trix Wallet"; "Ugly Blackheads Out in Seconds with Vortex"; and "Lose Weight Where It Shows Most" (see Chapter Nine).

Both of Gleason's titles went monthly in 1951, so it's no wonder they were among the few year-long successes during the Love Glut. They must have sold well. They all featured striking painted covers in 1950, many by Bob Fuje, following line-drawn covers on *Lovers' Lane* # 1 and 2 in 1949. The stories tended toward strong portrayals of emotions and relationships in contrast to the more exotic circumstances many other publishers offered.

Every now and then, one of the stories was a real knockout, such as "My High School Crush" in *Lovers' Lane* # 2 (Dec. 1949), illustrated by the accomplished Bob Lubbers. This 10-page tale would make anyone wish for more from Lubbers, who is best known for a series of sensational and highly collectible covers for the action-oriented publisher Fiction House in the late 1940s.

At the bottom of the first page of *Boy Meets Girl* # 1 (Feb. 1950), readers were invited "to send in your true story" for a $25 prize if accepted. How many were ever really accepted is problematical; this would be analogous to offering readers a $250 prize today! More likely, this was intended to deepen readers' involvement and bring them back. Since stories were not to exceed 300 words, the $25 prize would have been worth eight cents a word—a handsome rate in those days.

Quality Comics: Exotic and erotic

Publisher Everett "Busy" Arnold's line of Quality Comics, always one of the slickest of the Golden Age, was best known for two comic book icons—*Blackhawk* and *Plastic Man*—and continued its high production values into the romance comics era. Quality, though, suffered a severe implosion in 1950, perhaps as the result of both the declining popularity of Golden Age heroes and the effects of the Love Glut. The result: Quality cancelled or suspended 22 of its 30 titles late in 1950, including all 14 romance titles. At that point, all 14 had run from eight issues (*Heart Throbs*) to four issues (*Forbidden Love*).

Because of their high production values, Quality issues published during the Love Glut have long been among the most collectible romance comics. Issues published in 1950 all had photo covers, either of models or starlets, though seldom of recognizable Hollywood stars. Most of the photo covers featured *only* women in 1950, though Quality went to the more popular couples covers after the company rebounded from the glut. Some of the covers, such as the striking photo of Ava Gardner on *Broadway Romances* # 4 (July 1950), become crossover collectibles long before romance comics in general became popular with collectors.

Quality's art, including work by highly respected illustrator Reed Crandall and pinup cartoonist Bill Ward, was consistently excellent. Quality's stories tended toward themes involving the exotic or the scandalous. Most of the covers and stories didn't approach the level of bad taste that Fox exhibited, but not a few were too racy for pre-teens. Even so, Quality never posted warning labels on the covers.

Quality's romance themes

Quality took the unusual step of publishing themed romance titles among its 14 early titles. These ranged from *Campus Loves* to *Broadway Romances* to *Hollywood Diary*. Several companies tried the western romance category, but Quality took themes much further. None of the theme titles returned in 1951, however.

Campus Loves, which ran only five issues, is a particularly appealing period piece, featuring titles like "I Stole My Roommate's Man"; "Campus Cheat"; "My Shameless Deception"; "Can a 'Nice' Girl Win?"; and "Men Were My Guinea Pigs." In "I Paid the Price" in *Campus Loves* # 5 (Aug. 1950), there was the astonishing splash page scene of a young college professor spanking an insolent female student! The fact that he turned out to be her romantic salvation surely could have done little to sooth parental objections. It was this kind of story that the Comics Code regulators particularly objected to when they took over five years later.

Quality, also notorious for "lingerie panels," turned out an irresistible six-issue run of *Flaming Love*, cover-blurbed "Torrid Tales of Turbulent Passion" on # 2 (Feb. 1950). "Hash House Queen" was a typical title. The cover come-ons were among the most salacious in comics, such as this overwrought verbiage to advertise the story "Man Bait" in # 4 (June 1950), which featured a startling degree of "cover cleavage": "From Casablanca to Singapore, men's passions blazed at the mention of my name! [And doubtless other attractions.] Yet I was the one woman who made a mockery of love!"

Forbidden Love has long been among the most highly valued of romance comics, if only for its title and suggestive tone throughout the four-issue run. The story titles in # 3 (July 1950) offer an accurate reflection of the overly warm contents: "Kissless Bride"; "Girl-in-Waiting"; "Love for Sale"; "My Desperate Desire." The contents, if anything, warmed up in # 4 (Sept. 1950): "Brimstone Kisses"; "I Gave Him Everything"; "My Foolish Pride"; "Hate on Skates"; and "The Inner Fire."

"Hate on Skates" is one of several roller-derby tales from several publishers about the popular 1950s phenomenon. It told the tale of Dot Ferris, "just a waitress in Tim's Cafe back home," but on the banked track known as the whirlwind star Flash Ferris. Cat fights ensue until Dot/Flash's dashing boyfriend plants a punch on the kisser of a conniving promoter! The boyfriend literally takes Dot back to the farm, her roller derby days abandoned for true love. Such unlikely but creative epics are among the strongest appeals of 1950s romance comics.

Quality's flagship romance title, *Heart Throbs*, was the only one of the company's eight romance titles that National Comics picked up when it bought the company's titles at the end of 1956. *Heart Throbs* often offered the exotic, such as these titles in # 8 (Oct. 1950): "Island Magic"; Flame in the Desert"; and "The Sea Held Her Happiness."

Not too much imagination was needed for many of the titles in *Hollywood Diary* and *Hollywood Secrets*: "Stand-In for Heartbreak"; "Drama of Deceit"; "Sky Full of Stars"; and

Campus Loves # 5, Aug. 1950, copyright Comic Magazines, Inc. Unlike most large publishers, Quality tried to produce romance with themes.

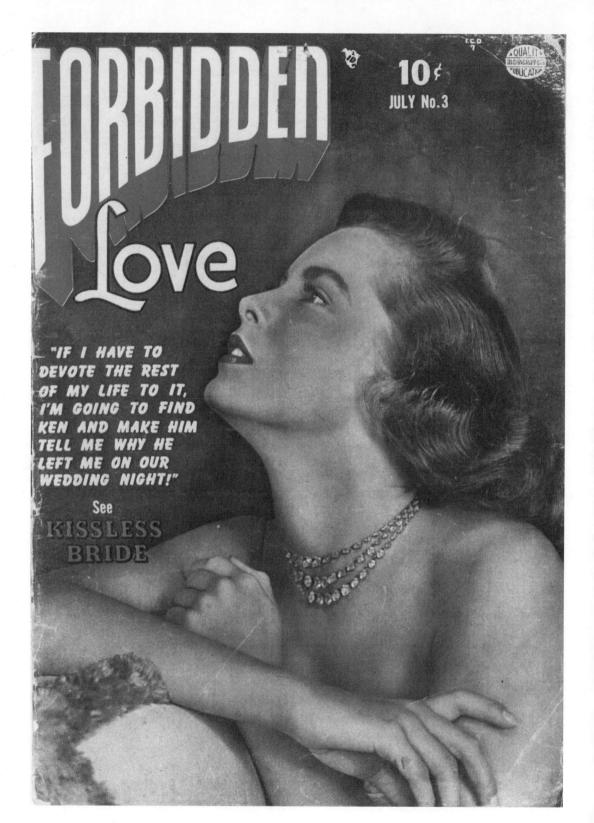

Forbidden Love # 3, July 1950, copyright Comic Magazines, Inc. The title overstated the case for this title's run of four issues.

"Enchanted Role." The logos were especially creative: A searchlight for *Hollywood Diary*, dozens of stars in the letters of *Hollywood Secrets*. One of the odder oddities in comics of the period was the cover of *Hollywood Secrets* # 5 (July 1950), featuring Lex Barker and an adoring Vanessa Brown as Jane in "Tarzan and the Slave Girl" (from RKO in 1950). Quality published this cover at the same time Dell Comics held the license for Tarzan's long-running title, one of the most popular in all of comics. Dell began its long series of Barker photo covers in January 1950, but Jane wasn't part of Dell's cover cast. The ever-wholesome chimp Cheeta was always OK, though.

Untamed Love offered tales with a moral, such as "I Longed for a Cave Man" in # 5 (Sept. 1950). After Fern Reston's "cave man" proves to be a wanton murderer, she realizes the man she left back home was the fellow for her and as the story bows out with a kiss, her once-and-future boyfriend holds a newspaper headlined by the death of her "cave man."

Love Scandals presented little epics of women who learned their lessons the hard way, such as "Flood Tide of Desire" in # 4 (Aug. 1950). The cover blurb said it all: "Men would do anything I wanted ... anything but inspire love in my designing heart!" Then there was "I Hated Being a Woman" in # 5 (Oct. 1950): "I was completely feminine, lovely to look at, adored by men ... yet I was wretchedly unhappy!" There was no hint of lesbianism, however; this one dealt with the tomboy Matilda Comstock, whose overly doting dad longed for a boy and responded at her birth, "We can make it Matty for short!"

Diary Loves, *Secret Loves*, *Love Letters*, *Love Confessions*—it seemed there was no end to Quality's contribution to the Love Glut. Then, abruptly, the company seemed to have abandoned love entirely, only soon to make the biggest comeback in the history of the romance comics industry.

Fawcett Comics: Happy cover couples

No company contributed as much to the Love Glut as Fawcett Comics, which published an industry-leading 73 romance issues in 1950, the same year it started its hugely successful Gold Medal line of original paperback novels. Fawcett published best-selling magazines such as *Popular Mechanics* and *Popular Science* along with *True Confessions* and others of its type, so comic books were only a part of the venerable firm's publishing empire in the 1940s and early 1950s. That's probably why the Love Glut did not affect Fawcett in quite the negative ways other companies suffered. Four of Fawcett's 17 titles survived cancellation or suspension and apparently thrived. *Sweethearts*, *Life Story* and *Romantic Secrets* made Fawcett the only company with three surviving monthly romance titles in 1950. A fourth survivor, *Romantic Story*, was a regular bi-monthly.

Sweethearts # 85 (March 1950) is typical of the Fawcett romance output, with stories entitled, "Enraptured Heart," "Dark Farewell," "The Guilt-Tainted Soul," and "I Betrayed My Love." Women typically suffer, suffer and suffer some more in Fawcett stories, in sharp contrast to the pleasant cover scenes. More often than not, shortsighted shallowness or greed led to a loss of love and problems that only modified thinking could resolve.

Fawcett tried two short-lived experiments in 1950—*Love Mystery* # 1–3 and *Negro Romances* # 1–3, both victims of the Love Glut. Both titles, sought after because of their scarcity, are self-explanatory. *Negro Romances* was the only comic book ever produced of its odd genre, though Charlton produced a single reprint issue (# 4) in 1955. Charlton acquired the rights to much of Fawcett's story inventory—and some of its characters and titles—after the company left the comic book business with five issues dated Jan. 1954, including the final appearance of the Golden Age version of the Marvel Family.

Inexplicably, Fawcett placed a full-page house ad for *Sweethearts* on the inside back cover of *Sweethearts* # 94 (Dec. 1950). The ad copy to the right of a tear-stained female face pretty much sums up the dispiriting Fawcett approach to romance: "Sheila Ryan's experience, and others like hers, can be yours without the *real-life Heartbreak* (with capital H and italics, no less!) that comes of a misguided love!" The balloon above Sheila's carefully-coifed head says it all: "No, don't pity me, Toni ... all that's ... sob ... happened to me I ... sob ... deserve. I destroyed love because I ... sob ... wasn't worthy of it.... Be happy with Ward and try not to think unkindly of ... sob ... me."

Harvey Comics: Before Richie, rich in romance

Most baby boomers remember Harvey Comics as the happy home of Richie Rich, Little Dot, Casper the Friendly Ghost, Sad Sack and other famously funny characters, along with a few newspaper strip heroes such as Dick Tracy and Joe Palooka. But during World War II, Harvey was primarily a super hero outfit, producing the likes of the Green Hornet and one of the relatively few costumed heroines, the Black Cat. She, like Wonder Woman from National Comics, was sometimes involved in romantic themes and boasted the not-to-be-underestimated power to fight crime in high heels. Before finding its financial way with funny people (and ghosts) of all types, Harvey tried to launch a romance comics empire during the Love Glut. Harvey eventually succeeded, but not before temporarily succumbing to the glut. All seven romance titles that Harvey started in 1949 were either suspended or cancelled in 1950.

In contrast to many of its competitors in 1950, Harvey persisted in publishing 36-page romance comics (including covers), making them less attractive than their 52-page competitors. Thus, Harvey specialized in the concise story along with emotion-drenched line-drawn covers. In *First Love* # 8 (April 1950), for example, there are four stories, none longer than six pages: "Too Hot to Handle" (about firefighters), "Love Starved" (about dentistry), "Confessions of a Telephone Operator" (a great period piece) and "Man of Many Loves" (covering a love triangle). The cover displays a bobby-soxer, a hay ride and a tear-stained girl telling herself, "If he loved me, he wouldn't treat me like this when he knows I'm love starved!" while counting the petals off a daisy in the time-honored fashion. Harvey romance titles often employed capable Golden Age artists such as Bob Powell and Lee Elias, so collectors have long paid a bit more attention to them than many others.

Harvey also published a title, *First Romance*, with a philosophical question atop the logo: "Is it better to have loved and lost ... than never to have loved at all?" The question should have been: "Is it better to have published and lost than not to have published at all?" The Love Glut must have struck Harvey rather suddenly, since the back cover of *First Romance* # 6 (June 1950) tries to entice readers to subscribe to all seven Harvey titles, all of which were discontinued or suspended that month! All seven were displayed in full cover glory.

Four titles—*First Love*, *First Romance*, *Hi-School Romance* and *Love Problems and Advice*—made it back within a year. But, despite the ad encouraging readers to subscribe for 12 issues (two years) or 25 issues (more than four years!), *Sweet Love*, *Love Lessons* and *Love Stories of Mary Worth* never returned. One can only speculate in amazement at the financial optimism represented by probably the only company ever to offer a four-year subscription to any comic book! The long-term rate of $2 for 25 issues did represent a 50-cent saving over the four years. Harvey, by the way, didn't give up on its four-year rate, advertising the same bargain a year later in the four romance titles that resumed publication. When *Hi-School Romance* resumed with # 6 (Dec. 1950) after a five-month layoff, Harvey advertised a "Miss Hi-School" contest. Harvey even published the photos of 10 semifinalists along with a ballot in # 8 (April 1951).

Also in # 6, Harvey plugged *Love Problems* # 7 (Jan 1951)—yet the cover showed a date of June 1950! The title was suspended with # 6 (May 1950), but nobody thought to adjust the cover date on the ad copy.

Charlton Comics: Not the real McCoy yet

Charlton, a low-rate, low-rent company destined to churn out comic books by the thousands in the 1950s, '60s and '70s, was still a tiny player in 1950. Even so, Charlton's only romance title, *Pictorial Love Stories*, tried something unique after taking over for the defunct *Tim McCoy Western* with # 22 (Oct. 1949). *Pictorial Love Stories* lasted only five issues and was yet another victim of the Love Glut.

Most romance comics did not run regular characters, but *Pictorial Love Stories* tried three in "Hotel Hopeful" (about soft-hearted boarding house maven Mrs. Lucinda—Aunt Mike—Michael); "Me—Dan Cupid" (a fantasy that pretends Cupid really exists!) and "Carter's Case Book" (about lovelorn editor Catharine Carter). Issue # 23 (Jan. 1950) also presented the tear-jerker "I Was a Small-Town Snob" along with a rather astonishing one-page "beauty brief" entitled, "Danger: Thin Shoulders!" The ending says it all: "Don't forget, girls ... thin shoulders lead to danger! Danger to your popularity! Be sure to try the above exercise for the upper body ... and look for the next helpful hint in *Pictorial Love Stories*' beauty briefs!"

Crestwood (Prize): First and often best

Correctly billed at the top of the front cover in 1950 as "the original love & romance comics magazine!" *Young Romance* became a monthly with # 9 (Feb. 1949). By 1950, *Young Romance* and its companion title, *Young Love*, were among the most daring of the romance titles and among the most original.

Young Romance # 22 (June 1950), with the cover-featured Simon & Kirby story "The Savage in Her!" was typical of what Crestwood, also known as Feature Publications and Prize, offered to perhaps older readers. "All my life, I had been two women! One—the daughter of a missionary, firm in her convictions and dedicated to her father's work.... The other—a hellcat! Fiery! Emotional! Wanting to love and be loved! I was never certain which of these women was really me ... until a wild, unprincipled scoundrel named Gary Donovan tried to waken 'The Savage in Me!'"

The other stories also offer a hint of more than mere heartbreak: "Sister Was a Stinker!"; "Child Bride!"; "Change Your Name to Mine!" and "I Never See Helen Alone!" Crestwood consistently offered the most breathless story titles in the industry, almost always with exclamation points. Likewise, the tempestuous classics in *Young Romance* # 23 (July 1950) were: "Gang Sweetheart!"; "A Woman's Honor!"; "One Last Fling!" and "Love on a Budget!" The cover displayed a hard-looking Bonnie and Clyde type pair, complete with cigarette arrogantly hanging from the young thug's lips as a moody thuggette smolders.

Simon and Kirby loved coming up with current-event themed sensations, such as "Hot Rod Crowd!" in # 28 (Dec. 1950), making Crestwood among the most collectible of companies. How could anyone resist a blurb like this one: "Hot Rod Crowd! Where DEATH was part of the game of LOVE!" The covers of the period also told readers: "Big 52 pages! Don't take less!" Crestwood's two western romance titles, *Real Western Romance* and *Western Love*, were victims of the Love Glut, but *Young Romance* and *Young Love* remained among the industry leaders in sales. Today, they're considered among the peak of the form by collectors and comic historians.

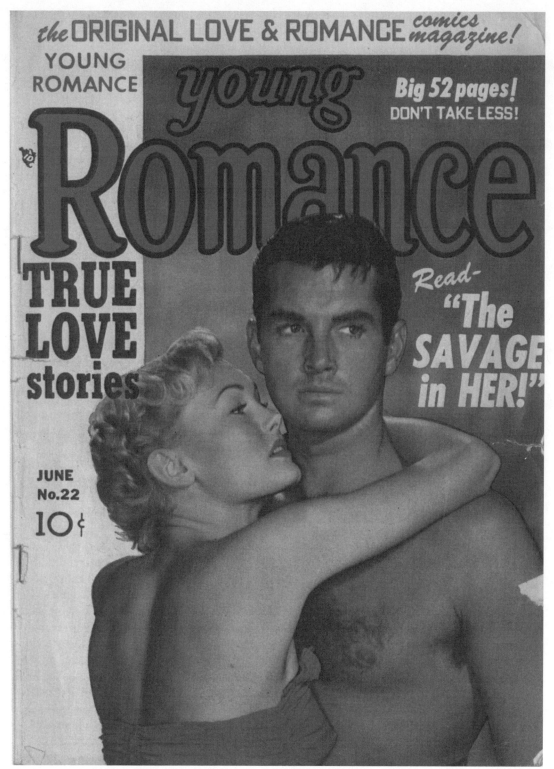

Young Romance # 22, June 1950, copyright Feature Publications, Inc. With stories like "The Savage in Her," *Young Romance* did not seem affected by the Love Glut.

Ace Comics: Transitional romance

Ace was never more than a second-tier comic book publisher, beginning with super hero titles in 1940. Like all the large firms, the Love Glut caught Ace, although the company recovered to become one of the industry's romance leaders until leaving comics in 1956 to concentrate on its growing paperback line. But in 1950, after Ace converted three of its teen humor titles to romance comics and started six other ventures in four-color love, the company entered the year with nine seemingly healthy titles. Six of the nine, however, soon were either cancelled or suspended.

After beginning its love line with lackluster line-drawn covers, Ace distinguished itself by appealing to the fashion sense of young girls with pulp-style painted covers of gorgeous female faces, complete with wonderful makeup and imaginative hats or ribbons. Many, if not most, of these covers were either pulp magazine holdovers, unused inventory or reprints, because Ace pulp covers of the 1940s looked just like the comics were to look by 1950. At any rate, these were among the most striking covers on the stands—truly fine works of commercial art.

Ace did not use the overwrought cover drama many companies relied on before the Love Glut struck down so many titles. But the stories were very much of a piece with the plethora of emotional love tales of the racks. The titles in *Real Love* # 30 (Feb. 1950) tell the tale: "I Wanted Him Back! "; "Out to Break Us Up"; "The Two Who Were Jilted"; "Her First Conquest"; "Overshadowed By My Sisters"; and "A Woman Scorned."

The art, seldom signed, was uniformly good, and the high word count of many stories was similar to Lev Gleason's style, minus much of the violence. Ace continued to stress stories of emotion, not adventure. In *Real Secrets* # 3 (Jan. 1950), the firm plugged all nine titles in an attractive house ad on the inside front cover, but Ace's "era" as a nine-title titan lasted less than a year. The company tried hard with a similar ad in *Real Secrets* # 5 (May 1950), but the Love Glut must have struck hard and quickly. Ace published 33 romance issues in 1950, but only five issues appeared dated for the final four months of the year.

ACG Comics: Human-interest love

For two decades through 1967, editor Richard Hughes successfully guided the American Comics Group. Famed among collectors for his fondness for unusual and original stories, Hughes often brought twists to romance stories he and others wrote. Hughes and ACG are best known for introducing the first regularly published horror comic, *Adventures into the Unknown*, in 1948. The theme of many of the pre–Comics Code horror stories of that title could be summed up as "girl and guy meet and beat ghost/vampire/zombie and live happily ever after." Hughes carried over the twin themes of romance and dangerous dramatics to his two successful romance titles, *Romantic Adventures* (later *My Romantic Adventures*) and *Lovelorn* (later *Confessions of the Lovelorn*). Both titles soon became monthlies, but they survived in 1950 as colorful bimonthlies. A third title, *Search for Love*, lasted only two issues before becoming a victim of the Love Glut.

"Beautiful Dreamer"—aside from being a nice pun—in *Romantic Adventures* # 6 (Jan.–Feb. 1950) was typical of ACG's human-interest stories. In a 13-page epic that involved espionage, fire, violence and rejection, elevator operator Harriet Wright learns that true romance isn't dressed up as a dashing Latin lover. In contrast to Ace's more realistic depictions of human emotion, ACG was often pure pulp—but highly entertaining pulp. Even today, many collectors find these stories fun to read, if impossible to take the least bit seriously.

In the amazingly hokey "From Rags to Romance" in *Romantic Adventures* # 7 (March–April

1950), the introductory blurb tells how odd this epic is: "Ever hear of Pygmalion, reader ... ancient sculptor who carved an ivory statue which magically became the living, vibrant Galatea? Well, his job was an easy one compared to mine! I'm Wayne Yardley, Park Avenue Playboy— who found his Galatea in the depths of the Florida swamps! It's a strange story—the story of the heart of a barefoot beggar girl—the tale of a man torn between two loves!" All's well that ends well when Our Hero outwrestles an alligator to rescue an illiterate swamp girl after 13 pages of her conflicts with the social set.

Plot? These stories absolutely overflow with it! Check these titles in *Romantic Adventures* # 8 (May–June 1950): "The Farmer's Daughter"; "The Girl Nobody Wanted"; "Close Your Heart to Love"; and "Bewitching Buccaneer." The later is a pirate romance! Only in the pages of the ACG romance titles could a story like that be found.

Search for Love # 1(Feb.–March 1950) and # 2 (April–May) offered much of the same format, but for some reason—or simply because of the Love Glut—this title failed despite the unusual title. Issue # 3 was advertised in ACG's mid–1950 titles, but the issue never appeared and the cover was used on another ACG romance comic.

Lovelorn offered "Stirring Stories of Real Romance," such as "China Doll" in # 3 (Dec. 1949–Jan. 1950), about how a tiny girl learns she doesn't have to scheme to find true love, and "Love Thy Enemy," about a two-fisted hero and heroine saving a lumber mill from criminals. It was pretty much the same formula that enabled *Romantic Adventures* to survive during the Love Glut. There were simply no more plot-filled, if unlikely, love stories than were found in the ACG titles.

Standard Comics: Pulp romance

Longtime pulp publisher Ned Pines's Thrilling Group took relatively late, tentative steps into romance comics. Pines started three romance titles in December 1949—*Thrilling Romances*, *Popular Romance* and *Western Hearts*—and added *Intimate Love* in January 1950. Pines also became one of the few publishers to add a romance title, the short-lived *Dear Beatrice Fairfax*, in the last quarter of 1950, defying the depression caused by the Love Glut. Perhaps because Pines published these titles at only bimonthly or quarterly intervals, all five made it into 1951, with a modest but significant total of 20 issues published in 1950. At the same time, Pines continued to publish dozens of pulp titles even though the field was dying and several other publishers, most notably Street & Smith and Ace, gave up pulps in 1949. Pines's well-established paperback line, Popular Library, continued to prosper in 1950 as well, making Pines the only prolific publisher in all three areas of popular culture in that pivotal year.

The Thrilling folks used beautifully painted covers for their romance pulps—many of them in a combination realistic/symbolic style by the wonderfully versatile and skilled Earle Bergey—but they bought photos for the covers of all of their romance comics except the five-issue run of *Dear Beatrice Fairfax*. That title, based on a King Features Syndicate comic strip by Vernon Greene, used gorgeous "wash" covers by Alex Schomburg, who is best remembered for the hundreds of collectible super hero covers he drew during the 1940s for Pines as well as Timely/Marvel, Harvey and a smaller publisher, Holyoke/Continental.

Standard's photo covers resembled Fawcett's in style, except that Standard purchased several romantic movie star stills whereas Fawcett's covers usually featured anonymous models. For example, the cover of *Intimate Love* # 5 (Jan. 1950)—the first issue—was identified on the cover as Beverley Tyler and Jerome Courtland from the obscure Columbia film, *The Palomino*. All of Standard's romance comics were only 36 pages—the publisher dropped the 52-page format earlier than most comic book factories. The stories were mostly mainstream romance, much like Ace, but seemed less attractive in 1950 because the art was often crammed into a format of eight panels per page. In that year, the remarkable Alex Toth's arrival was two years in the future at Standard, as was Nick Cardy's fine work.

Standard had a quirk that had nothing to do with seeking to elude paying for second-class mailing privileges. Beginning in the late 1940s, Standard began numbering most of its first issues either # 5 or # 11, seeking to convince news dealers that their titles had established more stability than they really had. Standard was a solid second-tier comic book publisher for nearly two decades—best remembered for colorful World War II super hero titles such as *The Black Terror* and *The Fighting Yank*—so it wasn't surprising the Pines people tried a trick or two to enhance their circulation.

National Comics (DC): Low-key but classy

National Comics is well respected by romance collectors for being one of the slickest purveyors of love during the post–Comics Code era, even though many 1950s and early 1960s stories tend to be merely mild fantasies. National, however, was only a minor player in the early years of romance comics. Two of National's titles in 1950—*Girls' Love Stories* and *Girls' Romances*—survived the Love Glut as bi-monthlies. *Secret Hearts* was suspended with # 6 (Aug. 1950) and did not resume publication until # 7 (Dec. 1951–Jan. 1952). A fourth title, *Romance Trail*, ended with # 6 (June 1950).

National's romance titles were among the most wholesome the industry offered, but the generally squeaky-clean company still seemed skittish about acknowledging its romance line, however small compared to National's huge influence on the industry as a whole. In 1950, the classic "Superman DC National Comics" circular logo disappeared from the romance covers, although ownership was acknowledged in the indicias. During that time, DC did not place house ads for its romance titles in other comics and vice versa. One would think that *Wonder Woman* would have been a natural to advertise in love comics, but such was not the case in 1950.

National also ran a complete list of all its titles in all of its comics except the romance line. The skittishness was obvious: Whereas *Girls' Love Stories* # 1 (Aug.–Sept. 1949) carried a complete list of DC titles on the inside front cover, the list was gone by the second issue. The logo and house ads for non-romance titles also disappeared. But National gave the reader one of the best 52-page issue bargains on the racks, since the company did not downsize to 36-page issues until late in 1951 (and then published many at 44 pages for a couple of years).

The titles in *Secret Hearts* # 3 (Jan.–Feb. 1950) give a good indication of the story themes, which almost always ended happily: "Sing Me a Love Song"; "Tomorrow's Tears"; "My Heart Was a Deceiver"; "Romance Rivals"; "Let Me Be Yours."

The first few issues of *Girls' Love Stories* and *Secret Hearts*—National's first two romance titles other than *Romance Trail*—must have sold well, because *Girls' Romances* # 1 (March 1950) began during the height of the Love Glut. All three titles were identical in theme and style, so perhaps when the company soon decided to drop one of them, it just seemed easier to keep the two comics with similar titles.

National used Fawcett-style "love-struck" photo covers in 1949 and 1950. When National went to illustrated covers early in 1951, they were consistently, if usually anonymously, among the most polished the industry could offer, often with at least mildly dramatic themes.

St. John: a shaky year

Gorgeous art by Matt Baker and outstanding writing by Dana Dutch could not improve St. John's financial fortunes in 1950, when its romance titles were at a low point from the standpoint of quantity. The small company plunged headlong into the burgeoning romance market in 1949, but encountered problems even before the Love Glut could be fully felt.

St. John's flagship title, *Teen-Age Romances*, was the company's only love comic to make it through 1950 with six bi-monthly issues (# 8–13), all among the most collectible of romance comics. *Pictorial Romances* (previously *Pictorial Confessions*) appeared only once that year (# 4, Jan. 1950) and *Hollywood Pictorial* (previously *Hollywood Confessions*) ended with # 3 (Jan. 1950). *Teen-Age Diary Secrets* # 8 (Feb. 1950) was the only issue that year except for the odd appearance of a digest-sized # 9 (Sept. 1950), which reprinted the digest-sized # 7 (Nov. 1949) with a different cover. All six issues of *Teen-Age Romances* in 1950 were oversize, a half-inch taller than regular comics, as were several later issues, meaning they are seldom found in fine or better condition. They were probably abused right on the racks while potential readers were flipping through the comics.

The Little Guys and Gals of 1950

Most publishers produced only a handful of romance issues during 1950, but they added up to more than 116 issues among them and contributed significantly to the overcrowded love on the racks. In addition to the three important small companies covered above—Lev Gleason, St. John and Charlton—no fewer than 13 other firms each turned out from four to 12 issues of romance comics. The names are a Who's Who of firms that were second-tier with regard to romance, although sometimes—such as EC and Archie—they were otherwise titans of the industry at some point. The often unlucky 13 in 1950 were Eastern, Hillman, Star, EC, Archie/Close-Up, Avon, Ziff-Davis, Youthful, Kirby, Orbit, Superior, Fiction House and Artful.

Eastern, the *Famous Funnies* people, apparently didn't feel the Love Glut at all, perhaps because they alternated bi-monthly issues of *Personal Love* and *Movie Love* for a total of 12 issues in 1950. Throughout their combined history of 55 issues, these two titles used nothing but romantic stars from the movies on their covers, making them noteworthy period pieces. Each issue of *Movie Love* condensed the stories from two romantic movies, most of them long forgotten by all but the most ardent film buffs. *Movie Love*'s covers for 1950 featured a mix of superstars and lesser lights: Dick Powell and Evelyn Keyes on # 1 (Feb. 1950); Myrna Loy and George Montgomery on # 2; Cornell Wilde, Lois Butler and Lon McCallister on # 3; Paulette Goddard on # 4; Farley Granger and Ann Blythe on # 5; and Jane Powell and Ricardo Montalban on # 6. Insets of stars from the second story were featured, as well. *Personal Love* featured movie stars on the covers, but the stories were densely-plotted mainstream romance, such as these little epics in # 1 (Jan. 1950): "Dual Love"; "I Stole Her Other Love"; "Last Chance for Love"; "Engaged to the Wrong Man."

Although story plots were often repetitive, it's amazing how many different titles the romance comic impresarios came up with. Well over 15,000 romance stories were published in the more than 3,750 romance issues from 1947–59, and it's quite likely that there were more than 5,000 different titles. It would be fun if anyone ever came up with an alphabetical list of all of them.

For the record, *Personal Love* covers featured these stars in 1950: Farley Granger and Cathy O'Donnell on # 1; Kathryn Grayson and Mario Lanza on # 2; Janet Leigh and Glenn Ford on

3; Deborah Kerr and Robert Walker on # 4; Tom Drake and Terry Moore on # 5; Audrey Totter and Richard Conte on # 6. Incidentally, # 6 (Nov. 1950) had the creative cover blurb, "Love is where you find it ... and you'll find PLENTY in this magazine."

Avon recycled several of its more suggestive 1940s paperback covers for its limited number of romance comics. But nothing worked for Avon during the Love Glut; all six of its early titles failed, including a 1949 one-shot entitled, *Complete Romance*. *Romantic Love* was suspended with # 3 (Feb. 1950) and did not resume publication until 13 months later. *Campus Romances* ended with # 3 and *Frontier Romances* with # 2, both March 1950. *Sparkling Love* had only one issue (June 1950). The oddest venture of all was *Betty & Her Steady*, marketed as a teen humor title with # 1 and a romance book with # 2 (March–April 1950), the last issue.

Star Publications, a 1949–50 start-up that sometimes gobbled up work from discontinued companies, featured elaborate, almost psychedelic covers by L. B. Cole and often primitive, bizarre inside work. *True-to-Life Romances* # 9 (Feb. 1950), the second issue, featured heroines with occupational challenges in "Stardust Can Blind You"; "Farewell to Love"; "Deadline for My Heart"; and "Love's Crashing Landing," dealing with a movie starlet, a model, a newspaper sob-sister and an airline hostess, respectively. Each story ended with a girl having learned her the real lesson of her star-crossed career, comforted in the arms of her man. Star's four titles all failed in 1950, though *True-to-Life Romances* returned in 1951. *Film Stars Romances* presented fictionalized stories of Hollywood, including a story in # 1 (Jan.–Feb. 1950) in which the director is named "Zarell Danutt."

Pulp publisher Ziff-Davis, best known for *Amazing Stories*, produced four romance comics in 1950 and then returned more than a year later. Like Standard, Ziff-Davis often started with a higher number, so *Cinderella Love* # 10 was the first issue in 1950. There were a pair of # 10 and 11 issues during the run of 11 total issues, since the title reverted to # 4 with the fourth issue. *Romantic Marriage* # 1 and # 2 (1950), the company's first romance comics, were edited by Jerry Siegel, the co-creator of *Superman* a dozen years earlier and a prime factor in the industry's success. He was marginalized after he and co-creator Joe Shuster lost a creators' rights lawsuit against National a few years earlier. Siegel's efforts at Ziff-Davis produced mixed results.

Our Publishing Company, often known as Orbit, was headed by a woman, Ray R. Hermann (sometimes known as Rae). The company was best known for producing one of the most infamous crime titles, *Wanted Comics* featuring "Mr. Crime," but it tested the romance market with eventually favorable results. *Love Diary* # 4 (Jan. 1950), the only issue for the first four months of the year, was typical of what makes the title collectible now, with cover blurbs like "Be Honest ... Are You a Moral Maurauder?" That was the title of a one-page essay by "Ray Mann" (usually Hermann).

Love Diary defied the Love Glut by becoming a monthly for the last five months of 1950 (# 7–11) after producing three issues in the first seven months. Covers like the glorious purple of # 9 (Oct. 1950) may have led to success, along with blurbs like "I could have known REAL LOVE with Don! But I lost him because all I could think of was myself! For I was a SPOILED DARLING!"

Hillman adapts a radio advice show

Hillman, a magazine and paperback publisher best known among comic collectors for creating *Airboy* and *The Heap* in the 1940s, could not make a go of the oddly named *Mr. Anthony's Love Clinic*. The title, an adaptation of a radio advice show, ran through # 5 (May 1950). But the company succeeded modestly with *Romantic Confessions*, which ran 25 issues until the company went out of the comic business in 1953. These 52-page, plot-packed issues of mainstream romance were among the better-written love stories of the period, stressing intense conflict and resolution.

The tiny publisher Kirby popped up seemingly out of nowhere to produce two titles covering 10 issues. Kirby failed in 1950 after less than a year despite two interesting 52-page experiments begun in 1949: *Enchanting Love* # 1–6 and *Golden West Love*, a western romance title that became the mainstream *Golden Love Stories* with # 4 (April 1950), its final issue. Kirby's production strongly resembled *Young Romance*, which was then pretty much the standard-bearer along with St. John for excellence in romance comics. Kirby's stories, though, were typical relationship-centered romance without the more exotic elements usually injected into *Young Romance*. *Enchanting Love* # 3 (Jan.–Feb. 1950) presented an atypical story with an unusual two-page splash: "My Heart Became a Wasteland," a western romance perhaps originally intended for *Golden West Love*. *Enchanting Love* # 5 (May 1950)—with the odd cover slogan, "A GOOD Kirby Comic"—presented a striking photo cover of leggy dancer Ann Miller from "On the Town."

Four of the most obscure romance "comics" published in 1950 weren't comics intended for youngsters at all, but rather attempts to horn in on the then-lucrative market for sensational digest-sized paperbacks with sleazy covers. The tiny company Artful/Harwell published a pair of 25-cent digests, *Honeymoon Romance* and *Confessions of Love*, that ran two issues apiece. The cover of *Confessions of Love* # 1 (April 1950) showed a terrified-looking woman clutched from behind by an obviously undesirable character, with the blurbs, "Should Brides Be Virgins?" and "My Wedding Night Was a Nightmare of Honeymoon Horror!" Likewise, *Honeymoon Romance* # 1 showcased the cover feature, "Sex Crimes on the Increase." These four issues are among the rarest romance issues and are highly sought after.

Like National Comics, the publishers of Archie did not present any obvious connections to their two short-lived romance titles, *Darling Romance* and *Darling Love*. With cover features such as "I Get What I Want!" on *Darling Love* # 3 (Feb.–March 1950), it's easy to see why Archie didn't want to claim them. The stories were filled with violent emotions—loaded with slaps, tears and regrets—quite a difference from the benign Archie titles. "I WANT My Soldier Boy," screamed the title of a story in *Darling Love* # 5 (June–July 1950), as did "Love's Oldest Sin" in *Darling Romance* # 4 (March–April 1950). The two titles advertised each other, but nobody could have known they were connected with the Archie folks. Their indicias told the tale: Close-Up was an Archie imprint, located at the home of Betty & Veronica—good old 241 Church Street in New York.

Pix Parade, a small publisher more commonly known as Youthful among other imprints, jumped into the love field in 1949 with *Youthful Love Romances*, which carried bylines for the writers on every story in # 1 (Aug.–Sept. 1949). Such writing credits weren't seen again as the title, soon renamed *Youthful Romances*, struggled for four more issues before a suspension. Pix Parade pulled a strange move, indeed, when it renamed *Youthful Love* # 1 (May 1950) as *Truthful Love* for # 2 (July 1950), the last issue. In an odd house ad in *Truthful Love* # 2 telling readers to "watch for the next issues!" the company pictured the two-month-old *Youthful Romances* # 5 and *Youthful Love* # 1, both May 1950! Indeed, there were to be no more issues of *Truthful Love*, and *Youthful Love* # 6 did not appear until February, 1951.

The only romance title from Fiction House, *Cowgirl Romances*, is covered in Chapter Six. Much of the art for *Cowgirl Romances* came from the Iger Shop, a prolific jobber of the 1940s operated by S. M. "Jerry" Iger, who briefly was a partner of the great comics pioneer Will Eisner before World War II.

Superior, which produced comics from 1948 to 1956, was the only significant Canadian publisher to circulate its titles on U.S. racks. Superior also used Iger shop art, as did Ajax/Farrell and Artful/Harwell in the 1950s, among others. Iger, in fact, was listed as Superior's art director in many indicias. Superior broke into the romance field with one title, *My Secret*, which became *Our Secret* with # 4 (Dec. 1949). Why? Most likely to avoid confusion with the plethora of Fox titles that began with "My."

Our Secret ran only through # 8 (June 1950) and became yet another victim of the Love Glut after running stories similar to the Fox titles. For example, the cover of *Our Secret* # 6 (March 1950) carries a picture of one Abdul Abulbul about to marry an American girl as another American girl rushes in to exclaim, "Stop! You can't marry him! Wait until you hear what I have to say." In this utterly bizarre featured story, "Forsaking All Others," the Arab intends to fool his American fiancée into become one of his wives. When his plans are threatened, the Arab tells her, "We shall simply rope her [the other American girl trying to break them up] to one of these trees, and go off in peace to tie our own nuptial knots." To which his thunderstruck fiancée replies, "Oh, goodness." Indeed! The story ends with the Arab put in his place and a two-fisted American named Bill set to marry the girl.

EC dallies with romance

EC, soon to become infamous for its unparalleled line of horror and science-fantasy comics, plunged into the love field with three titles in 1949. *A Moon ... A Girl ... Romance* (formerly *Moon Girl Fights Crime*, itself a change from *Moon Girl*) failed in 1950 after four issues, as did *Saddle Romances* (formerly *Saddle Justice*) following three issues. *Modern Love*, however, lasted through # 8 (Aug.–Sept. 1950) before the Love Glut caught up with it, too.

David Burlington, in *Comic Book Marketplace* # 80 (July–Aug. 2000), observed that in the EC romance comics, "The troubled and defiant teens depicted there seem about as rebellious to us as missionaries or insurance salesmen." Nevertheless, EC advertised its romance stories as "true love tales at their illustrated best" and "heart-rending scenes, poignant drama, and blissful moments!" Burlington points out that artists who never made it into the later, better-known EC comics, such as Walter Johnson and Bill Fracio, worked on EC romance along with the famed likes of Johnny Craig, Graham Ingels, Harry Harrison and Wally Wood. Burlington cites the "beautifully rendered" "Playtime Cowgirl" in *Saddle Romances* # 11 as especially noteworthy work by Harrison and Wood.

Burlington says, "These romance comics are not EC at its New Trend (horror, science fiction, war, etc.) best. However, they are simply good fun and can be enjoyed without undue comparison to Gaines's and Feldstein's later masterworks. The Ingels, Wood and Feldstein art is an appreciated bonus. EC romance comics are a nice collectors' adjunct to the more scrutinized and popular EC crime, horror, shock and science fiction fare."

"The Love Story to End All Love Stories"

Fittingly entitled, "The Love Story to End All Love Stories," this little satiric masterpiece, conceived and produced by EC's impish publisher William Gaines and editor Al Feldstein, foreshadowed the wonderful parodies in EC's *Mad Comics*, which started in 1952 and eventually became a national icon after *Mad* went to magazine size in 1955. The credit for "The Love Story To End All Stories" read "Blame this on Feldstein" (he was the artist, but the story was a teamup of Feldstein and Gaines). The EC indicia imprint that published *Modern Love* was called, of all things, Tiny Tot Comics. Thus, the story was taken "from the completely fictitious experiences of T. Tot"—the publisher of *Modern Love*.

The story begins, "One warm spring morning, when birds are twittering and buds are

Modern Love # 8, Aug.-Sept. 1950, copyright Tiny Tot Comics, Inc. This, the last EC romance issue, included one of the great satires in comic book history, a collaboration between publisher Bill Gaines and artist Al Feldstein.

bursting forth on green boughs, at the office of T. Tot, comic book publisher." T. Tot tells his two staffers—the images of Feldstein and Gaines!—that he is in love. T. Tot publishes crime comics like "Crime Ought to Pay" and "Crime Should Pay," according to his motto: "A comic book by Tot hits the spot!" "No more will we have to rely upon our crime comics for our paltry profits!" Tot tells his underlings. "Love will make us millions!" He is inspired by his love for the lusty, lovely young Cobina, who is far more interested in food and finances than she is in the love-struck Mr. T. Tot. But he, of course, is too blinded by love to see that.

Meanwhile, a rival publisher—Victor Fox, of course, disguised as "Mr. Wolf" and "V.W.," relies on the motto, "Wolf Comics Make 'Em Howl!" He publishes titles like *Crimes by Dogs*, *Crimes by Cats* and *Crimes by Criminals*. (One of Fox's real flagship titles before and during the Love Glut was the notorious *Crimes by Women*.)

Soon, as the story relates, "The Comic Book Industry Goes Berserk! Here is the greatest money maker since 'Soup-Or-Man.' Or, as one publisher says, 'Boost the print orders of my seventy-nine love titles to 1,000,000 each! From now on, call me Love Greasin'!'" Lev Gleason must have appreciated that. The story relates how "the number of love comics on the stands reaches staggering proportions. Soon, at the offices of Arnold Harvey Hermann [a melding of three real-life publishers' names], the bewildered publisher declares, 'Love is finished! Change the formats! Change the titles! Change the stories! Put out anything ... even ... horror!'"

T. Tot reaches the end of his rope when Jack Lyman and Joe Curry show up to tell him they are ruined. After these parodies of romance pioneers Joe Simon and Jack Kirby leap out of his penthouse window, T. Tot laments, "Oh, my poor tormented soul! Blood upon my hands ... honest kind editors' blood ... rival editors' blood! I drove them to it.... I did it!"

Soon declaring, "I hate love!" T. Tot finds he has gone bankrupt and can publish no further comics of any kind. His seven love titles have sold a grand total of 249 copies and he has thus lost $2,475,322.48. Given a gun by one of his staffers to commit suicide, T. Tot shockingly takes both staffers and the shocked Cobina with him, leaving only the office boy alive. In the final panel, the office boy directly advises the readers to let him know if they'd like to see more such stories—and provides the real address for E.C. Comics!

Thus did the overcrowded conditions cause the demise of most romance titles in 1950. But love would not be denied on the comic book racks. Publishers profited heavily from romance for many more years, but not from the short-lived specialized field of western romance.

• SIX •

Writers of the Purple Page
A Short-Lived Flirtation with Western Romance

In the scramble to find commercially successful replacements for the fading Golden Age super hero and newspaper reprint anthology comic books in 1949, several major publishers almost simultaneously tried an experiment unique in comics at that point: the mixed genre title. By 1949, pulp publishers had been cashing in on the combination of love and lariats for 25 years, since Clayton Magazines succeeded with the formula in 1924 with the debut of *Ranch Romances*. The magazine, which ran to 860 issues through 1971 under three publishers, was by far the most successful in its field and one of the most successful of all pulps. It was also the last of the pulps, outlasting others of all types by a decade.

It's a testament to the influence of the romantic western theme that elderly women still buy issues of *Ranch Romances* at antique shows or second-hand shops today, when they would otherwise have no interest in collecting or reading the old pulps. It's equally a testament to how dead the mixed genre is these days, however, that no pulp anthology has ever been published devoted entirely to the type of tale presented in *Ranch Romances* and its many sisters, aunts and nieces, so to speak, of the 1930s, '40s and '50s. When Fawcett Gold Medal Books presented an obscure paperback anthology entitled, *Western Romances* in 1974, only four of the dozen stories were plucked from pulps, and all four were from 1950s issues of *Ranch Romances*. The rest were from "respectable" slicks.

During the explosion of romance comics in 1949, several of the primary publishers tried to market western romance. But only two titles, both quarterlies, survived the Love Glut of 1950 to make it into 1951 on a regular basis—*Cowgirl Romances* from Fiction House and *Western Hearts* from Standard. It may have been no coincidence that Fiction House and Standard/Thrilling were among the final holdouts as prolific pulp magazine publishers, including western romance. Standard, in fact, picked up *Ranch Romances* from Warner Publications late in 1950, or that venerable publication might have bitten the pulp dust, too.

The tiny impact of western romance

In stark contrast to their pulp cousins, western romance comics had only a tiny impact on the comic book industry as a whole. More than 1,800 pulp western romance issues were published, or close to five percent of the more than 40,000 pulps produced in the 1920–60 period. The grand total of original western romance comics was 89 issues! There were, of course, western romance stories occasionally published in the mainstream romance comics, but not enough to be statistically significant. Many of these stories were probably left over from dead titles.

Crestwood, publisher of *Young Romance*, the first mainstream love comic, followed nearly two years later with the first romantic western. *Real West Romances* # 1 is dated April–May 1949. Crestwood, also known as Feature Publications or Prize, quickly added *Western Love* # 1 (July–Aug. 1949). Fawcett was the second to leap into market, with *Cowboy Love* # 1 (July 1949), followed by National's *Romance Trail* # 1 (July–Aug. 1949). All four of those titles were handsome 52-page presentations, complete with more than competent art and stories. They might well have been more successful but for an avalanche of competitors along with the effects of the Love Glut in 1950 (see Chapter Five). No fewer than 13 more western romance titles hit the racks with dates in the final quarter of 1949. Apparently, publishers both large and small must have felt that Crestwood, Fawcett and DC had latched onto something profitable.

Tiny Kirby Publications produced *Golden West Love* # 1 and prolific Marvel came out with *Cowboy Romances* # 1 in the same month, October. Marvel, always wont to flood the market with any theme that seemed likely to catch fire, quickly followed with *Romances of the West* # 1 in November, long before sales reports could have come for *Cowboy Romances*. Also in debut issues dated November, Star (the successor to Novelty Press) converted the long-running heroic title *Target Comics* into *Target Western Romances* with # 106 and Ace turned *Western Adventures* into *Western Love Trails* with # 7.

December debuts included Standard's *Western Hearts* # 1, Avon's *Frontier Romances* # 1, Quality's *Range Romances* # 1, Fawcett's *Romantic Western* # 1 and EC's *Saddle Romance* # 9, a genre switch from western crime to romance after the final issue of *Saddle Justice*. Also for December, Marvel decided to strike while the brand was steamy, or something like that, with *Love Trails* # 1, *Rangeland Love* # 1 and *Western Life Romances* # 1.

The two Cowgirl Romances

In what seems to have been an inevitable development, the 18th and 19th western romance types bore the same title—*Cowgirl Romances* from both Marvel and Fiction House! Marvel's version lasted one issue (# 28, Jan. 1950). Fiction House produced its *Cowgirl Romances* on a quarterly schedule, beginning with three undated issues copyrighted with 1950 dates, so it's possible Fiction House may have struck first.

The last of the original titles to appear was the first and only issue of the over-the-top *Flaming Western Romances* # 3 (April 1950) from Star, which had tried to avoid the burden of a new second-class postal permit for the two issues of *Target Western Romances*. Star, a third-tier publisher in 1949–54 best noted for horror and jungle comics and bizarre covers, was forced to play catch up with the postal authorities many times. That led to collecting chaos for those who avidly sought the many unique color-packed covers by L. B. Cole. It took a long while for enthusiasts to realize there were no *Flaming Western Romances* # 1 and 2.

Dell, a pre-eminent purveyor of western titles, followed in 1951 with the one-shot *I Met a Handsome Cowboy* (March). This may have been originally intended for one of paperback kingpin Dell's few failures: the unsuccessful digest-sized *As Told in Pictures* series, which ran only two issues in 1950. These were the anonymous digest, *Twice Loved*, and the nicely done *Four Frightened Women*, with illustrations by Robert Stanley of the adaptation of a mystery by George Harmon Coxe. *I Met a Handsome Cowboy* was adapted from a serial published in *Ranch Romances*, "Clouds over the Chupaderos," by Elsa Barker.

When the low-rent publisher Charlton gobbled up gobs of inventory art in 1954 after former industry titan Fawcett left comic book publishing, the Connecticut-based company tried titles in every possible genre. Most could do no better than brief runs in the 1954–57 period before the company stabilized. One of Charlton's experiments were four issues of *Cowboy Love*

(# 28, Feb. 1955, through # 31, Aug. 1955), using Fawcett reprints or inventory. After that, the pure (or even impure!) western romance was never seen again in comic books.

The complications of photo covers

The covers of the western romance titles have long appealed to collectors beyond the range of romance comics, especially because of the photo covers. Many of the photo covers came from the plethora of B westerns then still being produced by the likes of Republic, Columbia and Monogram/Allied Artists, giving these western romances crossover appeal to film buffs. Crestwood's two titles, the pioneering *Real West Romance* and *Western Love*, used such photo covers to handsome if sometimes puzzling effect.

Real West Romances # 2 (June–July 1949) identified the cover stars as Gale Davis and Rocky Shanan of the Republic film, *Death Valley Gunfighters*. The film's real title was not plural and the star on the cover is really Rocky Lane, whose birth name was Harry Albershart. Since Fawcett had recently began publishing *Rocky Lane Western*, one might assume that Crestwood was hesitant to identify the star correctly! *Real West Romances* # 3 (Aug.–Sept. 1949) also labeled the handsome western star with the same incorrect handle.

Covers for the western romance titles, in fact, were fraught with character perils. *Real West Romances* # 4 (Oct.–Nov. 1949) pictured Monogram stars Whip Wilson and Reno Browne, who were also cover featured on Crestwood's *Western Love* # 2 (Oct. Nov. 1949) and Standard's *Western Hearts* # 1 (Dec. 1949). Early in 1950, however, rival Marvel licensed Wilson and Browne to appear in their own titles, both of which lasted only three issues that year. Yet for *Western Hearts* # 9 (Dec. 1951), Standard used the same cover photo of the pair that appeared on Crestwood's *Real West Romances* # 4 two years earlier.

Real West Romances # 5 (Dec. 1949–Jan. 1950) cover featured a striking still of the young Audie Murphy and Gale Davis—possibly the best of all western romance covers—and # 6 (Feb.–March 1950) had a slightly seedy looking Robert Preston, crooked cigarette dangling from his lips, strumming a guitar for Cathy Downs in *The Sundowners*. For Preston, trouble in River City was 11 years in the future in *The Music Man*.

Unlike its other romance titles, National listed its six issues of *Romance Trail* with its mainstream comics and used the regular circular DC logo referring to "A Superman DC Publication." *Romance Trail* # 1 (July–Aug. 1949) began the *Harmony Ranch* series starring motherly Molly Adams, who solved romantic problems in all six issues while keeping an "open house for trouble" on her ranch property.

Monogram Pictures star Jimmy Wakely graced the cover of *Romance Trail* # 1 along with Wanda McKay. Wakely even included an announcement about his own National title, which was about to start, and the firm advertised its other westerns as well. Another lesser-known western actor, Jim Bannon, appeared on the cover of *Romance Trail* # 2 (Sept.–Oct.) along with starlet Nancy Saunders. From that point on, National didn't label the folks on the romantic photo covers, all of which were pleasant images of smiling couples.

The author thinks *Romance Trail* had the best western logo of all—"Romance" spelled with ropes and "Trail" with logs. Quality's *Range Romances* soon imitated the logo.

"Range Riders of the Month"

Like all Fawcett romance titles, the 11 issues of *Cowboy Love* and the three of *Romantic Western* featured only photo covers, mostly of unidentified models. Three of the 14 covers—

Cowboy Love # 1 with *Rocky Lane,* # 3 with Monte Hale and # 5 with William Boyd—featured the "Range Rider of the Month" on the back covers before the lure of advertising dollars conquered western love. In their multitude of films, Lane, Hale and Boyd (who played Hopalong Cassidy for many years) all were better known for displaying affection toward their horses than women. Fawcett must have thought western love would be hot indeed, for the company made *Cowboy Love* # 1–8 the only monthly issues of any western romance title.

Movie stills for western romance comics may have been hard to come by, for Quality pulled the trick of using Jane Nigh and Bill Williams from *Blue Grass of Kentucky,* a horse racing film, for the cover of *Range Romances* # 4 (June 1950). Even stranger, "cowgirl" Gloria Henry appeared on the cover of # 5 (Aug. 1950) in a still from *Kill the Umpire*—a baseball comedy! Likewise, the photo cover of Kirby's *Golden West Love* # 2 (Nov.–Dec. 1949) features a shot of Ruth Roman leaning on a mailbox from *Champion*—a classic boxing movie starring Kirk Douglas.

Some western romance titles are collected primarily for their covers. L. B. Cole, the colorful co-owner and art director of Star, drew most of his firm's covers. He illustrated the covers for *Target Western Romances* # 106 and 107 and *Flaming Western Romances* # 3, the company's three-issue *fling* with western romance. Fiction House's 12 issues of *Cowgirl Romances* also featured dynamic line-drawn covers, albeit unsigned. Several were by the talented Maurice Whitman, in the company's show-a-lot-of-leg style.

The 10-issue run of *Western Hearts* from Standard used primarily movie-theme covers, some identified and some not. Issue # 6 (March 1951) cover-plugged Irene Dunne and Fred MacMurray in *Never a Dull Moment*—a modern-day comedy about life in rural Wyoming. *Western Hearts* # 5 (December 1950) featured Hedy Lamarr and Ray Milland in *Copper Canyon*—the title of a Fawcett Movie Comic adaptation of the classic Paramount film published in the same year. Mona Freeman and Macdonald Carey, the other stars of *Copper Canyon,* were featured on the cover of Marvel's *Cowgirl Romances* # 28 (the only issue), meaning three different companies cover featured *Copper Canyon* at virtually the same time.

Marvel favored movie-star covers on all six of its short-lived western romance titles. Most of these cover stills, however, were from genuine western films, such as *Streets of Laredo* with William Holden and Mona Freeman on *Cowboy Romances* # 2 (Dec. 1949) and *The Kid from Texas* with Gale Storm and Audie Murphy on *Western Life Romances* # 2 (March 1950). There were times the editors at Marvel obviously took few, if any, pains to avoid duplication of cover featured story titles. Witness the likes of "The Cowpoke Who Jilted My Heart!" on *Love Trails* # 1 (Dec. 1949), which may have appeared on the stands at the same time as "The Cowpoke Who Lassoed My Heart!" on *Romances of the West* # 1 (Nov. 1949) and "He Rustled My Heart!" on *Cowboy Romances* # 2 (Dec. 1949).

Eastern Color, the *Famous Funnies* folks, did not venture into the purple page market while continuing *Movie Love* and *Personal Love.* It's interesting to note how Eastern stayed away from the western romance cover themes, although there were several noteworthy exceptions such as the smoldering pairing of Kirk Douglas and Patrice Wymore from *The Big Trees* on *Personal Love* # 14 (March 1952); Dale Robertson and Joanne Dru from *The Return of the Texan* on *Personal Love* # 15 (May 1952); and Dana Andrews and Piper Laurie from *Smoke Signal* on *Personal Love* # 33 (June 1955). Fawcett adopted 35 movies in its 1949–52 series *Fawcett Movie Comic* and *Motion Picture Comics,* including numerous westerns, but generally stayed away from the western romance theme.

"Unbridled passion"

Publishers worked hard to make a go of it with western romance, trying to convince girls that they had a hankerin' for stories of—as the blurb on Quality's *Range Romances* # 2 (Feb. 1950) promised—"Unbridled passion and death-defying devotion in the lawless country where primitive emotions held sway!" Publishers must have figured it would be tough to resist such a blurb about lurid tales of lust in the dust. Publishers seldom let inventory go to waste, as attested by *Popular Teenagers Secrets of Love* # 10 (Jan. 1952) from Star Publications. The marvelous L. B. Cole cover hides the reality that the issue consists entirely of western romance stories.

Fawcett provided a case of either deadline problems or frugality when the firm reprinted "The Tall Stranger" from *Cowboy Love* # 1 less than six months later in the company's second western romance title, *Romantic Western* # 1 (Winter 1949–50). "The Tall Stranger" typified some titles, which also tended to be metaphoric, such as "Rustled Rapture" in *Range Romances* # 5 (Aug. 1950) or downright corn such as "Frontier Flirt" in *Range Romances* # 4 (June 1950). Some of the titles were creative, such as "Cowtown Casanova" in *Western Love* # 4 (Jan.–Feb. 1950 and spelled "Cazanova" on the cover), "Wild Hosses and Ornery Women" in *Real West Romances* # 1 (Feb.–March 1949) and "The Blacksmith and the Belle" in *Romantic Western* # 3 (June 1950).

The Vixen strikes

One of the most memorable and outrageous of the western romances was the bizarre "I Was a Lady Bandit!" in Marvel's *Western Life Romances* # 2 (March 1950). In this story, Belle Chance sees her father murdered by a corrupt lawman and vows vengeance. But Belle's heart is rustled by a handsome hoodlum, who makes her realize she would be better off fighting the criminals. After becoming a costumed villain called the Vixen, she witnesses her bad boyfriend knock off the ne'er-do-well lawman. Stuck with an honest-to-goodness baddie, Belle tries to find a solution to her dilemma when a lawman realizes her masquerade as the Vixen and threatens arrest despite their growing affection. When Belle guns down her former boyfriend to save her new lover, she surrenders to him. Yet he resigns from his job as sheriff—shooting up his badge, no less—so the two of them can build a life together in safer surroundings.

When Ace converted the mainstream *Western Adventures* to *Western Love Trails* with # 7 (Nov. 1949), *Western Adventures* mainstay Sheriff Sal, an Annie Oakley knockoff, finds a fellow to love and lets him become sheriff so they can be married.

Fiction House's Cowgirl Romances *scores*

Of all the western romance comics, the essentially quarterly 12-issue run of Fiction House's *Cowgirl Romances*, 1950–52, is closest in theme and appearance to the western love pulps, in which titles with puns such as "He Lassoed My Heart" were rare, unlike so many of the comics. The pulps tended to feature conflict-laden stories with a strong love interest, rather than merely love stories set in the West.

Except for issue # 12 (Winter 1952–53), the lushly illustrated covers of *Cowgirl Romances* featured entirely different action-oriented themes, unlike most of the sweet-love themes on most of the western romance comics. Western romance pulps featured plenty of both types. Even # 12 presents intense conflict of a different sort, with famed cover artist Maurice

Range Romances # 2, Feb. 1950, copyright Comic Magazines, Inc. "Unbridled passion and death-defying devotion in the lawless country where primitive emotions hold sway"—and check out the horse's eyes!

Western Life Romances # 2, March 1950, copyright Classic Detective Stories, Inc. Marvel called this character "The Vixen" in an unusual romantic adventure that ended happily.

Whitman's striking vision of an angst-filled cowgirl cowering behind a tree as (presumably) her man goes into a clinch with another girl. Issue # 10 (Summer 1952) features perhaps the most memorable of the 12 covers, again a Whitman beauty. A handsome couple clings to each other, clothing torn, as he shoots toward the reader while a hungry wolf circles in the background.

Other than # 12, it's raw, pulse-pounding action and then some, very much in the Fiction House tradition. Issue # 1 (1950, no month) set the tone with a cowboy alerted to reach for his gun even while he is only a couple of inches from the lips of a cowgirl with her eyes closed. Issue # 2 (1950) is much different; a cowgirl leaps from a runaway buckboard toward a gun-wielding man on a horse. Issue # 3 portrays a cowboy on a high rock gunning for rustlers, while a girl alongside him reloads a rifle.

Fiction House often loved putting dramatic blurbs on its titles. *Cowgirl Romances*, though, didn't run a blurb until # 4 (1951), when "Bullets Sang Her Wedding-March" in "The Bride Wore Buckskin" appeared, above a striking image of a girl shooting her gun at an unseen enemy while branding a calf, with a cowboy and a rearing horse in the background. With a white background, this is a compelling cover.

Issue # 5 (1951) is a different theme entirely, with a masked outlaw carrying off a blonde as she struggles to get free while he is shooting at the hero. When the unauthorized reprint house IW reprinted this issue circa 1958 as *Frontier Romances* # 9, the blurb was the colorless "Boy Meets Girl ... Along the Frontier" with a leggy lass hanging onto a cowboy who is climbing a cliffside with a rope. It just showed that nobody could write cover blurbs like Fiction House. In a less socially conscious era, Fiction House often used caricatures that would be considered racist today. Such was the cover of # 6 (1951), on which a golden-tressed woman with a rope around her waist tries to avoid an evil-looking Latin. The ironic blurb is "She Fought Alone Against the Guns of Hate—Rose of Mustang Mesa." The seventh different cover theme in as many issues of *Cowgirl Romances* highlights # 7 (1951) as a gun-blazing, hog-tied cowboy tries to pull a cowgirl out of the way of a cattle stampede. Issue # 8 (1952) displays a girl with a gun in her right hand and a branding iron in her left trying to fight off two plug-ugly rustlers. On # 9 (1952), a buxom blonde grabs onto her hero aboard a horse while trying to fight off a knife-wielding, bearded villain. Issue # 11 features an angry girl aboard a horse about to whip a cowboy kissing a blonde in a lantern-lit stable. Of the 12 covers of *Cowgirl Romances*—the only western romance comic to reach a dozen issues—only the first cover does not feature a blonde!

Fiction House featured two short continuing strips in the first three issues, all 52-pagers before the company reverted to 36 pages. These were *Calamity Jane*, featuring Tony Tyler of the Tumbling Y, and *Halfway House*, starring a fearless, crime-busting hellion known as "The River Rose." She liked to describe Halfway House as "where the trail to nowhere starts" and "where Nevada law can't touch you." In tribute to the name of her ranch, the typically sassy Fiction House heroine Tony Tyler uses a slingshot and informs the reader: "And now, folks, take warning. I, Tony Tyler of the Tumbling Y, am my own boss, and anyone who says differently better remember I have this [her slingshot] and know how to use it!"

The colorful flavor of the titles of the longer stories in the first three issues is sheer Fiction House. The titles bear little resemblance to western romance comics from other companies: "Ride Fast for Wyoming," "A Kiss for Captain Lobo," "Beneath the Outlaw Moon," "Montana Rides the Gun Trail," "The Lady of Lawless Range," "The Rancho of Golden Dreams," "Maverick Guns from Arizona," "Daughter of the Devil's Brand" and "Gambling Queen of El Dorado."

"Rancho of Golden Dreams" in # 2 featured a happy ending in an unusual romance between a white lawman and a gorgeous Latina. Happy endings, though, were always the rule in *Cowgirl Romances*, unlike a smattering of sad endings in mainstream love comics. One of the best titles was "Two Hearts Against the Vigilantes" in # 10. Whitman, the Fiction House cover specialist who drew the covers for # 5 and # 7–12, also drew a rare eight-page story for # 12, "Ranch of Riddles."

In the breathtaking, non-stop action epic, "Daughter of the Devil's Brand," in # 3, circus trick shot Mary Colby is called on to play a combination of Robin Hood and Annie Oakley—complete with mask, six-shooter and short-short skirt—to rescue her elderly father from men out to bilk him. Sam Carter, sheriff of Dawson County where her heroics play out, wins her heart and Mary reverts to a female in love in the final panel with this promise as she embraces him and answers his plea for her love: "Get your branding iron out, Cowboy, for the answer's yes!" Ironically, the next town up the road in Old West Kansas from Oakley is— Colby.

The hard sell of love in the West

Fawcett's *Cowboy Love*, which ran 11 issues including an undated 1951 issue, and the short-lived companion title, *Romantic Western*, which lasted only three issues, featured nothing but happy endings. In stark contrast to Fiction House, all but two of the 14 Fawcett covers featured pleasant western themes of love-struck guys and gals along with horses, campfires and the like. *Cowboy Love* # 1 featured a tense, gun-toting cowboy and his equally tense girl, and # 6 showed a couple being held up by a gunman, matching the cover feature, "The Outlaw's Kiss."

The full-page house ad on the inside back cover of *Cowboy Love* # 7 (January 1950) is indeed odd, clearly showing artistically framed covers for *Cowboy Love* # 1 (July 1949), *Sweethearts* # 77 (July 1949) and *Life Story* # 7 (October 1949) instead of current issues. It's as if a Fawcett public-relations man decided any old issues around of the office would do instead of the January numbers of all three titles, even though an artist took the trouble to turn out an attractive page. The breathless blurb was typical of the larger early romance publishers: "REAL LOVE EXPERIENCES! Have never been presented with the DRAMATIC INTENSITY of these PICTURE LOVE-STORIES that bare the heart's most SECRET EMOTIONS!"

One of the most unusual stories in *Cowboy Love* is "Outlaw Girl!" in # 2 (Aug. 1949). Peaceful homesteader Jeff Benton knocks out a shady "gunman" who invades his home only to discover it's a beautiful girl. Tired, starved Amy Carter tells him she has been framed for a murder. He gallantly takes her to the neighboring couple to spend the night, then spends the rest of the story falling in love with her and tricking the man who framed her into confessing. To do so, however, he has to take her to jail, convincing her that all he wanted was a $1,000 reward until the despairing woman learns he has not been disloyal after all. "Yes, my love, and we've got a wonderful lifetime waiting for us," she tells him in the final panel. "I know now that all it takes to win in this world is faith, courage and love." So, even with the happy ending required of the western romance genre, it takes a man to teach a woman the error of her ways—so typical of the moral style in Fawcett's mainstream romance comics.

Marvel tried hard to market its short-lived line of six western romance titles, which had a combined total of only 11 issues over a six-month period. In *Rangeland Love* # 1 (Dec. 1949) a full-page house ad plugged all six titles, including one, *Cowgirl Romances*, which had not yet appeared. "America's Most Thrilling Western Romances," said the blurb, above a couple kissing with a background of a fence, a cactus, a mountain and an animal howling at the moon. Yes, that covers it all, doesn't it?

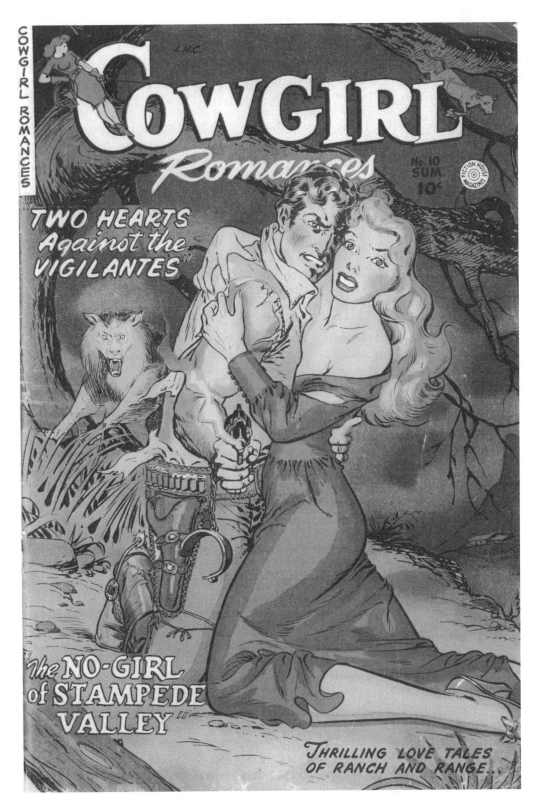

Cowgirl Romances # 10, Summer 1952, copyright Love Romances Publishing Co. Fiction House produced one of the few western romance titles with dramatic covers, such as this one by Maurice Whitman illustrating "Two Hearts Against the Vigilantes."

When it came to hard-sell covers, however, Quality was pretty much the king of hyper-bole. *Range Romances* # 2 promised the aforementioned "unbridled passion," then followed up by offering "pulsating, pistol-packed epics of passion and adventure in the wide-open spaces!" in # 4 (June 1950) and finally by plugging "stirring sagas of the West, filled with the rhythm of thundering hoofs and pounding hearts!" in # 5 (Aug. 1950). Alas, the stirring sagas ended with that issue.

"Wildcat of the West" in *Range Romances* # 5 told of Janey Dowling, who "preferred riot to romance" and didn't hesitate to knock down a wolf with the words, "Next time it'll be a bullet, not just a pistol-whipping!" But she's soft-hearted, too, as when she tells a handsome stranger who is the victim of robbers, "Shucks, I wouldn't turn a dog away if he was in trouble!" The handsome stranger eventually strikes gold and Janey doesn't have to be told twice to marry him.

Quality tried harder than most to come up with creative titles, such as "Petticoat Law" and "Tenderfoot Sweetheart" in *Range Romances* # 1. But the man still almost always ruled the western romance roost, such as in "Petticoat Law." In the town of Washupp, Sheriff Matt Westerly has his hands full with gunmen along with fearless Katie Ryan, a flame-haired dress-maker who tells him, "I'm warning you men! Either clean up Washupp—or we women will!" Ultimately, after the two of them take care of the town's gunslinging card-sharp, Matt lays down the law: "When we're married, no more blowing up and bawling me out! And no more trying to make me enforce your petticoat law! I'm the boss!" To which she replies, "All r-right, Matt! I promise! You'll be the boss in everything!"

Standard introduced its 10-issue run of *Western Hearts* with this message from the editor on the first page of # 1:

> Naturally, in those turbulent days, there were precious few pioneer girls to go around. Competition among the eligible males was so keen that many a maid was courted and married in an aura of gun smoke. And there was an ever-present element of danger in every courtship. A cowpuncher might be trampled in a herd's stampede, or shot by a crooked gambler or a bad man on the prod. He might throw in with a wild bunch and find himself outlawed, with *every* man's hand against him. So a cowgirl's romance was never a reality until the preacher spoke his piece. Life was also uncertain for the girls of the Western plains; they fought side by side with husbands and sweethearts against the savagery of the era, but still found time for romance. Hardship and strife were tempered by the strum of guitars and the crooning of rangeland love songs. Truly, the Old West was a land to test the power of love, for it demanded sacrifice and hard work from every girl who gave her heart to the man of her dreams.

One can vividly imagine how girls must have figured textbooks just couldn't match that description of life in the West! *Western Hearts* appeared quarterly through # 10 (March 1952), all with photo covers, but the stories generally had a cartoony feel and thus didn't seem as dramatic as most of those from other companies. Even so, only *Cowgirl Romances* outlasted *Western Hearts*. Standard's editor listed in the ownership statement of *Western Hearts* # 10, the remarkably versatile Joe Archibald, formerly wrote stories for several genres in the firm's vast pulp magazine line before going on to become the most prolific post-war author of young-adult sports novels in American history. Archibald wrote more than 40 novels dealing with athletics from the 1950s to the 1970s.

Being small didn't stop Kirby Publications from trying something different in *Golden West Love* # 1 (Sept.–Oct. 1949)—two western romances set in modern times. In the first, the word-heavy, 13-page "Heartbreak Trail," a woman returns to the man she loves in a western town, only to find him wheelchair-bound following a stampede. The story ends with a doctor's promise that he will recover his health, but it's uncertain whether he will recover his love for her, although she has faith he will. The second modern story, "I Hate You, My Love!" deals with social work in a western town and how it affects two people who find love in the end.

"The Tragedy at Massacre Pass"

Kirby went to even more unusual lengths in *Golden West Love* # 2 (Nov.–Dec. 1949) with four stories set in modern times, including the unrelentingly grim 13-page "The Tragedy at Massacre Pass." Gail Bender finds herself strongly attracted to misogynistic Dave Oakes at a roundup dance, but finds out that he's a woman-hater. "You're as handsome a woman as I've seen, Miss Bender! I mean that!" he tells her. "But, like all women, you're probably an extravagant, useless hussy! Never could understand why women were so no account!" To which she responds, "Ohhhh ... you ... you stupid, ignorant fool!"

She tells herself she can't help loving him and tries to convince him of the benefits of how she stands to inherit the most successful ranch in their area. His response: "Why, you husband-hunting little witch! Are you insinuating that I'd be interested in you because of your father's money? Do I look like an Eastern-type gigolo? Willing to be tied to a woman all my life just to be sure I have a meal ticket? Bah ... you're even worse than most dames!" Her reply as she slaps him: "I wish I were a man ... so I could give you a real beating!" To which he blurts out: "Just like a woman! Can't stand the truth!"

Eventually, she vindictively starts a rumor that nearly results in Dave being hanged for cattle rustling by a vigilante group led by her elderly father. Dave winds up hating her more than ever and her father goes to jail for seven years. Seldom have comics reflected misery more intensely than her thoughts in the final two panels: "My life is over ... there's no reason for living.... I've ruined Dad! He hates me! Even a lifetime of retribution can't undo the harm I've done! And all because of love ... because I wanted to hurt Dave! I can't understand how I could be so insane! I must face it ... a haunted life ... a life in shadows ... a life in bitter unhappiness ... and all because I let emotion rule me ... dictate what I knew in my heart was wrong ... wrong and hateful and sinful ... and ugly!" Whew!

Two of the other three modern westerns in # 2, "Price Tag on Love" and "Judas Kiss," told stories of the female protagonists' greed and the hard lessons they learned. The other, "A Woman Scorned," featured a man taught a lesson in courage by the woman he loves. "Judas Kiss" ended with a heavy handed moral caption: "Louise has been forgiven, and a much wiser girl, has set out to mend her life in full possession of the realization that money is not the road to happiness—that true happiness can only come about through forgetting greed and desire, and living in harmony with the people about her!"

Golden West Love # 3 (Feb. 1950) featured happy endings on all four stories, only one of which was set in the modern West. The stories featured plenty of violence and double dealing, but avoided tear-stained women in the final panels. The editors of *Golden West Love*, John Augustin and artist Tex Blaisdell, must have known they were producing unorthodox love stories. In all three issues, they took the unusual step of including coupons on which readers were asked to rate the three stories they liked best and also the one they liked least, along with an explanation of why they disliked it. They offered five $5 prizes for the best reasons—the modern equivalent of more than $50 for one sentence.

"Erotic spanking in a Western comic book"

Avon gave Dr. Fredric Wertham a rare and infamous image for his illustration insert in *Seduction of the Innocent* in 1954: the psychiatrist labeled it "Erotic spanking in a Western comic book." The panel became infamous precisely because it was such an uncommon image: spanking, erotic or otherwise, was almost never seen in any type of comics. It was typical of Wertham that he would use a 5-year-old extreme image in his gallery of offensive art (see Chapter Nine).

Collectors eventually discovered the original panel in "Tangled Love," the first story in the obscure *Frontier Romances* # 1 (Dec. 1949) from Avon. Even in worn condition, this issue *usually* goes for more than $50 because of its notoriety. Purely by coincidence, the reprint house IW (later known as Super) republished the issue with a different, much tamer cover circa 1958. IW produced several hundred issues of reprints or inventory art from a variety of publishers.

Avon was one of the first, and one of the best and most prolific, of the 25-cent paperback publishers in the 1940s and tended to feature exploitation-oriented covers even on literature. The same could be said of many of its romance comics. The painted cover of *Frontier Romances* # 1 displayed a passionate full-body clinch and kiss, with the ungrammatical but effective "She learned to ride and shoot, and kissing came natural." in large capital letters. This was a trick common to many publishers; the cover, in theory at least, could have applied to any of the stories.

"Tangled Love," like so many stories in the western romance comics, is heavy on words. It's the apparently modern-day tale of how young state legislator Rick Dennison finally convinces Laurie, the girl he grew to love, to see the wisdom of his plan to divert a lake to create an economically advantageous river for farm prosperity. Rick saves Laurie from drowning after a fall into the lake, then calls her a "spoiled brat an' mighty lucky to be alive" before he spanks her. She then slaps him furiously, not long after having succumbed to his attempt to kiss her before her fall. Later, her stubborn nature nearly causes both of them to be killed in a landslide caused by blasting. Ironically, the story, illustrated by journeyman artist Walter Johnson, is full of words young readers might not be familiar with, such as "humiliation" and "constituents." Most of the panels are dominated by word balloons; the art is secondary. Early on, Rick discovers Laurie in a two-piece bathing suit—definitely not something a nineteenth-century girl could have imagined!

The other stories in *Frontier Romances* # 1 were all entertaining little trifles with happy endings: "Heart-Wrangler!" "Ropin' in a Wild Cowpoke" and "Don't Fence Me In" (named for the popular song). "Ropin' " had a plot with a twist—a cowboy whom the girl berates as "boastful, crude and uncouth! ... a bearded savage!" eventually decides to clean up his act after much quasi-witty back-and-forth banter and battling between them about their qualifications for marriage. After the two of them survive a fire and rescue horses, the newly shaven cowboy tells her, "Oh, Gloria, darlin' I love you! I wouldn't care if you couldn't cook or ride or do anythin' around a ranch.... I love you and I want to marry you!" Accepting on the spot, Gloria tells the reader her thoughts, which might be considered the ultimate in generic writing: "He held me in ending," she says. "Mrs. Flash Gannon—purtiest, smartest wife in Red Dog!"

National's well-trod Romance Trail

National Comics didn't succeed with its six-issue run of *Romance Trail* in 1949–50, but it wasn't for lack of production values, including attractive photo covers. Every issue featured four stories, including the aforementioned *Molly Adams of Harmony Ranch* series, and the usual consistently solid art National became known for among collectors beginning in the late 1940s.

Every issue featured stories by either or both of the most accomplished artists ever to work in comics—Everett Raymond Kinstler and Alex Toth (who is inked by Frank Giacoia in a particularly gorgeous job in # 1). The supremely talented Kinstler went on to status unparalleled by any artist ever to work in comic books: He was commissioned to paint several presidential portraits, two of which hang in the White House, after beginning his distinguished career in 1940s pulps and comics. Kinstler's amazing career is well detailed in Jim Vadeboncoeur, Jr.'s outstanding collaboration with the artist, *Everett Raymond Kinstler: The Artist's Journey through Popular Culture, 1942–1962*. Kinstler's stories in *Romance Trail* # 1–3 and # 5 are highly collectible visions of a then-young artist's potential, helping to make this a scarce but sought-after series.

All 24 stories in *Romance Trail* are typically clean-cut, plot-packed National efforts. Like the vast majority of National's more than 3,000 romance stories covering 931 issues across 28 years, they all have happy endings. *Romance Trail*, in fact, offers a stunning contrast to Kirby's grim and gritty *Golden West Love* # 1–3, which were on the stands at the same time. The only thing these two series have in common is plenty of plot and dreamy titles. Otherwise, they're about as different as comic books of the same genre can be.

EC quickly kisses off western romance

Even EC briefly joined the western romance craze, producing *Saddle Romances* # 9–11 in 1949–50 before converting it to *Weird Science* with # 12 in one of the wilder title transitions in comic book history. Edited by publisher Bill Gaines, the three issues of *Saddle Romances* are eagerly sought by collectors if only because anything with the EC label is hotly pursued. Graham "Ghastly" Ingels, the avidly collected artist famed for his EC horror epics, drew stories in each issue plus the cover of # 9 (Nov.–Dec. 1949). Feldstein provided the covers of # 10 (Jan.–Feb. 1950) and # 11(March April). *Saddle Romances* was a continuation of the crime-themed western *Saddle Justice*.

The conflict-riddled stories, typically among the most compelling of their type, as were most EC epics, not surprisingly featured several of the most imaginative titles in the brief history of the genre. They included "Saddle in the Sky" and "Indian Love Call" in # 9, "I Loved a Murderer," "The Heart Robber" and "Romance Isn't for Tomboys" in # 10 and "Playtime Cowgirl" and "Cheating Cowboy Lover!" in # 11. Feldstein wrote two stories; credits for the other 10 have been lost even to EC experts.

Though western love was not destined to last long, mainstream romance comics rebounded well from the Love Glut of 1950 and became marketplace mainstays for years.

SEVEN

You Can't Keep a Good Girl (or Guy) Down

Before the Comics Code—How Romance Comics Rebounded in the 1950s

The aftermath of the Love Glut was like nothing that had ever occurred in American comic book publishing. Unlike the demise of horror and crime titles in the mid–1950s, the near simultaneous disappearance or suspension of more than 100 romance titles in 1950 did not involve censorship or the excessive outcries of outraged parents, teachers and librarians. It was simply a classic example of too much supply and too little demand, not to mention too little space available on the racks.

Although official circulation statistics have never been made available—most publishers of the period revealed only good news, not bad—it seems certain that overall comic book sales declined in 1950, perhaps for the first time since the industry began in the mid–1930s. Not that comic books weren't still profitable—or else why would eight companies have each published more than 100 issues (of all genres) in 1950? Comics were profitable, but just not enough to please the publishers.

The numbers involved are nothing less than startling, at least on the surface. There were 2,251 issues of all types in 1949 and 2,280 in 1950. There's little doubt, however, that comic book circulations continued to drop, if only incrementally, from year to year throughout the early 1950s. So why did total production of comic books continue to set records in the years after 1950? There were 2,623 issues with 1951 dates followed by 3,164 in 1952, the high for the first half-century of the industry's existence. Not until 1956, when 2,054 issues were produced, did comic book production fall below 1949 levels.

Baby Boomers helped stabilize comic circulation

One simple answer concerns steady population growth: the Baby Boom appeared beginning in 1946. There were many more potential young readers in the 1950s than in the 1940s, even though television definitely siphoned off a significant degree of interest in reading. Another answer is that comic books of the 1951–54 period grew more daring, with horror, crime and romance representing more than half the issues produced before the advent of the industry's self-censoring Comics Code Authority (see Chapter Nine). In addition, the nation's unparalleled post-war prosperity sprung loose many more dimes on a per capita basis than were available to most readers in the 1930s and 1940s.

Comic books reduced their standard page counts, including covers, from 68 (most made that first cut in 1943) to 60 pages to 52 to 36, until by late 1952, only a handful of comics were 52 pages. (The figures include covers because that's how all the comic book publishers referred to their titles on their front covers: "A 52-page comic magazine" and the like.) Yet their price point remained 10 cents until late in 1961. Pulp magazines, on the other hand, almost universally went to 25 cents in the 1950s—more than twice the price of many pulps 20 years earlier. Considering inflation, the 10-cent comic book, whatever its size, was one of the biggest bargains consumers could find in the 1950s.

In modern times, of course, the opposite is true of comics. Most current comic books cost $2.95 to $4 or more—30 to 40 times the price point of their counterparts 50 years ago. There are very few items purchased for mass consumption on a regular basis today that cost 30 to 40 times what they did in the late 1950s. That, of course, partially accounts for the fact that many comic books today have circulations 25 times less than they did 50 years ago. Modern comics are essentially a niche item. Anecdotes abound about elementary school classrooms, with surveys showing that few if any students in any classroom are reading comic books. The vast majority are now sold to young adults in comic book stores, which began to proliferate in the 1970s.

There's another factor in the relative stability of romance comics in the 1951–56 period. Notwithstanding the bloody Korean conflict of 1950–53, America was a relatively placid, prosperous land with an increasing emphasis on personal fulfillment, including romance. The explosion of both soap operas and situation comedies on television during the 1950s reflected this secure feeling, in a way not possible today.

When the number of prolific comic book publishers took a precipitous drop between 1954 and 1958, the influence and number of romance titles fell correspondingly (see Chapter Nine). By the middle of 1951, however, four-color romance was definitely back in bloom. Romance has never reached the levels of the 12-month period in the second half of 1949 and the first half of 1950; the market proved such frenzy was simply unsustainable.

A remarkable comeback for romance

Considering the severe slump caused by the Love Glut, the final 1951 count of 403 romance issues is nothing less than remarkable. There was definitely a market for love. In 1951, no single publisher produced more than the 53 issues or eight titles from industry pace-setter Fawcett. For all intents and purposes, it was seven titles, since the eighth was a single undated final issue of *Cowboy Love*. Marvel produced 45 issues and seven titles, all bi-monthlies except the nine-issue run of *True Secrets*. No significant new publishers entered the field in 1951, although Quality and Harvey returned to romance. All told, 28 publishers participated in the romance market, six more than in 1950, albeit including nine publishers with but a single love title.

There were no new trends in romance comics in 1951. The only development that even hinted of a trend was St. John's introduction of *Wartime Romances* # 1 (July 1951), one year into the Korean War. Two other publishers followed, with Quality's *True War Romances* #1 (Sept. 1952) and *G.I. Sweethearts* # 32 (June 1953, the first issue) followed by Superior's *G.I. War Brides* # 1 (June 1954). Superior's decision to publish a romance comic with military themes could not have been stranger, especially considering that "war bride" is a term applied to World War II, not Korea. Not only had the fighting in Korea subsided a year earlier, but Superior was a Canadian publisher! *G.I. War Brides* ran for a year, though # 8 (June 1955) and should be regarded as one of the oddest decisions in comic book publishing history. It was frequent, though, to see military themes mixed with romance in the mainstream titles of the early 1950s.

In striking contrast to the tumultuous romance comic events of 1950, the real story of 1951 was the remarkably emerging stability of the market for love. In addition to the titles resumed, 18 new titles were introduced and only five titles were discontinued. Two of the discontinued titles were one-shots from the tiny Canadian publisher P.L. Enterprises, *Co-Ed Romances* and *Love Life*, both dated November 1951. Fawcett's *Cowboy Love* and Archie's *Darling Romance* ran one final issue, both undated, and Standard's newsprint adaptation *Dear Beatrice Fairfax* ended with its fifth issue, which was # 9 since it began with # 5. In other words, no romance title of any significance was either discontinued or suspended in 1951! It seemed the publishers had found a most happy medium (pun fully intended).

Romance hit an all-time peak with 522 issues in 1952, the year of a record production of 3,164 comic books. One of every six comics was a romance comic, slightly less than the nearly one in four ratio of 1950. So why no Love Glut effect? The answer: Publisher stability was temporarily solid (the next few years would be a different story entirely) and the total number of romance titles in 1952 was "only" 86—far fewer than the 147 of two years earlier. In 1952, monthly totals did not vary nearly as dramatically as 1953, with a high of 53 and a low of 35.

The fall-off to 432 romance issues in 1953—albeit covering 82 titles—can be attributed almost entirely to the decision of magazine publishers Fawcett and Ziff-Davis to leave the comic book field. Fawcett's final five comic books (none of them romance) were dated January 1954. Ziff-Davis saw only one title survive, *G.I. Joe*, beyond 1952. Fawcett published only 13 romance issues in 1953 compared to 57 in 1952; Ziff-Davis went from 26 to zero.

Romance comics lumped in with crime and horror

By the time Dr. Fredric Wertham published his infamous screed against comics, *Seduction of the Innocent*, in 1954, the horror and crime comics were coming under intense scrutiny, up to and including hearings in Congress. It did not help romance comics that they were sometimes lumped with the "bad influences," but in truth most of them were already fairly tame even before the Comics Code Authority was created in September 1954. The stability of the 1954 market reflected that, with 440 romance issues and 80 titles.

Considering that the total of all comic books steadily dropped every year from 1953 through 1959, in the wake of the record high in 1952, romance comics more than held their own in 1953 and 1954 and even into 1955, when the total of 347 romance issues still meant that more than one in seven comics was devoted to romance (2,336 issues of all types were produced in 1955).

The situation was destined to change dramatically in the next five years, but it may not have been entirely due to a decreasing demand for romance comics. It's true that by 1959, with 160 romance issues published, only slightly more than half as many issues were in circulation as the 296 love comics that appeared in 1956, only three years earlier.

Several publishers leave in 1956

It's easy, however, to account for the difference from 1956 to 1959. Quality, which published 64 romance comics in 1956, left the industry at the end of the year and sold out to DC, which picked up only four Quality titles including one romance type, *Heart Throbs*. Ace, a leading romance publisher since 1949, abandoned comics late in 1956 to focus on its increasingly profitable paperback books. Lev Gleason and Superior also left comics in 1956. Marvel, popularly known as Atlas since late 1951, shrunk to a shadow of its former self in the wake of its 1957 implosion. St. John left the romance field after 1955, except for a brief three-issue return in 1957–58. Harvey stopped publishing romance comics in 1958 to concentrate on humor for the children's market, and Ajax/Farrell left comics entirely that year.

There was still a marginally healthy market for romance comics in 1959—the 160 romance issues accounted for better than 10 percent of the overall total of 1,511 issues that year—but there simply weren't enough publishers willing to produce four-color love. Dell (Western) didn't do romance; neither did Harvey or Archie by 1959. Those three publishers, all of whom focused on clean-cut humorous or adventure titles, accounted for nearly half (and perhaps more) of all comic book circulation.

That left mighty DC and three then-tiny companies—ACG, Prize and Marvel—to take care of the romance market in 1959 along with Charlton, which emerged as the new dominant commercial force with the quantity, if not always the quality, of its romance line. DC's five romance titles and 38 issues accounted for 10 percent of its total of 382 issues in 1959. Prize, with 16 love issues, was left with nothing but romance comics. ACG, with 20 romance issues, relied on love for half of its 40-issue production. Marvel, because it was limited by a distribution agreement with DC to 96 issues per year (eight every month), produced 12 romance issues with the bi-monthly *My Own Romance* and *Love Romances*.

Charlton? The king of the low-rent comics decided to make romance its special niche, in the wake of so few other companies remaining devoted to the genre. Since its days of short-run experimentation in numerous genres during 1954–57, Charlton had stabilized. With 289 issues of all types in 1959, Charlton trailed only DC and Dell in total production, and Charlton's 72 romance issues across 15 titles accounted for fully one-quarter of the company's entire total—and comprised nearly half of all romance comics published that year. It is instructive, however, to note that in 1959, only tiny ACG's *My Romantic Adventures* (11 issues) and *Confessions of the Lovelorn* (nine issues) appeared more than eight times among the 27 romance titles published that year.

A Marvel experiment

In 1949–52, *Girl Comics* was a hybrid experiment in romance and adventure from Marvel with a 12-issue run, as the author detailed in a "Nolan's Notebook" column for *Comic Book Marketplace* # 62. The run includes an outstanding cover of 17-year-old Elizabeth Taylor on the scarce # 3 (April 1950). That year, she received a significant career boost while appearing in her first major adult film role: *Father of the Bride*, with Spencer Tracy.

Girl Comics ran four issues as a romance title, then tried something different. *Girl Comics* # 4 (June 1950) plugged, "52 pages of Tender Love Tales" and "Stories of Life and Love ... as Thrilling as a Moonlight Kiss!" on the period-piece cover, which portrayed a teen couple enjoying records. It's this type of cover that still makes romance comics appealing to many collectors of items that reflect the flavor of their times.

Girl Comics # 5 (Oct. 1950) had entirely new blurbs: "Real Adventures of Real Girls!" and "Mystery, Adventure, Suspense" as the cover promised. In the final eight issues, *Girl Comics* indeed featured mystery, adventure and suspense, plus love themes, in a unique publication. Issues # 5–12 also reflected an industry-wide trend toward crime and horror themes. Girls often were portrayed as competent and ambitious, in part perhaps as the result of the influence of series books with independent, strong-willed heroines such as Kay Tracey and Judy Bolton, although some tales in *Girl Comics* resulted in a moral lesson.

With issue # 13 (March 1952), *Girl Comics* became *Girl Confessions*, one of Marvel's seven regular romance titles that year. Until then, though, there were 32 stories of female adventure

Girl Comics # 4, June 1950, copyright Cornell Publishing Corp. Period pieces such as this cover pulling out records are one of the attractions of romance comics.

in *Girl Comics* # 5–12, with almost that many different settings. Apparently, Marvel figured the title would sell better as a straight romance comic.

The author has cited the following stories as especially noteworthy in the eight adventure-themed issues of *Girl Comics*: In *Girl Comics* # 6 (Jan. 1951), "The Horns of Horror" was the strange tale of a girl whose father was accused of cowardice in the bull ring after he turned blind because of a genetic defect. She experiences the same genetic dilemma, but when she in turn goes blind in the ring, she manages to redeem both of their names by killing her last bull. The story doesn't make a lot of sense, but it presents well the concept of female bravery and honor. In the same issue, in a tale entitled, "The Victim was Me!" the female victim demonstrates such bravery that she saves her own life in addition to getting help from the hero. It wasn't often during this period that girls were shown in such a courageous, determined light.

Likewise, in *Girl Comics* # 7 (March 1951), there were the inspirational stories of a female teacher and a police woman who prove their mettle against insane criminals. In that same issue there was a clever psychological mystery entitled, "If a Girl Be Mad" (sounding like something out of a 1960s or '70s Marvel), along with the unorthodox story of a female traitor, "They Called Me a Spy." In that spy story, redolent of the Red Scare of the period, the girl stands in her prison cell in the last panel, bathed in a beam of sunlight and making the following declaration: "No matter what made me do it ... I realize now how terribly wrong I was! Bit by bit, I was selling away the freedom of America ... a freedom unequal in any other country in the world! I was sentenced to five years for conspiracy to commit espionage.... Imprisonment is teaching me the true value of freedom!"

One of the stories in *Girl Comics* # 8 (May 1951), drawn by Ann Brewster, has a cliché title, "Wings of Death," but it's an intriguing tale of how a girl and her brother save their small airplane business from criminals. In the same issue, a story entitled, "The Lonely One" shows how a girl learns the value of friendship in inspirational fashion. Marvel definitely had a sense that it was onto something unusual with *Girl Comics*. The hype on the cover of # 9 (July 1951) reads, "Only *Girl Comics* Can Give You Stories Like These." And, at the time, that was actually true in the comic book world. In *Girl Comics* # 10 (Sept. 1951), a railroad engineer's daughter bravely helps her father finish 40 years of unbroken trips even after he dies at the controls of the train! This one has to be read to be believed, so unbelievably bold and daring are the girl's feats. But the point is the girl is the hero, not her boyfriend. This was highly unusual in comics of the era.

Marvel comes back

Marvel, which became popularly known as Atlas by the end of 1951, did not lose faith in the romance genre despite the financial slowdown of 1950. In addition to the firm's experiment with *Girl Comics* and the erratic *True Secrets*, Atlas produced five bi-monthly titles in 1951. (Atlas was named for the cover symbol of Marvel's distribution arm.) These titles were *My Own Romance*, *Love Romances*, *Lovers*, *Love Tales* and *Love Adventures*. The stress on generic titles was probably no accident.

True Secrets began as *Love Secrets* in 1949 and was suspended with *True Secrets* # 3 (March 1950), but was resumed with # 4 (Feb. 1951) and became an oddity. Beginning with *True Secrets* # 6 (June 1951), the title became Marvel's first romance monthly, running through # 21 (Aug. 1952) when it was once again suspended. In addition, there was also an issue dated spring 1952 (# 16). In the 1970s and 1980s, it took dedicated collectors and art experts such as Atlas authority Jim Vadeboncoeur, Jr., to resolve these numbering and date mysteries.

Who can guess why *True Secrets* was selected to become Atlas's first monthly romance title? Such arcane decisions have been lost in the mists of time. Or, again referring to 1952, who can ever understand why *True Secrets* was discontinued with # 21? (It was actually only suspended, as it turned out.) In other words, the first Marvel monthly in 1951 mysteriously was abandoned in 1952. Another established title, *Love Tales*, ran monthly in 1952 from # 50 (Jan.) through # 58 (Aug.) before it was suspended, in addition to publishing # 53 with a spring date! At about the same time in 1952, however, *Lovers* became a monthly with # 41 (Sept.) and *Girl Confessions* went monthly with # 14 (May). The answer may be something as simple as better sales reports for certain titles. As if that weren't enough, *Love Adventures* became *Actual Confessions* with # 13 and lasted only two issues under the new title at the end of 1952.

When *Love Tales* was abandoned (actually suspended) with # 58 (Aug. 1952), it caused a long-running quandary for collectors until Atlas expert Dr. Michael Vassallo solved the mystery in 2006. *Love Tales* resumed with # 60 (Feb. 1955), leaving the long-unanswered question of what happened to the never-seen # 59. Vassallo, however, discovered that the art logged in for # 59 was instead published in *Lovers* # 42 (Oct. 1952), so *Love Tales* # 59 existed only as a book-keeping error! Since many collectors tend to be completists, discoveries such as this have been gratefully accepted by the collecting community as well as by historians.

During the 1951–54 period, Marvel produced 185 romance comics, demonstrating just how vibrantly commercial romance remained for this major comic book publisher. For the most part, these were among the most attractive examples of their genre during those years, with stories illustrated in glamorous fashion by solid professionals such as Jay Scott Pike, Morris Weiss and Al Hartley. Stories were almost always short, five or six pages. Though many stories had happy endings, there were plenty with the occasional "twist" outcomes that Marvel became well known for in other genres.

For example, in *My Own Romance* # 21 (March 1952), the remarkably grim "A Guest in the House" tells the grisly tale of a mentally ill woman who tries to break up her old friend's marriage. The man of the piece discovers how ill the visitor is when she plucks a nest of baby birds to death. This type of plot would never have appeared in a romance comic from National. In the same issue, in "The Sacrifice of Sheila Storm," a woman gives up the man she loves for the sake of his potential career in music. The last caption is sheer emotional agony: "The years have gone, but my great love still remains! He married Ethel and now is a world renowned pianist and composer! I go to his concerts as often as I can! I sit in the balcony and cry in the darkness!" And as if that wasn't enough mental torture for both the protagonist and the reader, she is pictured crying in the balcony, thinking to herself, "He's playing the lover's sonata ... our song! That's one thing I'll always have ... our song of love ... ours alone!" Such stories of unrelieved self-sacrifice, with overtones of martyrdom, were unusual in romance comics.

The cover of *My Own Romance* # 35 (Dec. 1953) features, "I Met My Dream Man!" with a startlingly handsome couple about to go into a clinch. The story, though, is far more complicated. The tale begins with a librarian determined to find out who was marking up a romance novel with comments like "women don't act this way" and "the girl in this situation is not reacting correctly in rejecting the man." She discovers a handsome young psychologist (who volunteers to pay for damage to the book). She falls in love with him, yet soon walks out in frustration at his antics and opinions. The story ends happily, though, when he admits the error of his ways—not a typical ending for a comic book romance story—and she takes him back. As they sail into a tunnel of love, she says, "You see, Lee, a girl likes to think she is always a bit unpredictable and mysterious to the man she loves!" To which he replies, "I predict wedding bells for us, darling ... and that's the last prediction I'll ever make! I promise!" Stories such as this one make Atlas comics worth reading just for the fun of it, outlandish premises or no.

Boy Meets Girl # 18, Dec. 1951, copyright Lev Gleason Publications, Inc. Before turning to more controversial covers, Lev Gleason featured painted covers with idyllic scenes, such as this one signed by Bob Fuje.

Quality's bizarre publishing patterns

Even after canceling all 14 romance titles in 1950, publisher Everett "Busy" Arnold's top-tier firm Quality Comics refused to give up on love on the racks. However, Arnold's romance publication patterns through the end of the company's existence in 1956 defy explanation. They are, in fact, about as puzzling as anything in romance publishing history.

In a decision dealing with publication frequency that can only be called surprising from a remove of more than half a century, Arnold authorized the return of *Diary Loves* and *Love Letters* in March 1951 and *Love Confessions* in May—and published them all monthly for the rest of the year! At Quality, only the best-selling heroic title *Blackhawk* already had such exalted monthly status in 1951. Quality had published all 14 of its original romance titles on a bi-monthly basis. Perhaps the continuing success of Crestwood's *Young Romance* and *Young Love*, also monthlies, inspired this astonishing business decision, or perhaps Quality figured that three monthly titles could be marketed more effectively than six bi-monthly titles. At any rate, Quality's decision must have reflected well on the financial books, for the company rebounded well from its casualties of the Love Glut to publish nearly as many romance issues as Marvel did in 1951–54—a total of 163 Quality love comics.

Quality brought back a fourth title, its original romance flagship *Heart Throbs*, with # 9 (March 1952) and published it monthly, with the exceptions noted below. Quality also started *True War Romances* with # 1 (Sept. 1952), apparently in answer to St. John's *Wartime Romances*, which started a year earlier. *True War Romances* must have been an immediate success, because *Diary Loves* morphed into *G.I. Sweethearts* with # 32 (June 1953), making Quality the only publisher ever to produce two concurrent titles with war-romance themes.

Baffling publication frequencies

Quality's decisions with regard to publishing frequency have long been baffling. For example, the company's five love titles were all monthly in 1952 and 1953—except there were no romance issues dated May or November in 1952 and none dated May, July or September in 1953. To have every romance title on sale during the same months would seem counter-intuitive regarding newsstand exposure, and it's a pattern no other publisher followed. National, for example, published best-selling titles in several different genres eight times a year beginning in 1954 instead of bi-monthly, but their appearances were staggered so that National's newsstand exposure was consistent month to month.

Quality, though, changed everything with the addition of *Brides Romances* # 1 (Nov. 1953) and *Wedding Bells* # 1 (Feb. 1954), giving the firm eight titles all the way through its demise as a comic publisher at the end of 1956. In 1954, all eight titles were published bi-monthly in a pattern staggered precisely to give Quality four titles on the newsstands every month—48 issues in all. This seems to make solid business sense, yet it was the antithesis of Quality's publishing philosophy in 1952 and 1953. Cover dates and on-sale dates, however, did not always correspond, so historians such as Jim Vadeboncoeur, Jr., call this a "mock mystery." The fascination of this publisher's odd patterns continues in 1955 and 1956. The pattern of four issues per month continued through June 1955, followed by no issues dated July and August but four issues dated September 1955.

Then followed a real comic book business mind-boggler—Quality published all eight of its romance titles monthly from October 1955 through May 1956. No company, before or after, ever published 96 romance comics over an eight-month span! It should be noted that Quality did use numerous reprints during this period, apparently making possible the romance overflow.

Quality then skipped June 1956 entirely with regard to romance before returning with eight issues dated July. There were no issues for August or September, but Quality finished with six October issues, two in November and six in December before the company's comic book division expired and was sold to National. Seven of the titles died—National picked up only *Heart Throbs* after it bought out Quality.

More happy endings

Quality continued its overwhelming penchant for happy endings when it first began publishing romance comics in 1949 (see Chapter Four), yet the company offered more variety when it returned to romance. For example, in the nine issues of *Love Confessions* in 1953, # 26 through # 34, all but one of the 36 stories ended with lovers joyfully in arms. The company continued to follow a 36-page issue format of four stories per issue, with typically polished production patterns although usually inked in such a heavy style that identification of some of the artists is difficult if not impossible even for experts.

The single 1953 story in *Love Confessions* with a tearful ending, "It Was Too Late for Love" in # 29 (April), was a remarkably naturalistic and convoluted nine-pager. This story could never have appeared after the Comics Code, with its strict rules dealing with the portrayal of marriage (see Chapter Nine). It told the tale of Phyllis and Don Brooks, a married couple with financial problems and bleak prospects as farmers. Phyllis leaves Don, returns to the city and meets Paul Larsen, a salesman with better financial prospects and the gift of blarney. "Don't ruin your life because of an idle dreamer, Phyllis!" he tells her after falling in love with her. "Let me arrange for a divorce! You said Don wouldn't contest it!"

"I could never fall in love with Paul," she has already thought to herself in the previous panel, "but he could give me everything I missed with Don! And he's such a wonderful person!" Her thoughts soon continue: "What did it matter if I didn't really love Paul! I visualized a pleasant home of my own and freedom from worry! At the time, it seemed like enough of a foundation for a happy marriage!" After they have a baby girl, Paul is content but Phyllis never stops thinking of Don. When they run into each other, he tries to win her back and nearly succeeds until she receives roses and a message from Paul, who is out of town: "To the two girls who make life worth living! See you Monday!" Her response: "Thank heaven for that message! Then and there I realized that I had no right to *play* the same cruel trick twice!" As she walks back from mailing a final farewell to Don, tearful Phyllis tells herself, "My heart was heavy as I walked home from posting that letter to Don! But I knew that I had done the honorable thing! Perhaps my reward will be a closer bond with my husband that will one day equal the love I cast aside!"

Many of Quality's romance stories in the early 1950s had glamorous settings, such as an auto race track or a gambling den, but they tended to avoid outright sleaze. However, kisses between a married woman and a single man were strictly a pre–Code phenomenon, and even then they were not especially common in romance comics. Remember, this was in an era when even married couples in the movies and on television were not shown sleeping in the same bed! The exotic and often bizarre nature of Quality's 1949–50 stories, before the temporary collapse of the firm's extensive romance line, was not nearly as much a factor in the 1951–54 period, except in occasional reprints. Most of Quality's stories became more realistic.

"I Was a Headline Girl"

Some stories, however, were as odd as ever, such as "I Was a Headline Girl," nicely drawn by the prolific Ogden Whitney in *Love Confessions* # 26 (Jan. 1953). This word-heavy, extremely melodramatic nine-pager is a good example of how some romance comics were too complicated for most young readers to follow and too illogical for many older readers to swallow.

Times-Herald sob-sister Jill Cameron, who describes herself as "probably one of the few women" to handle a big-city police beat, begins the story in love with detective-sergeant Tom Lambert, who is uncharacteristically portrayed as a middle-aged man with a black mustache. She falls for gang lord Frankie Orchid but realizes her error when she sees how he orders a man beaten up following the mysterious death of the notorious thug "One-Eye" Horton—a "rubout" ordered by Orchid. But she overhears Lambert taking a $5,000 bribe from Orchid and feels devastated about both men in her life. The story ends happily, though, as shown by a newspaper headline and two pictures of the men, one captioned "indicted" and the other "promoted." Lambert, it turns out, couldn't trust even Jill with his secret plan to prove Orchid guilty.

There are moments of the amazingly absurd, such as Jill's question to Frankie when she seeks an interview: "I'll write the truth ... are you a gang lord?" His answer: "Jill, you're sweet! But much too naive for a police reporter! But in answer to your question ... no, I'm not a gang lord! I would not know how to be one!" But the giveaway is that Frankie also has a mustache: a suspicious pencil-thin one in contrast to Lambert's bushy growth!

Love Confessions # 27 (Feb. 1953) also came up with an improbable doozy of a cover feature dealing with the familiar complaints of good guys who can't figure out why women chase shady characters: "I Fell for a No-Good Guy." ("No-Good" is hyphenated on the splash page but not on the cover, showing how erratic the editing could be.) The photo cover shows a clinging girl lighting a shady looking fellow's cigarette, but that only hints at this crime story's unlikely plot.

On the splash page, clean-cut Dave tells the girl he loves: "Lorna, please come back to me! Can't you see he's up to no good! You'll regret this later on!" To which she replies: "I can't help it, Dave! All I know is that I love him!" The no-good guy, Floyd, tells him: "Scram, Bub ... me and the little lady have some high livin' to do!"

When Floyd, fleeing from the police, carjacks Lorna (in the days before "carjack" entered the lexicon), he forces a kiss on her to convince police they are just a couple out for some healthy necking. "After he was gone, I put my fingers to my lips! They still tingled with the electric shock of his kisses ... it just doesn't make sense! The man's nothing but a common criminal ... yet I let him kiss me and I enjoyed it! And in spite of myself, I want to see him again! He's so unlike Dave, good, dependable Dave! There's a kind of animal excitement about the stranger! I'm, afraid Dave is rather dull compared to him!" But when Floyd fools Lorna into participating in a crime and is sent to jail, Dave tries to take the rap for her. Fortunately for all concerned, a detective with a dictaphone realizes the truth and arrests a knife-wielding Floyd as he tells Lorna, "I'm going to have to shut you up for keeps!" Lorna's narrative in the final panel says it all: "Suddenly Dave's lips were on mine, ardent yet so warm and tender! And from that exquisite kiss I knew this was love as it should be, sweet and rapturous ... the kind a woman wants from the man she will someday marry!" Such crime themes soon disappeared or were extremely muted in romance comics.

Ace and Harvey also rebound nicely

In addition to Marvel and Quality, two other publishers rebounded to produce prodigious volumes of pre–Code romance comics in 1951–54 while recovering from the negatives of 1950. Ace published 157 issues during those four years, though none of Ace's six titles were monthly, and Harvey produced 127 issues with a mixture of monthly and bi-monthly patterns for four regular titles before a fifth title, *Teen-Age Brides*, came along in 1953. Like Quality and Marvel, romance remained a staple for Ace and Harvey through 1956.

Harvey tended to be one of the most sensationalistic pre–Code publishers (see Chapter Nine). Ace, however, stuck primarily to its formula of relationship-oriented stories, almost always four to an issue, very much like Quality. Following the demise of the photo-cover-oriented Fawcett comic book line in 1953, Ace emerged as the only major romance publisher to use photo covers in 1954 (though publishers of fewer romance issues, such as Standard, also used them). Ace occasionally tried to use creative photos, such as the nose-rubbing shot of a grinning guy and gal on *Love at First Sight* # 31 (Nov. 1954).

In the seven 1954 issues of *Love at First Sight* (# 26–32), all 28 stories had happy endings—clearly a commercial necessity, many publishers figured. That was entirely typical of Ace. Most of the plots tended toward the realistic—in fact, some collectors have observed that Ace produced many of the most generic, dull stories in all of romance comics.

That doesn't mean they were bad, however. In the oddly titled, "The Grind and the Football Hero" in *Love at First Sight* # 29 (July 1954), a bookworm (female, of course) and a sports hero learn they are meant for each other after eight rather convoluted pages. "Hockey Hero" would have been a better title, for there is no football in the story! Instead, the jock, Toby Barr, is pictured participating in hockey and track. The story is not unrealistic, however, as each tries to accommodate the other's world. He tries to gain an appreciation for the fine arts and she won't let him pass up the big track meet. In the end, he turns down a professional hockey contract so that he can coach at Willowdale College, where she plans to teach. That might seem unrealistic today, in an era of multi-million dollar contracts, but most professional athletes in 1954 weren't paid that much more than typical workers.

Subdued sensationalism

Some Ace plots, though, were a lot less likely, albeit with subdued sensationalism such as "Dime-a-Dance Girl" in *Love at First Sight* # 26 (Feb. 1954). A newspaperman seeking a story falls in love with Linna, a dance hall girl, while working on an expose, but the guy who runs the dance hall also falls for her, much to the distress of his girlfriend. She threatens Linna (with what turns out to be a toy gun) and is rescued by the knight of the fourth estate. Eventually, they reach an understanding and she accepts his marriage proposal.

Considering how prolific Marvel, Quality, Ace and Harvey were in the 1951–54 period, it's intriguing to note how industry titan National—so well remembered by collectors today—had a far more tentative approach to the production of the genre in the immediate pre–Code era. This possibly could have been because National was the only 1950s firm still publishing an extensive line of super hero titles, featuring the icons Superman, Batman and Wonder Woman along with a few then-minor backup costume and super hero characters. After bringing back *Secret Hearts* with # 7 (Dec. 1951–Jan. 1952) after a one-and-a-half-year hiatus, National published exactly three titles, all bi-monthlies, and 18 romance comics per year through 1954. In retrospect, that's a highly conservative total for such a large publisher, but diversity of genres was a National hallmark throughout the 1950s.

Book It: Love Diary *and* Love Journal

Our Publishing Company, also known as Orbit, is best known for being one of the few firms to be headed by a woman, Ray R. Hermann. Our Publishing, located on Broadway one block from Harvey Comics, produced only two love titles, *Love Diary* and *Love Journal*, but they were among the more colorful romance comics of the 1951–54 period.

Hermann, listed as both publisher and business manager in early ownership statements, must have been an alert opportunist. In the second half of 1950, when so many other romance titles were succumbing to the Love Glut, she started publishing *Love Diary* monthly with # 7 (Aug. 1950) and didn't miss a month through # 28 (May 1952). Earlier, Hermann had been more careful, more frugal or both, because the fast six issues of *Love Diary* appeared sporadically in 1949 and 1950. She began a companion title, *Love Journal*, with # 10 (Oct. 1951). Both titles had solid production values, plot-packed stories with a variety of settings, and attractive covers. They were far better than most titles from other small companies.

"Big City Girl," nicely illustrated by Mort Leav in *Love Diary* # 12 (Jan. 1951), is typical of the solid plotting of most of the stories. Lois Jordan, a cigarette girl in a night club, loves the life of the big city: "I love it!" the long-legged beauty tells her boss in the splash. "The people, the noise, the excitement. I guess I'll always be a city girl!" But illness sends her to the country, where she finds Tom, who strongly attracts her with his kindness and character yet is a "simple farmer," as she calls him. Summoned back to the Hotshot Club by her impatient boss, she arrives too late and finds her job is gone. She also finds her old boyfriend is hardly the man she thought he was. "Larry doesn't matter and somehow the city doesn't, either! Those frantic people outside, scurrying around, they all seem so superficial!" She returns to the farm, finds the phlegmatic Tom in the middle of playing midwife to a cow, and unwittingly helps deliver "a beautiful young calf." She tells the reader in the final panel, "Tom and I are going to be married next month! And I know that I'll be a good farmer's wife! After all, I love that farmer with all my heart!"

There's a certain period-piece maturity involved even in stories with sensational titles, such as "I Was a Fat Girl!" in # 13 (Feb. 1951). "Clyde and I are married now," the erstwhile fat girl tells the reader in the last panel, "and we're terribly happy! I have learned how to take the ups and downs of everyday life without trying to compensate for them by indulging my appetite! If you are overweight, I hope my story will be an inspiration for you to reduce! Because you'll find that life can be truly wonderful, once you've licked the problem of being a lone, unwanted ... FAT GIRL!" The story, of course, reflects a stereotypical attitude; those who feel there's nothing wrong with being overweight would be offended. Even so, the story seems to mean well even though it was sex appeal, not health, that was at issue. This story is very much of its era.

In mid–1951, *Love Diary* began to plug itself above the cover logo as "The Fastest Selling Romance Magazine." It carried creative photo covers through mid–1952, then went to attractive line-drawn covers, several by future Marvel Comics star John Buscema. More than most love comics, there was a sensual, and often overtly sexual, sensibility to the covers. Occasionally, though, the story titles wouldn't match the cover at all, such as the innocent-looking girl on the phone adjacent to the featured title, "I Was a Pick-Up!"

Love Diary # 16 (May 1951) featured a surreal "photo cover" of a tiny man reaching out while kneeling in the hands of a giant woman to go with the story, "Wanted: A Man of My Own!" Hermann peppered most issues with advice columns, often using the name Ray Mann, in both text and illustrated form, along with lots of self-improvement tips. Ray Mann often asked readers to help solve a girl's problem and offered prizes for the best answer. The majority of the stories featured endings with a moral, albeit usually so obvious as to be often laughable today. By 1954, Hermann's little firm published only its love titles. *Love Diary* ran through # 47 (Dec. 1954) before Our Publishing seemed to vanish forever. Oddly, though, *Love Diary* returned with one more obscure issue, the Code-approved # 48 (Sept.–Oct. 1955). The cover, featuring a nondescript couple about to kiss, was only a washed-out version of the title's former vitality. The last issue reprinted "I Was a Fat Girl!" without any changes for the Comics Code. Hermann's 16 issues of *Love Journal* (# 10–25), which was essentially a bi-monthly, offered a similar format, but a different "male" advisor: Mark Ford. The covers tended to plug featured stories. *Love Diary*, on the other hand, emphasized self-improvement tips for girls.

"Tenement Girl" in *Love Journal* # 23 (March 1954) told the tale of Janice Green, a girl trapped in poverty, hoping to find an escape with a kind lawyer, Frank, whom she cares about before she learns the real meaning of passionate love with another tenement resident, Roxie Scott. But Roxie feels he's not good enough for her and hurts Janice badly in a breakup. The good-guy lawyer, realizing how much Janice really loves the other fellow, acknowledges that Roxie is ambitious enough to escape the tenements and lovingly surrenders Janice to him. The message of being unable to control the pull of love was told over and over in romance comics, in this case in Janice's words: "I want to be fair to you, Frank! I like you a lot—but I can't ever be in love with you! No matter how much of a fool Roxie made of me, I still love him!"

Beginning in 1951, *Love Diary* began to cover feature Ray Mann's advice with lures like, "Are You Really and Truly in Love?"; "Summer Is Golden Time for Romance!"; "How to Win His Love"; "How to Know If It's Love"; "How to Talk to Boys!"; and so forth. It wasn't easy for readers to find out "What Men Dislike About Women" in # 35 (June 1953) because the answer was buried in Ray Mann's advice column "Frankly Speaking": "Boys don't like girls who are aggressive and pushy," followed by a lecture about female insecurity.

Occasionally, the stories had a holier-than-thou feeling, such as the tale of "jazzman" Skeets Bradley. The woman who loves him hates the insecurity of his lifestyle: "I wondered about the concert! I guess in my mind I had vague notions of a prestige-packed audience waiting for Skeets' music ... the kind Benny Goodman or the other big men of *jazz* played to! When the next night arrived, it was with a sense of shock that I realized what the concert really was. It was nothing more than a local block party in one of the poorer neighborhoods! I was appalled by what I saw!" To win her love, Skeets had to see the light ... and did by becoming a dignified clarinet player with "the sweetest music" she ever heard.

Whimsy pays off

Except for the American Comics Group canceling *Search for Love* following two issues in 1950, the firm apparently was not affected by the Love Glut. The long-running *Lovelorn* and *Romantic Adventures* both seem to have become, if anything, stronger sellers in 1951–54, before ACG briefly descended into odd exploitation covers and stories late in 1954 (see Chapter Nine). *Romantic Adventures* continued bi-monthly in 1951 and became a monthly with # 18 (Feb. 1952), and *Lovelorn* appeared monthly from # 9 (Jan. 1951) on. Of course, it's likely that editor Richard Hughes may have noticed how many romance titles disappeared from the racks in the second half of 1950 and decided to take advantage. Romance, indeed, must have been good to ACG, for its two titles ran 85 issues in 1951–54. Contrast that with mighty National's romantic reticence. National published only 66 issues with love themes over the same period (two bi-monthly titles all four years, with a third bi-monthly title resuming in 1952).

The stories in each of ACG's two titles were not noticeably different, relying on Hughes' usual formula of unexpected plot twists and often offbeat characterization. These tales, many bordering in downright silliness, pretty much scream, "comic book," at the reader, yet they're invariably fun and seldom grim. It's hard to feel bad after reading an ACG story.

Until the second half of 1954, none of the 1951–54 ACG covers—all line drawings—would have had any trouble passing the Code. After trying to inject conflict on the covers of flagship *Romantic Adventures* through # 14 (May–June 1951)—usually with the theme of "frustrated odd woman out"—ACG did an abrupt about-face and began focusing on some of the cutest romantic cover themes in the industry, although not on every issue. These were all sans word balloons. *Romantic Adventures* # 15 (July–Aug. 1951) featured a tennis player writing, "20 love" on a scoreboard as a couple kissed on the court; on # 17 (Nov.–Dec. 1951), a group of leather-helmeted football players, apparently still in a game, grinned as a male cheerleader kissed his female counterpart. (One can just imagine the football coach having apoplexy.) On # 18 (Feb. 1952), one of the most amusing romance covers ever published showed a couple clinching in the snow as two snowmen "kissed" next to the cabin in the background. The last of these wordless covers appeared on # 29 (Jan. 1953), a pedestrian image of a smiling couple on skis. The cover of # 20 (April 1952) fetchingly used a word balloon—a guide at the top of the Empire State Building saying, "Where have you ever seen a view like that?"—with three tourists smiling at a couple high on a kiss. Korean War military themes occupied the covers of # 25 (Sept. 1952) through # 27 (Nov. 1952)—not an uncommon theme in romance comics.

ACG's stories were often framed from a definite point of view, usually to let the reader know why this story would be just a little different. For example, "Do-Good Girls" in # 15 (July–Aug. 1951) began this way: "Yes, I was different from other girls! For I didn't crave glamour, wealth, high adventure! Instead, I yearned to serve humanity, to dedicate myself to a great cause—to do good! But in my naive desire to serve, I almost betrayed myself, my love—and humanity! But let me start from the beginning...." ACG repeatedly tried to show how childhood influences affected characters, perhaps to give young readers a sense of their own possibilities and fallibilities. In this story, young Joan, raised by a kind uncle who was a brilliant scientist, sees him turn down a $100,000 salary to continue to work for a foundation at $4,000 so he can try to develop a cure for epilepsy. Ultimately, the idealistic young woman falls for both a young doctor and a smooth-talking older fellow who turns out to be a communist. When the communists try to kidnap her famous uncle, who by now is working on atomic energy, and imprison her, the dashing doctor saves her from an inferno she starts to save United States secrets: "Joan, darling, I love you for your sympathy for the underdog and for worthy causes! But from now on, I'm the only cause you're going to serve—for the rest of your life!"

The tongue-in-cheek nature of many ACG stories, which were definitely aimed at younger readers or those who enjoyed whimsy, make them enjoyable hokum. Many of them almost read as parodies of popular fiction. In *Romantic Adventures* # 16 (Sept.–Oct. 1951), "Campus Romance" is about as hokey as a story could possibly come. It's the tale of a fame-hungry girl whose press agent convinces her to feign love for a college football star. When her conscience gets the best of her after he falls for her, she admits the plot and leaves him in anguished guilt. But a flash on the radio, informing her how he refuses to play in the season's biggest game, convinces her to fly to the stadium. Arriving with his team down 13–0 in the fourth quarter, she forsakes her ambitions to tell him she realizes she loves him. He gets into uniform, runs wild to win the game at the final gun and claims a kiss on the field. "Harold was where he belonged—in my arms—his lips pressed hungrily to mine, our hearts pounding in unison to the accompaniment of the thundering roars of 100,000 cheering fans! And in our kiss was the thrilling promise of eternal love!" AGC did that type of story over and over again.

These themes of "little girl grows up" and "last-minute heroics" were combined in the astonishingly over-the-top "Love Makes a Hit" in # 17 (Nov.–Dec. 1951). Roberta "Robby" Harris, a tomboy known as "Little Slats" because she is the daughter of famed "Slats" Harris, manager of the big-league Bears, realizes as a girl that the next best thing to being a famous player is to marry one! Eleven pages, and a multitude of complications and years later, her love for an injured player who has learned a lesson about greed, Bucky Davis, inspires him to pinch-hit an inside-the-park homer to win the World Series. Before he can even get off the ground, she bursts onto the field, lands on him right at home plate and tells him, "You've won the game, Bucky, and my heart—forever!"

ACG was always full of surprises, even extending to the house ads. In *Romantic Adventures* # 19 (March 1952), the publisher plugs the new monthly schedule in an ad on the inside front cover. But the issue pictured is # 21—for May instead of April.

The titles of the stories in *Romantic Adventures* # 23 (July 1952)—the last 52-page issue—illustrate well the variety of the settings Hughes either used himself or encouraged. "Cover Girl" features a model; "Rodeo Romance" is self-explanatory; "Love Cheat" deals with a greedy sister who loses out to her honest sibling; "Stand-In for Love" involves actors and publicity; and "To Thine Own Love Be True" deals with a socialite finding her real love when she rescues him from a fire. ACG stories almost always end happily, but not before either the male or female encounters a crisis of self-examination and, often, an unlikely plot twist.

Romantic Adventures must have been perceived as an immediate success, because its companion, *Lovelorn*, started six months later with # 1 (Aug.–Sept. 1949). Early issues tended to cover feature exotic locales—Paris, the Northwest woods, a ski area, an Egyptian tomb, a historical pirate adventure, a cruise ship, a gypsy camp, a circus, and even a couple about to be guillotined during the French Revolution. ACG sometimes cheated; the issue with the guillotine cover, # 10 (Feb.–March 1951), did not have any such story or even text feature! Not to mention that the cover plugged it as an "all glamor issue," and yet glamour had little to do with the stories.

An over-the-top tale from ACG

Lovelorn # 11 (March 1951), the first issue listed monthly in the indicia—even though two issues had already appeared that year—featured a truly over-the-top story that illustrates how much plot Hughes could pack into 11 pages. "The Romance of Korea Kate" told of an American college student, Kate Parry, reared in Korea but sent to America after her father, a plantation owner, dies after taking a bullet in the face from a "communist agitator" in an unusually violent scene for a romance story. She was a great actress and athlete in Korea but is considered a "queer duck" in college because of her background. She develops a crush on Tod Murray, captain of the football team, and impresses him when she returns an errant pass: "Wow, what a pass! I never saw a girl handle a football like that!" When the tomboy shows up at a dance, gorgeous in a gown Tod had no idea she could fill out, he falls for her but drops her because of a trick played by his bitter former girlfriend. He joins the Army and is sent to Korea. Meanwhile, Kate is called on by federal officials to become "Korea Kate," needed to boost troop morale in radio broadcasts in Korea. One of her biggest fans is "Doughfoot"—Murray, of course!—and, inevitably, he rescues her from a communist assault. But, trapped and pinned down by the communists, she uses her brilliant throwing arm to destroy the troops with the last grenade they have left. In the final two panels, she wins the Congressional Medal of Honor but tells the reader, "The sweetest reward of all was the thrilling, pulsating embrace of my darling Tod—my husband-to-be!"

Whew! Contrasted with the brilliant Dana Dutch's tales of emotional and intellectual realism in the St. John comics of the same period, it's hard to believe such vastly different love stories could have been on the racks concurrently. ACG readers, though, must have loved them with the same fervor that made *Adventures into the Unknown* such a successful horror comic, more often than not with romantic sub-texts amid the vampires, werewolves and zombies.

In mid–1951, at the same time *Romantic Adventures* temporarily abandoned covers featuring

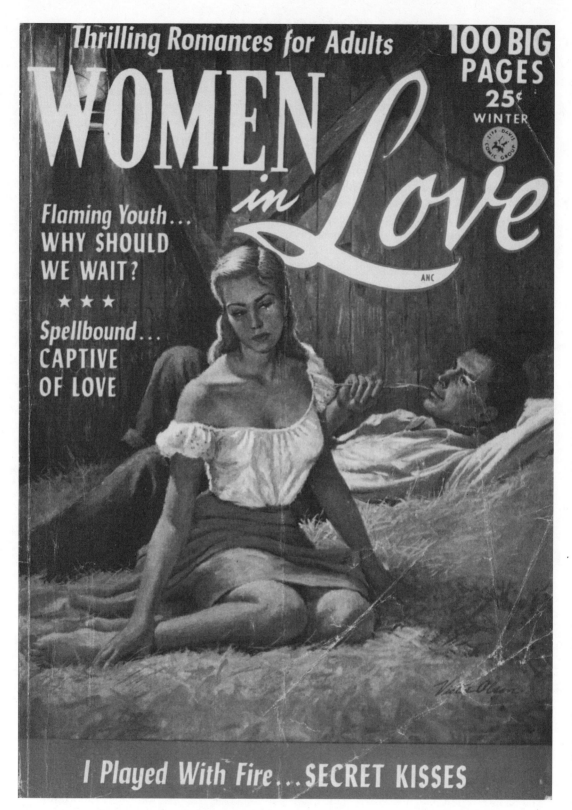

Women in Love # 1, Winter 1952, copyright Approved Comics, Inc. One of Ziff-Davis's final romance comics was this scarce 100-page giant.

romantic conflicts in favor of wordless but often amusing love scenes, *Lovelorn* adapted a similar policy. *Lovelorn* took a straighter approach, though, with gorgeous covers featuring kisses in a canoe, entering a tunnel of love, at a picnic, aside a swimming pool, and so forth. Like a few *Romantic Adventures* covers, occasionally crowds would get into the scene, such as the smiling college students admiring a kiss behind the back of a professor, who says, "I've never seen any of my mathematics classes so interested in my lecture before!" The love scenes made way for three consecutive covers with military themes (# 29, Sept. 1952 through # 31, Nov. 1952). Those were the identical months that *Romantic Adventures* cover-featured military themes, so it was a decision to take advantage of the headlines in Korea. ACG mainstay Ogden Whitney, who drew the patriotic costume hero Skyman in the 1940s, drew many of the firm's covers in the 1950s along with plenty of stories.

An unusual military theme

One of the military covers, showing a clinch in an office on # 31, featured a curmudgeonly commanding general entering the office in a rage when he sees the couple. The cover at first glance doesn't make a lot of sense, and doesn't match any of the stories inside. The point, though, seems to be to contrast the frustration of a graying general with the good fortune of the handsome single-stripe soldier.

"Love Asks No Questions" in # 31 is another of those occasionally outrageous plots Hughes loved so much. Penny Halliday, a reporter, lets the reader know right away "I want to tell you how I broke the most sensational scoop in the history of my paper, and almost broke my heart in the process!" She gets involved with a young man who has been ensnared by the gangster "Toothy" Vance. Convinced that he isn't a bad guy after all, the smitten fellow confesses all of Toothy's evil deeds, only to see Toothy himself show up to rub him out. A fight ensues, the young couple prevails, and the sob-sister soon has her editor screaming, "Stop the press! Get an extra out! Rip out the front page! Holy cow!" ACG even went over the top when it came to throwing three journalistic story clichés into one word balloon.

Like *Romantic Adventures*, *Lovelorn* soon abandoned both the amusing covers and the military themes to create garden-variety conflict on the covers, with a featured story title such as "My Imprisoned Heart!" on # 34 (Feb. 1953) and "Heart Throbs Were My Business" on # 36 (April 1953). Unlike a lot of publishers, ACG tried to lure the reader in with an extensive cover plug, such as this one for "My Beautiful Boss!" on # 39 (July 1953): "The world thought Rita Dunlop cold, ruthless—a stone-hearted Frigidaire with an adding machine for a heart! Read how she surprised even herself in the most fascinating love story of year—My Beautiful Boss!"

"My Beautiful Boss!" is *a doozy* of a tale, set up when the president of King Department Store decides to teach his playboy son a lesson by making him work for Rita Dunlop, the seemingly all-business head of the display department. Fireworks ensue and, several plot complications later leading to their breakup, Mr. King lets her know she can keep her job and tell him goodbye if she'll just forgive him. She finds his son pouring out his heart to a mannequin that looks like her, acknowledging his sins but also his frustrations with her cold nature. "So I'm just a cold, colorless, career girl, am I?" she blurts out, shocking him. "We'll see about that!" She tears off her suit down to her blouse, literally lets down her gorgeous head of hair, and dives on top of him when she realizes he isn't a worthless playboy, after all. "Do *you* think Denise [the girl he used to make her jealous] could do any better?" she asks him with a furious kiss. The story ends with Mr. King bouncing a grandchild on his lap and acknowledging the son's gratitude.

Fawcett's sales OK, but women still suffer

Fawcett, bolstered by deeper pockets than most comic book publishers, reacted in a logical way in 1951 after its 17 titles contributed heavily to the Love Glut in 1950. The company simply never stopped publishing its three monthlies—*Sweethearts*, *Life Story* and *Romantic Secrets*—and also continued the bi-monthly *Romantic Story* while canceling the other titles. Fawcett, in fact, was the only publisher throughout 1951 with three monthly romance titles, always with pleasant photo covers. Four other titles—*Cowboy Love* # 11, *Exciting Romances* # 4, *Sweetheart Diary* # 6 and *True Sweetheart Secrets* # 3—also survived with undated 1951 issues. *Cowboy Love* disappeared, but the other three titles reappeared as quarterlies with September and December dates that year.

Romantic photo covers

Fawcett's romantic photo covers, almost invariably featuring smiling lovers or single images of healthy-looking women who seem happy, continued to be at great odds with the company's raft of grim, intense stories usually dealing with relationships gone wrong. Many of the colorfully written stories were long, complex tales of foolish behavior, rejection and, more often than not, ultimate redemption. The Love Glut did nothing to change Fawcett's pattern of having selfish women learn from the men who most often take them back.

"Love's Last Gesture" in *Life Story* # 23 (Feb. 1951) is a consummate example of the Fawcett romance story, which invariably was more complicated than those found in most other love comics. This little epic packs a lot of pain and suffering into 11 pages. It's the story of Marge, a poor fisherman's daughter frustrated with her lot in life: "It isn't worth the struggle for the barest of necessities! The years pass quickly and I'll soon be as gnarled and wizened as the wood of the wharves!" Fawcett's female protagonists invariably had what they perceived as good reasons for their ambitions, even if they were often over-wrought rationalizations.

Marge finds a handsome, wealthy boat racer who falls for her, even though she doesn't share his passion for boating. But she has other motivations for agreeing to go off with him. "Do you love this Doug Morley, my dear?" her mother asks. "Why mention that?" Marge responds. "Would you rather I'd end up with what you and dad have—in an obscure little fishing village almost apart from the world?" But, during their engagement, Doug and Marge are thrown into the water during a boat race. She sees him struck by the mainsail and go under, her thoughts then nothing less than the astonishing (and ludicrous): "If I lose him, then once again, I'm nothing more than a poor girl from Milston who sold nets for a living! It mustn't be, it mustn't!"

Marge is rescued by Stan Mitchen, the man she blames for causing the accident with his boat. Stan turns out to be a handsome recent medical school graduate and invites Marge to be his first receptionist. A "suave older doctor," however, owns the rights to Stan's office space and callously gives the younger doctor the boot while keeping Marge on the job. But the doctor turns out to be a shady operator and, when he is arrested, Marge loses her position. She returns to Stan but rejects his gentlemanly overtures and seeks a job as a dancer, only to find men make unseemly passes in that profession, too. Unable to find a job, she tries to return to work for Stan months later, only to fly into a rage when he tells her he is engaged to someone else. Marge breaks down physically and mentally when she meets the other woman, Lorna, and reacts with rage. Marge quickly finds Stan treating her in a hospital bed because he feels he must from the standpoint of his oath.

The Fawcett man's message

Stan's message to Marge pretty much sums up Fawcett's approach to men in its love comics: "It's about time you faced the truth about yourself! You're weak—spiritless! You never loved Doug. It was only what his wealth would have provided. I misjudged you in the beginning! You haven't the courage to work out your own fate. You'll never know the meaning of happiness! You want to be nothing more than a parasite! So you attribute your own failings to me!"

Marge realizes he's right, but feels she must make up to him for the fact that she seems to have chased Lorna away. But Lorna informs Marge that it was Stan, instead, who broke up with her. Assuming that all is hopeless, Marge makes a statement repeated many times over in Fawcett romance comics: "I'm leaving now, Stan—forever! I promise I'll never interfere with your life again, never be a burden. All I can say is thanks—thanks—for showing me the right way." But Stan, realizing Marge has changed into "the girl I dreamed of," won't let her leave. As they kiss in the last panel, she tells the reader: "Even as his arms enfolded me and his lips warmly, ecstatically closed up mine, I vowed to devote my every living, breathing minute to making up to Stan for all the anguish I'd brought him—and to prove my love as no woman had ever before for any man!"

That might have been a tad bit overstated, to say the least, but it's amazing how much misery and misogyny, albeit usually with a happy ending, that Fawcett could cram into one comic book love story! The stories were almost never the slight tales of star-struck romance from numerous other publishers. No, it took a good deal of time to wallow in the seemingly inevitable self-caused misery of a Fawcett heroine and the noble motivations of the man who eventually rescues each female protagonist from her self-flagellation.

The formula, however, must have worked—or at least the glamorous covers did—because Fawcett led the industry on the overcrowded racks of 1952 with 57 romance issues, with its three monthly titles and four bi-monthlies (three of which released five issues because they did not become bi-monthly until March). But Fawcett phased out its comic book line in 1953.

Fawcett's final love comic

The firm's final love comic was *Romantic Story* # 22 (Summer 1953), the 235th Fawcett love issue. Ironically, this issue featured comical shorts of the little-known fillies Dizzy Daisy and Sarcastic Sue. There was more misery to the very end—in the last story of the last issue, "I Was a Contact Girl" (meaning escort girl). A long series of unethical business relationships left the protagonist telling the reader in the final two panels: "I threw away my chance to have a full, decent life! How can I face the dreary future? I have nothing to look forward to now, nothing! In a way, this [a dull job] is like serving penance! Maybe one day—I will find love again." Then, the final words in a panel: "That was two years ago that all this happened. Joe is happily married now and so is George Logan. As for me, I've learned one hard lesson. One must pay for the mistakes of the past, but in that paying learn to face the future with courage and hope!" There could have been no better summation of the Fawcett romance ethos.

Charlton eventually picked up *Sweethearts*, *Sweetheart Diary*, *Romantic Secrets* and *Romantic Story*, since the sheer commercial appeal of those titles was irresistible.

The Standard method

More than 20 years ago, comic art expert Jim Vadeboncoeur, Jr., became one of the first historians to draw attention to any of the old romance comics. In this case, he wrote short essays about Standard Comics in two issues of the reprint title *True Love*, published by independent Eclipse Comics. Eclipse was among the most prolific of the dozens of independent publishers who sprang up in the 1980s and '90s.

What interested Vadeboncoeur and other early romance collectors was the high caliber of artists employed by Standard for many of its love comics, including the likes of Alex Toth, after he left National in 1952, along with Mike Peppe, Nick Cardy, Vince Colletta and Ralph Mayo. They helped Standard recover nicely from the Love Glut. The company published 88 romance issues in 1951–54, a healthy total for a second-tier publisher and more than several larger publishers over that span. Standard's successful titles were *Popular Romances*, *Thrilling Romances*, *New Romances* and *Intimate Love*, all of which ran more than 20 issues on a bimonthly or quarterly basis.

Vadeboncoeur's viewpoint about romance comics was spot-on: As he wrote in *True Love* # 1 (Jan. 1986):

> They certainly weren't meant for the same audience that bought horror and crime books. They've never been popular with collectors or fans [this was certainly true at the time] though they were written and illustrated by many of the same people that fans collect. I think the answer is the obvious one: they were bought by young girls who were beginning to become interested in this thing called "love." Here in the comics was an illustrated primer to help de-mystify the concept; [to] show them how to act around boys, what to do and what not to do. Of course, no one bothered to tell them that these stories were representative more of how men wanted them to act and what men wanted them to do. After all, the preponderance of all comics were written by men and these were no exception. To be fair, these Standard stories are a bit more adult in approach than what was to come later [from other publishers after the Comics Code]. They dealt with women, not girls. They often discussed marital, not dating, situations. Women were portrayed with jobs, not attending school. There was a greater sense of the "real world" being portrayed and the fantasy element was love, not movie stardom or exotic preoccupation.

It's likely that no more perceptive observation about romance comics had been published up to that point in the mid–1980s, primarily because they had been all but ignored by the vast majority of comic book enthusiasts. By that time, comic book love on the racks was long gone.

Except for the five issues of *Dear Beatrice Fairfax*, a newspaper reprint experiment with gorgeous air-brush covers by Alex Schomburg, Standard used almost entirely upbeat, hearts-and-flowers photo covers for its romance comics (unlike its line-drawn covers for other genres). Movie stars occasionally appeared early on, but soon anonymous models appeared on most of the covers. This may have hurt, rather than helped, circulation since Standard romance covers bore a strong resemblance to those from Ace and Fawcett. Except for photo covers of famous stars, they generally don't enhance the title in the collectible market, either. Moreover, Standard offered seemingly skimpy 36-page issues beginning in 1949 instead of the 52-page products from several other companies until 1951 or 1952.

In many issues, Standard offered two or three short stories along with several one- or two-page featurettes, an atypical style for most romance titles of the time. *Intimate Love* # 17 (April 1952) was typical with "I Couldn't Fool Love" (eight pages), "Engaged to Trouble" (three), "Half-Pint Problems" (one), "Tomorrow We Marry" (three), "Secret Sweetheart" (seven), "Love Problems" (two), and "Winner at Love" (three), plus a one-page advice column and a two-page text story. Standard's stories often stressed the consequences of actions and feelings in relationships, rather than bizarre and unlikely circumstances and coincidences.

"Half-Pint Problems," dealing with older sisters' problems with siblings, ended with this common-sense line: "The whole trick is to treat youngsters as people and equals. With kindness and consideration, the problems usually disappear! Remember, you were once a kid yourself!" That last line indicates how romance comics were intended for girls of 16, not 6.

"Husband Unwanted" in *Intimate Love* # 20 (Nov. 1952) is an outstanding example of a realistic romance, distinctly within the realm of possibility. Ann Cameron, a small-town widow known for her aversion to men, meets Walt Adams, who eventually falls for her even though he intended to offer only friendship because of her feelings. On a picnic, she says, "It's lovely, but it's so familiar to me somehow." They share their first kiss, but she soon discovers "Ann and Jim" carved into a tree and feels trapped by her past. Later, Walt refuses to give up: "Not till we've talked! This isn't fair, Ann! I'm competing with a memory—with a ghost!" On the contrary, Ann confesses that her marriage was "miserable" to a man who turned out to be an unrepentant philanderer. Her line, "I don't trust men," doesn't prevent Walt from a last "But I love you, Ann—only you!" But she chases him away when she tells him that's also what Jim said. Yet she agonizes, realizes she does want Walt and tells the reader, "I had let cowardice rule and ruin my whole life!" The story ends with an appropriate kiss.

In the last Standard romance issue, *Intimate Love* # 28 (Aug. 1954), a noteworthy story entitled, "Man of My Own!" also featured an unusual but realistic outcome. Phil and Ruth buy their first home, located on "22 Paradise Path" in Coopertown, but soon begin to fight about finances and the flirtations (albeit still innocent) that go on at neighborhood parties. Ruth overspends to keep up with her neighbors, fearing they will think her cheap if she doesn't, until she realizes it's jeopardizing both their relationship and their home ownership. When her two friends show up for coffee, talking about their latest home-improvement projects Ruth finds the courage to tell them, "No! We'd love to have all that, but you see, we can't afford it! Frankly, we couldn't afford most of the things we bought, so I may have to get a job to help pay for them!" She also tells them she wants to spend more time with her husband and less time at parties. Her two friends are shocked—not at what Ruth says, but that they have found themselves in the same bind. "Ruth, you're wonderful to slap us down and bring us to our senses," one of her friends says. "And you're so right about the parties!" When she tells Phil that she fully intends to get a job, he tells her, "Okay, Darling! And I bet every girl in town will get one, too, just because you are!" Ruth tells the reader in the last panel, "I stopped his teasing with a kiss, and what a kiss that was! It thrilled me and made me feel sure that I still had my five rooms ... and love!"

For a woman to talk of getting a job to pay off her bills was far from typical in romance comics of the mid–1950s, when the vast majority of married women did not work in real life. Yet, in this story, it was the logical, responsible thing to do. When Standard decided to publish a new romance title in 1951, it might well have been entitled, *Exciting Romances* or *Exciting Love* (the company had a long running pulp with that title). For two decades, the company had been using "Thrilling," "Popular," "Startling" and "Exciting" in the titles of numerous pulps and later comics. But, just as Dell beat Standard to *Popular Comics* in 1936 (well before the first Standard comic was published), Fawcett somehow beat Standard to *Exciting Romances* in 1949. So, using a literal approach, Standard named the new love title *New Romances*.

Standard often eschewed # 1 for its first issues, so *New Romances* debuted with # 5 (May 1951). On the first page, the anonymous editor wrote a letter to the reader. "They [the stories] are written by people who have really loved the experiences they write about, and we hope that you may find an answer to your own problem which might be the difference between happiness and heartache. In other words, these stories about real people may show you how to make a better life for yourself and those around you. *New Romances* is not just for those who have suddenly discovered they are in love. It is also for those people who are adjusting themselves to marriage, for it is after the honeymoon when the real problems of life present themselves. And, of course, there is that critical in-between-time called 'being engaged'—or just dating."

Producing some of the most logical stories on the market in 1954 could not persuade Standard to continue to publish romance, even though the vast majority of its stories by that time could have passed the Comics Code with little trouble, unlike its horror, crime and war comics.

Complete Love Vol. 26, # 2, May-June 1951, copyright Ace Magazines. Many of Ace's 1950–51 covers featured painted beauties.

But the company's once huge pulp magazine line had shrunk to only a handful of titles, primarily romance and westerns, and perhaps a drop in pulp profits affected the comics, too. Standard published only 13 comic books in 1955, and eight featured the recently licensed *Dennis the Menace*.

Avon's artistic approach to violence

Avon was an early favorite among romance comic collectors for its pulp-style covers, often reprinted from its colorful line of 1940s exploitation paperbacks. In some ways, it's odd that Avon even stayed in comic books for so long (1947–56), because its small line of comics must have been dwarfed by its immensely profitable paperback empire. At any rate, after all six of its short-lived love comics were cancelled in 1949–50, Avon brought back *Romantic Love* with # 4 (March 1951) and started *Realistic Romances* and *Intimate Confessions*, both with # 1 (Aug. 1951).

All three titles were gone by the end of 1954, and there were only 33 issues among them. But collectors have celebrated their differences for years. They often featured stories that seemed more fitting for crime or war comics, and there was an overt sensuality to their covers that would never have survived the Comics Code. They also featured above-average art, most notably several compellingly illustrated short stories and a few unique covers by a young Everett Raymond Kinstler, who was far superior to the vast majority of artists appearing in romance comics of the era. Kinstler did an immense amount of work for Avon in numerous genres from 1950 to 1956, as detailed in the remarkable biography, *Everett Raymond Kinstler: The Artist's Journey through Popular Culture, 1942–1962* (2005) by Jim Vadeboncoeur, Jr., and Kinstler himself.

As the book details, Kinstler loved doing full-length stories—and produced dozens for several publishers—and he was also superb on romance stories, with perceptive pacing and the ability to effortlessly guide the reader through the story. One of the few compilations of romance reprints, *Teen Angst*, edited by Tom Mason for Malibu Graphics in 1990, features several Avon stories, including contributions from Kinstler and the talented Rafael Astarita. This reprint book was the first time many collectors gained exposure to Kinstler's romance work, along with that of Matt Baker for St. John.

Kinstler's pen-and-ink inside front cover shorts displayed his talents at their finest, but those eventually disappeared when Avon began to use advertisements on most of its inside front covers. Kinstler did "Our Love Was Battle-Scarred," a seven-page tale of romance during the Korean War in *Realistic Romances* # 8 (Nov. 1952). No war comic of the era ever produced more realistic images of combat, though the story has a happy ending with a marvelous "Kinstler kiss" image for the final panel. Kinstler's people seemed to move across the page. Kinstler also did the gorgeous "Girl on Parole" from *Realistic Romances* # 6 (June 1952). The facial images in this story are nothing less than striking, especially the one in which the parolee realizes it is her selfish, grasping boss who has double-crossed both her and the man she loves. From the standpoint of romance collectors, it's too bad Kinstler did so few stories in that genre.

A fatally flawed story

Astarita's eight-page "Fatal Romance" from *Realistic Romances* # 2 (Sept.–Oct. 1951) is a good example of Avon's willingness to try anything, nicely illustrated but poorly written in the extreme. It's a truly far-fetched tale, a fantasy that really belonged, if at all, in one of the crime comics that were flourishing at the time. It's the unique, "nourish" story of two carnival sharp-shooters who fall in love. "Both of us are crack shots! What's to stop us from making money—fast? What's the stop us from robbing a bank?" he asks her. "You can't be serious?" she asks him, only to commit to him in the next panel when he says, "Say you'll do it, honey, for me!" To which she responds, "I love you, Jim ... you don't have to ask!" This violent story wouldn't have a prayer of passing muster in the post–Comics Code era. Even worse, the woman comes across as a pathetically weak creature, incapable of deciding what's good for her.

The ending is predictable but amazingly grim for a romance comic: the two lie sprawled in death close to the Mexican border, having been shot by the police. The incredibly heavy-handed, not to mention unbelievably ungrammatical, comment by an officer in the final panel has to be seen to be understood: "Look at 'em! Both could have lived a long and happy life. Instead they chose crime—and a one-way ticket to the grave!" It's astonishing that any editor could have let pass "a one-way ticket to the grave!" That has to be one of the great redundancies of all time. Even before the advent of the Comics Code, this story would never have been allowed to appear in a romance comic by most publishers of the period. But it is a remarkable curiosity, perhaps inventory from a crime comic.

In his reprint volume, Mason's introductory essay accurately reflected why romance comics disappeared: "In addition, the loss of readers, particularly female ones, and the changing social mores of the country (specifically the rise of the women's movement, the sexual revolution of the '60s and the ascension of women into what were once typically male professions) made the romance comic seem incredibly out of touch." Later, he asks, "Can the romance comic exist today? Maybe, though certainly not as presented in its original form. Society has changed too much to buy into the attitudes these stories represent." Then he adds, apropos of one reason collectors still seek out romance comics, "Besides, 'bad' girls can be a lot of fun."

The essay also reveals why information in old books and fanzines about comics often needs to be double checked. The essay refers to *Captain Marvel* once being published weekly during the Golden Age (it was every other week at its peak) and also to Fawcett's production of *Cowboy Love* from 1945 to 1955 (it was 1949 to 1951). In addition, Fredric Wertham is spelled "Frederick." One of the problems with accurately presented information about romance comics for many writers has been their lack of the original material.

An astonishing Avon cover

One of the most astonishing covers ever to appear on a romance comic highlighted *Romantic Love* # 9 (Jan. 1952), one of the issues with gorgeous Kinstler inside-front-cover art, along with an eight-page story. This cover, featuring a blonde with a low-cut, art-deco-style dress bursting out of a newspaper want ad page and reaching out to the reader, was reprinted from one of the exploitation paperback novels published by an Avon subsidiary, *Helped Wanted—Male*, by Thomas Stone (who was actually Florence Stonebreaker). The title, "Help Wanted—Male," appears on the cover of the comic but not on any story.

The story Kinstler illustrated, "No Time for Love," is an interesting tale, a parody of sorts, of how a literary agent falls in love with a man who had sent her popular love stories for five years under the name Gloria Dare, his sister's married name. When Vivian asks Paul, "How did you write like that? How do you understand women so well?" he responds, "It's not simple to explain, Viv! Women are strange ... I observe them, then I observe them some more!" He quickly adds, before their first kiss, "Two people in love don't say trashy clichés under a moonlit sky. They don't have to! Their love speaks for them—like this!" Later, the story has Vivian asking herself, "Where is the contract with the Avon periodicals?" Love comics were

Romantic Love # 9, Jan. 1952, copyright Realistic Comics, Inc. Avon reprinted several of its painted paperback covers for use on comics, including this highly unusual example.

only rarely that self-referential, albeit ambiguously so. After a rival for Paul's love is uncov-ered sending in manuscripts that appall Viv, the story ends happily when Paul reveals the skull-duggery.

Although romance in comics rebounded in a big way in 1951 and 1952 after the disaster encountered in the second half of 1950, the years 1953 and 1954 were tougher for the indus-try. Following Fawcett and Hillman in 1953, second-tier publishers either toppled or left the romance field in 1954: Standard, Star, Avon, Harwell, Our Publishing, Magazine Enterprises. Several more were to follow within the next four years, most notably Quality, Ace, Harvey, Lev Gleason, Eastern and Superior. Meanwhile, a handful of tiny publishers also stubbornly tried to make a go of romance in the 1954–58 period before they, too, all faded away. These were, indeed, "minor-league lovers."

EIGHT

Minor-League Lovers

One-Shot Wonders and Other Short-Lived Flirtations

On the whole, romance comics were an unquestionably successful American commercial phenomenon, one often fondly remembered by the vast majority of female baby boomers. Yet fully two-thirds of all romance titles published over the 30-year period from 1947 to 1977 failed to make it beyond a dozen issues. More than two decades of research by myself, Dan Stevenson and Jim Vadeboncoeur, Jr., reveal that there were 301 distinct titles published in that three-decade period, if one includes a pair of short-lived Charlton reprint titles in the early 1980s after the "romance era" ended (see the company-by-company listing in the appendix). Of those 301, it's difficult to believe that only 103 titles lasted beyond a dozen issues. It's even more astonishing to realize that 113 titles ran no more than four issues! In other words, more than one-third of all romance titles bombed, even though the genre itself was one of the most profitable in the annals of comics.

On the other hand, a scant 15 romance titles ran more than 100 issues including *Young Love*, which needed two different publishers. Of those, National/DC was involved with seven, including four titles started when DC was National plus one picked up from Quality and two acquired from Crestwood/Prize. In contrast, consider that National alone published more than 100 issues across 11 titles devoted primarily or exclusively to Superman/Superboy, Batman and Wonder Woman. (But then, the total number of comic books in which those icons of three generations have appeared now exceeds more than the total of nearly 6,000 romance issues.)

Romance publishers, however, tended to publish several different titles at the same time rather than produce them monthly under fewer names, the way character-driven comics have always been produced. That offered the consumer the illusion of variety. Bi-monthly publication also meant longer shelf life. In addition, since newsstands and other outlets did not receive all titles before the advent of comic book stores and the direct market, consumers might have been frustrated trying to acquire every issue of a smaller number of titles. Long-time comic book fans and collectors often tell stories of having to frequent several outlets in the 1960s and earlier to avoid missing an issue of favorites such as *Superman* or *Spider-Man*, not to mention lesser known characters. The huge number of romantic obscurities—the author, tongue firmly in cheek, coined the term "osculations of obscurity" for *Comic Book Marketplace*—accounts for much of the growing fascination of collectors with short-run romance. Minor-league lovers, as it were.

There were, of course, a multitude of reasons for all these short runs. Several of the 33 publishers (many more, if you want to count sub-publishers created for tax purposes) lasted only briefly. Others, such as Fox, went into romance comics near the end of their existence. Timely/Marvel/Atlas, the third-ranking romance publisher with 562 issues from 1948 to 1976—

not counting the humorous and even occasionally "serious" romantic flirtations of the likes of *Millie the Model* and *Patsy Walker*—suffered from economic implosions in 1950 and 1957.

Slight disparities in counts

There will, of course, be slight disparities in the title counts of any two collectors or historians. The author used a common-sense approach, recognizing the realities of commercial gambles. Comics with only a minor adjustment in their titles, such as Lev Gleason's *Boy Meets Girl/Boy Loves Girl*, are counted as one title. But a totally different title even if the numbering is continued, such as Charlton's *Intimate/Teen-Age Love*, was counted as two, since Charlton clearly did not consider *Intimate* a commercially viable title after only three issues (or perhaps the Comics Code Authority made the suggestion in the still-stultified atmosphere of 1958). Likewise, *Young Romance* from Crestwood/Prize and National/DC is counted as two titles, since the latter publisher took on a new financial challenge when assuming publication. In that case, it was not much of a risk in 1963, but it still represented at least a leap of financial faith in the genre, and in the new publisher's ability to market the title successfully.

Issues that were intended to be one-shots, such as DC's *Super DC Giant* # 17 and 21 (cover titled *Love 1970* and *Love 1971*), were not counted as separate romance titles, but are counted in the publisher's totals. There were only a handful of such, including the odd likes of non-romance publisher Dell's *I Met a Handsome Cowboy* in 1951 as part of the *Four Color Series*. Unless you count some of Dell's adaptations of *Zane Grey*, which included the occasional love scene, that was the only romance issue ever to come from the publishers, who became Gold Key in 1962 (when a separate Dell imprint emerged with the breakup of Western and Dell).

And although rebound giants from Fox, St. John and Fawcett (which did only one) appear in the appendix, they are not counted in the above survey, since they are not original stories and were not intended as ongoing series. Nor are the 34 known reprints counted from IW/Super in the late 1950s and early 1960s, since none of those are original.

The author made a few arbitrary decisions, counting as one those titles that never really changed such as two issues from the obscure McCombs people of *Love Problems and Advice*, which was picked up by Harvey with # 3 in 1949 in perhaps some sort of commercial connection with McCombs. In fact, McCombs used the same artists and had the same New York address as Harvey and advertised its romance flagship *First Love* in *Love Problems* # 2. On the other hand, the all-romance issue of the teen humor title *Junior Miss* # 37 from Timely/Marvel in 1949, counted as one of the one-issue wonders, reverted to the apparently more commercially successful humor format for its final two issues. The logic is simple: # 37 was not a teen humor comic. Avon's *Betty and Her Steady* was cover-marketed as teen humor with # 1 and as serious romance with # 2, albeit with mixed genres inside. And as for the 19 issues of Timely/Marvel's romantic heroine *Venus, Goddess of Love* (the "real" thing, by the way!) despite the romantic covers on a few issues, the author calls that fantasy, not romance.

One-shot romance wonders

During the era of the greatest influence of romance comics, the 1950s, most titles were at least moderately commercially successful if they enjoyed runs of at least a year or two after they regained their newsstand legs in 1951. One-shots were the exception, not the rule. But in the decade from 1949 to 1959, there were some 25 non-reprint romance one-shots, not to mention a goodly number of short-run series. Some of these bear examination, if only because they rank with the most obscure publications in the history of American magazines.

Many collectors love one-shots. They seem more exotic than the usual comic book. There have been hundreds of one-shots in the history of comics, and some collectors have acquired several boxes of them by dint of trolling conventions, comic-book store bins, mail-order price lists and Internet auctions. Many such short-lived comics were intended to be one-shots, or at least as a series of comics unconnected by official publishing schedules. Others appeared near the end of a failing company's days. Still others may have resulted from changes in editors or shifts in financial goals. For some one-shots, though, there is no apparent or logical explanation.

The one-shot list

Not all collectors define one-shots the same way, so the following list of one-shots may seem arbitrary to some readers, although several issues earn the distinction without a doubt. Here are the issues the author considers to be one-shots, listed by year:

1949: *Complete Romance* # 1 (Avon); *Love Trails* # 1 (Timely); *Adventures in Romance* # 1 (St. John; the comic changed genre with # 2 and was titled *Spectacular Adventures*).

1950: *Sparkling Love* # 1 (Avon); *I Love You* and *Young Marriage* (Fawcett); *Honeymoon* # 41, *Real Experiences* # 25 and *Cowgirl Romances* # 28 (Marvel, with numbering continued from titles of different genres).

1951: *My Love Life* # 13 and *My Secret Life* # 27 (Fox, both Sept. 1951, part of a handful of Fox titles that all inexplicably appeared once after it had appeared the publisher had died in 1950); *Co-Ed Romances* # 1 and *Love Life* # 1 (P.L).

1952: *My Real Love* # 5 (Standard); *Pictorial Love Stories* # 1 (St. John); *Dearly Beloved* # 1 (Ziff-Davis); *Women in Love* # 1 (Ziff-Davis, an uncommon original romance giant).

1953: *Daring Love* # 1 (Stanmor; this continued as *Radiant Love* # 2, but I still consider it a one-shot for arbitrary reasons); *3-D Love* # 1 (MikeRoss).

1954: *3-D Romance* # 1 (MikeRoss); *Sorority Secrets* # 1 (Toby).

1955: *Negro Romances* # 4 (Charlton; a reprint of *Fawcett* # 2 from the three-issue 1950 series); *My Secret Confession* # 1 (the only romance comic from the tiny publisher Sterling).

1957: *Romances of Nurse Helen Grant* (Marvel); *Giant Comics* # 2 (Charlton, the only romance issue).

1958: *Secrets of True Love* # 1 (St. John).

Tough to find

None of these comics could be called easy to find; many are considered scarce or rare.

Yet they all have their fascinations for collectors and comic book historians, and so should not be ignored. One of them, *Daring Love* # 1, with the famous "roll in the hay" cover, boasts the first published artwork of Steve Ditko, who went on the great fame with thousands of pages of compelling art and famously co-created *Spider-Man* and *Doctor Strange* at Marvel in the 1960s. *Daring Love* # 1, at one time among the most obscure of all comics, has become the Holy Grail for romance collectors.

P.L. apparently had connections with a Canadian publisher of the late 1940s called D.S. Why P.L.'s two romance titles lasted only issue can be explained easily enough: the publisher quickly went out of business after they hit the racks. The same, however, can't be said of Standard's *My Real Love* # 5, the only one-shot among the company's 111 romance issues from 1949 to 1954. Perhaps the title was abandoned because of its similarity to Ace's long-running *Real Love*, which was established in 1949.

Title confusion also may have led to the one-issue status of Marvel's *Cowgirl Romances* # 28 and *Love Trails* # 1, since Fiction House also pumped out *Cowgirl Romances* and Ace came first with *Western Love Trails*. On the other hand, Marvel's *Honeymoon* # 41 and *Real Experiences* # 25 were both continued from comics with different genres. They were attempts to evade purchasing postal permits and quickly disappeared along with many other titles from the same publisher in 1950 (see Chapter Five).

When *Dearly Beloved* and *Women in Love* appeared in 1952, Ziff-Davis was soon to decide to leave the comics field except for *G.I. Joe*, which lasted until 1957. Ziff-Davis sold its romance titles to St. John.

3-D Love and *3-D Romance*, published under the Stereographics imprint as part of a short-lived experiment by the entrepreneurial artistic team of Mike Esposito and Ross Andru, were victims of the short-lived 3-D craze, not to mention possible under-capitalization. The two artists, who later gained fame for their imaginative work for National on *The Metal Men* and *Wonder Woman*, among many others, also published *Heart & Soul* # 1–2 and the satire *Get Lost* # 1–3 in 1954 under the MikeRoss imprint.

The bizarre Sorority Secrets

Perhaps the most unexpected romance title ever to hit the racks was Toby's *Sorority Secrets* # 1 in 1954. Talk about possibly limiting your story options and your target audience. In 1954, only a small fraction of American women attended college, though other women may have wanted to read about them. Toby, a small publisher destined for demise the next year, planned a second issue of *Sorority Secrets* but instead used the material as part of issue # 20 of *Great Lover Romances*, which had a generally undistinguished 22-issue run.

It's hard to believe that in the year after the Supreme Court decided the landmark Brown vs. Board of Education case, Charlton would unearth reprint material for *Negro Romances* # 4 (Fawcett published # 1–3 in 1950). But then, the Civil Rights Act was a decade in the future, and segregation remained very much the norm in much of America in 1955. The name immediately became *Romantic Secrets* with # 5, taking the title of another longtime Fawcett publication.

Sterling, which published a grand total of 22 comic books in 1954–55, has the distinction of being the only publisher ever to produce one (and only one) romance comic, *My Secret Confession* # 1.

Romances of Nurse Helen Grant, the first "nurse love" comic book (more came in the 1960s), appeared at the worst possible time for fans of nurses, romantic or otherwise. What might have been the second issue was among dozens killed in the Marvel implosion of 1957. Nurses would become the popular subjects of romance paperbacks in the 1960s, but in 1957 it's possible that the book series adventures of Cherry Ames and Sue Barton inspired the brief appearance of Helen Grant. If there was any inventory art, it may never have been published.

Charlton experimented with numerous 25-cent giants in the late 1950s, including a romance one-shot in 1957 as part of a three-issue series entitled *Giant Comics*. It's not certain whether the material consisted of reprints, which would have been in effect similar to the rebound Fox and St. John 25-cent romance giants of the 1949–50 period.

St. John, publisher of many of the most collectible romance comics from 1949 to 1955, bowed out with the less-than-memorable *Secrets of True Love* # 1 in 1958, following two equally unremarkable issues of *It's Love, Love, Love*.

Sorority Secrets # 1, July 1954, copyright Toby Press, Inc. Toby came up with a spicy title for a routine comic dealing with campus life.

A multitude of minor efforts

During the era of romance comics, 1947 to 1977, a dozen publishers produced more than 100 romance issues each, with totals ranging from Charlton's 1,422 and National's 931 to Fox's 125 (including rebound giants) and Standard's 111. (See the appendix.) Those 12 publishers accounted for the vast majority of the total of original (non-reprint) romance comics for those three decades. Yet no fewer than 27 other publishers also entered the market, with totals ranging from Lev Gleason's 98 issues in two titles to Sterling's single issue of *My Secret Confession*.

Many of these publishers, such as Lev Gleason, Hillman, and Avon, were prominent second-tier outfits in several genres. Others, such as Archie Publications, EC, Magazine Enterprises and Fiction House, were significant comic book publishers who flirted only briefly with romance. Still others, such as Mainline and MikeRoss, were short-lived independent businesses conducted by ambitious artists. And some publishers, such as Sterling and Kirby, published only a handful of comics of any type.

It's intriguing to note that beyond the top 20 publishers with regard to the number of issues, the remaining 19 publishers (led by Comic Media's 40 issues) produced a grand total of 268 issues—about four percent of the total market. That represents numerous romantic business dreams that went largely frustrated by the often difficult nature of the comic book market.

Simon & Kirby's experiment with Mainline

Seven years after introducing the romance genre to comics with *Young Romance* in 1947, Joe Simon and Jack Kirby in 1954 created their own short-lived line of comics, Mainline, including four issues of a romance title, *In Love*. The effort was there, but their timing was poor, what with the comics industry in heavy financial flux amid strong national criticism, and the Comics Code Authority about to take over.

S&K tried something different in the first three issues of *In Love*, which was taken over by Charlton. They plugged the innovation as "a book length love novel" and led off *In Love* # 1 (Aug.–Sept. 1954) with "Bride of the Star," a baseball romance. It was far from the first sports story in romance comics, but it was the longest athletic epic to that point—20 pages in three chapters.

Just as they had used the word "adult" on the covers of the first three issues of *Young Romance*, S&K introduced *In Love* with the prominent blurb in the upper left-hand corner, "ADULT reading! NEW! Different! Daring!" They ran the same blurb on # 2 (Oct. Nov. 1954) but ran no cover teasers in # 3 (Dec. 1954–Jan. 1955) except "Full Length Love Novel" at the top of the cover. Comics, incidentally, often failed to hyphenate compound modifiers such as "full length"; this is as good an example as any.

A final ADULT label

This may have been the last time "ADULT" appeared in a newsstand romance comic blurb, since romance comics were clearly geared for younger readers following the imposition of the Comics Code in 1955.

The low-rent publisher Charlton, which scooped up so many titles from dead and dying publishers, took over *In Love* with # 5 (May 1955) and changed the title to *I Love You* with # 7 (Nov. 1955). While *In Love* was a Mainline title, however, there was no cover logo or any attempt at all to tell the reader that here was a title produced by a publisher new to the comics field. It wasn't until # 4 (Feb.–March 1955) that a small stamp-sized logo, "another Simon & Kirby Smash Hit," appeared on the cover. By that time, *In Love* had become a typical anthology title, with four short stories.

"Bride of the Star" was a more than competent if somewhat improbable story dealing with the marriage of Pat Brown, daughter of the owner of the major league Blue Sox, and Warren Parker, a brash rookie pitcher. In an entirely different context, a big-league team called the Blue Sox, created by former pulp magazine writer Duane Decker, had already become the most famous mythical professional squad in American sports fiction, but perhaps S&K didn't know of them, since Decker's books were targeted for young adults. Decker's Blue Sox performed in a thirteen-book series from 1947 to 1964 dealing with the problems and personalities of individual players, and the eighth book in the series appeared in 1954.

Although two-part and three-part stories began becoming more common in comics, most notably from National, later in the 1950s, they were still a comic-book rarity in 1954. At that point in romance comics, they were non-existent, so S&K's idea had considerable merit. The comics apparently did not sell well, though.

"Bride of the Star"

"Bride of the Star" began with a wild throw from Parker nearly beaning Pat Brown, who blurts out, "I've seen some of you dugout wolves use even cruder methods to gain a girl's attention!" to which Parker replies, "I wouldn't put it past them, but I've got more important things to do ... there's not much of a future playing third base for West Falls."

That conversational error was jarring, since no where else in the story is Parker anything but a pitcher. Otherwise, though, the story is solid, dealing with Parker's disinclination to accept anything resembling special favors from the man who becomes his father-in-law, the team owner. When Parker encounters rough times in his second season after a promising rookie year, this leads the stubborn couple to break up. They have too much passion to stay apart, and Parker finally returns to the mound because "my arm is strong and ready ... all I needed was a rest!"

Parker gains the pitching victory and wins over skeptical teammates in his first game back. The best writing in the story follows when he asks Pat what she thought. Responds Pat, with painful honesty: "I ... I almost wanted you to lose! I wanted to know how you'd stand up in defeat!" He comes back with an equally mature, honest comment: "I was thinking about that too, Pat! But that doesn't mean so much to me any more! The only thing I want to win is your respect and your love!" That causes her to continue, "Now you're talking like a real major leaguer ... darling!" Pat, who narrates the story, tells the reader at the end while kissing Warren: "We both made mistakes! Too many of them! But Warren was the man of spirit again—the man I loved! And no matter how the game [meaning the sport itself] went from that moment on, we couldn't lose! For I had found the man I loved!"

Interestingly, even though this is a pre–Code story, there was little or nothing to it that the Comics Code could have objected to. The most improbable aspect of the story was the cover, on which a bare–chested Parker lifts Pat in a clinch—in the locker room!—as another player and a man in mufti (a sports writer?) look on with disapproval. The cover blurbs were deceiving and not at all what the story was about: "She had to share her husband with a million women fans who adored him!" and "An intimate peek at the men and women who live and love behind the scenes of big league baseball." Even so, the story is still far better than most fare offered in love comics of the period.

The story "Marilyn's Men" in # 2 was 20 pages in three chapters and "Artist Loves Model" in # 3 was 18 pages in two chapters. "Marilyn's Men" was pure soap opera, dealing with a woman and her relationships with her erratic brother, a man who loves her and a third man she comes to love. Unlike "Bride of the Star," there's nothing especially memorable about it. On the other hand, "Artist Loves Model" is a compelling look into the frustrations of an aspiring comic-strip artist on two levels, involving creativity and romance.

The painful life of Inky Wells

"Artist Loves Model" is almost painful to read, dealing in detail with both the aesthetic and romantic frustration endured by young artist Inky Wells (!). After 20 pages of emotional pain seldom portrayed in comics, Inky realizes that the once immature woman he loves, former gossip columnist Donna Dreame, has learned a lot about life and that he must have her after all. It seems as though they are parting forever, but the final panel says otherwise: "Inky watched her as she turned the corner, and then he started after her. He didn't know why. Donna wasn't much good for anything. She couldn't write. She was even a rotten model. But he needed her! He loved her!"

Unlike # 1, the cover blurb on # 3 is far more accurate: "Here is the jungle life of the city … LOVE born of the struggle for the fast buck! You'll be shocked, intrigued and charmed by the people you meet here." Avoiding a "happily ever after" ending in # 1 and # 3 stamped these stories as worthy efforts and certainly far different than most romance comics of the 1954–55 period were offering. The chapter titles offer a hint of what S&K were trying to accomplish. For # 1, they are "The First Pang of Love," "Falling Star" and "The Challenge." In # 3, they are "Search for Inspiration" and "The Girl … Cute and Cunning."

Issue # 4, with four short romance stories, offered little to distinguish it from other romance comics on the stands. It was the first Code-approved issue, led by the twist story "Wolf Bait" with the blurb, "small town girl … man of the world … big city." This could be summed up as "small town guy turns out to be narrow-minded heel and big city slicker turns out to be empathetic hero." It's too bad this experiment failed, for Simon & Kirby offered hints of the graphic novels to come from so many others more than two decades later. Of the dozens of short-run romance titles from 1947 to 1977, *In Love* is perhaps the most different and noteworthy.

Short-run romance and obscure osculation

All of the following early short-run titles could be called case studies in the art of obscure osculation (kissing).

As the author pointed out in a "Nolan's Notebook" column in *Comic Book Marketplace* # 80 and 81, among the scarcest 1950s romance issues are *Heart and Soul* # 1 (April–May 1954) and # 2 (June–July 1954). They were self-produced in thoroughly professional corporate style and published in Sparta, Illinois—where most comics were printed—by the young Ross Andru and Mike Esposito. *Heart and Soul* was among the few romance comics to include even a phone number in the indicia. For a good time, call Chickering 4-4195! The indicia to *Heart and Soul* # 1 listed the publishers (Andru and Esposito), the general manager and the circulation manager, along with the art director (Esposito) and the script editor (Andru). That might be a record for a 1950s indicia! The second issue, however, listed only the title's editor: Martin Thall, a partner of Andru and Esposito.

None of the four stories in *Heart and Soul* # 1 or the three tales in # 2 are signed, although Andru and Esposito clearly did some of the art along with Thall. Two of the titles in # 1 are

Heart and Soul # 1, April-May 1954, copyright MikeRoss Publications, Inc. The famed artistic team of Mike Esposito and Ross Andru self-published this.

remarkable for their originality (such as "Gigolo") and their banality ("Second Love"). The Comics Code surely would never have accepted the title "Gigolo." Especially a story that ends with an unshaven, unkempt gigolo drinking alone in a bar, saying "Here's to you, baby! You were right ... Ex-Gigolo meets Gigolette ... and loses!" while the bartender mutters, "Boy! Why is it my place attracts all the bums!"

"You know, our romance comics were really adult," Esposito told Jim Amash for an interview published in *Alter Ego* # 53 (Oct. 2005). "They were very dramatic; they were not sugarcoated like DC's were at the time, very pretty-pretty. Ours were not pretty, because Ross didn't think pretty. Neither did I and neither did Martin Thall. Martin's inking was very strong; it had a very hard line. I liked it." In the same interview, Esposito said that although they reprinted about a half-million copies each of *3-D Love* and *3-D Romance*, they sold poorly. "Now about 5 percent?" he said. "Nobody bought them; nobody even looked at them."

The Canadian outfit P.L. Publishing Co. apparently had some connection with the D.S. Publishing Co., the small late–1940s firm that produced nifty, short-run crime comics with titles like *Exposed* and *Whodunit*. *Co-ed Romances* and *Love Life* were both dated November 1951. They listed editorial offices in New York but were printed in Canada. They were typical romance fare of the period, with four ordinary stories in each issue, all with unsigned art of no great distinction. Both covers featured the themes of female rivalry for a man.

Sterling Comics, the folks who created the solid four-issue super hero title *Captain Flash* and the two-issue horror classic *Tormented*, also did a romance one-shot entitled *My Secret Confession* # 1 (Sept. 1955). Romance comics with titles beginning "My" were a tradition at this point. However, the title *My Secret Confession* had never been tried. This Sterling one-shot looked very much like an issue from Standard circa 1954, with art and a cover from Mike Sekowsky. One intriguing aspect of *My Secret Confession* is a full-page house ad plugging "The Big 3"—*After Dark*, *Surprise Adventures* and *Captain Flash*. They weren't big enough, though, since *After Dark* folded with # 8 (Sept. 1955, the third issue), *Surprise Adventures* with # 5 (July 1955, the third issue) and *Captain Flash* with # 4 (July 1955). It's doubtful whether many readers of *My Secret Confession* cared about *Captain Flash*. But if they did, you can imagine their frustration in trying to find a comic that had already gone off the stands forever—at least off newsstands that promptly removed their old titles by the time this house ad ran in *My Secret Confession*.

Another intriguing little-known romance title is *Enchanting Love*, which ran six issues in 1949–50 from obscure Kirby Publishing Company in New York. This tiny company had nothing to do with Joe Simon or Jack Kirby, who were busy pumping out romance comics for Crestwood (Prize) during this period. Kirby Publishing's editors were listed as John Augustin and the artist Tex Blaisdell.

Kirby published one other romance title—the four-issue run of *Golden West Love*, which became merely *Golden Love* for its final issue. All 10 romance comics from Kirby Publishing featured photo covers, including a nice movie still shot on the cover of # 3 (Jan.–Feb. 1950) of the immortal James Stewart and the famed Italian actress Valentina Cortesa from the 1949 film, *Malaya*, which was one of Stewart's most obscure efforts. Cortesa looks as if she's ready for a nice, long nap in the grasp of Stewart, who seems to be musing, "Lookie what I found!" with a typically wry Stewart smile.

Romance mysteries of tiny publishers

Collectors have puzzled for many years over the multiple mysteries presented by the tiny related groups Artful/Harwell, Youthful/Trojan/Ribage, Story/Master/Merit/Premier and

Heart and Soul # 1, April-May 1954, copyright MikeRoss Publications, Inc. "Gigolo" was one of the more unusual stories of the pre–Code period—and would never have passed the Comics Code Authority a year later.

Gilmor/Stanmor/Key. All told, these four publishers produced a total of 117 known romance comics ranging from late in 1949 to early in 1956.

Youthful/Trojan is the best known of the four groups. This group's titles include *Youthful Romances* # 1 (Sept. 1949) through # 18 (July 1953), *Youthful Romances* # 5 (Sept. 1953) through # 9 (Aug. 1954), *Youthful Love/Truthful Love* # 1 and 2 (May and July 1950), *Youthful Hearts* # 1 (May 1952) through # 3 (Sept. 1953), *Daring Confessions* # 4 (Nov. 1952) through # 8 (Oct. 1953), and *Daring Love* # 15 (Dec. 1952) through # 17 (April 1953). Youthful's version of *Daring Love* is not to be confused with the highly collectible Stanmor one-shot *Daring Love* # 1 (Oct. 1952).

Youthful/Trojan produced several of the ugliest comic covers and art in history. Poses were awkward, to say the least. Stories were sometimes so bad they hurt. For example, *Truthful Love* # 2 (July 1950) has artwork by Walter Johnson and Howard James that is among the worst ever seen in comics. The issue also has a bizarre house ad with the covers of *Youthful Love* # 1 (May 1950) and *Youthful Romances* # 5 (April 1950), saying, "Watch for the next issues!" Not only are these the past issues, but here was an example of a comic that had just changed its title from *Youthful Love* to *Truthful Love* in huge letters on the cover, yet—telling the reader to watch for the next issue under its old title! What were these editors smoking?

Youthful Hearts # 1 (May 1952) has far better art, with stories by Harrison/Bache, Goldfarb/Baer, a very young Doug Wildey and a clinker—a remarkably poor job, worthy of any third grader, by one Stephen Kirkel. The Wildey piece, graced by a fine splash page of a circus girl set to leap through a ring of knives, is excellent work.

An excruciating lack of quality

The early issues of *Youthful Romances* (known as *Youthful Love Romances* at the start) are excruciating for lack of quality. This title was hardly missed as a victim of the Love Glut after # 5 (April 1950). Like so many publishers during the Love Glut era, Youthful resumed publication in 1951 with # 6 (Feb. 1951). This issue includes one story that looks as if *Wonder Woman* artist H. G. Peter had an imitative admirer, sort of like "Wonder Woman's Holiday Girls Go Romantic." Wally Wood, who did intriguing work for Youthful's *Captain Science* comic of the same era, looks as though he helped create the cover of *Youthful Romances* # 8 (Aug. 1952).

Youthful's weak art and period-piece stories, which included supposedly real-life tales of famous pop crooners, all continue in *Youthful Romances* through # 14 (Oct. 1952), when the title did one of the most confusing switches any comic-book detective ever had to sort through. Pix-Parade, the sub-publisher of *Youthful Romances*, changed the title to *Daring Love* with # 15 (Dec. 1952), but the *Youthful Romances* title and logo continued exactly the same under new publisher Ribage with # 15 (Jan. 1953).

One would think this would be enough to confuse the postal authorities, but they may have caught on, for *Youthful Romances* continued through # 18 (July 1953)—the fourth issue under the Ribage indicia—before changing to the correct # 5 (Sept. 1953), which features a full inside front cover house ad for Master/Merit's *G.I. Jane* # 2.

Not only that, but *Youthful Romances* # 5 has a story entitled, "Dangerous to Kiss!" with lettering and art straight out of an American Comics Group title such as *Lovelorn*. Apparently, somebody got signals crossed at the art shop! Or perhaps ACG rejected that story from the Sangor Shop.

Artful/Harwell was bought out by both Ajax and Charlton at the end of 1954. Artful's regular romance comics history began with *All True Romance* # 1 and *Dear Lonely Heart* # 1, both dated March 1951. For unclear reasons, their second issues did not appear until October 1951. After that, *All True Romance* was published regularly through # 20 (Dec. 1954), when Harwell, otherwise known as Comic Media, sold the rights to Ajax. The reason that Ajax started with # 22 apparently was that *All True Romance* had two # 7 issues in Sept. and Nov. *1952*, with the first dated November inside (although there is no # 8).

Dear Lonely Heart ran through # 8 (Oct. 1952), then was resumed by Harwell under the title *Dear Lonely Hearts* with # 1 (Aug. 1953) and ran through # 8 (Nov. 1954) before also being sold to Robert Farrell's second-tier Ajax line. That adds up to 40 Artful/Harwell books, most of which have competent art (much from the Iger shop) and utterly emotion-drenched stories.

A startling bondage splash page

Dear Lonely Heart # 1 (March 1951) has a startling bondage splash page for the crime-romance story, "So This is Love!" If Dr. Fredric Wertham had seen this, he surely would have prominently featured it in *Seduction of the Innocent*. The page is unsigned, but it's typical Iger shop work, similar to that seen in Ajax and Superior titles. In all honesty, the author can't imagine the parent of a teenager seeing this and reacting with anything other than dismay.

Dear Lonely Heart # 2 (Oct. 1951) has a similarly shocking Li'l-Abner-type splash for a story entitled, "The Good Looker An' Me!" This one ends, "Ohhh ... Yore crushin' me ... But don't stop, darlin' ... Don't ever stop!" Indeed!

The second incarnation of this Harwell title, with the name changed slightly to *Dear Lonely Hearts*, features a lot of solid work by Kenneth Landau, Bill Discount, Marty Elkin and others. In *Dear Lonely Hearts* # 6 (June 1954), there's a Harwell house ad including a comic book title supposedly called *Little Amigo ... The Original Hot Tamale*! No one has ever discovered any copies of this politically incorrect title. Was it published under another name? Collectors of obscurities continue to speculate.

The mystery of the missing issue

Gilmor/Stanmor/Key, published by Stanley P. Morse, is yet another puzzle.

As far as veteran collectors know, there is only one major mystery still unsolved relating to 1950s obscurities, as related by the author in several issues of *Comic Book Marketplace*. Stanmor's *Diary Confessions* # 13 apparently was never published, even though *Diary Confessions* # 12 (Nov. 1955) and # 14 (April 1956) do exist. Stanmor's funny book fadeout in 1956 probably prevented issue # 13. Stanmor, owned by magazine entrepreneur Stanley Morse, was actually a fairly significant newsstand comic book publisher in 1955. In fact, the little company published 56 comics in 1955, more than twice as many as its 27 issues in 1954. In 1955, Stanmor released slightly more comics than the much better known EC, Ace, Ajax, Prize and Magazine Enterprises.

Just to show how confusing comic book data can become: Stanmor produced a whopping 18 titles in several genres in 1955, but only four titles continued into 1956—*Diary Confessions* # 14 (and possibly # 13, which would be Feb. 1956 if it exists), *Battle Fire* # 6 (and possibly # 5 and # 7), *Flying Aces* # 5 (and possibly # 4) and *Navy Task Force* # 8. *Battle Fire* # 4 is dated Oct. 1955 and # 6 is dated May 1956, but collectors have no evidence of either a # 5 (which would be dated Jan. or Feb.) or a # 7 (which would have been published later than any other issue from Stanmor). Likewise, *Flying Aces* # 3 is dated Nov. 1955 and # 5 is dated March 1956, but # 4 seems to be non-existent. Meanwhile, *Navy Task Force* did not skip an issue, but did go from # 7 (Dec. 1955) to # 8 (April 1956). *Navy Task Force* # 8, by the by, was an exact reprint of Stanmor's *Navy Patrol* # 1 (May 1955) except for the advertisements.

Stanmor's missing months

Stanmor apparently suffered a financial blip and thus did not publish any comics dated in January through March of 1956. Perhaps the work was done—including the numbering of the missing issues—but possibly these comics were never actually published. Another hint that *Diary Confessions* # 13 may not exist: In the indicia to # 14, it says "formerly *Ideal Romance*," repeating information listed in the indicia to *Diary Confessions* # 9 following the title change from *Ideal Romance* # 8. Yet the indicias to *Diary Confessions* # 10, 11 and 12 do not make any reference to the title change, nor would they have been expected to.

There's also an intriguing and confusing statement of ownership in *Diary Confessions* # 9. The title is listed as *Diary Confessions*, but the statement is dated Oct. 1, 1954—surely well before *Ideal Romance* # 8 hit the stands with its Feb. 1955 date, and long before the title change to *Diary Confessions* with # 9 (May 1955). Some statements of ownership list the former title of a current comic—Charlton did that often—but few, if any, other statements began with a future title change other than *Diary Confessions* # 9.

Stanmor comics occasionally ran reprints—in fact, *Diary Confessions* # 10 bannered "All Stories Brand New" even though the tale of "Rich Man's Daughter" was a reprint from *Tender Romance* # 1 (Dec. 1953).

The mystery of Love Mystery

Perhaps Fawcett's little-known *Love Mystery* does not quite match up to Charlton's *Space Western Comics* (1952–53) with regard to the most bizarre genre pairings. Even so, the three-issue run of romance and intrigue from the publisher of *Captain Marvel* was an original concept in comic books, as originally detailed in a "Nolan's Notebook" column for *Comic Book Marketplace* # 120.

Of the 17 romance titles with which Fawcett overwhelmed readers in 1950, the last four introduced were the three-issue run of *Negro Romances*, the one-shot titles *I Love You* and *Young Marriage*, and the three-issue run of *Love Mystery*.

Too many of Fawcett's love stories, nicely illustrated though they were by the likes of George Evans and Marc Swayze, involved themes of girls being redeemed by a boy's wisdom, such as "I Was Selfish" or "I Was Blinded by Money" (see Chapter Seven). In contrast, the six little epics in the three issues of *Love Mystery* were different. Not always well written, but they were at least different. There were "The Case of the Missing Buddha" and "Terror at Tarn House" in # 1, "Nightmare" and "Twelve Hours to Murder" in # 2, and "Fatal Fascination" and "Death Take All" in # 3. These were 36-page comics (including covers), unlike the fat 52-page Fawcetts more typical of the year 1950, but each *Love Mystery* had 30 pages of comics, plus a two-page text feature.

Love Mystery seems to have been marketed to older teenagers and adult women, since the stories were far wordier and much more densely (if not always logically) plotted than the vast majority of love comics, which tended to be read primarily by females about 10 and older. All three back covers plugged *True Confessions*, Fawcett's long-running text magazine, although most other Fawcett romance comics also carried similar ads for *True Confessions*.

There was a sensationalized back cover ad for *True Confessions* on the back of *Love Mystery* # 2. Bannered over a dropout photo of a teenage girl clinging to a boy at the wheel was the term, "Teenicide!" in two-inch letters. The blurb began, "This girl and her boy friend discovered what happens when teenagers, carried away by wildfire romance, defy the law and their parents. Her tragic story appeared in True Confessions." Then the ad ended with this equally dumbfounding, dignified observation: "Stories to help you make a better life for yourself and those you love.... There is no finer, more exciting entertainment for sale at any price." Talk about trying to have it both ways!

The most unusual stories are "The Case of the Missing Buddha" in # 1 and the unusual "Death Take All" in # 3. "Buddha" involved the attempts of a secretary (strikingly beautiful, of course) and a private detective (a classic hunk) to solve the mystery of the murder of her boss. The culprit was a double-dealing female office manager who learned the rival of the boss had been hiding diamonds in a Buddha statue. The secretary and detective wind up tied up in adjoining panels on the bottom of the penultimate page. As the detective finds a way to free himself, the secretary wonders, "If only he loved me ... perhaps I could better face the prospect of death!" When she sees him escape, she fears he has deserted her, only to see him come back with police in tow. Her response: "Oh, Neil, my dearest! Untie my arms so I can put them around you!"

A strange horse-racing story

Harvey workhorse Bob Powell, who earlier was so effective on sports strips in Street & Smith's long-running 1940s title, *True Sport Picture Stories*, did a rousing 15-page horse racing mystery for *Love Mystery* # 3, "Death Take All." This is by far the most amusing story in *Love Mystery*. There were more than a few romance comic stories involving baseball and football, and lots involving horses, cowboys and dude ranches, but for some reason not too many involved horse racing. "Death Take All" goes behind the scenes with a reporter (handsome, of course) and his investigation into a crooked trainer who tries to defraud a good guy horseowner and his daughter (beautiful, of course).

Some of the lines in this tale are priceless. Early on, when our reporter is trying to get the girl out of the way of a rearing horse, he inadvertently trips her and says, "There goes my dignity! Just as I was trying to play hero??" (Right, two question marks, and for a sentence that is not a question.) To which she responds, "I prefer slightly vulnerable heroes anyway!!" (Right, two exclamation points.)

Later, when the baddies try to frame our hero, he tells a cop who has arrived on the scene, "I'm a newspaper reporter, officer. I just got a flash there was a story out here!!" The line inexplicably works, enabling the hero to buy the time he needs to solve the crime, unleash the correct horse in time to win the big stakes race, and corral the girl.

Avon: Not So Steady with Betty

Another odd short run is Avon's *Going Steady with Betty* # 1 (Nov.–Dec. 1949), which changed its title to *Betty and Her Steady* with # 2 (March–April 1950), with a serious romantic cover. These two issues are part teen humor, part romance, and both tough to find. The two-issue run was not unusual for Avon—and perhaps the reason the cover theme changed from teen humor in the debut issue to serious romance in the second issue was because of the flak received from Archie Comics, which had been telling the tales of vivacious Betty Cooper for eight years to that point. Archie published the first issue of *Archie's Girls Betty & Veronica* as an undated one-shot in 1950.

Painted covers, painted ladies

Pulp magazine publisher Ziff-Davis tried to distinguish itself during its brief fling with comics in 1950–52 with painted covers on many of its numerous short-run titles, during a period when painted covers stood out on crowded racks. These colorful covers, many by famed pulp artist Norman Saunders, have long made Ziff-Davis popular with collectors.

Ziff-Davis published 42 romance issues, with numbering and date patterns that can be described only as truly odd. Like Standard Comics, the publisher sought to imply established success to retailers by starting several of its titles with 10 and 11. This wasn't meant to avoid postal mailing permits, but for unknown reasons Ziff-Davis often would return to regular numbering, leading to collector confusion.

Who could possibly explain why Ziff-Davis began its fling with romance in 1950 with the undated *Romantic Marriage* # 1 and the undated *Cinderella Love* with # 10? *Romantic Marriage* ran through # 17, but *Cinderella Love* was numbered this way: # 10–12, then # 4–11. Furthermore, *Romantic Marriage* ran only five sporadic issues through # 5 (Aug. 1951), then went monthly for the rest of its run: # 6 (Oct. 1951) through # 17 (Sept. 1952). Likewise, *Cinderella Love* ran monthly from # 6 (April 1952) through the second # 10 (Aug. 1952), then finished with # 11 (Fall 1952). *Perfect Love* began with # 10 (Sept. 1951), switched to # 2 (Nov. 1951) and was monthly from # 4 (March 1952) through # 7 (Aug. 1952), before finishing with # 8 (Fall 1952). Adding to the confusion, there is also a *Perfect Love* # 10 (Dec. 1953) from St. John! In the early days of serious collecting of romance comics, this would cause collectors to ask often befuddled retailers, "Is that issue the Ziff-Davis *Perfect Love* # 10 or the St. John *Perfect Love* # 10?"

As if those patterns weren't odd enough, Ziff-Davis added three titles to the crowded racks of 1952: the one-shot 100-page giant *Women in Love* (Winter 1952), which had no number either on the cover or in the indicia; the one-shot *Dearly Beloved* # 1 (Fall 1952), and the brazenly exploitative *Strange Confessions* # 1 (Spring 1952) through # 4 (Fall 1952).

Scarce and Strange Confessions

Strange Confessions # 1–4, all of which are justifiably labeled "scarce" in the Overstreet Price Guide, boast photo covers that feature story titles bordering on the salacious. They are scarce because they were either unsuccessful commercially, or are locked up in collections as the exploitative oddities they are. Titles like *Strange Confessions* tarred the vast majority of "innocent" romance comics.

In an era when married couples were not allowed to be shown in the same bed in mainstream Hollywood films, the photo cover of *Strange Confessions* # 2 (July–Aug. 1952) is astonishing. A woman in a low-cut gown lies invitingly supine on either a couch or a bed as a man, apparently in a dinner jacket, is an inch from kissing her. Both have eyes wide open. Directly above her forehead is the blurb: "I Was Starved for Affection: I COULDN'T SAY NO." The other blurbs were "I Hated His Kisses: HE BOUGHT MY LOVE" and "Heartbreak Ahead … BACKROADS OF ROMANCE."

The photo cover of # 1 displays an exotic young tart, with gloves and come-hither body language amid a background of appropriately red curtains. The blurb: "Flaming Youth in TARNISHED KISSES." Other blurbs were "I Couldn't Resist His DANGEROUS EMBRACE" and "THE MAN I COULDN'T MARRY." For this title, which promised more than it delivered inside with routine stories, "couldn't" was the operative word!

The blurbs on # 3 (Sept.–Oct. 1952 on the cover, but incorrectly # 2 July–Aug. inside because Ziff-Davis failed to update the indicia) were "The Man I Couldn't Resist: MY SOUL IN BONDAGE"; "Love Led Me To Shame ... REFORMATORY GIRL" and "I Was The Girl Boys Talked About ... EVERYBODY'S SWEETHEART." The seven-page "Reformatory Girl" tells the slight tale of a girl in panic because she feels she'll be unjustly accused of a theft and the infatuated man who rescues her from a fall over a ravine.

Issue # 4 played on the crime angle: "Cornered ... I WAS A GANGSTER'S MOLL"; "My Secret Shame ... SCANDAL'S CHILD" and "Out Of The Depths ... SLUM GIRL." The gangster's moll goes to jail, wondering in the last panel: "I'll serve my time without complaining! I can only pray that it will make me worthy of love ... the kind of love I want! It must be waiting for me somewhere in the world! I wonder?" Even in the most sensational of pre–Code comics, the bad actors of either sex almost always either come to a deadly end or realize the error of the ways, usually with a heavy-handed moral. The other three stories end happily.

The jumbled bookkeeping of Ziff-Davis produced another oddity in *Strange Confessions* # 4: Not once, but twice, does the same full-page ad appear plugging, "Sensational NEW Story by MICKEY SPILLANE!" "The Veiled Woman" appeared in the new digest size magazine *Fantastic*. This short story by former comic-book writer Spillane, his only appearance in a genuine science fiction magazine, appeared in *Fantastic* # 3 (Nov.–Dec. 1952), so maybe it was worth plugging twice! Ironically, it was Signet/New American Library, not Ziff-Davis, that made Spillane well known with his infamous Mike Hammer paperback novels.

Women in Love

The era of 25-cent giants had begun in earnest from funny animal kingpin Dell, but Ziff-Davis tried to get a piece of that action with several giants including *Women in Love*, the last romance issue the company released before St. John took over the Ziff-Davis love franchise. *Women in Love* includes only two interior pages of advertising and a full dozen short stories, all with happy endings, including the unique "I Was a Greenwich Village Character." In the era shortly before the beats appeared, a magazine art director's wife, Della Harriman, becomes fascinated with the struggling artists in Greenwich Village and leaves the art director when he constantly criticizes them. But she finds that her husband is correct, after all, and that the grasping, scheming Truslow Benedict is inept with more than just modern art. Has the name Truslow ever appeared in any other American fiction? At any rate, Truslow's frustrated and soon-to-be ex-girlfriend, annoyed that he has invited the estranged wife to his apartment, fetches the art director. He quickly rescues Della from the cowardly Truslow's clutches just as he grabs her and tells her, "Names can't hurt me, you little fool! What do you think I brought you here for—a lecture? You knew what you were doing." The art director tells Della she has won a contest with her work, but not before he lets her know, "No, Della, I didn't come before because, well, a man has his pride, too! I waited until I had a good excuse to come—just in case you really didn't want me!" The excuse, of course, was her winnings in the art contest. The entire story, though, was just another excuse for a man's-wisdom-saves-foolish-girl plot.

Hollywood Love Doctor

Like Ziff-Davis, Toby Press was a second-tier comic book publisher that lasted only a few years (1949–55) and was best known for publishing the likes of *Billy the Kid*, a licensed John

Wayne title, *Felix the Cat* and *Li'l Abner*. Toby plunged into love with *Great Lover Romances* # 1 (March 1951), which was led by a tale of "Dr. Anthony King, Hollywood Psychiatrist." Dr. King continued to solve the romantic problems of his patients in early issues, including the two issues in which *Great Lover Romances* inexplicably morphed into *Young Lover Romances* # 4 (June 1952) and # 5 (Aug. 1952) before returning to *Great Lover Romances* # 6 (Oct. 1952) through the last issue, # 22 (May 1955). (Toby also suffered from bookkeeping problems, dating # 21 April 1954 instead of the correct 1955.)

Perhaps for tax reasons, Toby Press published a few comics under the Minoan imprint, including four issues of *Dr. Anthony King, Love Doctor* in 1953–54. He was still *Hollywood Love Doctor* in the indicia, however, even though he either narrates or gets directly involved with a variety of people in most of the stories in his own title. The folks the pipe-smoking Dr. King tries to help are, for the most part, at least out of the ordinary. For example, he helps "Scandal Girl," a gossip columnist, find honesty and love in # 2 (1953, no month given). In the extraordinary "Beanpole," he helps Karen, a girl of six feet (or perhaps taller), find love with Roger, a short man. When Dr. King introduces the two and they both think it's a joke, he tells why he's bringing them together: "Because you're both suffering from the same complex. One feels too short for women, one feels too tall for men. But if you go out together, you'll find out how much you have in common." And so they do. Karen even realizes, after one date (and one kiss) with a taller man, that the man she really wants is Roger. She is, however, shocked when she learns Dr. King has sent the taller man to test her emotions. The questionable ethics of that situation are left for the reader to decide, for Dr. King makes no apologies for meddling in the life of his patients. In the final panel, Roger tells Karen, "Darling, on this couch we're the same size. Our lips are the same size and our hearts are the same size." To which the well-meaning Dr. King tells the reader, "Karen omitted one thing. The clue to their lifelong happiness. Their love was the same size, too!" *Love Doctor* # 4 (May 1954), the last issue, appeared a full year after # 3. Dr. King helps a girl overcome her infatuation with an old actor and assists girls with problem dreams, amnesia and a clumsy approach to life. It's difficult to imagine why the publisher would expect to make a commercial success of this belated final issue, but apparently it didn't sell well, because it's one of the more obscure love comics of the pre–Code period.

Mr. Anthony's Love Clinic

Before there was Dr. Anthony King, there was the five-issue run of *Mr. Anthony's Love Clinic* from the second-tier comic publisher Hillman. Hillman was better known for a variety of magazines and paperbacks but nonetheless achieved great commercial success with the Golden Age World War II costume hero Airboy, which lasted until the company abruptly left comics in 1953.

The cover blurb on *Mr. Anthony's Love Clinic* # 1 (Nov. 1949) explains it all: "Real Stories from Life as told to John J. Anthony ... Director [of the] Marital Relations Institute and Conductor of the *Famous Radio Hour* heard weekly by millions of people." (The complexities of the use of capital letters were often lost on comic book writers.) The first cover displayed a photo of two anguished people speaking to a man in front of a microphone and featured the story, "I Ran Around."

Mr. Anthony was apparently the Dr. Laura of his era, dealing with a wide variety of personal problems, although he didn't appear in every story in the short run. Issue # 1 listed five of Mr. Anthony's "Ten Rules to Marriage Happiness," with long-winded explanations dealing with spiritual guidance, personal attractiveness, age to marry, physical fitness and likes and dislikes, followed in # 2 (Dec. 1949) by Mr. Anthony's extensive advice on compromise, money, parent fixation, children and the family. The cover of # 2 featured "I Know What's Best for My Sister."

"Love Hits a Home Run" at Premier

Though there was never a comic book entitled *True Love* until independent publisher Eclipse produced two issues of that title in 1986, reprinting stories from Standard Comics, one of the final small publishers of the mid–1950s period came close. Premier Comics, which was affiliated with the Story/Master/Merit folks, published 11 bi-monthly issues of *True Love Confessions* from # 1 (May 1954) through # 11 (Jan. 1956). Premier's circular logo was similar to the much better-known EC Comics. The covers after # 1 were highly unusual in that they featured several panels centered around one large scene, all from the featured story. During the 1954–56 period, no other comics consistently featured romance cover styles of this type.

Kurt Schaffenberger, best known for his hugely popular work on Fawcett's *Captain Marvel Junior*, National's *Lois Lane* and *Superboy* and ACG's science fiction and fantasy stories, was largely in between work with those companies when he contributed 6-page stories to *True Love Confessions* # 1, 4 and 5 and covers for # 9, 10 and 11. These romance comics are so obscure that the massive "Schaffography" in his biography, "Hero Gets Girl!" (2003) by Mark Voger, listed only the covers for # 9 (a wonderful baseball scene) and 10. The biography warned, however, that his body of work was so large that the list couldn't be complete.

True Love Confessions was generic, similar to the large Ace line with a penchant for relationship-driven stories rather than tales with a twist or a heavy-handed lesson. They were pretty much generic romance comics, with a handful of exceptions, and there were hearts-and-flowers endings to 42 of the 44 stories (there were four short stories in each issue).

One of the stories, though, was remarkable for its improbability. Whoever wrote the six-page "Love Hits a Home Run" in # 9 (Sept. 1955) penned one of the most whimsical and far-fetched baseball stories of all time, not to mention used one of the strangest metaphors. As the story opens, Marion has brought her 17-year-old sister, Debbie, along with her girlfriends, to ogle the dashing Duke Halsey, the star of a team never named in a league not identified. His home run lands in Debbie's lap and, as Debbie narrates, "There was Duke, smiling at me!" Duke comes over—as though this would ever happen during a real game!—to tell her, "Good catch, little girl! Come around after the game and I'll autograph it for you!" Marion insists on getting the autograph, but Duke gives Debbie a pass for Saturday's game.

"And when game time came," Debbie narrates, "I secretly borrowed Sister's high heels and clothes and makeup!" Naturally, she catches another ball. Duke later invites her to dinner and autographs it after again talking with her right after the catch: "You should really catch for our team, Debbie!" A few dates and kisses later, Debbie's mother forbids her to date Duke because a newspaper says he's engaged to someone else. But it turns out that it was "last year's newspaper"—a mean-spirited trick by Marion. Debbie races to the next game, catches yet a third ball hit by Duke, and accepts his invitation for another autograph. "It's the marriage license I'm going to autograph, Darling," he tells her, having been informed of the truth by Marion. But what are the odds of one girl catching home runs—by the same player, no less—in three consecutive games?

The Ajax oddities

Ajax, also known as Farrell after publisher Robert Farrell, produced an entire comic book "library" of funky short-run romance series from 1954 to 1958. The Ajax logo in the upper-left corner resembled the logo of comic book giant Dell. Farrell's attempts at comic book publishing date from the 11-issue series of *Captain Flight Comics* in the mid–1940s under the Four Star imprint. He really didn't get going until the 1950s, beginning with the masked western hero *Lone Rider* # 1 (April 1951), apparently trying to take advantage of the popularity of *The Lone Ranger* on television and in the best-selling Dell comic book series.

Farrell tried publishing a little of everything in the 1950s, including super heroes, funny animals, westerns, war and horror comics, but none of his titles ran monthly. They may have suffered from distribution problems, for some readers don't remember seeing them on the racks. The Comics Code forced Farrell to change his horror title *Voodoo*, which lasted 19 issues in 1952–54, to *Vooda*, a jungle heroine who lasted three issues. Romance, though, was the genre Ajax tried to use as its cash cow, if it ever had one. When it came to minor-league love, Ajax was the king. Of the approximately 320 Ajax issues in the 1950s, 70 issues were devoted to romance.

What made Ajax's romance books especially intriguing, though, was the fact that he published those 70 issues covering 11 different titles! He used two titles, *My Personal Problem* and *Secret Love*, in two different series. Many of those issues are hard to find. It took the author more than 20 years to complete a set of all 70, and then only with the help of Dan Stevenson. It would seem to have made more economic sense to publish more issues under fewer titles.

The first Ajax romance comic was *Bride's Secrets* # 1 (March–April 1954 on the cover, April–May in the indicia). Since the 19-issue run dealt with stories of dozens of brides, the misuse of the apostrophe in the title is a glaring example of Ajax's grammatical deficiencies. The date confusion is also somewhat typical of Ajax. *Bride's Secrets* was the only Ajax romance title to run from 1954 to 1958, although it appeared sporadically, perhaps in relation to the publisher's economic fortunes. There were only two issues of *Bride's Secrets* in 1956, for example. Farrell was listed as the publisher throughout and Ruth Roche as editor. Roche formerly wrote for S. M. "Jerry" Iger, who supplied the best-selling line of Fiction House anthology adventure titles in the 1940s, and Fiction House published its last few comic books in 1954.

Unique conversational covers

Ajax had a cover conversational style unique in comic book history. The protagonist would use the title of the lead story (all in colored, capital letters) in her word balloons or thought balloons. For example, on the cover of *Bride's Secrets* # 19 (May 1958), a tear-stained woman, presumably a bride, is telling her husband, a librarian, "Your job may deal with books ... I guess MY CATEGORY IS LOVE!" She's shown holding a magazine (the price is 50 cents, even though it looks like a book) titled, "The Home Superb."

The breathless tone of most Ajax stories is set with the blurb on the cover of # 1, which portrays a big-busted bride (Fredric Wertham wrote of "headlight" covers) in an awkward kiss with a man who seems less than thrilled. Both people have their heads up, yet their eyes closed, and his nose is about to connect with her ruby-red lips. "At long last it was my wedding day," reads the blurb. "But suddenly a fear of his kisses filled MY TREMBLING HEART!"

The final story in # 1, "Our Honeymoon Was Over," dealt with a couple's economic problems. The wife's boss tries to buy her away from her low-earning husband, but, after a contretemps, they realize they love each other in the final few panels. "I know it's rough going on my salary, honey," he tells her, "but we're building from the bottom up! You've got to want it, to make it come true." After she acknowledges her "terrible mistake," they make up with a kiss, and she submits to him completely: "Oh, David, you wait and see how good a wife I'll be from now on!" Imagine that story appearing in a romance comic two decades later! When this story was reprinted in *Bride's Secrets* # 16 (Aug. 1957), it was retitled, "How to Hold Onto a Dream!"

Iger's art studio produced the always-anonymous art for Ajax, using heavy inking and a generic style, similar to art produced for Artful/Harwell and Canadian publisher Superior, among others. Occasionally, though, arms and legs would extend into adjacent panels and there would be other experimental panel shapes compared to most comics of the time. Yet Ajax issues were as commercial as comics could be; *Bride's Secrets* # 1 opens with full-page ads on the first two pages! Few, if any, other publishers ever tried that. Including the covers, 11 of the 36 pages were advertisements.

In the first six issues, all of which appeared before the Comics Code, only one of the 24 stories had anything but a lovers-in-arms ending (or at least lovers reconciled). "Breaking Hearts Was My Game" in # 5 (Dec. 1954–Jan. 1955) turned the usual little-girl-loves-little-boy formula on its head. "I was nine and I adored Tommy Brooks," narrates the heartbreaker, Diana Flynn. "But he was always with my cousin Lisa. One day ..." Portraying the kids in flashback, this nine-year-old (!) then says, "I hate Lisa! I'm going to get Tommy away from her!" She fakes an ankle sprain and coaxes Tommy to carry her books home. "There were a lot of Tommys after that," the adult Diana, complete with low-cut gown and cigarette in holder, tells the reader. "I always wanted someone else's man—and I got them!" As an adult, though, she eventually becomes Lisa's victim when Lisa's husband-to-be deliberately tricks Diana into telling a gossip columnist that she's going to marry Felix Kuttner, a "handsome young architect," as the column says. Felix soon reveals the trick: "I'm not going to marry you, Diana! Now or ever! The whole thing was a little game! I mean that Lisa planned it! To get even and teach you a lesson! Cruel, maybe, but you deserve it! And I'm going to marry Lisa next week!" In the final panel, with Diana in tears, she tells the reader: "That was my lesson! I'm alone now, in a bleak and lonely house, waiting for another chance at love! I wonder if it will ever come ..." In romance comics, two wrongs sometimes made for a most disturbing "right."

Throughout the 19-issue series, the only other story with an unhappy ending was a unique one-pager in # 12 (May 1956). A whirlwind romance, capped by a proposal, is sealed with a ring that turns out to be a "worthless trinket." She sends him a "goodbye, jerk!" letter, only to receive a genuine diamond ring in the mail with a letter: "Dear Prue ... Here is my big surprise! The ring you are wearing will always have great sentimental value, but this one will have more! It was my mother's ring." She calls him to tell him of her "terrible mistake" and professes her love, but he has read her letter and says, "I'm sorry, Prue! If you felt that way, it wasn't the kind of love I want ... goodbye!"

Ajax expands

When Ajax first began to expand its romance line by picking up *All True Romance* from defunct publisher Comic Media, the numbering skipped from Comic Media's # 20 (Dec. 1954) to Ajax's # 22 (March 1955). There were 21 issues from Comic Media, including two # 7 issues in 1952. *All True Romance* # 22 oddly includes a statement of Farrell's ownership dated Sept. 28, 1954, even though Comic Media's # 20 should have been on the racks. *Lonely Heart* # 9 (March 1955), the first Farrell issue after being picked up by Ajax, indicates Farrell as publisher and is signed Oct. 1, 1954.

Ajax's fourth love title debuted as *Bride's Diary* # 4 (May 1955), formerly *The Flame* # 3, as the indicia indicates. Ajax then started four new romance titles: *My Personal Problem* and *Today's Brides* (both # 1, Nov. 1955) and *Secret Love* and *True Life Romances* (both # 1, Dec. 1955). But Ajax may have run into financial problems in 1956, for there were only 21 romance

Bride's Secrets # 8, June 1955, copyright Excellent Publications, Inc. Gossips on the phones in the background make for an unusual cover in the early post–Code era.

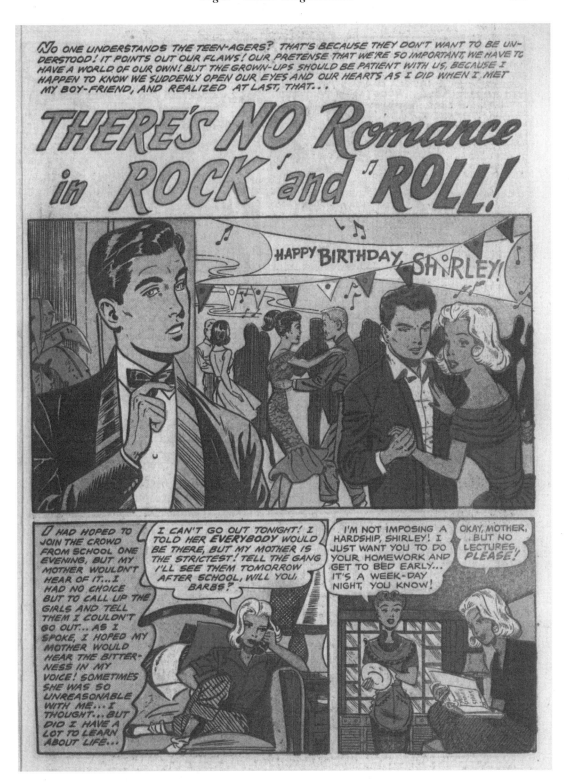

True Life Romance # 3, Aug. 1956, copyright Ajax Publications. The ultimate period piece: In "There's No Romance in Rock and Roll," the boy who disliked the new music won out!

issues produced sporadically among the eight titles. Ajax followed with only 12 romance issues in 1957 and eight in 1958.

Ajax's often tear-stained covers usually portrayed extreme emotional upheaval, including one of the line's few original covers—*Bride's Secrets* # 8 (June 1955) in a twisted takeoff on Norman Rockwell's famed "telephone face covers" for the *Saturday Evening Post*. The teary bride shouts into a phone, "It's not true! Don't believe them! I am not a two-timer!" as nine women, two looking especially nasty, supposedly gossip on phones. There are, however, no men in the gossip picture. A similar cover for *All True Romance* # 23 (May 1955) portrays eight men and women apparently making fun of a teary blonde. Like *Bride's Secrets* # 8, this was strangely negative for a Comics Code-approved cover.

"There's No Love in Rock and Roll!"

One of the great—or at least greatly strange—period pieces of all time is Ajax's 6-page "There's No Romance in Rock and Roll!" in *True Life Romance* # 3 (Aug. 1956). The introduction is narrated by a teenager: "No one understands the teen-agers? That's because they don't want to be understood! It points out our own flaws, our pretense that we're so important, we have to have a world of our own! But the grown-ups should be patient with us, because I happen to know we suddenly open our eyes and our hearts as I did when I met my boyfriend and realized at last that ... there's no romance in rock and roll!"

Shirley, a defiant daughter of irritated parents, insists on dating a boy who prefers rock and roll, which more or less debuted two years before this issue hit the racks. Shirley, however, ultimately decides a square-shooter—who prefers good (i.e. adult) music—makes both her and her parents happy. Says Shirley in the final panel, "Gee, I can't believe that I ever enjoyed that horrible rock and roll stuff—it's just plain noise!" To which her new fellow responds, "Right! It'll never take the place of a sweet love song ... by the way, let's get some records to share." It's no wonder that this story was reprinted in *My Terrible Romance* # 1 in 1994 by the small independent publisher New England Comics.

Also in *True Life Romance* # 3 is a full-page house advertisement urging the reader to pick up all eight of "the best in love magazines!" Ajax reckoned without its financial problems, because six of the eight titles were soon cancelled and the other two disappeared for six months. Ajax's bookkeeping sometimes baffled collectors for years. For example, the Ajax issues of *All True Romance* extend from # 22 through # 30 (July 1957), then shift to # 3 (Sept. 1957) and # 4 (Nov. 1957) before correctly continuing with # 33 (Feb. 1958) and finishing with # 34 (July 1958). Ajax went out of business with that month's issue and the last of the "minor-league lovers" was never seen again. In 1959, only commercial giants National and Charlton and tiny publishers ACG and Crestwood/Prize and a greatly shrunken version of Marvel remained in the romance comic field. Funk, though, was largely gone forever.

Thrilling Love, Dec. 1937, copyright Standard Magazines, Inc. Campus love is epitomized by a co-ed clinging to a football hero, complete with leather helmet.

Top, left: Miss America # 2, Nov. 1944, copyright Miss America Publishing Corp. Dolores Conlon, a 15-year-old model, wears a costume representing the super heroine Miss America. Patsy Walker debuted in this issue. *Top, right: My Date* # 1, July 1947, copyright Hillman Periodicals, Inc. This Simon & Kirby project once was considered the first romance comic, but now it's recognized primarily for teen humor. Two months later, S&K's *Young Romance* # 1 hit the racks and made history. *Left: Young Romance* # 1, Sept.-Oct. 1947, copyright Simon and Kirby. "For the more ADULT readers of COMICS." The first true romance comic.

Glamorous Romances # 41 (# 1), July 1949, copyright A.A. Wyn, Inc. Not many comics advertised title changes on their covers, but Ace apparently wanted everyone to know the teen humor title *Dotty* was now a romance comic.

Dear Beatrice Fairfax # 8, July 1951, copyright King Features Syndicate. Alex Schomburg, famed for drawing covers with super heroes and science fiction themes, briefly tried his hand at romance for this five-issue series (this is actually the fourth issue).

Top, left: Real West Romances # 2, April-May 1949, copyright Crestwood Publishing Co., Inc. Photo covers of romantic scenes were typical during the brief heyday of western romance. *Top, right: Love Diary* # 13, Feb. 1951, copyright Our Publishing Co. editor and publisher Ray Hermann's two romance titles often focused on aspects of self improvement in a variety of ways, such as in "I Was a Fat Girl!" *Right: Wartime Romances* # 1, July 1951, copyright St. John Publishing Co. Published during the Korean War, this started a mini-trend.

My Secret Confession # 1, Sept. 1955, copyright Sterling Comics, Inc. A classic one-shot: this was tiny Sterling's only romance title.

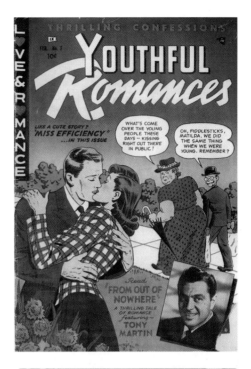

Top, left: True Love Confessions # 9, Sept. 1955, copyright Premier Magazines, Inc. Kurt Schaffenberger, who later portrayed Lois Lane's pursuit of Superman, turns in a nice sports theme cover. *Top, right: Youthful Romances* # 7, Feb. 1954, copyright Ribage Publishing Corp. Romance comics seldom had humorous covers such as this one. *Bottom, left: Young Romance* # 170, Feb.-March 1971, copyright National Periodical Publications, Inc. Lily Martin, "The Swinger," is a mod girl trapped between heaven and heartbreak. *Bottom, right: Young Romance* # 194, July-Aug. 1973, copyright National Periodical Publications, Inc. "Full Hands, Empty Heart" told of an ill-fated interracial romance.

Young Love # 126, July 1977, copyright DC Comics, Inc. This was the last of National/DC's 931 romance comics and essentially ended the romance era.

NINE

Cut That Cleavage!

Before and After the Comics Code Authority

Perhaps no better example exists than *Romantic Hearts* # 9 of what some romance comics had become in the days before the Comics Code Authority imposed self-censorship on the industry. It's ironic that *Romantic Hearts* # 9 (second series), dated November 1954, may have been sitting on the stands in September, at the very time the Comics Magazine Association of America folks were meeting in New York, finalizing the requirements for their new Comics Code stamp of approval. That stamp began appearing on most comics early in 1955.

The classic cat fight cover on *Romantic Hearts* # 9—one of the few in the history of romance comics—represented an apparently unintentional parody of pretty much everything the Fredric Wertham-inspired critics would have abhorred, though the issue appeared well after the psychiatrist's anti-comics screed, *Seduction of the Innocent*, hit bookstores earlier in 1954. There were, of course, numerous passive-aggressive conflicts and tears on the covers of old romance comics, but this was something different—one of the wildest, weirdest covers ever slapped on a comic book that purported to deal with real life (as opposed to fanciful notions of vampires and space pirates).

The cover art, not signed, shows one woman—with cleavage bursting in a drawing that can charitably be called a bit anatomically exaggerated—knocking another woman against the rail of an excursion boat while shouting, "You keep away from Jim! He brought me on this outing. He's my man, you understand—all mine!" Meanwhile, Jim is casually standing in the background thinking, "There go the girls fighting over me. I never should have given them both the same line—" Talk about a classic male chauvinist pig!

This unorthodox cover was part of the second series of the *Romantic Hearts* title, produced by Master Comics, the same folks who published the bizarre Master/Merit horror comics of the era. Oddly, the cover-featured story, "River Girl," did not come close to featuring any cat fights. However, the good guy of the piece does wind up knocking the bad guy over a boat rail—seconds after the thug had slapped the heroine. In the same issue, a story subtly entitled, "I Wanted a Caveman," is one of the worst anyone could imagine. As the splash shows one guy laying into another with a left hook, the woman in front blurts out, "I finally got Bob to fight for me! He really loves me!" Ironically, Master Comics (the *small* company, not the long-running Fawcett title starring Captain Marvel Junior) was located at 480 Lexington Ave. in New York. That was then the hallowed address of National (later DC) Comics, which published many of the mildest and least controversial of all pre–Code romance comics.

Romantic Hearts was a good example of the type of book the Comics Code Authority wanted to censor, or preferably eliminate. The first series ran from # 1 (March 1951) through # 10 (Oct. 1952) and was published under the imprint of Story Comics and did not even carry a publisher's logo on the cover. The second series, using the same oversized title logo as the

Romantic Hearts # 9, Nov. 1954. copyright Master Comics Inc. Most conflict on the covers of romance comics was implied, but this one features a rare cat fight.

first series, ran from # 1 (July 1953) through # 12 (July 1955) and appeared under the imprint of Master Comics. (Some issues of # 1 appear to say # 11, with the same date, so the cover may have been recycled, with # 11 scratched to become # 1.) Story Comics was listed at 7 E. 44th St. in New York in the final issue of the first series; Master was listed virtually next door at 11 E. 44th St. in the first issue of the second series.

Couples embraced in passionate kisses

Until the cat fight cover on second series # 9, the first 18 issues of *Romantic Hearts* all displayed identical themes—couples embraced in passionate kisses, with dismayed rivals for love in the background. Conflict and tension, anyone? By the time of the final issue, # 12 of the second series in 1955, the influence of the Comics Code was clearly felt. The feeling of conflict was set up with a tear-stained woman in the foreground of a television stage, thinking, "He isn't just speaking the words of the script. He means them! He really loves her ... not me!" Meanwhile, a woman in a chaste embrace looks into the eyes of a fellow who says, "Darling! Darling! We were meant for each other. My heart is yours alone."

The four stories in the Code-approved # 12 (July 1955)—"Too Old for My Man!"; "Flight from Love"; "No Love for Me!"; and "Go West for Love!" displayed no leg or lingerie and certainly nothing remotely resembling cleavage. That issue, published under the imprint Merit Comics (connected to Master) was among the last to be seen from that sensationalistic little outfit. Compare those tame titles to the effects portrayed in *Romantic Hearts* # 6 (Feb. 1952) from the first series. The cover promised the thrills of "Love Messed My Life" and "Horror of False Kisses," but the inside four titles were different, if no less sensational: "Love Was My Sin!"; "Glamor Killed My Lover"; "I Gave Away My Love"; and "I Wanted to Die for Lost Love." Nowhere inside was anything involving the suggestive cover image of a cheerleader dropping her megaphone while a muscular basketball player grabs her as a horrified co-ed, dressed in a flaming red blouse with cleavage aplenty, thinks, "That little cheerleader is not as innocent as she looks. I'll get him yet no matter how bad I have to be!!" (Double exclamation points, indeed.) To complete the picture—as if the reader needed further dialog—the hunky hoop hero exclaims, "Being hugged by you is even better than winning the game! !" while the big-busted, short-skirted cheerleader tells him, "You won my kiss, Ray, and I love you so!" Alas, there were no basketball shots or kisses by cheerleaders in any of the stories inside. That was atypical for romance comics, which often boasted a cover theme based on one of the stories inside.

Even before romance comics became more popular with collectors, comic book fans were well aware of the differences between the pre– and post–Code art and story themes, especially with the smaller (and often more daring) companies. For example, *Ideal Romance* # 6 (Oct. 1954), from Key Publications, an imprint of the Stanley P. Morse comic book publisher, needed no word balloons in its depiction of a couple—he with grasping arms and eyes looking directly down toward her cleavage and she with bedroom eyes—about to turn out a lamp. *Ideal Romance* for inexplicable reasons changed from *Tender Romance* # 2 to *Ideal Romance* # 3. Then, with the advent of the Comics Code, issue # 9 became *Diary Confessions* (May 1955). Since cleavage and overt conflict were out, apparently the publisher thought "confessions" might sell more comics than "romance" in the title. In retrospect, it's a little surprising the Comics Code did not ban titles with "confessions" the way it did with "horror" and "terror."

Even well before the Comics Code was created, it was obvious that some publishers were sensitive to the criticism addressed to romance comics, among so many others. When Pix Parade sold *Youthful Romances* to fellow tiny publisher Ribage with # 15 (Jan 1953), cleavage and passion disappeared, to be replaced by wholesome and even humorous images, such a kid brother smiling on the stairway while big sister pulls back from a good night kiss in *Youthful Romances* # 17 (May 1953).

Interestingly, the postal authorities apparently forced the new publisher to buy a separate mailing permit—as the indicia indicates—since *Youthful Romances* became # 5 (Sept. 1953) following # 15–18. Issue # 7 (Feb. 1954) shows a young couple kissing while an older couple passes by, with an overweight "battle-ax" stereotype muttering, "What's come over the young people—kissing right out there in public?" To which her husband replies, "Oh, fiddlesticks, Matilda, we did the same thing when we were young, remember?"

Pre–Code, post–Code and the new rules

The industry's financial troubles, potential response to censorship, and other complications limit a comparison of romance comics and their often racy covers in the pre–1955 period before the coming of the Comics Code with the immediate aftermath on 1955–56 Code-approved issues. Fortunately, however, several companies offer a compelling opportunity for comparisons.

When the Comics Code was enacted in September 1954, by the Comics Magazine Association of America, the more risqué romance comics and their advertisements were distinctly targeted with specific standards, along with the general standards that resulted in the elimination or drastic toning down of the notorious crime and horror titles. Although the majority of romance stories did not deal directly with serious crime (as opposed to, say, a teenager's mistakes such as shoplifting lipstick), the Code effectively eliminated crime plots. Likewise, the slaps and other violence women endured in some comics vanished, such as the sins of many of the Fox issues of 1948–50. "All lurid, unsavory, gruesome illustrations shall be eliminated," read a line in the "General Standards" section. Since that is somewhat subjective, it was left up to editors (first) and censors (second) to determine what was lurid, unsavory or gruesome.

Another general standard also affected some romance stories: "Inclusion of stories dealing with evil shall be used or shall be published only where the intent is to illustrate a moral issue and in no case shall be presented alluringly nor so as to injure the sensibilities of the reader." In other words, stories of "bad boys" and "bad girls" had to be soft-peddled at best.

The Comics Code section on dialogue forbid "profanity, obscenity, smut, vulgarity or words or symbols which have acquired undesirable meanings." Excessive slang was discouraged. In addition, "Special precautions to avoid references to physical afflictions *or* deformities shall be taken."

The remaining two sections of the Comics Code, covering costume and marriage and sex, forced wholesale changes in the emphasis of some romance titles. Other publishers, such as National, were essentially unaffected in the 1954–55 adjustment.

Under "costume," the rules could not have been clearer: "Nudity in any form is prohibited, as is indecent or undue exposure." That's why even something as seemingly innocent in our world today as cleavage almost never shows up in post–Code 1950s comics. "Suggestive or salacious illustration or suggestive posture is unacceptable." No more roll-in-the-hay covers, for example. "All characters shall be depicted in dress reasonably acceptable to society." No more lingerie panels, even when seemingly appropriate. "Females shall be drawn realistically, without any exaggeration of any physical qualities." Breasts consistently became significantly smaller.

Finally, the "marriage and sex" section resulted in thoroughly watered-down stories:

"Divorce shall not be treated humorously nor represented as desirable."

"Illicit sex relations are neither to be hinted at nor portrayed. Violent love scenes as well as sexual abnormalities are unacceptable."

"Respect for parents, the moral code and for honorable behavior shall be fostered. A sympathetic understanding of the problems of love is not a license for morbid distortion."

"The treatment of love-romance stories shall emphasize the value of the home and the sanctity of marriage."

"Passion or romantic interest shall never be treated in such a way as to stimulate the lower and baser emotions."

"Sex perversion or any inference to same is strictly forbidden."

Wertham was merciless in his criticism of the pre–Code romance books. (*Seduction of the Innocent* came out a few months before the Comics Code was created.) "Love comics do harm in the sphere of taste, esthetics, ethics and human relations," he wrote. "The plots are stereotyped, banal, cheap. Whereas in crime comics the situation is boy meets girl, boy beats girl; in love comics it is boy meets girl, boy cheats girl—or vice versa."

Comparing censorship and the lack of it

Nine noteworthy publishers of romance comics survived into the 1955–56 post–Code period with a significant number of comparable issues from those published in 1953–54: National, ACG, Ace, Harvey, Atlas/Marvel, Quality, Crestwood/Prize, Charlton and St. John. A handful of smaller publishers also provide possible comparisons: Gleason, Ajax, Mainline, Toby, Gilmor, Master/Merit and Premier. It's worth noting that, other than a romance one-shot from tiny Sterling, not a single new publisher of romance titles emerged in 1955. For that matter, not a single significant publisher of romance comics appeared throughout the remaining two decades of corporately published love titles.

It's also instructive to count the publishers, both large and small, who discontinued all their romance titles in 1953–54 (and, in some cases, left the comics business entirely): Fawcett, Standard, Star, Avon, Fiction House, Artful/Harwell, Youthful, Ribage, Magazine Enterprises, Hillman, MikeRoss and Orbit (except for one odd single 1955 issue). By the end of 1958, the only publishers of romance remaining were National, Atlas/Marvel, Charlton, AGC, and Crestwood/Prize. Three left the romance market that year—Harvey, Ajax and St. John. Harvey continued to publish dozens of non-romance titles; the other two folded.

From "savage" to "old enough"

The post–Code efforts of Simon & Kirby became tame, considering they tackled so many bold themes in Crestwood's *Young Romance*, the pioneering romance comic in 1947, and *Young Love*. Cover features like "The Savage in Her!" (*Young Romance* # 22, June 1950) were reduced to the likes of "Old Enough to Marry" (*Young Romance* # 80, Dec. 1955–Jan. 1956). Post-Code issues of *Young Romance* featured either idyllic cover images or only a hint of conflict, with disappointed and/or tear-stained women in the background. Occasionally, Simon & Kirby would inject a welcome dose of humor, such as on the cover of *Young Romance* # 92 (Feb.–March 1958), showing a librarian kissing a man checking out a book entitled, "It's Fun Being Single," while a yearning woman in the background holds a volume entitled, "Marriage Is the Thing."

When *Young Romance* and *Young Love* remained bestsellers in the industry in 1952, Crestwood added a third romance title, *Young Brides*. The pre– and post–Code contrast is astounding. The early issues featured the cover themes, "Teen-Age Mother"; "Wait for the Doctor"; "Dear John: I Love Someone Else" and "Under Twenty-One." One of the last pre–Code issues, # 19 (Nov.–Dec. 1954), featured a passionate kiss on a beach. Yet # 22 cover-featured a fully dressed woman darning socks for her adoring (and equally fully dressed) husband on a couch! The last issue, # 30 (Nov.–Dec. 1956), displayed a couple taking time out for a chaste kiss in front of a stroller with twin babies as an elderly couple looked on with approval. Images of such domestic bliss were rarely seen on pre–Code comics, which counted so hard on conflict and controversy for sales.

Oddly, in 1957 Crestwood discontinued *Young Love* and *Young Brides* in favor of the first issues of *All for Love* (which became *Young Love* again in 1960) and *Personal Love* (which became *Going Steady* in 1960). Title changes, at times, were inexplicable.

The Gleason switch

In the pre–Code period, some publishers dramatically shifted their emphasis from relatively innocent covers and stories to suggestive and/or racy themes. One such publisher was Lev Gleason, who was notorious for publishing *Crime Does Not Pay*, the first comic dedicated to realistic crime (as opposed to the more fanciful criminals in *Batman*, for example). The two Gleason romance titles provided stark contrasts in their six-year history.

The first 18 issues of *Boy Meets Girl* featured Norman Rockwell-style covers mixing dreamy girls or couples (romance comics almost never featured only males). Issue # 18 (Dec. 1951) oddly juxtaposed a colorful autumn scene of a sweet young thing on a swing with her boyfriend in the background with the featured story blurb: "Pick-Up in the Park."

Everything changed with *Boy Meets Girl* # 19 (Jan. 1952) with a series of passionate photo covers through # 24 (June 1952). The blurb on the cover of # 19 is a stark departure from the previous 18 issues: "I loved Roger, that I knew, but I couldn't forget Al's dark, dangerous passion, even when Roger held me in his arms." The title? "Morning, Noon and Love." Issue # 20 followed up with this: "I was called THE ONE-KISS GIRL. But when I really fell in love for the first time I broke all the rules."

The title changed to *Boy Loves Girl* with # 25 (July 1952), and it sometimes got much racier. Issue # 28 featured "Phone Call on My Wedding Night," with a girl in bed, in lingerie, talking into a phone: "But Dennis, this is my wedding night! Please, please ... Terry's coming right back! I'll call you later!" Terry, of course, is pictured looking shocked in the doorway. Many publishers, especially National, consistently avoided such extreme suggestiveness, even in pre–Code days, but others apparently couldn't resist the commercial value of sensationalism. That is why love comics in general, even the relatively innocent titles, came in for such harsh criticism along with those with crime, horror and terror themes.

Gleason tried hard for variety in its sensationalism. *Boy Loves Girl* # 30 (Jan. 1953) cover featured the type of period piece collectors love, "Romance at the Roller Derby." Issue # 32 (March 1953) displayed four women's faces with the four themes, "I Couldn't Escape My Past," "I Tried to Cheat Love," "I Paid for My Mistake," and "I Was Tormented By Guilt." Issue # 33 (April 1953) showed a couple in a car-clinch, with the blurb, "I exchanged a few moments of bliss for heartbreak and disgrace!" That's an amazing contrast to the issues of two years earlier.

Once the Comics Code Authority entered the scene, however, Lev Gleason could not have made a more dramatic about-face. The last seven issues of *Boy Loves Girl*, # 51–57 in

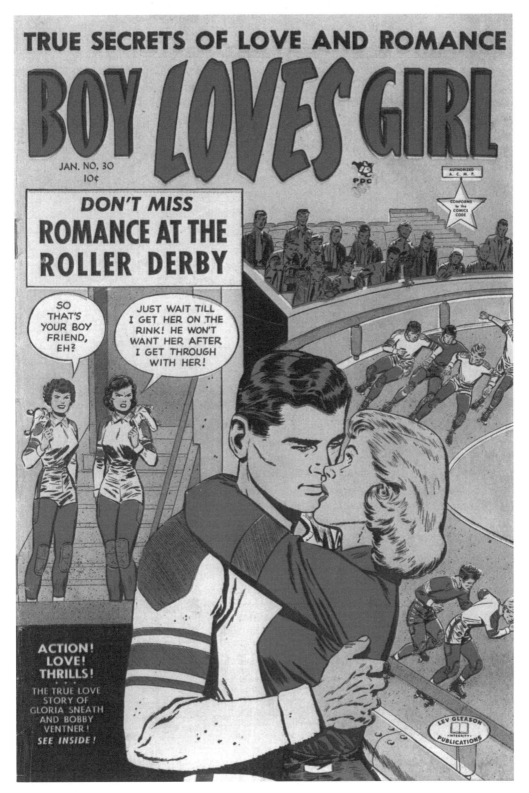

Boy Loves Girl # 30, Jan. 1953, copyright Lev Gleason Publications, Inc. "Romance at the Roller Derby" featured physical conflict between females—something not generally allowed when the Comics Code took effect two years later.

1955–56, featured happy couples except for the tear-stained face in the foreground on # 57 (June 1956), shortly before the company stopped publishing comics. The only excitement reflected by the cover of # 56 (Feb. 1956) was the blurb at the top of the cover, "More exciting than a movie ... more thrilling than T.V." Which more or less summed up many of the problems comics were then enduring, since most of them clearly were neither more exciting than a movie nor more thrilling than television to the younger generation.

Lovers' Lane, the cleverly titled Gleason companion title, for some reason didn't make it beyond # 41 (June 1954). *Lovers' Lane* followed the same sweet-sour pattern of *Boy Meets Girl*. *Lovers' Lane* # 19 (Dec. 1951) featured the odd juxtaposition of a smiling couple on the dance floor with the feature blurb, "Three Wrong Guys—And a Girl Who Tried to Be Good." Issue # 23 (April 1952) went it one better (or one worse): "I Was No Angel—I had a confession to make to the man I was going to *marry*—and I was scared to death!" Then there was this title featured on # 28 (Sept. 1952): "Shabby Angel—The Story of a Bad Girl...." The three dots may have gone over the heads of younger readers, but ...!

A classic case study in censorship

Diary Confessions # 12 (Nov. 1955), a scarce issue from tiny Stanmor near the end of the small company's run in comic books, provides a fascinating study in Comics Code reprint mandates. The story entitled, "Skin Deep!" is a quirky five-page human-interest tale about how a homely girl and a blind man find love. "Skin Deep," however, was reprinted from Stanmor's pre–Code issue of *Tender Romance* # 2 (Feb. 1954), when the story was titled, "Ugly" in inch-high letters. "Ugly" was signed by artist Sal Trapani. That alone was unusual—most Stanmor stories were not signed. Yet in the "Skin Deep" reprint, the box with Trapani's signature was removed.

The splash page of "Ugly" shows homely Belinda Sauer (even the name is not attractive) sobbing on the school steps because she overhears one varsity letterman telling another, "That beast! I'd rather go stag than be seen with her!" In the reprint version, the words "that beast" have been eliminated. There is no other change in either lettering or art, until after Belinda has met a blind soldier named Ken and they inevitably kiss on the fourth page. Then we see how the Comics Code really worked. This part of a sentence was eliminated in the cutline above the panel in which they first kiss: "and the fires of passion were consuming my very being!"

Post-Code teen girls, obviously, were not to be "consumed" by reading about "the fires of passion." The story ends as Ken is predictably cured of his blindness, yet still loves Belinda for who she really is.

Not so Superior

Other than Dell Comics and Classics Illustrated (Gilberton), only one publisher escaped the purge of the Comics Code. This was not for long, however, though whether romance comics had much to do with the fate of Superior Publishers is uncertain. Superior, a small Canadian publisher of comics sold in the United States from 1948 to 1956, was an unusual publisher, producing comics in Canada and routinely also selling them in the United States. Except for the sharp-eyed readers who saw "printed in Canada" in the indicia, probably few readers even suspected any differences.

There was one other difference: Superior did not subscribe to the Comics Code, a decision that ultimately may have forced the company's product off the stands. The last issues of

Secret Romances # 27 (July 1955) and *G.I. War Brides* # 8 (June 1955) appeared shortly after the Code took effect. But the remaining Superior romance title, *My Secret Marriage*, actually went monthly for a few issues with # 14 (July 1955), the same month *Secret Romances* expired. *My Secret Marriage* ran through # 24 (July 1956), leaving odd little Superior with only one title: the inexplicable *U.S. Fighting Air Force*, published by Canadians! That peculiar title ran 10 monthly issues in 1956 before abruptly expiring with # 29 in October.

Superior's use of Iger shop art meant production values were sometimes adequate, if seldom more than that, although some collectors would call that being kind. Superior's covers, though, were among the dullest and poorest in the industry. Many covers looked like the product of a mediocre high school artist with a heavy, muddy inking style. The effects of the Comics Code showed on the covers, however. If anything, they got worse artistically and certainly duller and drabber. Before the Code, Superior seemed to specialize in suggestive covers portraying men leering at women who acted as though they liked being leered at.

Superior's 1955–56 interiors, in contrast, were the only romance comics in the post–Code era still loaded with lingerie and cleavage. Most stories had happy endings, though there were exceptions—unusual in the post–Code period. "My Greedy Heart" in *My Secret Marriage* # 24 (July 1956), the last Superior romance issue, ended with the selfish protagonist thinking in shock, "I've never really loved anybody ... I'm just a faker, through and through ... but that's all over, now! I've learned my lesson! I'll make it up ... this is a new girl from now on! I want to be loved, too ... and I see, now, you have to be worthy of it or it will never happen!"

Superior Comics tended to have benign advertisers, unlike the often worrisome "girls' products" in many other pre–Code romance comics (more on this soon). But later issues of the romance titles featured one of the most unusual back cover ads ever seen on a love comic: a pitch for a $4.98 "Novena Rosary Cross of the Seven Sorrows." The address of the company selling them was located in the same Toronto building as Superior Comics!

At ACG, from calm to crazed to calm

The small but sturdy American Comics Group produced its usual quota of unorthodox stories for its two long-running love titles, *My Romantic Adventures* and *Confessions of the Lovelorn* (originally *Romantic Adventures* and *Lovelorn*). There was often more characterization, albeit with a tongue-in-cheek feel much of the time, in ACG stories than in other publishers' work, but ACG tales also featured some of the most complex plots in the industry.

Most of the pre–Code covers tended to be clean-cut images of either dreamy romance, mild conflict between rivals, or clever sight gags. For example, the cover of *Romantic Adventures* # 21 (May 1952) featured a couple kissing in front of a television set with a couple in the same clinch on the screen. Issue # 28 (Dec. 1952) showed two marionettes "kissing" of front of a couple smooching. The first 48 issues were very much in that mold until a sudden, shocking switch in emphasis, heralded by top-of-the-cover theme changing from "The Magazine of Youth and Love!" to "True Love Confessions!"

When the title became *My Romantic Adventures* with # 49 (Sept. 1954), the cover feature was "Jailbird's Romance," displaying a distressed, big-breasted blonde in handcuffs in front of a judge, who tells her, "You dare talk about love—with the killer's brand on you for all the world to see?" The blurb read, "Has a murderess a heart? Read the bombshell answer in 'Jailbird's Romance' ... the most sensational confession of outlaw love ever published!"

This would never have passed the soon-to-be-imposed Comics Code. But the next issue was even more shocking, considering how tame this title had been for so long. The cover feature of # 50 was "Love of a Lunatic," with a yellow-tinged female lunatic's face screaming and withered hands clutching bars. The blurb: "The most amazing confession you've ever read! Love of a Lunatic ... the true story of a woman's anguish!" Below that, a flashback of the same woman telling her man, "How can I tell him that ... I'm going insane?" But this stunning shift in emphasis lasted only these two issues. Featured titles in *My Romantic Adventures* soon reverted to the milder likes of "The Time of My Life!" and "Romance and Racquets."

The grim "Jailbird's Romance"

"Jailbird's Romance," a fully developed 12-page story, is one of the grimmest little epics ever to appear in a romance comic. It could just as well have appeared in one of the goriest crime titles. Angel Morelli, the protagonist of the piece, is bad to the bone from childhood on. She seems to find love and redemption, only to be blackmailed and framed by a former gang partner, whom she shoots just before she goes insane at the end. "Thank heavens I found out what she was in time, or that—that might have been me!" says her erstwhile, clean-cut lover as Angel stands over the body of the baddie. This entire story, nicely illustrated by ACG mainstay Ogden Whitney, is amazingly downbeat. It's extremely difficult to imagine that ACG could have intended this for any young reader.

On the other hand, "Love of a Lunatic" is a remarkably sensitive 12-page story, albeit often grimly illustrated by Whitney, dealing with the difference between treatable mental illness and true insanity. "I won't say thanks, Doctor," the heroine says at the end before walking out with the love of her life, "just God bless you!" after he tells her, "Your guy's waiting outside!" The contrast between "Jailbird's Romance" and "Love of a Lunatic" is stunning, considering they ran in consecutive issues. Oddly—and maybe not so oddly after all—in the middle of "Love of a Lunatic" is a full-page advertisement for the book, *The Marilyn Monroe Story*, with "The Intimate Inside Story of Hollywood's Hottest Glamour Girl" along with "39 gorgeous, intimate, wow! photos." One can only imagine the consternation of a parent whose 13-year-old daughter (or son!) mailed off $2 for that book.

ACC's brief emphasis on shock was obviously deliberate, for the same policy existed concurrently with *Lovelorn*. When the title changed to *Confessions of the Lovelorn* with # 52 (Aug. 1954), the featured story was "I Sold My Baby," complete with gossiping faces and taunting fingers pointed at an anguished young mother with an infant in her arms in something of a parody of Norman Rockwell's happier themes. *Confessions of the Lovelorn* followed with three more issues in this vein, featuring "Heart of a Drunkard" in # 53, followed by the slightly less sensational "The Wrong Side of the Tracks" in # 54 and "I Take What I Want" in # 55. Soon, though, the title returned to Code-approved stories such as "The Man in My Past" and "My Own Heart."

"Heart of a Drunkard," showing a disheveled woman drinking alone in a bar, certainly ranks with the most disturbing images of the pre–Code period. The young woman did recover to find happiness in the 13-page story, and it is indeed a tad more sensational on the cover, like the others, but it's still a story that would have been flatly rejected by the Comics Code. Why ACG made this brief shift to the extreme will forever be a mystery, especially since some publishers already were reining in their more sensational elements in the wake of the firestorm engendered by Wertham's *Seduction of the Innocent*. It's somewhat unsettling to realize that these 1954 ACG sensations and Wertham's screed were being sold at the same time. Stories like "Heart of a Drunkard" surely convinced legions of parents, teachers and other comics critics that Wertham was onto something meaningful.

ACG's brief flirtation with grim, sensationalistic stories remains one of the great mysteries of comic book history. Economics may have had something to do with it, for the Comics

My Romantic Adventures # 49, Sept. 1954, copyright Best Syndicated Features, Inc. Ogden Whitney captures the spirit of the highly unusual "Jailbird's Romance"—a story that would not have been possible a few months later under the new Comics Code Authority.

Confessions of the Lovelorn # 53, Sept.-Oct. 1954, copyright Regis Publications, Inc. "Heart of a Drunkard" was an unusual story to come from ACG, which quickly returned to tamer fare.

Code was about to result in the elimination and/or conversion of the company's horror comics into gentler fantasy/science fiction fare.

Quantity from Quality

Quality Comics, best known for publishing *Blackhawk* and *Plastic Man* from the early 1940s until the company left comics at the end of 1956, led the industry in romance issues produced in the years immediately before and after the Comics Code. Whatever the commercial effects of the code, it was difficult to say with Quality, since the company published eight titles covering 49 issues in 1954 and eight titles covering 52 issues in 1955. Quality did convert *G.I. Sweethearts* to *Girls in Love* and changed *True War Romances* to *Exotic Romances* in 1955, but that was most likely a commercial decision—the fighting in Korea ended nearly two years before the change.

In both 1954 and 1955, Quality surely led the industry in tears per female on the covers. The company stressed emotion out front and in the stories, too. The stories tended to the nonsensational and driven by conflicts in relationships. When reprints were used in 1955–56, lingerie and cleavage in early stories tended to be the primary problems for the artists who did touch-up work.

In the 12-issue run of *Girls in Love* in 1955–56 (# 46–57), either tears or a shocked face were featured on 11 of the covers, so inner turmoil was the hook. Even the cover of # 56 (Oct. 1956) was a study in tension in the featured "High School Crush." A smiling, handsome young teacher reads in front of a star-struck girl who looks up thinking, "Oh! Mr. Dryden is so handsome! I don't care if Chuck is jealous ... I love Eliot Dryden and I think he likes me!" Meanwhile, Chuck looks on with balled-up fists and dismayed expression.

The ending of "High School Crush" is astonishing, following a fistfight at a dance between Eliot and Chuck. The school principal discharges the hunky teacher but his job is saved by Julia's admission that she was the cause, having forced her attentions on the instructor. "Oh, I see!" the principal says. "In that case, let's forget the whole thing! Run along, young lady ... and take your football hero with you!" But Julia tells Chuck she doesn't love him, and Eliot shows up to thank her, then says, "If you don't mind marrying an old man of twenty-four when you graduate school, I'll be waiting!" And as she falls into his arms, Chuck turns to the reader and says, "Whaddya know! Looks like you'll be getting two official documents soon ... a graduation diploma and a wedding license!"

It's hard to tell what's more ridiculous—the redundant phrase "graduation diploma" or the principal's acceptance of a teacher fighting with a student for any reason. And even though he quickly acknowledged it was wrong, three pages earlier Eliot briefly kissed Julia, unable to resist her approach. The principal apparently never did find out about that! The censors were looking for lingerie, not logic.

Interchangeable titles

Quality's eight post–Code titles were virtually interchangeable, even though titles like *Wedding Bells* and *True War Romances* hinted at themes. Perhaps, then, the lone romance title DC picked up along with *Blackhawk* and two other adventure titles was chosen for its name—*Heart Throbs*. This title, which was Quality's first romance comic, had cleaned up its act well in advance of the coming of the Comics Code, as the titles on # 26 (Jan. 1954) clearly show: "Unwanted Love," "Almost a Bride Twice," "Kissless Partner," and "Nothing But a Memory."

Unlike some romance publishers, Quality seldom used exclamation points in its titles, leaving those to publishers with a bent for the artificially dramatic. For the most part, pre–Code and post–Code Quality are pretty much the same.

Quality ran "I Was Too Tall" in *Heart Throbs* # 31 (Nov. 1954) and followed a year later in # 38 (Dec. 1955) with "Tearful Dates," which could have been entitled, "I Was Too Short." The Comics Code, with its stress on avoiding pointing out physical imperfections, may have preferred the "Tearful" title. But then, Quality simply wanted to avoid repeating the title in reverse. Both stories ended with the women realizing that being tall and short didn't matter to the men they loved; in fact, the fellow at the end of "Tearful Dates" took the girl home to meet his height-challenged mother!

A similar story ran in *Love Confessions* # 37 (June 1954) entitled, "I Was the Homely Sister." This title likely wouldn't have been seen after the Comics Code arrived, yet the way the girl was drawn, she was far from homely. She wasn't as glamorous, but she was quite attractive, so perhaps "homely" was used in a more generic way. The story itself would have had no problem with the Comics Code, but the word "homely" probably wouldn't have been allowed.

Chances are, if you thought up virtually every romantic complication you could, Quality published a story dealing with the situation. It's no wonder Quality published 358 romance comics in a little more than seven years. By the end of this outstanding company's run in 1956, only Marvel had published more.

Marvel romance: heavy on beauty and dreams

Marvel publisher Martin Goodman's output rivaled Quality for the bulk of its romance comic production in the years immediately following the establishment of the Comics Code. The difference was that Marvel, unlike Quality, did not depend nearly as heavily on the romance genre for commercial success.

Marvel, using the familiar Atlas imprint in the upper left-hand corner, led the industry with 389 issues of all genres in 1955 and 431 in 1956, a record total over any two-year period in the first 50 years of comics publishing. This covered close to 100 different titles in those two years—some short-lived, such as *Meet Miss Bliss*, and others long-established, such as *Marvel Tales*. The total number of romance comics—not counting humorous titles such as *Patsy Walker* and *Meet Miss Bliss*—in those two years was 99 issues, or slightly less than one-eighth of the company's output. When the Atlas distribution company fiasco resulted in Marvel's implosion in 1957, editor Stan Lee used primarily inventory material in 1958 for the long-running *My Own Romance* and *Love Romances*.

Pre–Code Marvel romance titles in the 1952–54 period, following the turmoil endured at the company in 1950, tended to be similar to National's, confining with often nicely illustrated stories by now established pros like Jay Scott Pike, Chris Rule, Morris Weiss and Vince Colletta. These stories were usually long on mild conflict, albeit with contrived touches such as auto accidents, and short on sensationalism. Most of the stories could have been reprinted in post–Code issues with only minor touchups. Even the titles often fell short on titillation. For example, *My Romance* # 24 (Sept. 1952) offered "Be Still My Heart," "Dangerous Kisses," "A Man for Amy," "My Lost Love," "Overanxious" and "Two Men Love Joan!"

There was virtually no difference between the pre–Code issues of *My Own Romance* # 41 (Dec. 1954) and # 42 (Feb. 1955) and the post–Code # 44 (June 1955) and # 45 (Aug. 1955). All four titles were sheer romance, albeit with a hint of conflict as another woman looks on in # 41, and the titles were interchangeable. Like most Marvel titles, the stories tended to be short—four or five per issue—with a tight focus on plot developments.

Post–Code Marvel romance comics had an endearing quality of generic love about them. What kept them from being as repetitive as those from Quality, Harvey and Ace was the variety of art. Marvel titles seem to offer more kisses per panel and/or cover than romance issues from other companies. *My Own Romance* # 47 (Oct. 1955) epitomizes the company's output: "With Open Arms!"; "My Own True Love!"; "My Dearly Beloved!" and "The Night We Kissed!" And on the cover, of course, a tender kiss.

In a development that doubtless frustrated many of the artists, post–Code bathing suit scenes at Marvel, like most publishers, had to avoid almost any hint of cleavage. The beach-kiss, hot-dog-roast cover for *My Own Romance* # 45 showed no cleavage even though the girl was wearing a low-cut bathing suit and clearly was full-busted.

The uncensored Frank Frazetta

The iconic artist Frank Frazetta was represented in romance comics with seven stories published in *Personal Love* # 24–25, 27–28 and 32 from Eastern in 1953–55 (not to be confused with the later title of the same name from Crestwood) and sister title *Movie Love* # 8 and 10 in 1951. Eastern lasted only briefly into the post–Comics Code period, and these stories were not reprinted (at least in color) until Fantagraphics Books unearthed four of them in a 1987 one-shot comic book, "Frank Frazetta's Untamed Love," named after the title of one the stories.

Frazetta, so well known for his images of Conan, Tarzan and the like beginning in the 1960s, worked in a variety of comic book genres in the 1940s and the first half of the 1950s, but did no other work in the romance genre.

One of the stories reprinted, the seven-page "Too Late for Love" from *Personal Love* # 25 (Jan. 1954), was a marvelous tribute to 1950s pinup queen Bettie Page. The other reprints were entitled "The Wrong Road," "Empty Heart" and "Untamed Love." Even before the Fantagraphics reprint was published, Frazetta enthusiasts were well aware of his body of work. Fans had long sought out these romance issues from Eastern, along with his series of eight classic Buck Rogers covers for *Famous Funnies* # 209–216 in 1953–55.

The Fantagraphics reprint issue was the first time many collectors had a chance to see and savor Frazetta's romance imagery. "Breathtaking" only begins to do his lush work justice, and it's fortunate that the Comics Code never had a chance to ruin any reprints of these stories (although his last story, in *Personal Love* # 32, was in the first Code-approved issue). For an enthusiast, to imagine Frazetta's work being spoiled is not a pleasant thought. No one can imagine "Cut that cleavage!" could ever be applied with any justice to Frank Frazetta!

Interestingly, Fantagraphics provided no biographical information and no hint of where these four Frazetta stories came from. Frazetta was such an icon that it may not have been deemed necessary. Fantagraphics did sneak in one witty comment about the romance genre in the copyright notice in the indicia: "Any similarity between names, characters, persons, institutions and emotions in Frank Frazetta's *Untamed Love* # 1 and those of any real persons, institutions and emotions is purely coincidental."

The fadeout of a fine company

St. John was among the solid second-tier outfits in the pre–Code period, but the firm was doing a slow fadeout in the mid–1950s, especially following a disastrous flirtation with the failed 3-D format. St. John produced 30 romance issues in 1954 but only 17 in 1955, the year publisher Archer St. John died. Yet the firm provides one of the better comparisons of pre– and post–Code covers and story titles.

An index provided by St. John authority John Benson, with artist identification by Jim Vadeboncoeur, Jr., shows that of the 17 romance issues in 1955, including the post–Code issues, the highly collectible artist Matt Baker continued to produce original covers for every issue of the firm's four titles that year: *Cinderella Love, Diary Secrets, Going Steady* and *Teen-Age Romances*. All four titles were cancelled late in the year. All 17 issues used either material produced originally by Ziff-Davis, for which St. John had purchased the rights, or reprint material from pre–Code St. John issues. The reprints of pre–Code material in post–Code books are among the most instructive in the industry from the standpoint of studying censorship, or rather the lack of it.

Baker's post–Code covers from 1955 are consistently upbeat and pleasant images of romance, with no hint of the more naturalistic and sometimes controversial Baker cover art from the pre–Code period. Even one of the established titles, *Teen-Age Temptations* # 9 (Aug. 1954), was changed to the far less suggestive *Going Steady* # 10 (Dec. 1954), even before the Comics Code stamp appeared.

Some of the cover-feature blurbs in 1953 and 1954 issues of *Diary Secrets* likely would not have been allowed by the Comics Code, including "Did I Give My Lips Too Freely" in # 17; "That One Wild Night" in # 22, and "I Wanted Too Much Love" in # 24. In stark contrast, Issues # 26 through # 30 carried only romantic images and no blurbs except for the much tamer "My One Little Mistake" and "I Wouldn't Give Up My Secret Love" in # 30 (Sept. 1955).

All five issues of *Going Steady* (# 10–14) carried no cover blurbs. *Teen-Age Romances*, the company's flagship and among the first few original romance titles, ended with a tame by-the-fireplace cover, with the couple merely holding hands, in # 45 (Dec. 1945). That was St. John's last romance issue except for an abortive three-issue comeback in 1957–58. The cover of # 45 is a stark contrast to the highly suggestive cover of # 38 (July 1954), showing a boy getting into the back seat as a girl says, "There's no room here, Mack.... Go curl up on the front seat and keep the headlights on!" To which he responds, "But we're stalled here for the night ... so let's make the best of it!" This was similar to the cover of # 33 (Sept. 1953), in which a baseball player in uniform tells a girl, "Everything's fixed, honey! We leave after the game." She responds, "All ... all right, I told Mother I was spending the night with Mary." Such dialog would never have been allowed by the Comics Code.

Teen-Age Romances # 44 (Aug. 1955), a Code-approved issue, reprinted four stories from the pre–Code # 25 (Sept. 1952), providing an example of changes. Two of the titles were changed from "I Was a Child Bride" to "I Had to Live and Learn," and from "Too Loose to Love" to "Love Came Last." On the other hand, "Discarded Sweethearts Are an Easy Mark!" and "Kid Sister" went unchanged. The dialog in "Child Bride," a tale about how a woman learns responsibility to her child following an auto accident, was generally approved, but low-cut dresses were modified.

In # 43 (May 1955), the first code-approved issue of *Teen-Age Romances*, the stories were reprinted from *Teen-Age Romances* # 6 (Oct. 1949), though the titles were originally changed in 1952 for *Diary Secrets* # 14. "It Doesn't Pay to Steal Kisses" became "Foolhardy and Headstrong." "Rx for a Broken Heart" emerged as "Breaking All the Rules." "Was I a Fool to Go on Loving Him?" was changed to "Love Challenge." "I Lived a Lie!" became "The Risk I Had to Take." It's interesting to note, however, that Baker's tasteful art and Dana Dutch's realistic writing required virtually no adjustments by Code personnel.

In the Code-approved *Going Steady* # 14 (Oct. 1955), "Blinded by My Ideals" originally appeared as "I Gave Romance the Run–Around" in *Teen-Age Romances* # 10 (June 1950). "Unfair to My Boyfriend" was originally "I Betrayed My Sweetheart" in *Teen-Age Romances*

Teen-Age Romances # 42, May 1955, copyright St. John Publishing Corp. Matt Bakes makes creative use of a blackboard theme in the early post–Comics Code period.

Teen-Age Romances # 38, July 1954, copyright St. John Publishing Corp. Matt Baker draws a highly suggestive cover in the last days before the Comics Code arrived.

19 (Dec. 1951). "Love's Worst Enemy—Suspicion" had been "Pitfalls of Jealousy" in *Teen-Age Romances* # 21 (April 1952).

None of the stories in the nine-issue pre–Code run of *Teen-Age Temptations* were reprinted, although a few were reprints themselves. Since they all appeared in 1952–54, they may have been considered too recent to reprint. Benson says most St. John's title changes stemmed merely from a desire to avoid repeat titles. Many of the story titles surely would have been changed, such as "They Branded Me Immoral," "I Married a Bigamist," "The Price of Sinful Dates" and "I Tempted the Wrong Boy." "I Married a Bigamist" in # 7 (April 1954) told of a woman's acceptance by her husband, Fred, even after he learns she had been inadvertently married to a bigamist, Hal. Fred shoves the smarmy bigamist in the face and turns toward her with acceptance. There was a line of her thought process after she left the bigamist, shocking for the day, that the Comics Code would have strictly forbidden: "What if I were to have a baby ... Hal's baby! Then I'd never be able to hide the truth of that night!"

St. John was well aware of the dangers of quickly outdated material. None of the stories in the 18-issue run of *Wartime Romances* were reprinted except for content in # 1 (July 1951), which reappeared in two 1954 pre–Code issues. The best material available on St. John is by Benson in *Romance Without Tears*, a book of reprints of Dana Dutch's stories, mostly illustrated by Matt Baker, with a perceptive essay on Dutch, whose contribution to realistic romance writing was unmatched in comic book history. Benson followed with an informative companion book on St. John, the highly recommended *Confessions, Romances, Secrets and Temptations* (2007).

Photo covers before and after the Comics Code

Only one comic book publisher, Ace, used photo covers to any extent on romance issues in the first two post–Code years. That gave comics from Ace a unique look, especially for new readers who weren't accustomed to the heavy use of photo covers in the early years of the genre. More than any other publisher, Ace depended on romance in the immediate aftermath of the Comics Code. Of the 80 issues released by Ace in 1955–56, 63 were devoted to romance, with six bi-monthly titles. Each issue had a photo cover, almost all featuring couples, with virtually no difference between pre–Code and post–Code styles. Most Ace romance comics featured four short stories, similar but not as good as St. John's style of plot-driven, relationship-oriented stories long on emotions and short on contrived heroics, such as rescues or fights. The interior art, usually unsigned, was usually at least of journeyman quality.

For the most part, Ace used either line-drawn covers or nicely painted versions for its 1949–52 issues before switching to photo covers. It seems likely the switch was done to avoid paying cover artists. Indeed, many of the painted covers may have been reprinted from the publisher's 1940s love pulps—another way to save money.

Little Dot, Little Audrey *and lots of love*

Following the imposition of the Comics Code, one top-tier publisher in particular focused on the market for the youngest children. Parents of the mid–1950s soon teamed to look not only for the clean entertainment provided by Dell and National, but to Harvey as well, especially for stories of little kids and equally little ghosts and goblins, such as *Little Dot, Little Audrey, Richie Rich, Casper the Friendly Ghost, Spooky* and *Hot Stuff.* Harvey, though, also published a few of the more bizarre horror titles, such as *Witches' Tales* and *Black Cat Mystery,* in pre–Code days along with five long-running romance titles in both the pre– and post–Code periods. Unlike most publishers, Harvey's romance titles tried to provide thematic distinction— *First Love* and *First Romance, Hi-School Romance, True Love Problems and Advice,* and *True Brides' Experiences* (plus a couple of variations of that title). Harvey's cover style was almost entirely line drawn, although often in somewhat sketchy or basic styles, especially in the post–Code period.

First Love was Harvey's flagship title and the sixth romance title to begin overall, with # 1 in February 1949. The title ran 88 issues through 1958, plus # 89 and # 90 in 1962–63. *First Love* began innocently enough, but the title soon featured racy themes. Issue # 12 (May 1951) heralded this change with a cover featuring a half-naked showgirl (and her boyfriend hiding behind a curtain) confronting a modestly attired redhead. The clean-cut miss pleads, "Please— he's here—I know he's here—he means nothing to a floozie like you—he's too young, too inno-cent—" To which the alluring floozy responds, "Get out! You silly little girl!" The story title fits: "I Lost My Pride!" The featured story, however, is not included inside the comic book!

This Harvey stuff most definitely was not clean-cut material a la National and ACG. Nor were editing standards high. Issue # 12 opens with a splash of a vicious looking fellow with his arm around a girl's neck near the edge of a cliff. The title: "I Had to Run Away." No such scene, however, appears in a little epic dealing with the rescue of the girl by her father and her bitter recriminations. The second story in the issue, "Hasty Wedding," ends with a girl ask-ing the reader about her future after she marries the "wrong" brother. In her query to the reader, the girl says, "And that is the dilemna [*sic*] I face." So much for a love of spelling.

First Love # 13 was an astounding contrast to many of the cleaner romance comics on the stands. There's a roll-in-the-hay cover, complete with the fellow's arms clinched just south of a blonde's large breasts. Inside were titles such as "Confessions of a Runaway!" and "I Joined a Teen-Age Sex Club!" "Runaway" ends with a happy marriage, a baby and a reconciliation with the girl's parents; "Sex Club" finishes with a former member in the arms of the reporter who exposed the club. Two other tales, "Torment" and "Robbed of Love," end with sad-eyed girls who have learned the lessons of love the hard way.

It's no wonder that for *Seduction of the Innocent,* author Fredric Wertham used a particu-larly violent panel of a father slapping his daughter in "Forbidden to Love Him" in *First Love* # 35 (Dec. 1953), Not that this particular image can be defended, but what Wertham did not say was that the story ends with the young man winning the Medal of Honor winner for mil-itary duty and her parents acknowledging they were wrong as the young couple offer a prayer during their marriage "for the right of all men, everywhere, regardless of race, creed or color, to live—and love—in peace!" This story's unusual hook: the girl had fallen in love with an "Indian" (today referred to as a Native American) and her parents were horrified. The mother's racist reaction: "My own daughter and a heathen Injun."

Jim Vadeboncoeur, Jr., has done research that indicates almost all of Harvey's post–Code mate-rial seems to be reprints, including many seemingly controversial pre–Code stories. Plenty of touchup work was done, however, to accommodate the Comics Code. "Forbidden to Love Him" was reprinted in *First Love* # 68 (Sept. 1956), less than three years after it first appeared. The title wasn't changed, but the infamous slapping panel was redrawn to make it seem as though the father-daughter confrontation was merely verbal. In the previous panel, the father's comment, "Make bargains with us, will you! Offer us deals like some ... some squaw!" became in the reprint, "Susan, why must you be so obstinate'?" And in the slapping panel, the father's "I'll teach you! I'll teach you to do as you're told!" became merely, "I'm sorry, Susan—but that's the way I feel!" On the same page, the mother's comment about a "heathen Injun" became just "heathen." In those same two issues, the other titles in # 35—"Desire Me," "Weak With Wanting" and "Kisses for Sale"—became in # 68 "My Heart's Desire," "Love Was Found Wanting" and "Your Kiss."

First Love # 13, July 1951, copyright Harvey Features Syndicate. "I Joined a Teen-Age Sex Club!" was typical of many pre–Comics Code stories, though its title was racier than most.

Sometimes, the introductory blurbs in the pre–Code versions were simply dropped entirely, such as this example from *Hi-School Romance* # 19 (Feb. 1953): "A girl has to go a long way—do a lot of things sometimes—to get the things she wants! And I wanted success more than anything else in the world! But one day the ugly truth caught up to me, and I knew I WENT TOO FAR!" In the reprint in # 43 (Sept. 1955), everything is replaced by blank white space and the story is retitled, "Broadway Lights." In the same story, two of the panels are merely replaced by a blob of black with a rewritten caption! On the same page, a caption with phrases such as "the cheap thrills I had substituted for abiding love" became blank space. In the same issue, the title, "Treacherous Kisses," was retained but the blurb beginning "caught in the trap of a scandalous love, I struggled to regain my self-respect, to free myself from the lure of passion!" likewise became blank space. And even when a title and caption were deemed OK for the reprint, in "Hidden Heartbreak," the cleavage of a girl in a low-cut gown in the splash panel was eliminated in the touchup. Whether dealing with titles, blurbs, wood balloons, *or art,* there was often work ordered by the Comics Code censors!

Criticism of sensationalistic romance themes may even have convinced Harvey to change the title of *Teen-Age Brides* to *True Brides Experiences* with # 8 (Oct. 1954), even before the Comics Code took effect. The title soon became *True Bride-to-Be Romances,* with happy-couple cover images for the most part. Likewise, *True Love Problems and Advice* became *Romance Stories of True Love* with # 45 (May 1957).

In the first few years of *Hi-School Romance*'s run, the title often featured covers of guys and gals who looked nothing like typical high school students, in much the same way late 1950s films about juvenile delinquents often starred actors in their 20s. Later, the title began to live up to its name with stories like "Second-String Sweetheart" in # 34 (Dec. 1954). It's a high-school football epic in which the girl takes up with a no-goodnik player who gets booted off the team. As the good-guy football player who does love her says after she confesses her shame and says she feels small, "No, you're big in your honesty! Rick's got to learn that he isn't the center of the world, and you—you, Ann, have to learn that I love you!"

Even something as innocent as a girl playfully poking one leg in the air while talking with her boyfriend on the phone in her bed—the leg was bare to mid-thigh—was redrawn to show both legs clothed and clamped together on the bed! The original panel was in *First Love* # 27 (April 1953) and the revision was in # 61 (Feb. 1956), which "reprinted" all four stories in # 27. In the story, "Sinful Surrender," the introductory blurb read, "Don's battling fists meant a free ticket to a gold-plated world—his strong arms brought security and fame! But suddenly I was caught in a stranglehold of passion that ruined everything! I was trapped by the guilt of my Sinful Surrender!" In # 61, this story became "Foolish Dream" and the blurb was altered to read, "Don was the only man I ever loved ... his strong arms were security and happiness to me. Was I wrong to love him? Was it all a Foolish Dream?"

All in all, there were hundreds of changes in the post–Code Harvey romance comics, and collectors have long enjoyed making the comparisons. Yet wholesale touchups of stories only a few years old were still apparently better than paying for entirely new stories. Interestingly, about the time the Comics Code came along, Harvey took its logo off the covers and used a heart with "true love" in the upper left-hand corner. "Harvey Famous Name Comics," as they often advertised, apparently wasn't proud of publishing even Code-approved romance comics.

Comic book advertisements: the problem of "problem bosoms"

Dr. Fredric Wertham was so concerned about situations resulting from advertisements in comic books that he devoted a chapter in *Seduction of the Innocent* to what he considered the

First Love #27, April 1953, copyright Harvey Features Syndicate. This pre–Comics Code boxing story is entitled, "Sinful Surrender."

First Love # 61, Feb. 1956, copyright Harvey Features Syndicate. The post–Comics Code reprint of "Sinful Surrender" emerged as "Foolish Dream."

commercial exploitation of children. Part of the chapter dealt specifically with ads common in certain publishers' romance comics before the advent of the Comics Code in 1954, which was established several months after the publication of *Seduction*.

Wertham has been roundly castigated for faulty cause-and-effect analysis in his book, but his points about advertising, especially ads directed to girls in the romance comics, weren't nearly as far off the mark—and sometimes not at all. He wrote:

They [comic books] play up these very words [such as "problems"] which should be avoided. Advertising people tell me that in the profession this is called the "emotional appeal." And that is precisely what it is—ruthlessly playing on the emotions of children. They ask children whether they are not "self-conscious" about one minor or fancied ailment or another, thereby, of course, deliberately *making* them self-conscious or unhappy. They [the comic book ads] promise to help [children] if they are ashamed about some little, or perhaps even non-existent, blemish, thereby, of course, causing them to feel unnecessarily ashamed. They frighten the girls by insinuating to them that they have "problem bosoms." This phrase alone thrown at twelve- or thirteen-year-old girls is enough to precipitate a severe and distressing hypochon-driacal reaction. No wonder [children] are willing to spend money on all sorts of pills, ointments and gadgets!

The Comics Magazine Association of America, in establishing the initial set of rules for the Comics Code previously referred to in this chapter, included "a code for advertising matter."

"Good taste shall be the guiding the principle in the acceptance of advertising" was the catch-all guideline, followed by several explicit prohibitions. With regard to romance comics, three of the points were directly salient: "Advertisement of sex or sex instruction books are [*sic*] unacceptable." "Nudity with meretricious purpose and salacious posture shall not be permitted in the advertising of any product. Clothed figures shall never be presented in such a way as to be offensive or contrary to good taste or morals"; and "Advertisement of medical, health or toiletry products of questionable nature are [*sic*] to be rejected. Advertisement of medical, healthy or toiletry products endorsed by the American Medical Association, or the American Dental Association, shall be deemed acceptable if they conform with all other conditions of the Advertising Code."

Wertham cited numerous advertisements he considered especially offensive to adolescent girls, especially those involving concern for their breast size or shape, their weight, or their skin condition. The ads he saw came from comics published before 1954. But how prevalent were these ads in issues published with 1954 dates? How much effort did publishers make to avoid running ads that clearly could hurt—or at least fail to help—the concerns of the girls who read romance comics?

Let's take a look at both 1954 and 1955, before and after the Comics Code, and see how the various companies handled the situation. Some companies, such as National, eliminated these ads entirely. Others generally did a good job of policing the worst of these ads.

Minor publishers, major offenses

In *Romantic Hearts* # 4 (Jan. 1954) from minor publisher Master Comics, a weight reduction plan using chewing gum is advertised! "This wholesome, tasty delicious Kelpidine Chewing Gum contains Hexitol, reduces appetite and is sugar free. Hexitol is a new discovery and contains no fat and no carbohydrates." This type of ad for mail-order products was common in comics and dated to a patent-medicine tradition begun in the nineteenth-century. In issue # 5 (March), two full-page ads directed at boys appeared, one of them a common Charles Atlas muscle-building plan. This was not uncommon in pre–Code romance comics, even though very few boys read them. Such placements were most often probably the result of selling to a company's entire line of comics. There's also a full-page ad to "lose ugly fat" through the use of "a tasty wafer called Meltabs." In the post–Code # 12 (July 1955), Kelpidine returns, only this time with candy instead of gum, along with the same weight-gain ad contained in # 5, but the rest of the ads are innocent enough.

Astonishingly, small publisher Stanmor's *Ideal Romance* # 4 (June 1954) contained no tasteless ads directed at girls, but a full-page ad was devoted to the problems of baldness! One can only marvel at the inefficiency of placing such an ad in any comic book, much less a romance title. A full-page ad with one-inch high red letters cautioned against pimples in *Ideal Romance* # 5 (Aug. 1954). When the title changed to *Diary Confessions*, the first four post–Code issues (# 9–12) contained nothing offensive.

Tiny publisher Trojan/Ribage came up with three ads some critics would have seen as disconcerting in *Youthful Romances* # 8 (May 1954): "Lose Ugly Fat" (in huge, black letters advertising Dr. Parrish's Tasty Tablets); "Rubber Waist Nipper Reduces"; and "Young Form Bra." *Youthful Romances* # 9 (Aug. 1954), the last issue, has a frank full-page ad for a new "tummy trim" girdle with pictures that would be quickly proscribed in the post–Code era (although this ad did turn up briefly elsewhere), plus ads to solve the problem of "fat legs!" and to hype *Dropex* Reducing Cocktail.

Reforms of the Comics Code

Quality Comics went through obvious ad censorship. Quality carried ads such as these in its eight romance titles in 1954: a full page ad for bras to help "small bust" (in large letters) problems, plus a different ad for the "young form bra" along with the tasteless girdle ad in *Youthful Romances* # 9, plus the usual pimple-elimination ads. There were also ads for "a glamorous Hollywood wardrobe" from Frederick's of Hollywood (!) and a weight-loss ad headlined, "She Once Had Thin Legs! Now I Have Fuller Calves, Shapely Thighs, Hips and Ankles." Yet in Quality's post–Code 1955 issues, the racy ads disappeared, to be replaced by appeals to buy dolls, dresses and movie star photos, along with still-acceptable weight-loss and pimple-reduction products. Pimples were not a problem for the Comics Code; bras and girdles eventually were. The stories in "Boy Loves Girl" often remained violent and suggestive until being subjected to the Code for the final seven issues (# 51–57). In those issues, the only thing slightly suggestive was a half-page bra ad in one issue. Like ACG, Gleason took a lot of ads from a wide variety of sources; unlike ACG, almost none of the ads mentioned "unmentionables."

The big guys: National, Atlas and Harvey

Marvel usually carried lots and lots of ads, including many for the "unmentionables." *My Own Romance* # 42 (Feb. 1955), the company's first love title, had 10 pages of advertising, including the covers, with a full-page ad for a "waist-cinch bra." In the first year of the Comics Code, the company defiantly produced back-page ads in # 44, 45 and 49, among many other Atlas issues, for girdles or bras. Eventually, though, Marvel for the most part acquiesced, although occasionally continuing to run "emotional appeal" ads directed to girls, such as the one headlined, "Wipe Off Ugly HAIR in minutes!" in # 51 (March 1956).

Harvey, eventually so synonymous with clean fun in the 1960s but the producer of frequently racy pre–Code romance comics, followed the same ad-acceptance policy that Marvel did in the pre–Code period. But the 1955 post–Code issues of its first love title, *First Love* # 50–60, continued to run the occasional controversial ad, such as the one for "Cornfo Guard." But those were soon gone, too, at Harvey.

Dell (Western) usually didn't carry ads at all, except sometimes on the back covers, during the 1950s. Dell, which didn't publish romance comics, decided it did not need to subscribe to the Comics Code, but that decision apparently did not cost Dell anything, since the company had such a sterling reputation for clean comics. Dell's back-cover ads, usually for kid-friendly products such as breakfast food and bicycles, certainly never showed anything remotely related to bra size or weight loss. The lack of these controversial ads, in fact, at least subconsciously had much to do with convincing parents there was nothing harmful in a Dell comic, even if it had a two-fisted Western hero such as Red Ryder on the cover.

Like Dell, National enjoyed a virtually squeaky clean reputation by 1954, except among people like Wertham who simply did not like comics, although National's stories in the 1940s were often considerably more vibrant and violent than near the end of the pre–Code period. National was never shy about running a variety of ads, but the 1954 issues of flagship romance title *Girls' Love Stories* (# 27–32) show how clean these ads were. There was not a bra, girdle, weight-loss or pimple had to be found! There was literally nothing to clean up. The ads directed at girls primarily sold dresses. Of the companies that did subscribe to the Comics Code when it was established at a meeting in September 1954, National was the only company that did not run even remotely controversial ads.

It may not be a coincidence that the companies that seemed to benefit most from the establishment of the Comics Code, Dell and National, faced no economic dislocation with regard to changes in advertising. There were other problems, such as circulation numbers, but advertising wasn't an issue. Meanwhile, what had been a minor company in the pre–Code era, Charlton, was poised to fight it out on the post–Code newsstands with the big companies.

• TEN •

The Bland Leading the Bland
When Tears Began to Flow Freely

In the wake of the self-censorship imposed by the Comics Code Authority, romance comics had little choice but to become far more homogeneous. To be sure, there were often abuses in the pre–Code period of 1947–54. Yet many romance comics became far less interesting beginning in 1955, with the tear-stained face—virtually always female, of course—representing what little conflict was allowed in post–Code issues. Tears flowed far less frequently in pre–Code days, when woman were more likely to raise their eyebrows, sneer and/or ball their fists while muttering in the direction of their rivals, "I'll find a way to get that sneaky little witch!" or words very much to that effect.

When publisher after publisher left comic books in the 1953–58 period, there were no significant replacements for many years, until the era of independent publishers began in the late 1970s and 1980s. There were significant developments in romance, yes. Significant replacements, no. By 1959, all of the remaining traditionally large comic book publishers—National, Dell, Harvey, Archie and Marvel (albeit a severely truncated Marvel since late 1957)—had been publishing comics of many types in high volume since the Golden Age of the 1940s. All of the large publishers, that is, except Charlton, a 1940s song magazine publisher that began to produce a handful of comics after World War II.

Charlton's first successful romance title (and second overall) was *True Life Secrets*, which ran from # 1 (April 1951) through # 29 (Jan. 1956) when it became, of all things, *Long John Silver*, based on a briefly popular television pirate show. Early issues of *True Life Secrets* had some of the worst art ever to appear in comics, but the title somehow survived on a bi-monthly basis.

Early on, *True Life Secrets* was very much in the mold of the more risqué comics, with titles such as these in # 7 (May 1952): "My Fatal Weakness," "Flames Fed My Foolish Heart," Pick-Up Girl," "The Curse of Being Misjudged" and "My Undecided Soul." Another highlight—or lowlight—was a violent roller derby story in # 15 (Sept. 1953). In this little epic; the "winner" of a violent cat fight on skates did not know the "loser" was married to the man the "winner" was chasing.

The covers became ever *more* suggestive until Charlton swiped an old Fox image for the cover of *True Life Secrets* # 23 (Nov–Dec. 1954). As two male hands reach out with a string of pearls and diamonds, a brunette with outrageous blue eyeshadow asks, "And just what must I do to get those?" One can only imagine mother or father discovering 12-year-old Linda or Laurie reading that one!

When Fawcett left comics in 1953, Connecticut-based Charlton picked up most of its titles. Charlton thus jumped from a modest total of 56 issues in various genres during 1953 to 124 in 1954—more than all but four publishers. That total included six issues of *Sweethearts*,

Fawcett's flagship romance title. In one of the odder numbering decisions of the day, Charlton's first issue of *Sweethearts*, # 122 (March 1954), picked up the numbering from Fawcett, then reverted to # 23 (May 1954) and continued onward.

Charlton takes advantage

When publishers continued to disappear over the next four years, Charlton took full advantage in the late 1950s and continued to put out new romance titles, becoming by far the bulk leader in the genre, though National remained far superior from the standpoint of production values. Movie fans would have said Charlton was an inflated Monogram; National was a consistent MGM. But Charlton's romance titles must have been immensely profitable, if only because there was so relatively little competition and yet still a fairly healthy market.

In fact, if the market had not been somewhat healthy, how could Charlton had emerged as the all-time king of romance comics? Charlton produced 1,420 romance issues, though only 254 appeared before 1960. In contrast, National (DC) finished with 931 romance issues through the end in 1977, including 243 before 1960.

Charlton was simply the only one left standing with a wish to fill the romance market niche heavily, particularly in the super hero revival-heated days of the Silver Age (1956–69). While National and Marvel published thousands of super hero comics, along with many other types, Charlton produced only a handful of super heroes but became by far the leading purveyor of romance beginning in the late 1950s. Charlton published 130 romance issues in 1958 and 1959 combined; DC produced 76. Charlton produced more love titles in 1959—15!—than any publisher since the Love Glut days of 1950. In fact, of the 160 romance comics published in 1959, Charlton issued 72.

The only Charlton title that even hinted of anything other than hearts and flowers in 1959 was *Teen Confessions*. In fact, it must have sold pretty well, because the company went that title one better and started *Teen-Age Confidential Confessions* and *High School Confidential Diary* in 1960. If confessions were good for the soul, confidential confessions were even better!

Collectors still recall Charlton

Charlton is often popular with collectors today, if only because Charlton is what so many of them remember when it comes to romance. Readers born in the second half of the baby boom (1956–64) don't remember 1950s comics first-hand at all, much less romance comics. Gen-X fans, of course, are collecting four-color artifacts their parents might have read, at least when it comes to romance comics. The beginning of Gen-X in the late 1970s neatly coincides with the end of romance comics.

And yet ... many romance collectors say if you've seen or read one Charlton, you've seen or read them all. Still, they have an amazingly funky appeal for some readers. In fact, John Lustig, a highly amusing Seattle writer with a lot of comic book credits, bought the rights to the inventory of the art for the old Charlton title *First Kiss* and created a most clever strip called *Last Kiss*. He did this by noticing that Charlton's art styles lent themselves the re-wording the balloons with his witty satires. After publishing four of his own comic books and running the strip in *Comics Buyer's Guide*, Lustig broke into a metropolitan market in 2007 when the *Seattle Times* bought his strip for Sunday publication in its Northwest Living section.

Marvel only dabbled in the romance market in the 1960s, when the likes of *Spider-Man* and the *Fantastic Four* ruled the company's output, so that left only National to compete commercially to any meaningful degree with Charlton during the final two decades of romance comics. In fact, tiny Crestwood (Prize) sold its remaining two titles, *Young Romance* and *Young Love*, to National in 1963, giving the iconic publisher of *Superman* and *Batman* seven romance titles. (Some female collectors like to fondly add *Superman's Girl Friend Lois Lane* to that list of romances.)

Meanwhile, the tiny American Comics Group dropped *Confessions of the Lovelorn* with # 114 in 1960 but held onto *My Romantic Adventures* through # 138 in 1964. ACG, still the undisputed king of unusual romance stories, offered plenty of variety in its human-interest tales, yet published only 31 issues of *My Romantic Adventures* in 1960–64. The scarcity of those issues, in contrast with the far more plentiful nature of Charlton and National romance, says a lot about how poorly ACG's productions must have sold while being overwhelmed by the sheer volume of the competition.

Charlton tried an intriguing experiment in 1958, when the Connecticut-based firm briefly published several of its titles in 68-page editions for 15 cents. Until four years earlier, National had done the same thing with *World's Finest*, which featured stories of Superman and Batman, and Comic Cavalcade, a super hero and later a funny animal title. And 15 cents for 68 pages in 1958 was the best bargain in comic book history, comparable to 68 pages for a dime through 1943. In fact, at the same time those 68-page Charltons were on the stands, Dell was trying to squeeze 15 cents from the kiddies (or their parents) for several of its more popular titles, all of which were 36 pages (except the 100-page giants, which remained a bargain at a quarter). Dell's experiment ultimately failed, as did Charlton's 15-cent attempt. Charlton quickly was back to 36 pages, like everyone else.

One issue, 12 stories

In the 68-page *I Love You* # 17 (Feb. 1958), instead of using the space to develop real plots, Charlton crammed the issue with 12 of its typically short stories, none more than six or seven pages. That issue probably did set a single-comic book record for last-panel kisses—all 12 tales! At the top of the cover, the blurb read, "Daring—Adult." In one respect, that was certainly true—none of the tame stories was about teenagers, despite the two images of ponytails on the cover.

The same smiling teen girl with a blonde ponytail at the top of the cover of *I Love You* # 17 also appeared, albeit as a brunette, at the top of the 68-page *Stories of Brides in Love* # 7 (also 68 pages) and several other Charlton 68-pagers, all of which ran short stories. But on the cover of the 68-page *Secrets of Love and Marriage* # 7 (Feb. 1958), she was a redhead!

In the wake of the film *High School Confidential* in 1958, Charlton released *High School Confidential Diary* # 1 (June 1960), offering a look at "reckless rebels tearing at life," as the cover blurb promised. Someone at Charlton must have been looking at posters of the many juvenile delinquent films of the late 1950s and early 1960s. Issue # 2 (Aug.) promised a glimpse at "secret yearnings of troubled teens," which was just about the most suggestive sentence the Comics Code ever allowed! The title lasted 11 issues until Charlton removed "High School" and made it just *Confidential Diary* with # 12. So much for secret yearnings!

High School Confidential Diary # 1 included a three-page non-fiction story entitled, "Something to Think About," urging readers to study hard so they could get into college. At a time when high-paying manufacturing jobs were plentiful, and when fewer than one-quarter of all high school students wound up with any college experience at all, much less a diploma, the story included a statement that was nothing less than astonishing: "Remember this: we live in a time when an individual must have a college background to get anyplace and fulfill his destiny."

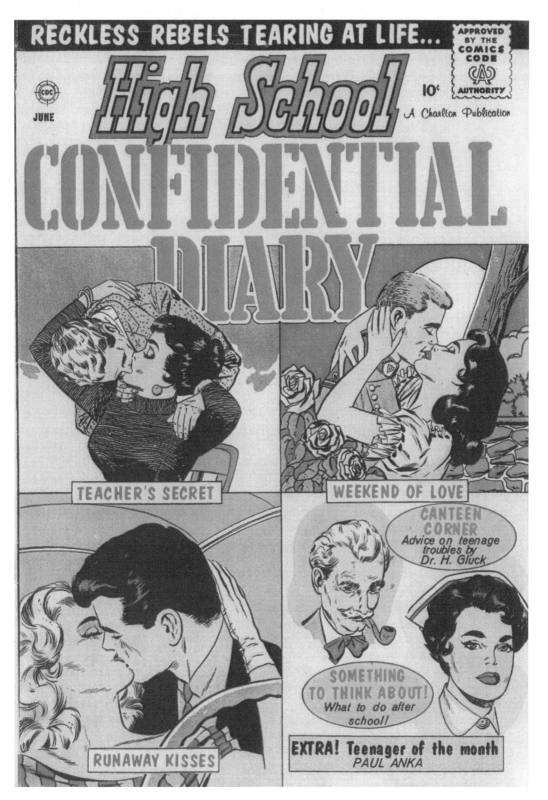

High School Confidential Diary # 1, June 1960, copyright Charlton Comics Group. The Comics Code did not prevent some publishers from trying to inject romantic controversy, spurred by the popularity of films about juvenile delinquents.

There was also a rather astonishing two-page advice column, "Canteen Corner," written not by a fake female advice counselor (as was the usual custom) but by one "Dr. Harold Gluck." There were no credentials for the good doctor, but he did give advice to a boy about not wanting to beat up his rival for a girl, and to a girl about not hogging the family phone! In the same issue, the story about the "teenager of the month" told the story of singer Paul Anka, who turned 19 shortly after this issue hit the racks.

This same debut issue had an even more astounding lead story called "Teacher's Secret," in which a young school principal advises a county commissioner of education named Mr. Grundy (shades of Archie!) to stop harassing a young teacher who seems to be interested in one of his high school students. The young principal wound up telling the story of how he fell in love with and eventually married one of his high school teachers. Somehow, the following line got past the Comics Code: "Oh, Eddie, you're adorable! I ... don't care if I am your teacher! I ... love you too!"

Issue # 2 of *High School Confidential Diary* offered nothing even close to that unusual tale, but the deceptively titled "I Was a Cheat" was different, telling the tale of a girl who takes test answers from boys. When she finally falls in love with a boy but he learns of her cheating, he tells her off and she ends the story moaning, "Bruce, darling, come back to me ... come back!"

Elvis gets cover exposure

In one of the oddest of the Charlton romance comics, *My Secret Life* # 19 (Aug. 1957) assumed its numbering from *Young Lovers* # 18, which was actually the third issue and featured Elvis Presley on the cover. *My Secret Life* debuted with a rather astonishing image—a woman in a low-cut gown and mink—that could have come off the old Fox title of the same name. This cover, though, had the cleavage taken completely off. Like many earlier Charlton romance issues, this one contained a reprint (or inventory) story from Fawcett, in which a girl once again learned her lesson from her husband-to-be.

When Charlton's revival of *Negro Romances* lasted only one issue (# 4)—perhaps the Comics Code objected to this reprint of # 2 in the three-issue Fawcett series—Charlton started *Romantic Secrets* with # 5 (Oct. 1955). The cover was, for Charlton and the Comics Code, highly unusual. As a man and woman speed down the road, he's thinking, "I'll not wait any longer ... "I'm going to propose now," and she's thinking, "This is torturing me ... I'll tell him right now that I'll never see him again!" Alas, the stories had nothing to do with the clever cover.

Every now and then, though, Charlton would come up with a totally unexpected surprise. Such was the photo cover of *Romantic Secrets* # 27 (June 1960), with a man nuzzling a woman's cheek, and the photo cover of *Secrets of Young Brides* # 19 (May 1960). This must have been an experiment, because photo covers were almost never used by any publisher in the post–1956 period. There was also a highly unusual peacetime era cover for *Romantic Story* # 37 (Nov. 1957), in which a woman cries in front of a picture of a sailor while holding a Navy telegram saying, "regret to inform you."

After the Beatles came to America in 1964, their images were illustrated in a few comic books, including Charlton's *Summer Love* # 46 (Oct. 1965, the real first issue). In # 47 (Oct. 1966), unable to come up with a genuine Beatles angle, Charlton used a poster of the quartet to inspire a girl in "The Beatles Saved My Romance." The girl was hesitant to marry the star of "Dave Dare and His Devils" (!) until he pointed to a poster, telling her three of the Beatles were married. The poster also appeared on the cover in what seemed like an attempt to convince the reader into thinking the Beatles really were featured in a story. One can only assume not a few readers were disappointed.

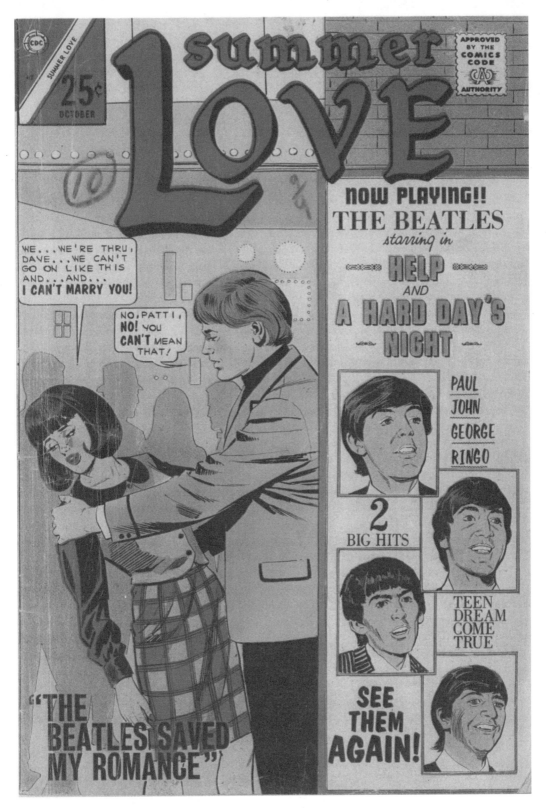

Summer Love # 47, Oct. 1966, copyright Charlton Comics Group. By the time this issue hit the racks, the Beatles were on the verge of making their final appearance in America.

Charlton put a photo of Sal Mineo (on a drive-in movie screen, no less!) on the cover of *Sweethearts* # 39 (Aug. 1957), in the wake of his smash success in *Rebel Without a Cause*, followed by singer Tommy Sands on the cover of # 40 (Nov. 1957). Ricky Nelson appeared (on a television set) on the cover of *Sweethearts* # 42 (March 1958). Nelson was not yet in the movies; he was still starring in television's long-running *The Adventures of Ozzie and Harriet*. Singer Jimmy Rodgers followed up by appearing in a girl's daydream on the cover of *Sweethearts* # 46 (Dec. 1958).

Charlton dominates the 1960s and '70s

Dan Stevenson has compiled an exhaustive database of all comic book issues through the 1980s. This shows just how commercially successful Charlton made romance in the two-decade period when essentially only Charlton and National/DC were invested in comic book love. Of Charlton's 1,420 romance issues, 1,140 appeared from 1960 to 1976 (plus 26 issues in 1979–83). Stevenson counts 26,978 corporately published comics in the 1960s and '70s (underground comics are a separate field entirely), so that means there was a four percent chance that any given comic book on the racks during those two decades was a Charlton romance issue.

During the 1960–77 period, National/DC produced 688 romance issues; all seven of its long-running titles made it into the 1970s. Marvel, meanwhile, published only 117 love comics. Clearly, Charlton felt there was more to be gained by marketing romance, among other non-super hero genres, since Marvel and DC had by far the most folks in costumes running and flying around. These Charlton romance issues clearly must have sold well, because they are common at comic book conventions, although the handful of Charlton completists have been known to experience extreme frustration trying to find a given issue.

Stevenson's statistics for the two decades show how romance diminished in influence despite Charlton's attempts. He shows 8.84 percent of the comics in the 1960s were romance but only 4.42 percent of the total issues sold love in the 1970s. That, by numerical coincidence, is exactly half. His figure for the 1950s is 10.55 percent, which is actually much more influential than it seems, especially since Charlton's 254 romance issues represents slightly more than one percent of Stevenson's total of 23,339 comics in the 1950s. (The few issues still in question as to existence are statistically insignificant.) Look at Charlton's almost always generic version of love on the racks this way: In one decade, Charlton's romance issues became more than four times as influential in the comic book field, even though National's production values were far more memorable (see Chapters 11 and 12).

Nurses and doctors on call

In the 1960s, when medical shows became popular on television, Charlton converted other titles to nurse comics, though none lasted long. Applying bandages and kisses equally were the likes of *Cynthia Doyle, Nurse in Love* from # 66 (Oct. 1.962) through # 74 (Feb. 1964); *Nurse Betsy Crane* from # 12 (Aug. 1961) through # 27 (March 1964); *Three Nurses* from # 18 (May 1963) through # 23 (March 1964), and *Sue and Sally Smith, Flying Nurses* from # 48 (Nov. 1962) through # 54 (Nov. 1963), along with *Dr. Tom Brent, Young Intern* with # 1 (Feb. 1963) through # 5 (Oct. 1963) and *Young Doctors* from # 1 (Jan. 1963) through # 6 (Nov. 1963). (The film *The Young Doctors* was released in 1961.) There was also a *Registered Nurse* one-shot dated Summer 1963.

Charlton doubtless would have liked to include Doctor Kildare, then one of television's top-rated shows, but television adaptation specialist Dell gained the franchise and produced nine issues from 1962 to 1965, though they weren't marketed especially to romance readers. Charlton, in contrast, knew it would be almost exclusively girls who would buy the company's nurse and doctor titles, so there was plenty of romance to go with recuperation. For some reason, the medical romances all seemed to go south at the same time and they were all gone early in 1964, never to be revived at Charlton. The mainstream romance titles, of course, continued to present plenty of medical romance tales.

Nurse Betsy Crane # 16 (May 1962) was typical of Charlton's approach to the dilemma of nurses on the job: On the cover, a horrified Betsy encounters a doctor and nurse in a clinch. "Bill ... Patty ... how could you?" she asks as the other nurse, taken back, blurts out, "Oh Betsy!" In the story "A Broken Trust," Betsy promises the parents of 18-year-old nurse-in-training Patty Hilton that she will watch over her. When young intern Bill Amherst and Patty begin to fall for each other, Betsy convinces Bill that he needs to back off for the sake of Patty, her parents and her career. Patty, distraught over Bill's sudden lack of attention, tearfully tells Betsy she is "devoted to nursing and to Bill too!" After watching Patty's further training, Betsy changes her mind, even though Patty's parents become upset after Bill and Patty declare they want to marry. Betsy lectures the parents: "If a girl is mature enough to decide on a career and can be entrusted with the health and lives of others, then she is mature enough to be entrusted with her own life!" The parents see Betsy's wisdom and give the young couple their blessing. It all makes sense in a Charlton sort of way, but any parent of a teenage nursing prospect might have been a bit taken aback by this story. Betsy is definitely the responsible type. In the 12-page lead story, "Cautious," beautiful Betsy Crane receives a marriage proposal from a man she has rescued from the ravages of malaria. She has to turn him down (there were still 11 more issues of the title to go!). When a fellow nurse tells her, "I hope you weren't being too cautious this time, Betsy!" the heroine in white responds, "Cautious? Maybe, but what is destined to be, will be. I have my work. This I'm sure is meant to be!" The same issue also had the three-page "Dr. Forsyth's Beauty Clinic," with health tips for girls, typical of the upbeat fillers in Charlton's nurse and doctor comics. The only nurse title following the Charlton set was Marvel's brief run of *Night Nurse* from # 1 (Nov. 1972) through # 4 (May 1973).

Charlton's long running successes

Charlton was well known for producing dozens of short-run experiments in the 1950s and '60s, but several of its 1950s romance comics enjoyed long runs into the 1960s and '70s, including *Brides in Love, First Kiss, I Love You, Just Married, Love Diary, Romantic Secrets, Romantic Story, Secrets of Young Brides, Sweethearts, Teen-Age Love* and *Teen Confessions*. Charlton began other long-running successes in the 1960s, such as the topically named *Career Girl Romances*, which ran 55 issues from # 24 (June 1964) through # 78 (Dec. 1973). The title, which probably wouldn't have made it in the more domestic 1950s, was the longest-running romance title started in the 1960s or '70s. Although there were plenty of "career girls" in comics of the 1950s, no title indicated such until Charlton came up with it.

My Romantic Adventures *Hangs In*

If you ask most comic collectors which romance title ran the most issues in the first decade following the imposition of the Comics Code Authority, you'll almost certainly be given a title such as *Girls' Love Stories* from National or *Sweethearts* from Charlton (if you get an answer at all). Very few fans would get the correct answer, because *My Romantic Adventures* quickly slipped into obscurity in the mid–1960s.

After its last pre–Comics Code issue, # 52 (Feb. 1955), *My Romantic Adventures* from ACG ran 88 more issues until it expired nine years later with # 138 (March 1964) following a run of 15 years. At the time *My Romantic Adventures* vanished, it held the record for total number of issues of a romance title. (*Young Romance*, the first of the genre in 1947, published # 128 that same month.)

ACG's long-running companion title, *Confessions of the Lovelorn*, disappeared with # 114 (July 1960), so *My Romantic Adventures* was an oddity, indeed. Even stranger, ACG apparently had cancelled *My Romantic Adventures* with # 115 (Dec. 1960), only to bring it back with # 116 (July 1961). There was no change in format and no explanation was offered by legendary ACG editor Richard Hughes, nor was there any dramatic plug for the title's return on the cover. *Romantic Adventures* became *My Romantic Adventures* on the cover with # 49 (Sept. 1954), yet the change wasn't made in the indicia until # 72 (Dec. 1956).

In the first few years following the arrival of the Comics Code, *My Romantic Adventures* used tears to illustrate emotional conflict no fewer than 18 times on the first 39 Code-approved issues, from # 53 (March 1955) through # 91 (July 1958). In fact, there were tears on five consecutive issues (# 87–91). Then the tears pretty much disappeared, being featured, if at all, on faces in the background. Only six of the 47 covers from # 92 (Aug. 1958) through # 138 featured tears. Instead, the publisher counted on odd stories and tales with familiar themes, such as "The Ugly Twin" in # 103 (July 1959), to sell the title, along with a few reprinted and/or redrawn covers used along with new stories.

The fascination of ACG

The unexpected nature of ACG stories never ceases to fascinate. That may account for some of its success, since *My Romantic Adventures* was simply different from any other romance comic on the racks in the post–Code era.

The story "Longhair Loves Cat!" in # 116 is typical. Eva Stevens, a "longhair" oboe player in the symphony, is heckled by Larry Brent, a "cool cat" who directs the Jim-Jam *Jazzlers*, a jazz band. Eva returns the favor, only to be booted by Brent. But something happens when he forces a kiss on her, and she finds herself showing up at his concerts and even changing her hairstyle. Yet he rejects her: "You're a longhair and I'm a cool cat, and never the twain shall meet! You couldn't come into my world any more than I could come into yours, so let's leave it at that!" At that point, the unlikely coincidence that so many ACG stories depend on occurs: Eva encounters an accident involving the star oboist in Larry's band and decides to replace him. She jams with the best of them, true love ensues, and they wind up performing half the time in each other's musical groups. It could happen only in an ACG story. Ridiculous, but fun.

In "The Ugly Twin" in # 103, twin girls Dale and Wendy Ravenal, both gorgeous beauties in show business, are rivals for Ron and good-hearted Wendy wins out over grasping Dale. But a plane crash into the ocean leaves Dale unhurt but mars Wendy with facial injuries, white hair and poor vision. After much conflict and angst in an 11-page tale, Wendy takes the advice of a plastic surgeon and finds ways to look attractive again—contact lenses, a dramatically different hairstyle and a brighter outlook—and Ron ultimately realizes he loves her, after all.

"The Ugly Twin" is about as unlikely as any ACG tale, but it's what the plastic surgeon says to Wendy that's most meaningful: "There's nothing I can do for you anymore—except tell you that looks are largely a matter of mental attitude! Go around shrinking from the world and acting like the ugly twin, and that's what you'll be!" ACG, via the prolific Hughes, often presented such morals in the middle of otherwise unlikely stories, and readers seem to have reacted well to them. It's always fascinating that in the middle of absolute hokum with regard to logical fiction can be found nuggets of real-life wisdom. That's why ACG stories can be pretty much regarded as parables.

Romance mixed with tongue-in-cheek humor

There was a wonderful tongue-in-cheek quality to many of ACG's stories, which are often played for humor as much as romance. For example, in "Female of the Species" in *Romantic Adventures* # 106 (Oct. 1959)—a story greatly unlike anything to be found in contemporary titles from National, Charlton, Marvel or Crestwood—college student Steven Hastings receives a lesson in the need for marriage mixed with misogyny from his curmudgeonly uncle: "A woman is a cowardly, trembling sort of thing—but necessary! She has no brains, no thoughts or ideas of her own! She must know her place, defer to you in everything, speak only when spoken to, and obey your every wish! That's all—now go out and find yourself one to marry!"

Steven meets a remarkable girl, Janet Miggs. (That's an inside joke for ACG readers, since the popular science fiction story, "Mr. Miggs from Mercury," appeared in *Forbidden Worlds* # 42, April 1956, a few years earlier.) She saves him from an undertow and a bear with improbable heroics. When she accompanies him to talk with space scientists, he tells her, "I realize you can not understand a discussion of this sort! I'll try to explain it to you later!" To which she responds, "I'm afraid that I'll have to disagree with what was just said! The moon is approximately 200,000 miles distant [actually, about 240,000—so much for comic book accuracy]—feasible for rocket transport! As for the stars, please bear in mind the nearest one is 4 light years away [actually 4.3]." And so on ... flabbergasting Steven.

What he doesn't know, when he continues to try to stifle her, is that she's a lion tamer at the circus. Eventually, she realizes how brave he is, he realizes how intelligent and accomplished she is, and they wind up saying, "darling" and "honeypie" during a final-panel kiss. The cover of issue # 106 is symbolic with Steven as a caveman worshiped by Janet as a cavewoman—perhaps the oddest cover in the history of romance comics. Issue # 115 (Nov.–Dec. 1960) had an equally bizarre fantasy entitled, "Miss Hercules Finds a Man," about the love affair of a girl with super strength and a small town farmer.

When the book, *Forbidden Adventures: The History of the American Comics Group*, by Michael Vance was reprinted by Roy Thomas in *Alter Ego* # 61 (Aug. 2006), ACG fans who had not read the original volume learned how Hughes had hired an invaluable young assistant editor, Norman Fruman, who played a key role with the romance titles.

"As Hughes's assistant editor in the early 1950s, Norman Fruman wrote many of the scripts for *Lovelorn* and *Romantic Adventures*," Vance wrote. "In fact, he wrote for all of the ACG books, with the exception of the humor titles, averaging two stories a week for many years. He and Hughes even instituted an advice to the lovelorn column in the romance titles." That, of course, was not unusual; most romance publishers used such text pieces, filled with generally common-sense advice. The advice, however, might not have occurred to the typical young reader.

In his interview with Fruman, whom Vance noted later became a professor at the University of Minnesota, Vance gives the reader an idea of what working for ACG's romance comics was like. As Fruman told Vance, "Generally, we were writing for the unmarried woman, working-class girls, and also teenaged girls, although the stories were often sophisticated; like the movies with white tie and tails were also directed at working-class women, as fantasies. We never got into the territory of being improper in any way."

Fruman also told Vance of the 1954–55 period when he encountered surprises following the censorship imposed by the Comics Code: "Much to our surprise, that also involved our love stories. And although I was all for the industry policing itself, and felt it simply was not going to do it without pressure, I very soon learned—and have been on a kind of intellectual seesaw ever since—what happens when you have a board of censors which goes far beyond its mandate, and it did so with our love stories. And it actually took the outrageous form of censoring the occasional story we had in which parents and children were in conflict. It just seems to me that was disgraceful. They had no right to do it. There was nothing immoral or improper unless you take the position, as you might now (chuckle) that family values are endangered. But these were completely innocent matters [in the 1950s]. But once they started interfering in that way, they had almost no resistance from the profession, which just wanted peace."

ACG discontinued *Confessions of the Lovelorn* in 1960, before circulation figures of comics were required to be printed in the annual ownership statements. However, the last such statement to appear in *My Romantic Adventures*—in # 131 (April–May 1963)—indicated the title was holding its own with the firm's three fantasy titles. The statement in # 131 indicated an average of 162,250 issues of every issue had been sold in the 12 months preceding September 1962. Vance's research showed the numbers were 178,600 for *Forbidden Worlds*, 165,200 for *Adventures Into the Unknown* and 159,500 for *Unknown Worlds*, but perhaps *My Romantic Adventures* took a bigger drop in 1963.

The end of ACG, but Marvel tries a romance revival

Even though it held the record for issues of a romance comic by the time it expired with # 138 in 1964, *My Romantic Adventures* apparently had become lost in a barrage of comics from National and Charlton. Its unorthodox style of stories seemed dated by that time. The same might have been said of Marvel's longest running romance title, the oddly titled *Love Romances*, which last appeared with # 106 (July 1963) amid a flurry of Silver Age super hero icons-to-be from Marvel. (*The Amazing Spider-Man* # 1 appeared four months earlier.)

ACG went out of business in 1967 but Marvel gave romance another fling at the beginning of the 15-cent comic book era (and the beginning of what has become known as the Bronze Age of the 1970s) with *My Love* # 1 (Sept. 1969) and *Our Love Story* # 1 (Sept. 1969). Those titles apparently filled a gap, or at least they provided the only ongoing alternative to National (by then DC) and Charlton, before Marvel killed them off with *My Love* # 39 (March 1976) and *Our Love Story* # 38 (Feb. 1976).

When Ernst Gerber published the *Photo-Journal Guide to Marvel Comics* in 1991, with nearly 4,000 photos of the covers of the issues published after the Atlas era ended in 1957, he included a handful of *Millie the Model* and *Patsy Walker* covers, and even a couple of the romantic soap opera *Night Nurse*, but the post–Atlas love comics from "the House of Ideas" (i.e., Marvel) didn't merit a single mention. That was merely a reflection of the lack of collector interest in romance, even though it has picked up in recent years. *My Love* and *Our Love Story* can be tough to find, and they aren't valuable, although some collectors seek them out for polished glamour art by John Buscema, Gene Colan, and John Romita, all of whom were well established in comics by that time, all having drawn far more publicized comic books.

Marvel didn't spare the talent

In Jerry Boyd's "Bullpen Romances," an article in *Back Issue!* # 13 (Dec. 2005), the writer talks of how Marvel used top talent in this attempt to revive romance: "Stan 'The Man' Lee

Confessions of the Lovelorn # 79, March 1957, copyright Best Syndicated Features, Inc. Ogden Whitney's cover reflects the human-interest themes prevalent in post–Code comics.

handled all the early writing for both titles, and with John Buscema, Don Heck, Gene Colan and Romita on interiors, it was wonderfully apparent that the House of Ideas (as Marvel was then dubbed) didn't separate their talent pool into those who did love comics and those who didn't (by this time, all of those artists had appeared on major heroics strips for Marvel). It was that major difference that made their two books so memorable and special. The Man's dialog, though he'd been happily married for years, was hip, and his yarns as vibrant as his super-hero material." That explains why some Marvel collectors still seek out these lushly produced issues, which sparkled far more than those from Charlton and were just different enough from those published by DC to stand out on the racks.

My Love and Our Love Story both often used reprints, as did a number of other titles during an era when the publisher was expanding. By 1969, the company's printing limitations as the result of its deal with National (following the implosion of 1957) had been expired for some time and Marvel was turning out a multitude of both original and reprint titles. In the years of the start and finish of its final two romance titles, Marvel more than doubled its production (from 249 issues in 1969 to 507 in 1976). So it wasn't that Marvel couldn't print romance comics in 1976; these comics just simply weren't selling well enough to justify continuing them.

"Unlike sword-and-sorcery, horror, and cosmic battles, there was no room to maneuver creatively (in the romance comics)," Boyd wrote. "Comics Code restrictions and conventional thinking kept events fairly predictable and sales, Romita comments, 'probably were not as high as the publisher hoped they'd be, and that's all reasons needed' (for cancellation)."

Romita, whose sparkling style graced National's romance stories in the 1950s and '60s, achieved fame when he took over as the artist on Spider-Man in 1966. "By late 1972, however," Boyd writes, "Romita was art director and he was a little disappointed in the quality of art the fledgling illustrators (Marvel then employed) exhibited. The Jazzy One observes, 'We were unable to give the (love) project the attention it needed and couldn't continue to impose on our top artists to do double duty, and using young artists on romance work was not wise. The work on those stories required subtlety and glamour not easy to find in young adults. Just my opinion, of course.'"

The Steranko surprise

Marvel would occasionally pop up with a romantic surprise, such as appearances by Jack Kirby in the 1960s (when he was so busy with the likes of Fantastic Four and Thor) and the single romance story illustrated by the marvelous Jim Steranko and "as narrated to" Stan Lee, the editor who ran Marvel from the 1940s to the 1960s and produced and edited untold thousands of stories.

Steranko's epic "My Heart Broke in Hollywood!" in Our Love # 5 (June 1970) was the epitome of "hip" romance of the era, complete with psychedelic bell-bottoms and a fetching mini-skirt in the splash panel. The story fairly screams, "Forget what you've seen before!" All tears, kisses and pastel backgrounds, this cool little seven-pager gives us the tale of Victoria and Wendy, who have been invited along with their drama class to see the famous director Artur Lavelle. Artur's kiss, demonstrating to others how to feign love under the arc lights, convinces Victoria she will be the one chosen to act in his film.

But the hip Wendy wins the role. Except ... Artur wipes away Victoria's tears and tells her, "Yours will be a lifetime contract, my darling—if you just say the word! I can always find an actress—but I've finally found the star my heart has searched for—to take the role of—my wife!" Victoria, literally swept off her feet, tells the reader who sees a panel filled only with a chair marked "the end," "I know my story is not a typical one! I know it might not happen to every girl who reads these words! But it can happen, if you have hope—and faith—and if you dare to believe—in the miracle of love...."

It is, of course, the height of silliness, the apex of fantasy, since Artur and Victoria barely know each other. Three decades later, they did it on television in the reality show "Who Wants to Marry a Millionaire?" But it's fun, different and obviously done with a light heart. Not long after, Marvel even reprinted the story in *My Love* # 23 (May 1973).

In the 1960s, an unusual message

Marvel tended to produce gorgeous, fluffy, short romances, but they could have unusual messages such as the six-page "A Regular Gal!" in *Love Romances* # 101 (Sept. 1962), which boasts a pretty Kirby cover to accompany the story. What this hard-boiled story essentially says is, "Play hard to get, play the diva, play the field and have fun, and you'll be sought after by the college boys." Throughout her school days, gorgeous redhead Karen has won praise from adults and peers alike as "a regular gal," one willing to help in any way needed. The pattern continues in college until she overhears a boy telling another, "I thought of taking Karen to the prom [do colleges have proms?], but heck, she's so regular, she's almost like a sister! I could never kiss her in the moonlight!" Tears flowing, she tells herself, "What a fool I was! I should have known, I should have realized, that it's fine to be a 'regular gal' up to a point, for boys don't feel romantic about 'regular gals.' They fall for girls who have some glamour and mystery about them!"

Then, in a scene worthy of war-torn Scarlett O'Hara vowing never to be hungry again, she gets up off the ground, wipes her eyes clear and says, "Well, I've learned my lesson! I missed out on this prom! But I'll never miss out on another one! I swear it!" She learns how to say no—three times in three panels—and the boys' interest perks up. "From then on," she tells the reader as she wiggles her hips into a bright light, "life was a lot more romantic for me, a lot more romantic indeed...." This is clearly not a story that would have appeared in the late 1940s or early 1950s.

"I Love You Too Much!" in # 102 is also unusual, out-and-out dramatic rubbish along the lines of "They had to destroy the village to save it." It tells the tale of Sheila and Ken, who fall deeply in love, causing him to abandon plans for medical school. His father calls on Sheila and convinces her that she must abandon him in order that his potential be fulfilled. The agony and martyrdom go on and on until Sheila is pictured in five panels on the last car of a train vanishing on the horizon: "Oh, Ken, my darling! My own dearest darling! If only I could reach out and touch you, if only I could tell you I'm leaving because I love you, because I adore you! But someday I pray you will understand! Someday, when you are a doctor at last! And then your heart will tell you what mine is saying now. It will tell you that I'll return! Nothing will keep me from you, nothing on earth, my beloved! Wait for me, my own true love! For I'll be back—I swear it! And we'll never be parted again!" The drama makes for a good story, but the logic is ridiculous. Today, of course, the message could be, and should be, "Ken, we can't be married yet, but I'll wait for you if you'll wait for me!" Or perhaps, "Ken, we're going to have to make sacrifices, but why can't we have both marriage and studies?" The other two stories, it should be noted, ended with lovers in arms, giving the reader a little of everything in one issue.

Marvel converted its original romance title, *My Own Romance*, to *Teen-Age Romance* with # 77 (Sept. 1960). It lasted only 10 issues, through # 86 (March 1962), to be replaced on Marvel's then-limited publishing schedule by, of all things, *The Incredible Hulk* # 1 (May 1962).

The first story, "A Teen-Ager Can Also Love," was a flashback tale of teenager Jill and her love for a crooner, Danny Morgan, obviously patterned along with lines of Frank Sinatra. "It happened a long time ago when I was young!" she tells the reader, flashing back to her parents criticizing the crooner over her shoulder as she watches him on an anachronistic large-screen television! Large-screen televisions—in fact, maybe any commercial television—didn't exist during her flashback period, since the story refers to Morgan being struck with an illness during a U.S.O. Tour in the South Pacific. The story is typical wish-fulfillment, filled with the coincidence of Danny coming to Jill's hometown and how she meets him, helps him and eventually wins his love.

Mary Dixon's mistake

"The Mistake of Mary Dixon," harking back to Marvel's habit of using a girl's name in many of the firm's early romance titles, was grim but far more realistic. The story says a lot in only five pages. Mary, a spoiled child and now a spoiled young woman, and Frank Dixon fall in love; he was "the only man who ever made my heart do somersaults." But their tastes and values clash, so much so that Mary tells herself in the moonlight on a date, "I think I'm going to have to change Frank! I love him very much, but I won't sacrifice my tastes for him! I'll have to teach him to like what I like!" The reader can guess what happens: Frank has the gumption to place happiness over hormones. He tells her, "In short, if I marry you, I'll have to deny my own personality, and that's too big a price to pay, even for the woman I love! So that's why I've decided I'm not going to marry you!" But Mary, and perhaps the reader, has learned a lesson. "If I ever fall in love again, I'll not make the same mistake! I'll not think that loving a man gives me the right to mold him! I'll accept and respect him for what he is, if I ever get another chance!"

Marvel probably wouldn't have sold many romance comics if every story ended in tears like that one, but it was a tale that needed to be told (and was, many times over). There was a similar story, signed by Jack Kirby and Stan Lee, in *Teen-Age Romance* # 85 (Jan. 1962) entitled, "She Who Laughs Last." The other three stories in the issue, however, end happily, so Marvel isn't *entirely* about morals. Likewise, "Too Many Kisses" in # 83 (Sept. 1961) revealed the feelings of a boy who felt he couldn't stand to be a girl toy. "My sorority sister had been right! There are no such things as harmless kisses—at least, not to boys!" Wendy's sin was simple: she kissed Tom passionately on the first date, just as the other boys had told Tom she would.

In the same issue of *Back Issue!* magazine in which Boyd covered romances, the clever, irreverent writer/artist John Lustig speculates that without the high number of romance stories worked on by the folks at Marvel, editor Stan Lee's success with the "hip" super heroes of the early 1960s might have been diminished. "If Stan and Jack [Kirby] hadn't pumped out '50s romances, would they have ever thought to infuse their super-hero comics with the sort of romantic angst that made Marvel such a success? ... Would we have ended up with a Spider-Man without a Mary Jane Watson? A Daredevil without a Karen Page? Or a Thor without that insipid, annoying Jane Foster? [Oh, please!] Face it, Tiger! We'll never know!"

The best-remembered romance comics of the 1960s and 1970s, however, have always been those from DC. But even that venerable firm had to make major changes to survive in the final decade of love on the racks.

ELEVEN

Hippies, Harpies and Heroines
National Comics Takes Charge in the 1960s and '70s

Of all the romance comics publishers, National Comics seemed the most consistently wholesome. DC Comics, as National has been known since the 1970s, produced the love comics most likely to be accepted in the typical home of the 1950s and 1960s. Of course, anyone who was intensely anti-comics wouldn't approve of them, but National nonetheless established a reputation similar to Dell Comics for clean-cut entertainment even before the Comics Code Authority stamp began appearing early in 1955. National, with a far more diverse line than Dell, subscribed to the Code Authority. Dell did not, claiming there was no need since "DELL COMICS ARE GOOD COMICS is our credo and constant goal," as the company advertised. Dell, however, did not publish romance comics with a few marginal exceptions.

National stories, while often beautifully produced, were "lightweights" in theme and texture compared to much of the company's competition in the 1950s and early 1960s. In the late 1960s, however, National began tackling themes with much more bite, both to appear more topical and perhaps to differentiate the venerable firm's romance comics from the generally blander but higher-volume product offered by Charlton.

When National began reprinting pre–Code stories in various genres in the 1960s and 1970s, only marginal adjustments were usually needed, in contrast to those from the likes of Harvey. This would certainly have been true of National's romance stories, but the company rarely saw the need to reprint them without touchups to adjust for fashions and hairstyles.

Whereas there was intense interest among devoted collectors and more casual readers alike in the history of National's super heroes, there was virtually no demand for romance reprints. In addition, the company's early romance stories from the 1949–54 period would doubtless have seemed obviously dated—if only from the standpoint of hair and clothing fashions—10 to 20 years later. National, however, constantly recycled romance plots and verbiage.

National's romance line was remarkably stable and thus must have sold consistently well. Beginning in 1952—when *Secret Hearts* resumed with # 7 (Dec. 1951–Jan. 1952) after a hiatus of one and one-half years—the company produced *Girls' Love Stories*, *Girls' Romances* and *Secret Hearts* on a bi-monthly basis through late 1957, when those three titles along with *Falling in Love* began to appear eight times per year. National started publishing *Falling in Love* in 1955. The company picked up a fifth romance title, *Heart Throbs*, with # 47 (April–May 1957) after Quality Comics left the business in 1956.

By 1963, when National picked up the venerable *Young Romance* and *Young Love* when Crestwood left comics, that gave National seven titles in a year when less stable but more prolific Charlton published 20! By then, however, National and Charlton had the market essentially to themselves.

Heart Throbs reprints old DC stories

It wasn't until 1965, with the publication of Jules Feiffer's *The Great Comic Book Heroes*, that books began to appear dealing with comic books from the perspective of pop cultural nostalgia and/or collectibility and value. A limited number of comic book conventions, mostly in New York, also began to occur in the mid–1960s, by which time several fanzines had been in print for a few years. By the end of the 1970s, when comic book fandom, comic book stores and the direct market were all going strong, dozens of volumes dealing with comic books had been published, the vanguard of hundreds to come. Yet it wasn't until 1979 when a handful of fans were startled by the appearance of the first book on the subject: *Heart Throbs: The Best of DC Romance Comics* from Fireside Books and Simon and Schuster. The book appeared only two years after the final DC romance issue was published. The volume either apparently did not sell well, or had a limited printing, for copies now go for premium prices many times the original cost. The book was published at $6.95, but the author bought her copy on a remainder table for $1.98.

Heart Throbs was a companion title to two other volumes of DC reprints dealing with the company's famous war and science fiction comics, originally printed when the company was officially known as National and unofficially as DC. The idea, apparently, was to spotlight material that had not been reprinted in books. Since the 1970s, hundreds of hardcover and softcover books and graphic novels have appeared with DC reprints, but *Heart Throbs* remains the only volume ever produced solely devoted to DC romance reprints. That says it all about the non-commercial viability of the topic. *Heart Throbs*, in fact, was the only significant book devoted entirely to romance comics until John Benson's *Romance Without Tears*, dealing entirely with St. John stories, appeared in 2003. In graphic-novel softback form, Malibu Graphics published the reprint volume *Teen Angst* and Eclipse produced *Real Love*, both in 1990.

Naomi Scott edited the 256-page *Heart Throbs* and wrote short, perceptive commentaries that still stand up well. It's not clear whether her statement, "All the romance comics had one thing in common—they were wholesome," was intended only in reference to DC stories or to the market in general. If she was referring only to DC, she was certainly correct. She continued:

> The stories were about good, clean romantic fun. Maybe that's what made them seem so funny to us back in the never-never land of prepubescence. Sex was *never* a subject for discussion. In fact, most of the romance stories were about single men and women. Marriage was certainly discussed, but the story usually ended with John and Mary in each other's arms, making plans for their wedding. Occasionally a story about a married couple appeared, but not often. And heaven help you if you were a divorced woman—you were branded a hussy, a tainted woman, and automatically excluded from the society of decent folks. Readers wanted romance and Mr. Right, not the humdrum life of a married couple. Who wanted to read about the problems young marrieds had when the romance had gone out of their marriage? Romance was the key word. Will they marry? Does he love her? Does she really love him? Will they get back together?

Indeed, National was among the few primary purveyors of romance comics who did not produce at least one title dealing with young married couples. Nor did National ever publish "theme" romance comics—other than its six-issue fling with *Romance Trail*—such as comics with "teen-agers" or "war" in the title. Instead, National stuck to generic titles, albeit with stories that run the gamut of all possible permutations of romance.

In her introduction to *Heart Throbs*, Scott also included an important statement that seldom, if ever, had appeared in any book about comics: "Interestingly enough, romance comics were written and drawn primarily by men. Even the advice columns, with bylines attributed to Jane Ford and Julia Roberts, were written by men. Over the years there were women artists and story editors, but until recently the comic industry was dominated by men. That may have had something to do with the romance comic point of view—and why we (as girls) were never quite sure they were right."

The artists drew from life

Scott's points about the art in romance comics were also spot on: "Just as romance stories came from real life, so did the art. The artists drew their wives, sisters, mothers, neighbors and friends for the romance comics. And just as there was a formula for romance comics, so there was a formula to romance art. There were ideal images for men and women in the romance comics, and if you look closely, you'll notice that most of the characters conform to this ideal. The typical romance women were wholesome and had very regular features, and so did the men. No need to worry about a bad complexion, braces, or prominent features. Romance characters were nondescript enough that it was easy to fantasize about them—and identify with them, too."

Scott summed up the appeal and style of romance comics as well as anyone ever has. Even though romance comics tried to become more topical during their last decade of existence, she added an accurate comment about their demise: "Romance comics *were* popular for almost thirty years because they showed a simpler life. Love, romance and marriage were ends in themselves; problems were limited to finding the right mate, the person who would share the rest of your life. They satisfied a kid's need to know what was ahead, to know that dreams could come true and that life was a simple matter once you found your man. They were done in the same spirit as the Doris Day and Debbie Reynolds girl-next-door films of the fifties. In the late fifties and early sixties, television was stealing a large share of the comic market—action-adventure comics, as well as romance. But the changing morality of the sixties and seventies killed romance comics forever."

History has proven Scott's observations correct in the ensuing three decades. Even the market for romance reprints has never been strong. People interested in these artifacts of a long-gone era are forced to seek out the original comics. The National/DC titles, by dint of their high production values, are among those most sought after. One of the best ways to acquire a representative example of fashions, mores and pop cultural trends of the 1947–77 period is to build a large collection of romance comics.

When comics historian Les Daniels produced *DC Comics: Sixty Years of the World's Favorite Comic Book Heroes*, a detailed and entertaining coffee-table history, in 1995, romance comics received a two-page entry of 300 words in the 256-page volume. This, too, accurately reflected the relative unimportance of romance comics to collectors and fans.

Included, however, was this revealing paragraph: "When DC finally attempted a full-fledged love title, editor in chief Irwin Donenfeld made the unprecedented decision to hire a woman as editor. 'The romance magazines really appealed to young girls,' he says, 'so I felt a woman would have a better handle on what a young girl would be like, better than a guy like Bob Kanigher, who was doing the war books.'" (Kanigher did not introduce the war books until 1952 and Donenfeld was referring to 1949.)

Daniels continued: "Actually, Kanigher would eventually become editor of the love line for a while, but that event was many years after Donenfeld appointed Zena Brody as editor and launched *Girls' Love Stories* (Aug.–Sept. 1949). Other women who would rule the romance roost included Ruth Brandt, Phyllis Reed and Dorothy Woolfolk [who had worked at All American Comics as Dorothy Roubicheck and before marrying prolific comics writer William Woolfolk]. They helped open doors for the many women who occupy important positions in the [comics] business today, long after love comics have become only a memory.... Now every-one laughs at love comics, but for some strange reason everyone remembers them as well." This information, not widely known until Daniels published his book, was one of the first exam-ples of recognition for DC's female editors.

Pop art icon Roy Lichtenstein famously used panels from several DC romance comics in the 1960s. "While [Andy] Warhol concentrated on content, Lichtenstein concerned himself with form," Daniels wrote. "In the stylization of comic book panels, Lichtenstein saw an abstract quality of design that matched the archetypical simplicity of certain ritualistic story elements. Ignoring the spectacle provided by the super heroes, he chose to concentrate on the elemental passions on view in the less popular genres of love and war. Pulling single panels out of their comic book context, Lichtenstein found pure pictures of a civilization's stereotypes in garish graphics depicting weeping women and murderous men.... Of course, Lichtenstein's paintings were more than simple copies, even if he has referred to his material as 'swiped.' He refined and redesigned his found images, altering details of composition and sometimes com-bining elements from several different panels. He also emphasized the mechanical aspects of comic book reproduction by applying color in dots that parodied the printing process. His tech-nique was to draw a small version of his picture, then project it onto a canvas for painting, enlarged so 'we can see how abstract and unreal it really is.'"

Though DC continued to produce seven titles until the final issue of *Secret Hearts* in 1971, Charlton cut back so severely that the total number of romance comics fell to 90 in 1965. Clearly, love titles were on their way out, though the issue count did rise to as high as 156 in 1972. The 90 issues produced in 1965—50 by DC, 47 by Charlton—were a low for the indus-try since the first few groundbreaking love comics in 1947–48.

DC makes romance more topical

It's especially intriguing, then, that DC tried to salvage its love line by making the titles more vibrant in the late 1960s, even in the face of greatly diminished competition. It is these themes of "hippies, harpies and heroines" that collectors and pop cultural historians find fas-cinating today. It is instructive to look at the run of National's flagship romance title, *Girls' Love Stories*, which ran an unbroken 180 issues from 1949 to 1973, the record for one title under the same publisher. Many middle-aged American women will remember *Girls' Love Stories* from their youth, even if they haven't seen a comic book in 50 years.

Girls' Love Stories ran a variety of photo covers on its first nine issues, but with the intro-duction of line-drawn covers with # 10 (March–April 1951), the themes seldom varied for well over a decade. The cover feature on # 10, entitled, "Kiss Love Goodbye," showed a distraught young women about to dab her eyes with a handkerchief as she watches a couple walk away behind the closed gates of an estate, with a "no trespassing" sign a few feet away. The sym-bolism could not have been more obvious!

From that point on, the covers almost invariably displayed two girls—one of them often teary-eyed—and a guy, though occasionally a couple would stand alone in an embrace. A por-trayal of conflict, or implied conflict, was the rule. On one of the few covers where the conflict went beyond tears and/or the passive-aggressive style, one woman is shown shaking another above the cliffside of a roaring river as a man rushes in from the background (# 15, Feb. 1952). For the cover of # 18 (Aug. 1952), National illustrated *Romance of a War Nurse* with a teary nurse and an injured soldier carried by two medics. Such drama, so common in the love comics from other companies, was the exception in National's books.

The appeal of the conflict was obvious from the back-page house ad in *Girls' Love* # 19

(Oct. 1952) for *Girls' Romances* # 16 (Sept.): "Have you ever known the pangs of jealousy? [With "Jealousy" in huge letters]. I thought Jack only had eyes for me ... but I was wrong! Other girls flocked to him—and he melted under their charm! If you have ever doubted your sweetheart's love, then you can understand my heartache ... there was only one course for me to follow. Read my story and find out what I did!"

Other than fashions, virtually nothing changed in *Girls' Love Stories* for more than 15 years. Comic book publishers generally figured a "generation" of readers lasted four or five years, or roughly children from 8 or 9 years of age to 12 or 13. Romance comics may have attracted more older readers, mostly females, than most comics in the 1950s. In the 1960s, though, it was the super hero books, especially the "hip" Marvel titles, that attracted older, mostly male readers in high school or college.

Johnny Romita, Sr., who gained fame drawing *Spider-Man* for Marvel in the second half of the 1960s, reflected on the sameness of romance comics while telling Andy Lee about his stint at National in an interview in *Comic Book Marketplace* # 24 (June 1995): "So I went over to DC in 1958 [the year after Marvel's implosion]. At DC, I just did love stories for eight years. It was almost like a living death. It is the most boring stuff and the challenge (at first) was to make it look exciting even though nothing is happening. Nothing ever happened in those books—just a lot of soulful looks, a lot of tears. So, I took some pride in jazzing them up to the point where I became their main artist in the romance department. I even got offered the job of romance editor. It's funny, when we talked about it, I didn't really want it, but I was afraid to turn it down, thinking this might be a great future. While we were talking about it, it suddenly occurred to me, if I was the one doing most of the artwork, if I took this job I'd be losing my best artist?"

Romita eventually became among the best known of the National/DC romance artists along with Everett Raymond Kinstler and Alex Toth in National's first few years with the genre. Dozens of others contributed art to National's love efforts, though they are virtually all better known for their work in other genres and/or work for other companies: Bob Oksner, Irwin Hasen, Gil Kane, Jay Scott Pike, Gene Colan, Irv Novick, Tony Abruzzo, Mike Sekowsky, Mort Drucker, Frank Giacoia, Kurt Schaffenberger, Art Saaf, Vince Colletta, and many, many more. Most of National's romance stories are unsigned.

April O'Day, Hollywood Starlet

The first heroine appeared in *Girls' Love* # 104 (July 1964) with the debut of April O'Day, Hollywood Starlet. The popularity of soap operas, along with dwindling circulation, may have spurred the appearance of a regular character for the first time in *Girls' Love*. "Stand-In for Heartbreak," the title of the April O'Day story in # 105 (Aug. 1964), pretty much says it all. National wanted even more conflict in the title. From the time April was introduced as a young girl in the first story, she had distinctive white hair until colors began to appear near the end of her run in # 115 (Nov. 1965). Further adventures were promised, but April did not return.

In *Girls' Love* # 125 (Feb. 1967), the annual statement of ownership listed the average circulation as slightly over 205,000, including 563 subscriptions. That was not especially high for those days, although better than some DC titles, but such a figure would be inconceivable today, when only the best-selling super hero sensations of the moment can hit figures that high. But standard 36-page comics were 12 cents in those days; that meant a gross sale of about $25,000 per issue, to be shared among publisher, distributor and retailer. It's no wonder many newsstands considered comic books to be "loss leaders" by this time, and it's no wonder why prices began to increase exponentially beginning in the 1980s, when corporate comics opened the decade at the 50-cent level.

In one year, the circulation had fallen off more than 10 percent, according to the figure of 178,000 in *Girls' Love* # 133 (Feb. 1968). By # 158 (April 1971), the figure was 158,000. It was not surprising, then, that the title was cancelled shortly after the 122,000 listed in # 177 (April–May 1973). DC soldiered on in 1974 with only two romance titles, *Young Love* and *Young Romance*, and those were published only bi-monthly.

As hard as it might seem to believe in our era of iPods and rock bands, the first indication of a rock band in the life of a girl appeared on the cover of # 136 (July 1968), with three Beatles clones in the background of a conflict between two men and a girl. It was about that time that some of the men's hair began to look a little longer. The cover of # 142 (April 1969) hinted at a different kind of conflict—a straight-arrow boy in the foreground thinking to himself, "She knows I love her! Why does she torture me this way?" as a girl and guy—both in long hair and bell-bottoms—embrace on a campus walkway. The lead story, "Thrill Chick," is a 10-page epic about how a spoiled blonde is rescued by "Mr. Nice Guy," as she calls him at school, from a tough guy who uses her as his getaway driver in a robbery. This type of contrived drama, so common in the 1950s in other romance titles, was exactly what DC tried to avoid for a long time.

A black face first appears on a *Girls' Love Stories* cover with # 159 (May 1971) in the story "Someone to Love." This was a tale that would have been unthinkable only a few years earlier, in which a black girl and a white girl team up and both wind with the boyfriends they want. The story ends with the white girl whispering, "Psst! Angela ... isn't it a riot? Men are all alike!" To which the black girl responds, "You better believe it, Celia! We girls will win it every time!" Blacks would soon become common in DC romance issues. A text feature in # 159 also contained a theme that most likely would not have appeared much earlier: "Do You Know When to Kiss?"

The DC logo began appearing near the end of 1970, a year or so after the price had increased to 15 cents. When the company experimented with a 52-page, 25-cent format for about a year from mid–1971 to mid–1972, most DC titles included reprints from the 1940s and 1950s, but the romance titles seldom did. The price went down to 20 cents for the final 10 issues of *Girls' Love Stories* in 1972–73, but the page count shrunk to the long-standard 36, so the reader actually got less for her money.

National's takeover of *Young Romance* and *Young Love* in 1963 revitalized those titles, which had long since had become marginalized even though Joe Simon was still editing them. *Young Romance* # 125 (Sept. 1963), the first National issue, looked like any other title from the company. But in # 126 (Nov. 1963), National introduced its first serial character: "Meet Bonnie Taylor, the lovely airline stewardess who flies in and out of romantic adventures!" National used that blurb on six consecutive issues. Bonnie ran through # 139 (Dec. 1965–Jan. 1966), until finally meeting the pilot of her dreams, as one of the first serial characters in any romance title.

In the early 1960s, well before the advent of women's liberation, being an airline stewardess was one of the more adventurous jobs a woman could take, at least from the standpoint of meeting handsome (and well-heeled) pilots and other professional men. People of modest means were seldom seen on airlines in those days!

Young Romance # 157 (Dec. 1968–Jan. 1969) may have startled girls with its cover feature, "My Mother ... My Rival!" with a middle-aged blonde in a mini-skirt dancing with a young fellow in a Nehru jacket as her daughter sobs on the sideline. The story wasn't nearly as sensational, dealing with a mother who enjoyed the company of young people and made her daughter jealous until both came to their senses. However innocent the story may have been, DC would never have touched that title not long before.

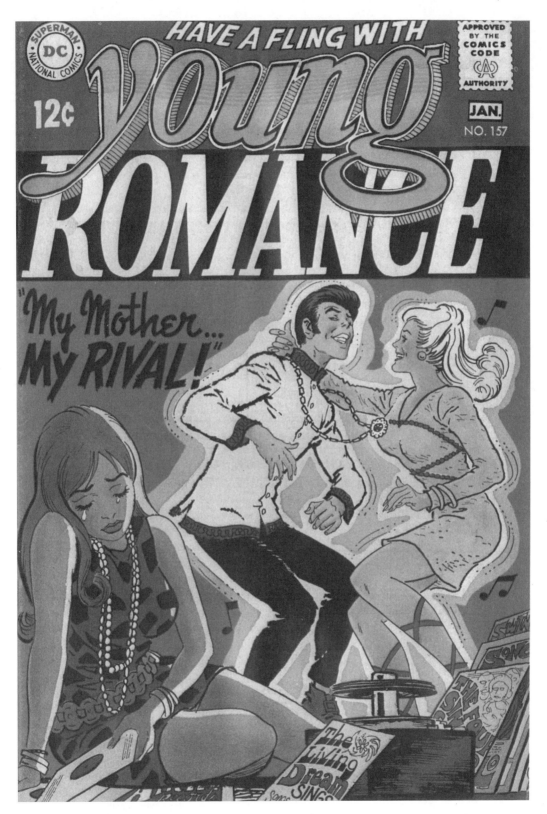

Young Romance # 157, Dec. 1968-Jan. 1969, copyright National Periodical Publications, Inc. "My Mother, My Rival!" might not have been seen on most post–Code comics only a few years earlier.

"The Swinger" in Young Romance

Sophisticated readers, younger and older alike, might have done a double-take at the blurb on the cover of *Young Romance* # 170 (Feb.–March 1971): "Introducing Lily Martin, 'The Swinger,' a girl trapped between Heaven and Heartbreak!"—with Lily hitch-hiking in bell-bottoms while wearing a headband and carrying a guitar in a story no doubt inspired by the Woodstock rock festival. Surely the Comics Code folks, who somehow approved this title, got an earful! Though her return was promised, "The Swinger" never came back.

Young Romance # 171 (April–May 1971) featured another story and cover that would have shocked readers only a few years earlier. "Strangers in Love" was one of the first stories of ethnic romance, ending in happiness for Brad (a white man with a rich uncle) and Maria (a poor Latina) after the uncle realizes on his deathbed that they were meant to be together, after all.

When DC reprinted a romance story in *Young Romance* # 172 (June–July 1971), "advice columnist" Laura Penn introduces it by saying, "Love is love, no matter where or when it happens! Young Love never changes. It was the same when your mother was a girl as it is for you today, with only a few changes in fashions, makeup, cars, etc. *Young Romance* has allowed me to bring you a classic love story. Heartache for Three appears here exactly as it did when your mother read our love stories twenty years ago!"

Robert Kanigher, who wrote *Wonder Woman* for many years and made a name for himself as the longtime editor and writer for National's outstanding war comics, also edited the romance books for a spell toward the end of their days at DC. In *Young Romance* # 194 (July–Aug. 1973), Kanigher wrote a 13-page story of interracial romance between a black nurse and a white doctor, "Full Hands, Empty Heart." Rejected by both black and white worlds, the couple falls in love but he is killed trying to save her from a drug-crazed patient. "If we don't learn to love each other, the world will always be a jungle," she says, holding the dead doctor. (This followed the movie tradition of ill-fated interracial romances.) At the end, returning to the forlorn folks in the emergency room, she says, "In some worlds there's no color, only people."

Kanigher also penned an unusual 18-page tale for *Young Love* # 104 (June–July 1973). "Veil of Love" told of an ill-fated love affair between a motorcyclist and a woman who realizes she must follow her call to fulfill her vows as a nun. Although never done in poor taste, this type of controversial tale attempted to keep the romance genre alive after DC decided serials weren't the answer.

When romance genre pioneer Joe Simon briefly returned as editor of *Young Love* with # 106 (Oct.–Nov. 1973), he produced a story that looked very much like one of his epics from 25 years earlier, but the cover tease was truly bizarre: "Give me lib or give me love. I was a girl in hot pants, driven to steal a boy's job—a boy I loved! I was the—Daughter of Women's Lib." Another story in the same issue dealt literally with hair issues: "Imprisoned by Frizz!" Both tales ended with the traditional theme of lovebirds overcoming obstacles to find happiness.

When National also took over *Young Love* from Crestwood with # 39 (Sept.–Oct. 1963), a series entitled, "The Private Diary of Mary Robin, R.N." was introduced, with the blurb, "an exciting new feature of the life and loves of a beautiful young nurse in a great metropolitan hospital!" When this feature debuted, Doctor Kildare had been a huge hit on television for two years and nurse stories were all the rage in magazines and paperbacks. The stories were usually told in "two-part novelettes" and ran through *Young Love* # 52 (Nov.–Dec, 1965), ending at the same time as the Bonnie Taylor, airline stewardess, stories finished in *Young Romance*.

"The Life and Loves of Lisa St. Claire"

A new series, "The Life and Loves of Lisa St. Claire," started in *Young Love* # 68 (July–Aug. 1968) and returned in # 70 after being interrupted by # 69, which was a 25-cent DC romance reprint issue, with a cover promising stories of "jealousy, heartbreak, rage, loneliness and [in a heart-centered image] love." Lisa finally made peace with her father and found true love in # 78 (Jan.–Feb. 1970).

National's other two original mainstream romance titles, *Girls' Romances* and *Secret Hearts*, were interchangeable with the flagship *Girls' Love Stories* in the 1950s and early 1960s, as were mid–1950s additions *Falling in Love* and *Heart Throbs*, which National began publishing with # 47 (April–May 1957) as the only one of defunct Quality's eight romance titles picked up. The five titles benefited from some of the best production values of any romance comics, but they were certainly virtually identical in art styles and story themes. That is why the new continuing characters in *Young Romance* and *Young Love* differentiated those titles after National acquired them in 1963.

Throughout most of the 1950s, National consistently put out more than three dozen titles at any one time, primarily bi-monthlies, while fulfilling market niches in every genre after focusing primarily on super heroes until the late 1940s. National surpassed 300 issues annually for the first time in 1953, with 303, and followed with 341 in 1954 and 356 in 1955 while reacting first to attacks on pre–Code comics and then having to make relatively minimal adjustments with the coming of the Comics Code Authority stamp in 1955. Financially stable National, in fact, had been publishing very little that was objectionable to the Comics Code and thus benefited immensely from the demise of so many other companies in the 1953–58 period.

The first slightly different issue of *Girls' Romances* was # 99 (March 1964) with the introduction of its first series character, who was a fantasy image for most girls compared to the airline stewardess in *Young Romance* or the registered nurse in *Young Love*. "Thrill to the true-to-love story of Wendy Winthrop, television model, as she pursues her heart in and out of the loopholes of her romantic career in 'The Name of Love.'" Unlike the more successful film starlet April O'Day, Wendy inexplicably lasted only two issues, even though her return was promised at the end of the story in # 100 (April 1964).

Readers might have been startled to see images of the Beatles on the cover of *Girls' Romances* # 109 (June 1965), although they weren't identified out front. National fudged on this one; the Beatles made a cameo appearance in a star-struck girl's daydreams in the 13-page story, "When My Dreams Come True." That was the one of only two "appearances" of the Beatles in a National romance title. *Heart Throbs* # 101 (May 1966) was the other.

Hippies make the scene

On the racks during the summer of 1968, one year after the Summer of Love, readers found the first cover reference to hippies in *Girls' Romances* with an unusual two-part story, "My Time to Love," in # 135 (Sept.) and # 136 (Oct.). In retrospect, the tale of middle-class Karen and hippie guitarist Kip seems amazingly innocent and full of stereotypes, but it was topical in its time. Kip, reacting to Karen's urging that he enroll in college to make something of himself, fires back "and become a nice three-button-suit creep with a pipe, two kids and a wife who's queen of the PTA! I'm not a machine! I'm a man! I can't live tied down to some split level in the suburbs!" Yet in the second half of the story, after achieving success with the rock band Tumbleweeds (!), Kip enrolls at the same college as Karen's straight-arrow suitor and tells her parents he intends to marry her "whether they like it or not." To which Karen replies, "Oh, Kip—now you're acting the way I dreamed you would!" As the story ends with their kiss, the caption reads: "When the time for love comes, a boy suddenly turns into a man and a girl changes into a woman!" And a hippie goes straight, of course! That was about as radical as *Girls' Romances* got until the end of its run with # 160 (Oct. 1971), four months after the demise of *Secret Hearts* with # 153, leaving National (by now DC on the covers) with five romance titles.

Secret Hearts broke into the serial ranks in # 96 (June 1964) with Amy Ames, "Miss Listening Heart" of the *Daily Star*. Ames, a novice reporter, was forced on the editor after saving the publisher, a widow, from drowning in a boating accident. In a scene right out of 1930s movies, the editor decides he has just the place for Amy: "Every day we get hundreds of letters from people asking us to solve their heartaches! Everyone who had this job has either quit or been carried away in a straightjacket! It's yours! Unless you want to quit—right now!" Amy lasted through # 109 (Jan. 1966), after skipping # 108, but she never did find her own true love.

At least National had a good reason for ending Amy's adventures. In *Secret Hearts* # 110 (March 1966), National began "Reach for Happiness," plugged on the cover as "the one and only serialized story in any romance comics magazine!" (That was temporarily true, since DC had dumped all of its previous series.) National's epic about Danville Corners was the company's knockoff of Peyton Place, which had been a hit on television for more than a year when the first episode of "Reach for Happiness" hit the racks.

"Reach for Happiness" included blurbs like, "Teenage rebels fight for their right to love" in episode 13 in *Secret Hearts* # 122 (Sept. 1967). The plot became so complex that National inserted a one-page update about the cast. "Reach for Happiness" ran 29 consecutive episodes through *Secret Hearts* # 138 (Sept. 1969). The ending was unorthodox for the time period, to say the least: On the final page, heroine Karen asks hero Greg, "Oh, Greg, Greg, Greg, my darling—will you marry me?" To which our man of few words replies, "You bet I will!" And in the final panel, we read: "Danville Corners ... a typical small American city ... where people in all walks of life go about their business of working, loving, crying and laughing, as they ... Reach for Happiness!" It was probably no coincidence that the original run of Peyton Place ended in June 1969—shortly before the final episode of "Reach for Happiness" hit the racks.

Secrets Hearts began "20 Miles to Heartbreak" by penciler Alex Toth and inker Vince Colletta in # 141 (Jan. 1970) and # 142 (March), then concluded the story in *Young Love* # 79 (April 1970). *Secrets Hearts* then began "For Singles Only" in # 143 (April) and concluded it in # 144 (June). *Secret Hearts* also took the unusual step of running a full-length 26-page, three-part "novel" in # 147 (Oct. 1970) entitled, "Cry, Soul: Cry, Love."

Secret Hearts *is the first to be cancelled*

Secret Hearts obviously tried hard, but circulation dropped to an average of 140,927 with only 53 subscriptions, as listed in the ownership statement in # 150 (March 1971). The title expired with # 153 (July 1971), the first of DC's seven romance titles to depart. Such a circulation in comic books today would be cause for great celebration, but in 1971 it wasn't good enough to make the desired profit.

DC produced a lot of giant reprint comics in the 1960s and 1970s, including three romance one-shots—*Super DC Giant* # 17 (Oct. 1970), entitled, "Love 1970," and *Super DC Giant* # 21 (Jan.–Feb. 1971), entitled, "Love 1971." Collectors especially treasure Nick Cardy's sizzling "beach love" cover for # 17. DC followed up with the undated *DC 100-Page Super Spectacular* # 5 in 1971, simply entitled, "Love Stories." That issue included a seven-page story of African

Girls' Romances # 135, Sept. 1968, copyright National Periodical Publications, Inc. This is one of the first references in romance comics to hippies, in the year following the "Summer of Love" in San Francisco.

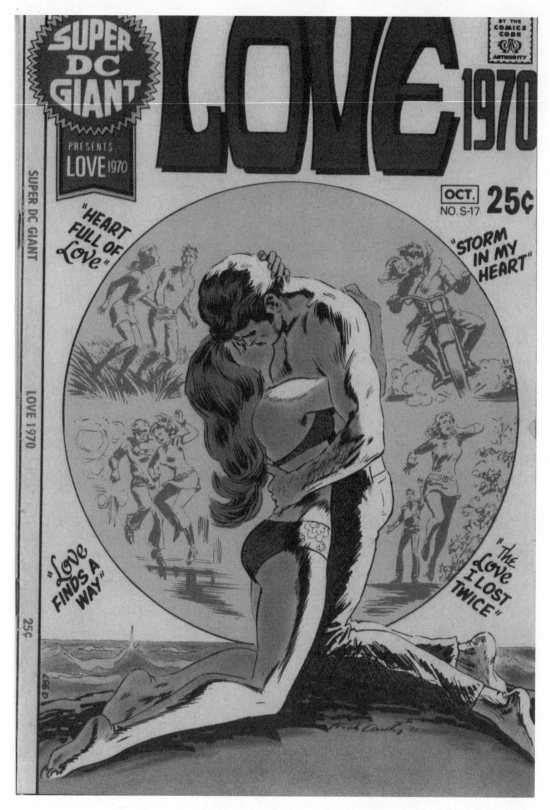

Love 1970, Super DC Giant # S-17, copyright National Periodical Publications. Artist Nick Cardy perfectly captures the sizzling spirit of summer love.

American lovers, "The Other Girl." These three issues must not have sold well, because all are labeled as scarce in the *Overstreet Comic Book Price Guide.*

Falling in Love, National's fourth romance title, debuted in October 1955. The market must have been good, in the wake of the imposition of the Comics Code, because this title offered nothing to distinguish it from the company's other love comics. There was a nice touch on the cover of # 75 (May 1975) with a girl standing by a newsstand displaying all of DC's romance titles. *Falling in Love* was the only National romance title that did not attempt a serial or continuing characters.

Falling in Love # 118 (Oct. 1970) offered an unbelievable period piece entitled, "I Found My Love at the Woodstock Festival"—published one year after the festival. This little epic starts with a campus protest at "Barrett College—ivy-covered, peaceful, straight"—until heroine Sally discovers hero Robin leading a wild campus protest until the police arrest him. Incredibly, one of the student protest signs reads, "Down with Dippy Deans!" Invited later to join him at Woodstock, she gets stuck in a monumental traffic jam until she is offered a ride by a motorcyclist who proclaims himself, "Zack Barton, practicing hippie, guitar player, zen master, and lover!" Numerous complications later, Sally and Robin both grow up enough to find both purpose and each other. "Peace ... and love ... I learned to do my thing!" the hero declares as they fly off in a helicopter. *Falling in Love* faded out with # 143 (Nov. 1973).

The Beatles as a backdrop

The first issue of *Heart Throbs* to distinguish itself was # 101 (May 1966) with a Beatles cover. They were only a backdrop on a movie date, however, not really in the story. But four months after "Reach for Happiness" began appearing in *Secret Hearts, Heart Throbs* offered something more substantial with the first episode of "3 Girls ... Their Lives ... Their Loves" in # 102 (July 1966). DC took the unusual step of making the serial title part of the logo and the serial ran 22 episodes through # 123 (Dec. 1969–Jan. 1970). After romantic adventures and misadventures aplenty of the three career girls, they all found marital happiness. DC ended the serial with an empty room scene and the blurb: "For rent: lavish penthouse apartment in exclusive area ... suitable for sharing by single girls sharing a career in New York ... and romance ..."

Heart Throbs # 128 (Oct.–Nov. 1970) featured a cover—and thought balloon—that would never have appeared on a DC love title only a few years earlier. The featured story, "No Love for Miss Goody Two-Shoes," is introduced by the blurb, "Can a girl with old-fashioned ideas about love 'make it' in today's hip scene?" as the girl in question, spotting another couple in a clinch, thinks to herself, "That's the fourth man I've caught Carol kissing at this party! How can she do this to Rick? She's supposed to be engaged to him!" By this time, the Comics Code had been loosened a bit, or that comment never would have made it.

The same could be said for the dialog expressed by a couple (in a dune buggy!) on the cover of *Heart Throbs* # 136 (Dec. 1971). "I love you—why won't you DO what I want?" asks a long-haired hippie sort, to be answered by "I love you, too! But I'll NEVER do that!" DC covers, though, were almost never that suggestive, even in the "mod" 1970s, and certainly never even in the period before the Comics Code.

Heart Throbs # 146 (Oct. 1972) became *Love Stories* # 147 (Nov.) for no discernable reason other than perhaps a change in editors from Dorothy Woolfolk to Deborah Anderson. *Love Stories* lasted six unremarkable issues, until # 152 (Nov. 1973), while fading out concurrently with *Girls' Love Stories* and *Falling in Love*. Suddenly, DC went from five romance titles to two. Only *Young Romance* and *Young Love* would make it into 1974. Not long after, the romance era in comics was over.

• TWELVE •

Where Love Has Gone
The End of Young Romance and Young Love

The last year romance comics made any sort of impact at all on the market was 1973, when the total of 125 romance issues from Charlton, DC and Marvel represented less than seven percent of the 1,946 issues published in all genres. The romance totals were only 45 issues in 1974, 82 in 1975 and 53 in 1976, representing a combined total of 180 of the 5,500 issues produced by the corporate comic book industry over that three-year span. That's about three percent.

The vast majority of comics produced in the mid–1970s were super hero comics or variations thereof involving a high degree of fantasy. And by fantasy, that doesn't mean fantasies of love and romance. Yet only 20 years earlier, romance comics far, far outnumbered super heroes, in the period between the end of the Golden Age of the 1940s and the Silver Age, which began in 1956 but didn't get going in earnest until the second generation of Marvel super heroes came along in the early 1960s.

While the Marvel and Charlton products presented up-to-date fashions and the occasional bright story, DC's *Young Romance* and *Young Love* were perhaps the best of the remaining love comics in the mid–1970s. That was fitting, if only because those titles pretty much started it all nearly three decades earlier.

Starting in the 1970s—now that 12-cent comics were permanently a thing of the past, soon to be followed into the dustbin of economic history by comics selling for 15 and 20 cents—DC displayed a willingness to experiment with issue sizes and price points. So much so, in fact, that it was difficult to predict what the next DC issue of any title would cost. But in the early 1970s, 50 cents was still considered a high price for any comic—that would be about the same as $3 to $4 today, what most comics now cost—so DC took a real chance with both *Young Romance* and *Young Love* at the start of 1974.

Both surviving romance titles were converted to DC's 100-page *Super Spectacular* format for 50 cents, beginning with *Young Love* # 107 (Dec. 1973–Jan. 1974) and *Young Romance* # 197 (Jan.–Feb. 1974). This was the first time any company had produced 100-pagers on a regular basis, rather than sporadically or as rebound/reprint giants. The price soon rose to 60 cents and the format lasted through *Young Romance* # 204 (March–April 1975) and *Young Love* # 114 (Feb. March 1975) for a total of 16 romance giants.

Most of the stories (which included some reprints) were fairly typical stuff, but every now and then there was an eye-popper, at least compared with traditional DC fare. For example, *Young Romance* # 197 cover-featured, "'That Strange Girl,' the story they dared us to print!" As a girl paints on a ladder, another tells a friend, "Don't waste your time, Fred ... Liz isn't interested in boys ... You know what I mean!" Liz, though, turns out to be very much interested in Fred after they solve their communication problems. The story ends with Liz telling

Young Romance # 197, Jan.-Feb. 1974, copyright National Periodical Publications, Inc. "That Strange Girl" (the title inside) merely turned out to be shy.

the reader, "If any girl reading my story feels that you're different, because you despair of ever learning what it is to be in love, I wish you one thing ... that you too can find a boy like Fred!" In those days, no one would dare suggest a girl might be interested in a Frieda!

"Greaser's Girl": Something Different

In *Young Love* # 110 (June–July 1974), "Greaser's Girl" told the time-honored tale of a good girl attracted to a bad boy, but only until she learns a straight arrow is really the man for her. "You're one of us now! The other guys won't go near you!" a scuzzy "greaser" on a motorcycle screams to her on the cover.

In his short return stint as editor, Joe Simon, who co-created the genre for comic books 27 years earlier with Jack Kirby, peppered the cover of *Young Love* # 112 (Oct.–Nov. 1974) with story teases such as, "My dreams burned with her passion ... Never Been Kissed!" and "I had to settle for her leftovers ... The Pretty One!" not to mention, "One Boy After Another" and "I Was Only His Plaything!" But the 100-page format apparently wasn't the answer and both *Young Romance* and *Young Love* returned to the 36-page format late in 1974 for what had become the standard price of 25 cents ... nowhere near as good a deal for the money. It took nearly seven years for most comics to go from 12 cents (in 1962) to 15 cents (in 1969). But it took only five years to jump another dime, and the 25-cent price point didn't last long. By the end of the 1970s, regular-sized comics were at least twice that much.

Simon filled both titles during his two-year stint as editor with sensational-sounding stories: "Too Much for Me"; "Hitch-Hiker"; "Tough Girl!"; "The Gossip Mongers"; and "I Bought a Boy!" followed by other editors who titled stories, "Love Behind Bars!" "Biker's Girl" and others of the type. But the times—and the relative lack of readers—had caught up with romance comics, and *Young Romance*, once dubbed, "the first and the best," expired with # 208 (Nov.–Dec. 1975). Marvel soon published the last issues of *My Love* (# 39, March 1976) and *Our Love Story* (# 38, Feb. 1976). The entire field was left with DC's *Young Love*—which soon suspended publication in 1976 before making one final stab at success—along with nine bi-monthly titles from Charlton, none of which made it into 1977.

A few years earlier, DC became the last publisher to experiment with cross-genre romance, publishing four 52-page issues each of *The Secret House of Sinister Love* and *Dark Mansion of Forbidden Love* with 25-cent prices. This attempt to cash in on the then-popular gothic romance paperback market apparently failed, for both titles were converted to weird mystery comics with the fifth issues. Many collectors categorize those as gothic-romance titles in the horror/weird category, since DC had resumed publishing horror comics—albeit with themes not nearly as gross as some pre–Code publishers flirted with—in the late 1960s. DC also introduced its long-running *Ghosts* title concurrently with the two gothic titles in 1971, so there was no question the publisher was trying to take advantage of the then-popular world of the weird.

For some time, *Young Love*, taking a cue from ABC's "Wide World of Sports," billed the title as "The Agony and Ecstasy of Young Love" on the cover. But that was dropped with # 120, which was dated "Winter 1976" and copyrighted 1975. Issue # 119 (Jan. 1976) featured "Love Behind Bars!" (with an indeterminate ending to be decided by the reader) and # 120 highlighted "Too Old, Too Young" (the woman was too old ... until the last panel!). The frazzled economics of the mid–1970s comic book industry were on display when *Young Love* returned with # 121 (Oct. 1976), featuring "Biker's Girl." That issue ran 52 pages for 50 cents, less than two years after the reader had been offered 100 pages for 60 cents.

Young Love *finally disappears*

As for 1977, the entire total of romance comics published in the industry that year consisted of the final four issues of *Young Love* (# 123–126). That, for all intents and purposes, was the end of love comics. Charlton did try nine issues of *I Love You* and seven issues of *Secret Romance* in 1979–80, and put out *Soap Opera Romances* # 1–5 and *Soap Opera Love* # 1–3 in 1982–83. Charlton itself soon disappeared.

DC billed the final issues of *Young Love* in 1977 as "Stories of romance for today's young woman!" below a new, larger logo. A reprint serial, "20 Miles to Heartbreak" penciled by the wonderful Alex Toth several years earlier, nicely spiced # 122–125, and a sequel to "Love Behind Bars!" appeared in # 124 (March 1977) entitled, "Love Behind Bars II!"

Issue # 126 (July 1977) featured a suggestive tone for the final love stories in DC's history: "C.B. Romance"; "I Won't Kiss That Evil Way!"; "Love in Peril"; and "My Boyfriend's Best Friend Was My Rival!" But, in what had become a three-decade tradition, they all ended happily ever after for each set of lovers. Who could have guessed that was the end of more than 4,000 romance stories and more than 900 issues from DC?

The final six issues of *Young Love* really were decent romance comics, albeit a bit sensationalized, showing DC was trying right up to the end. The folks in charge may not even have known the end was at hand with # 126 since the letters column told of awarding 10 contest winners one-year subscriptions to *Young Love*, and another reader was informed how to subscribe! Readers were even asked, "We'd like to hear what you think of our efforts on *Young Love*, and what you think we could do to make it a better comic. And if you have a problem you need some advice on, we'll try to help you."

Comics historian and artist Trina Robbins, in *From Girls to Grrrlz: A History of Girls' Comics from Teens to Zines* (1999), summed up DC's romance plight this way: "With the dawn of the seventies, DC Comics made a last-ditch attempt to keep their shrinking love comics audience. They hired new, younger artists, including Elizabeth Berube, probably the last woman to draw for love comics, who contributed charming neo-retro-style pages of fashion and beauty tips. They featured stories with themes more in keeping with a new morality of the times: unwed mothers, prostitutes (they though never used the word) and lesbians (but God forbid they should use the word!). They even used the word brassiere, not used in comics since [Marvel's] *Patsy Walker* had mentioned it fifteen years earlier."

Nothing, though, could help romance comics. In the late 1970s, after love on the racks and everything else in comics became an anachronism at drug stores and newsstands, the growth of comic book specialty stores and the direct market saved the comic book as an American institution. But circulation of all types, from Disney to Daredevil, continued to plummet from the market force it once was. Publishers began to sell comics to the specialty stores on an unreturnable basis through distributors. This proved practical for the most popular super hero comics and a few others, along with the growing ranks of the non-corporate independents in the 1980s, but comic book stores weren't about to stock love comics, other than marked-up back issues. Most of the readers or romance comics were female; the early comic book shops were frequented mostly by fellows of all ages who famously became known as "fanboys" in the industry.

Why girls outgrew romance comics

Dick Giordano, a longtime artist and editor at both Charlton and DC, talked with writer John Lustig for an article entitled, "The Death of Romance (Comics!!)" in *Back Issue!* # 13

(Dec. 2005). "When I left DC in the late '60s, romance titles were among the best-sellers in the DC lineup," Giordano said. "When I returned to a DC editorial post in 1980, they were gone. I'm not sure why they went away, but a guess that girls simply outgrew romance comics is probably correct. The harder question then becomes why?" Giordano gave Lustig his answer: "[The content was] too tame for the more sophisticated, sexually liberated, women's libbers [who] were able to see nudity, strong sexual content, and life the way it really was in other media. Hand holding and pining after the cute boy on the football team just didn't do it any more, and the Comics Code wouldn't pass anything that truly resembled real-life relationships."

Later, Giordano told Lustig how nothing could have prevented romance comics from becoming cultural artifacts. "No, I think the time for romance comics was past and no amount of doctoring could change that. On the other side of that statement: The sales success of anime and manga in this country is largely attributable to a female audience. This *might* be the time to approach the idea of romance graphic novels for a young-adult bookstore audience. Just not with my money!!!!!!!" Lustig's use of the seven exclamation points is telling, because love comics would, indeed, be a huge financial gamble in the modern world.

As the industry matured through the growth of independent comics, many of which dealt with relationship issues, women readers, not to mention writers and illustrators, became far more involved in comics in the 1990s and beyond than they were in the 1970s. Comic conventions began to attract many more females, some of whom still enjoy digging out old romance comics for fun, and now any large comic convention has plenty of females in attendance. Our modern *Seinfeld* and *Friends* society, though, has long since moved beyond the type of stories romance comics used to publish. And though love is still very much part of illustrated stories, there will never again be the type of romance or easy availability of love on the racks there once was.

Appendix: Catalog of American Romance Comics

By Dan Stevenson, Michelle Nolan and Jim Vadeboncoeur, Jr.

Romance comics published or circulated in America from 1947 through 1983 are listed by company.

Ace (April 1949 to Nov. 1956)

All Love # 26 (May 1949) through # 32 (May 1950). 7 issues.

All Romances # 1 (Aug. 1949) through # 6 (June 1950). 6 issues.

Complete Love Magazine Vol. 26 # 2 (# 158) (May-June 1951) through Vol. 32 # 4 (# 191) (Sept. 1956). 34 issues.

Dotty # 40 (May 1949). 1 issue.

Glamorous Romances # 41 (July 1949) through # 90 (Oct. 1956). 50 issues. (Formerly *Dotty*.)

Love at First Sight # 1 (Oct. 1949) through # 43 (Nov. 1956). 43 issues.

Love Experiences # 1 (Oct. 1949) through # 5 (June 1950); # 6 (April 1951) through # 38a (June 1956) and # 38b (Aug. 1956). 39 issues.

Real Life Secrets # 1 (Sept. 1949). Becomes *Real Secrets* # 2 (Nov. 1949) through # 5 (May 1950). 5 issues.

Real Love # 25 (April 1949) through # 76 (Nov. 1976). 52 issues.

Revealing Romances # 1 (Sept. 1949) through # 6 (June 1950). 6 issues.

Ten Story Love Vol. 29 # 3 (# 177) (June-July 1951) through Vol. 36 # 5 (Sept. 1956). 33 issues.

Western Love Trails # 7 (Nov. 1949) through # 9 (March 1950). 3 issues.

—Ace total: 279 issues

Ajax/Farrell (March 1954 to June 1958)

All True Romance # 22 (March 1955) through # 30 (July 1957); # 3 (Sept. 1957) through # 4 (Nov. 1957); # 33 (Feb. 1958) through # 34 (June 1958). 13 issues. (Purchased from Comic Media).

Bride's Diary # 4 (May 1955) through # 10 (Aug. 1956). 7 issues.

Bride's Secrets # 1 (April-May 1954) through # 19 (May 1958). 19 issues.

Dear Heart # 15 (July 1956) through # 16 (Sept. 1956). 2 issues. (Formerly *Lonely Heart*.)

Lonely Heart # 9 (March 1955) through # 14 (Feb. 1956). 6 issues. (Purchased from Comic Media).

My Personal Problem # 1 (Nov. 1955) through # 4 (Nov. 1956). 4 issues.

My Personal Problem # 1 (Oct. 1957) through # 3 (May 1958). 3 issues.

Secret Love # 1 (Dec. 1955) through # 3 (Aug. 1956). 3 issues.

Secret Love # 1 (April 1957) through # 6 (June 1958). 6 issues.

Today's Brides # 1 (Nov. 1955) through # 4 (Nov. 1956). 4 issues.

True Life Romances # 1 (Dec. 1955) through # 3 (Aug. 1956). 3 issues.

—Ajax/Farrell total: 70 issues

American Comics Group (April 1949 to March 1964)

Lovelorn # 1 (Aug.-Sept. 1949) through # 114 (July-Aug. 1960). 114 issues. (Becomes *Confessions of the Lovelorn* with # 52, Aug. 1954.)

Romantic Adventures # 1 (March-April 1949) through # 138 (March 1964). 138 issues. Becomes *My Romantic Adventures* with # 68 (Aug. 1956).

Search for Love # 1 (Feb.-March 1950) through # 2 (April-May 1950). 2 issues.

—ACG total: 254 issues.

Archie (Sept. 1949 to 1952)

Darling Love # 1 (Oct.-Nov. 1949) through # 11 (1952). 11 issues.

Darling Romance # 1 (Sept.-Oct. 1949) through # 7 (1951). 7 issues.

—Archie total: 18 issues

Avon (Sept. 1949 to Oct 1954)

Betty & Her Steady # 2 (March-April 1950). 1 issue (first issue was teen humor).

Campus Romance # 1 (Sept.-Oct. 1949) through # 3 (Feb.-March 1950). 3 issues.

Campus Romance, no number (1953). 1 issue.

Complete Romance # 1 (1949). 1 issue.

Frontier Romances # 1 (Nov.-Dec. 1949) through # 2 (Feb.-March 1950).

Intimate Confessions # 1 (July-Aug. 1951) through # 8 (March 1953). 8 issues.

Realistic Romances # 1 (July-Aug. 1951) through # 8 (Nov. 1952); # 15 (April-May 1954) through # 17 (Aug.-Sept. 1954). 11 issues (no # 9–14).

Romantic Love # 1 (Sept.-Oct. 1949) through # 13 (Oct. 1952); # 20 (March-April 1954) through # 23 (Sept.-Oct. 1954). 17 issues (no # 14–19).

Sparkling Love # 1 (June 1950). 1 issue.

Sparkling Love, no number (1953). 1 issue.

Women to Love, no number (1953). 1 issue.

—Avon total: 47 issues

Charlton (Oct. 1949 to June 1983)

Brides in Love # 1 (Aug. 1956) through # 45 (Feb. 1965). 45 issues.

Career Girl Romances # 24 (June 1964) through # 78 (Dec. 1973). 55 issues.

Confidential Diary # 12 (May 1962) through # 17 (March 1963). 6 issues. (Formerly *High School Confidential Diary*.)

Cowboy Love # 28 (Feb. 1955) through # 31 (Aug. 1955). 4 issues. (Purchased from Fawcett.)

Cynthia Doyle, Nurse in Love # 66 (Oct. 1962) through # 74 (Feb. 1964). 9 issues.

Dr. Tom Brent, Young Intern # 1 (Feb. 1963) through # 5 (Oct. 1963). 5 issues.

First Kiss # 1(Dec. 1957) through # 40 (Jan. 1965). 40 issues.

For Lovers Only # 60 (Aug. 1971) through # 87 (Nov. 1976). 28 issues. (Formerly *Hollywood Romances*.)

Giant Comics (only romance edition) # 2 (Fall 1957). 1 issue.

Haunted Love # 1 (April 1973) through # 11 (Sept. 1975). 11 issues.

High School Confidential Diary # 1 (June 1960) through # 11 (March 1962). 11 issues.

Hollywood Romances # 46 (Nov. 1966) through # 59 (June 1971). 14 issues.

I Love You # 7 (Sept. 1955) through # 121 (Dec. 1976); # 122 (March 1979) through # 130 (May 1980). 124 issues. (Formerly *In Love*.)

In Love # 5 (May 1955) through # 6 (July 1955). 2 issues. (Purchased from Mainline.)

Intimate # 1 (Dec. 1957) through # 3 (May 1958). 3 issues.

Just Married # 1 (Jan. 1958) through # 114 (Dec. 1976). 114 issues.

Love and Romance # 1 (Sept. 1971) through # 24 (Sept. 1975). 24 issues.

Love Diary # 1 (July 1958) through # 102 (Dec. 1976). 102 issues.

My Only Love # 1 (July 1975) through # 9 (Nov. 1976). 9 issues.

My Secret Life # 19 (Aug. 1957) through # 47 (Sept. 1962). 29 issues. (Formerly *Young Lovers*.)

Negro Romances # 4 (May 1955). 1 issue. (Purchased from Fawcett.)

Nurse Betsy Crane # 12 (Aug. 1961) through # 27 (March 1964). 16 issues.

Pictorial Love Stories # 22 (Oct. 1949) through # 26 (July 1950). 5 issues.

Registered Nurse # 1 (Summer 1963). 1 issue.

Romantic Secrets # 5 (Oct. 1955) through # 52 (Nov. 1964). 48 issues. (Purchased from Fawcett.) (Formerly *Negro Romances*.)

Romantic Story # 23 (May 1954) through # 130 (Nov. 1973). 108 issues. (Purchased from Fawcett.)

Secret Romance # 1 (Oct. 1968) through # 41 (Nov. 1976); # 42 (May 1979) through # 48 (Feb. 1980). 48 issues.

Secrets of Love and Marriage # 1 (Aug. 1956) through # 25 (June 1961). 25 issues.

Secrets of Young Brides # 5 (Sept. 1957) through # 44 (Sept. 1964). 40 issues. *Secrets of Young Brides* # 1 (July 1975) through # 9 (Nov. 1976). 9 issues.

Soap Opera Love # 1 (Feb. 1983) through # 3 (June 1983). 3 issues.

Soap Opera Romances # 1 (July 1982) through # 5 (March 1983). 5 issues.

Sue and Sally Smith # 48 (Nov. 1962) through # 54 (Nov. 1963). 7 issues. (Formerly *My Secret Life*.)

Summer Love # 46 (Oct. 1965) through # 48 (Nov. 1968). 3 issues. (Formerly *Brides in Love*.)

Sweetheart Diary # 32 (Oct. 1955); # 33 (April 1956) through # 65 (Aug. 1962). 34 issues. (Purchased from Fawcett.) (Formerly *Cowboy Love*.)

Sweethearts # 122 (March 1954). 1 issue. (Purchased from Fawcett.)

Sweethearts # 23 (May 1954) through # 137 (Dec. 1973). 115 issues.

Teen-Age Confidential Confessions # 1 (July 1960) through # 22 (Feb. 1964). 22 issues.

Teen-Age Love # 4 (July 1958) through # 96 (Dec. 1973). 93 issues. (Formerly *Intimate*.)

Teen Confessions # 1 (Aug. 1959) through # 97 (Nov. 1976). 97 issues.

Teen Secret Diary # 1 (Oct. 1959) through # 11 (June 1961). 11 issues.

Three Nurses # 18 (May 1963) through # 23 (March 1964). 6 issues.

Time for Love # 53 (Oct. 1966). 1 issue.

Time for Love # 1 (Oct. 1967) through 47 (May 1976). 47 issues.

True Life Secrets # 1 (March-April 1951) through # 29 (Jan. 1956). 29 issues.

Young Doctors # 1 (Jan. 1963) through # 6 (Nov. 1963), 6 issues.

Young Lovers # 16 (July 1956) through # 18 (May 1957). 3 issues.

—Charlton total: 1,420 issues

Comic Media/Artful (April 1950 to Dec. 1954)

All True Romance # 1 (March 1951) through # 20 (Dec. 1954). 20 issues (two # 7s, no # 21).

Confessions of Love # 1 (April 1950) through # 2 (July 1950). 2 issues (digests).

Dear Lonely Heart # 1 (March 1951) through # 8 (Oct. 1952). 8 issues.

Dear Lonely Hearts # 1 (Aug. 1953) through # 8 (Nov. 1954). 8 issues.

Honeymoon Romance # 1 (April 1950) through # 2 (July 1950). 2 issues (digests).

—Comic Media total: 40 issues

DC Comics/National Comics (July 1949 to July 1977)

Dark Mansion of Forbidden Love # 1 (Sept.-Oct. 1971) through # 4 (March-April 1972). 4 issues.

DC 100-Page Super Spectacular # 5 (1971). 1 issue.

Falling in Love # 1 (Sept.-Oct. 1955) through # 143 (Oct.-Nov. 1973). 143 issues.

Girls' Love Stories # 1 (Aug.-Sept. 1949) through # 180 (Nov.-Dec. 1973). 180 issues.

Girls' Romances # 1 (Feb.-March 1950) through # 160 (Oct. 1971). 160 issues.

Heart Throbs # 47 (April-May 1957) through # 146 (Oct. 1972). 100 issues. (Purchased from Quality.)

Love Stories # 147 (Nov. 1972) through # 152 (Oct.-Nov. 1973). 6 issues. (Formerly *Heart Throbs*.)

Romance Trail # 1 (July-Aug. 1949) through # 6 (May-June 1950). 6 issues.

Secret Hearts # 1 (Sept.-Oct. 1949) through # 6 (July-Aug. 1950); # 7 (Dec. 1951-Jan. 1952) through # 153 (July 1971). 153 issues.

Sinister House of Secret Love # 1 (Oct. Nov. 1971) through # 4 (April-May 1972). 4 issues.

Super DC Giant # S17 (Sept.-Oct. 1970) and # S21 (Jan.-Feb. 1971). 2 issues.

Young Love # 39 (Sept.-Oct. 1963) through # 120 (Winter 1975-76); # 121 (Oct. 1976) through # 126 (July 1977). 88 issues. (Purchased from Crestwood.)

Young Romance # 125 (Aug.-Sept. 1963) through # 208 (Nov.-Dec. 1975). 84 issues. (Purchased from Crestwood.)

—DC/National total: 931 issues

Dell (March 1951 to May 1963)

I Met a Handsome Cowboy (Four-Color) # 324 (March 1951). 1 issue.

Private Secretary # 1 (Dec. 1962-Feb. 1963) through # 2 (March-May 1963). 2 issues.

—Dell total: 3 issues

EC (Sept. 1949 to April 1950)

Modern Love # 1 (June-July 1949) through # 8 (Aug.-Sept. 1950). 8 issues.

A Moon, a Girl... Romance # 9 (Sept.-Oct. 1949) through # 12 (March-April 1950). 4 issues.
Saddle Romances # 9 (Nov.-Dec. 1949) through # 11 (March-April 1950). 3 issues.
—EC total: 15 issues

Famous Funnies/Eastern (Jan 1950 to June 1955)

Movie Love # 1 (Feb. 1950) through # 22 (Aug. 1953). 22 issues.
Personal Love # 1 (Jan. 1950) through # 33 (June 1955). 33 issues.
—Famous Funnies/Eastern total: 55 issues

Fawcett (Oct. 1948 to Summer 1953)

Cowboy Love # 1 (July 1949) through # 11(1951). 11 issues.
Exciting Romances # 1(1949) through # 12 (Jan. 1953). 12 issues.
Girls in Love (May 1950) through # 2 (July 1950). 2 issues.
I Love You # 1 (June 1950). 1 issue.
Life Story # 1 (April 1949) through # 47 (April 1953). 47 issues.
Love Memories # 1 (1949) through # 4 (July 1950). 4 issues.
Love Mystery # 1 (June 1950) through # 3 (Oct. 1950). 3 issues.
Negro Romance # 1 (June 1950) through # 3 (Oct. 1950). 3 issues.
Romantic Secrets # 1 (Sept. 1949) through # 39 (April 1953). 39 issues.
Romantic Story # 1 (Nov. 1949) through # 22 (Summer 1953). 22 issues.
Romantic Western # 1 (1949) through # 3 (June 1950). 3 issues.
Sweetheart Diary # 1 (1949) through # 14 (Jan. 1953). 14 issues.
Sweethearts # 68 (Oct. 1948) through # 121 (May 1953). 54 issues.
True Confidences # 1(Fall 1949) through # 4 (June 1950). 4 issues.
True Stories of Romance # 1 (Jan. 1950) through # 3 (May 1950). 3 issues.
True Sweetheart Secrets # 1 (May 1950) through # 11 (Jan. 1953). 11 issues.
True Tales of Romance # 4 (July 1950). 1 issue. (Formerly *True Stories of Romance*.)
Young Marriage # 1 (June 1950). 1 issue.
—Fawcett total: 235 issues (see rebound giants)

Fiction House (1950 to Winter 1952-53)

Cowgirl Romances # 1(1950) through # 12 (Winter 1952-53). 12 issues.

Fox (Sept. 1948 to Sept. 1951)

I Loved # 28 (July 1949 through # 32 (March 1950). 5 issues.
My Confessions # 7 (Aug. 1949) through # 10 (Jan.-Feb. 1950). 4 issues.
My Desire # 30 (Aug. 1949) through # 32 (Dec. 1949); # 3 (Feb. 1950) through # 4 (April 1950). 5 issues.
My Experience # 19 (Sept. 1949) through # 22 (March 1950). 4 issues.
My Great Love # 1 (Oct. 1949) through # 4 (April 1950). 4 issues.
My Intimate Affair # 1 (March 1950) through # 2 (May 1950). 2 issues.
My Life # 4 (Sept. 1948) through # 15 (July 1950). 12 issues.
My Love Affair # 1 (July 1949) through # 6 (May 1950). 6 issues.
My Love Life # 6 (June 1949) through # 13 (Aug. 1950). 8 issues.
My Love Life # 13 (Sept. 1951). 1 issue.
My Love Memoirs # 9 (Nov. 1949) through # 12 (May 1950). 4 issues.
My Love Secret # 24 (June 1949) through # 30 (June 1950). 7 issues.
My Love Story # 1 (Sept. 1949) through # 4 (March 1950). 4 issues.
My Past # 7 (Aug. 1949) through # 11 (April 1950). 5 issues.
My Private Life # 16 (Feb. 1950) through # 17 (April 1950). 2 issues.
My Secret Affair # 1 (Dec. 1949) through # 3 (April 1950). 3 issues.
My Secret Life # 22 (July 1949) through # 27 (May 1950). 6 issues (existence of # 27 for May 1950 is not confirmed).
My Secret Life # 27 (Sept. 1951). 1 issue.
My Secret Romance # 1 (Jan. 1950) through # 2 (March 1950). 2 issues.
My Secret Story # 26 (Oct. 1949) through # 29 (April 1950). 4 issues.
My Story # 5 (May 1949) through # 12 (Aug. 1950). 8 issues.
My True Love # 65 (July 1949) through # 69 (March 1950). 5 issues.
Women in Love # 1 (Aug. 1949) through # 4 (Feb. 1950). 4 issues.
—Fox total: 106 issues (see rebound giants)

Harvey (Feb. 1949 to March 1963)

First Love Illustrated # 1 (Feb. 1949) through # 88 (Nov. 1958); # 89 (Nov. 1962) through # 90 (Feb. 1963). 90 issues.

First Romance # 1 (Aug. 1949) through # 6 (June 1950); # 7 (June 1951) through # 52 (Nov. 1958). 52 issues.

Harvey Comic Hits (*Girls in White*) # 58 (June 1952). 1 issue.

Hi-School Romance # 1 (Oct. 1949) through # 5 (June 1950); # 6 (Dec. 1950) through # 75 (Nov. 1958). 75 issues.

Hi-School Romance Datebook # 1 (Nov. 1962) through # 3 (March 1963). 3 issues.

Love Lessons # 1 (Oct. 1949) through # 5 (June 1950). 5 issues.

Love Problems and Advice Illustrated # 3 (Oct. 1949) through # 6 (April 1950); # 7 (Jan. 1951) through # 44 (March 1957). 42 issues. (Purchased from McCombs.)

Love Stories of Mary Worth # 1 (Sept. 1949) through # 5 (May 1950). 5 issues.

Romance Stories of True Love # 45 (May 1957) through # 52 (Nov. 1958). 8 issues. (Formerly *Love Problems and Advice Illustrated*.)

Sweet Love # 1 (Sept. 1949) through # 5 (May 1950). 5 issues.

Teen-Age Brides # 1 (Aug. 1953) through # 7 (Aug. 1954). 7 issues.

True Brides' Experiences # 8 (Oct. 1954) through # 16 (Feb. 1956). 9 issues. (Formerly *Teen-Age Brides*.)

True Bride-to-Be Romances # 17 (April 1956) through # 30 (Nov. 1958). 14 issues. (Formerly *True Brides' Experiences*.)

—Harvey total: 316 issues

Hillman (Oct. 1949 to May 1953)

Mr. Anthony's Love Clinic # 1 (Nov. 1949) through # 5 (April-May 1950). 5 issues.

Romantic Confessions # 1 (Oct. 1949) through Vol. 3 # 1 (April-May 1953). 25 issues.

—Hillman total: 30 issues

IW/Super Romance Reprints (circa 1958–64)

These issues reprinted comics from several different companies. Numbering was not consecutive.

Dream of Love # 1, 2, 8, 9; *Frontier Romances* # 1, 9; *Hollywood Secrets of Romance* # 9; *Intimate Confessions* # 9, 10, 12, 18; *Love and Marriage* # 1, 2, 8, 10, 11, 12, 14, 15, 1.7; *My Secret Marriage* # 9; *Realistic Romances* # 1, 8, 9; *Romantic Love* # 2, 3, 8; *Teen Romances* # 10, 11, 15, 16, 17; *Young Hearts in Love* # 17, 18.

—Total: 34 issues

Kirby (Sept. 1949 to July 1950)

Enchanting Love # 1 (Oct. 1949) through # 6 (July 1950). 6 issues.

Golden Love Stories # 4 (April 1950). 1 issue. (Formerly *Golden West Love*.)

Golden West Love # 1 (Sept.-Oct. 1949) through # 3 (Feb. 1950). 3 issues.

—Kirby total: 10 issues

Lev Gleason (Oct. 1949 to June 1956)

Boy Loves Girl # 25 (July 1952) through # 57 (June 1956). 33 issues. (Formerly *Boy Meets Girl*.)

Boy Meets Girl # 1 (Feb. 1950) through # 24 (June 1952). 24 issues.

Lovers' Lane # 1 (Oct. 1949) through # 41 (June 1954). 41 issues.

—Lev Gleason total: 98 issues

Magazine Enterprises (1953 to Oct.-Nov. 1954)

Dream Book of Love A-1 # 106 (June-July 1954); A-1 # 114 (Aug.-Sept. 1954); A-1 # 123 (Oct.-Nov. 1954). 3 issues.

Dream Book of Romance # 5 (A-1 # 92) (1953); # 6 (A-1 # 101) (April-June 1954); # 7 (A-1 # 109) (July-Aug. 1954); # 8 (A-1 # 110) (Sept.-Oct. 1954). 4 issues.

—Magazine Enterprises total: 7 issues

Mainline (Aug. 1954 to March 1955)

In Love # 1 (Aug.-Sept. 1954) through # 4 (Feb.-March 1955). 4 issues.

—Mainline total: 4 issues

Marvel Timely/Atlas (Sept. 1948 to March 1976)

Actual Confessions # 13 (Oct. 1952) through # 14 (Dec. 1952). 2 issues. (Formerly *Love Adventures*.)

Actual Romances # 1 (Oct. 1949) through # 2 (Jan. 1950). 2 issues.

Best Love # 33 (Aug. 1949) through # 36 (April 1950). 4 issues.

Cowboy Romances # 1 (Oct. 1949) through # 3 (March 1950). 3 issues.

Cowgirl Romances # 28 (Jan. 1950). 1 issue.

Cupid # 1 (Jan. 1950) through # 2 (March 1950). 2 issues.

Faithful # 1 (Nov. 1949) through # 2 (Feb. 1950). 2 issues.

Girl Comics # 1 (Oct. 1949) through # 12 (Jan. 1952). 12 issues.

Girl Confessions # 13 (March 1952) through # 35 (Aug. 1954). 23 issues. (Formerly *Girl Comics*.)

Honeymoon # 41 Jan. 1950). 1 issue.

Ideal (A Classical Comic) # 5 (March 1949). 1 issue.

Junior Miss # 37 (Dec. 1949, romance issue). 1 issue.

Love Adventures # 1 (Oct. 1949) through # 2 (Jan. 1950). # 3 (Feb. 1951) through # 12 (Aug. 1952). 12 issues.

Love Classics # 1 (Nov. 1949) through # 2 (Feb. 1950). 2 issues.

Love Dramas # 1 (Oct. 1949) through # 2 (Jan. 1950). 2 issues.

Love Romances # 6 (May 1949) through # 106 (July 1963). 101 issues. (Formerly *Ideal*.)

Love Secrets # 1 (Oct. 1949) through # 2 (Jan. 1950). 2 issues.

Love Tales # 36 (May 1949) through # 58 (Aug. 1952); # 60 (Feb. 1955) through # 75 (Sept. 1957). 39 issues. (# 59 does not exist.)

Love Trails # 1 (Dec. 1949). 1 issue.

Loveland # 1 (Nov. 1949) to # 2 (Feb. 1950). 2 issues.

Lovers # 23 (May 1949) through # 86 (Aug. 1957). 64 issues.

Molly Manton's Romances # 1 (Sept. 1949) to # 2 (Dec. 1949). 2 issues.

My Diary # 1 (Dec. 1949) to # 2 (March 1950). 2 issues.

My Love # 1 (July 1949) to # 4 (April 1950). 4 issues.

My Love # 1 (Sept. 1969) through # 39 (March 1976). 39 issues.

My Love Special # 1 (Dec. 1971). 1 issue.

My Love Story # 1 (April 1956) through # 9 (Aug. 1957). 9 issues.

My Own Romance (My Romance # 1–3) # 1 (Sept. 1948) through # 76 (July 1960). 76 issues.

Night Nurse # 1 (Nov. 1972) through # 4 (May 1973). 4 issues.

Our Love # 1 (Sept. 1949) through # 2 (Jan. 1950). 2 issues.

Our Love Story # 1(Oct. 1969) through # 38 (Feb. 1976). 38 issues.

Rangeland Love # 1 (Dec. 1949) through # 2 (March 1950). 2 issues.

Real Experiences # 25 (Jan. 1950). 1 issue.

Romance Diary # 1 (Dec. 1949) to # 2 (March 1950). 2 issues.

Romances of Nurse Helen Grant # 1 (Aug. 1957). 1 issue.

Romances of the West # 1 (Nov. 1949) through # 2 (March 1950). 2 issues.

Romance Tales # 7 (Oct. 1949) through # 9 (April 1950). 3 issues.

Romantic Affairs # 3 (March 1950). 1 issue. (Formerly *Molly Manton's Romances*.)

Secret Story Romances # 1 (Nov. 1953) through # 21 (March 1956). 21 issues.

Stories of Romance # 5 (March 1956) through # 13 (Aug. 1957). 9 issues.

Teen Age Romance # 77 (Sept. 1960) through # 86 (March 1962). 10 issues. (Formerly *My Own Romance*.)

True Life Tales # 8 (Oct. 1949); # 2 (Jan. 1950). 2 issues.

True Secrets # 3 (March 1950) (formerly *Love Secrets*); # 4 (Feb. 1951) through # 21 (Aug. 1952); # 22 (Feb. 1954) through # 40 (Sept. 1956). 38 issues.

True Tales of Love # 22 (April 1956) through # 31 (Sept. 1957). 10 issues. (Formerly *Secret Story Romances*.)

Western Life Romances # 1 (Dec. 1949) through # 2 (March 1950). 2 issues.

Young Hearts # 1 (Nov. 1949) through # 2 (Feb. 1950).

—Marvel total: 562 issues

McCombs (1949)

Love Problems and Advice Illustrated # 1 (June 1949) through # 2 (Aug. 1949). 2 issues. (Purchased by Harvey.)

—McCombs total: 2 issues

MikeRoss (Dec. 1953 to July 1954)

Heart and Soul # 1 (April-May 1954) through # 2 (June-July 1954). 2 issues.

3-D Love # 1 (Dec, 1953). 1 issue.
3-D Romance # 1 (Jan, 1954). 1 issue.
—MikeRoss total: 4 issues

MS Distributors (1954)

My Love Secret # 53 (1954). 1 issue.

Our Publishing Co. (July 1949-Oct. 1955)

Love Diary # 1 (July 1949) through # 47 (Dec. 1954); # 48 (Oct. 1955). 48 issues.
Love Journal # 10 (Oct. 1951) through # 25 (July 1954). 16 issues.
—Our Publishing total: 64 issues

P.L. Publishing Co. (Nov. 1951)

Co-Ed Romances # 1 (Nov. 1951). 1 issue.
Love Life # 1 (Nov. 1951). 1 issue.
—P.L. total: 2 issues (printed in Canada)

Prize/Crestwood (Sept. 1947 to July 1963)

All for Love # 1 (April-May 1957) through Vol. 3 # 4 (Dec. 1959-Jan. 1960). 17 issues.
Going Steady Vol. 3 # 3 (Jan-Feb. 1960) through Vol. 4 # 1 (Sept-Oct. 1960). 5 issues. (Formerly *Personal Love*.)
Personal Love # 1 (Sept. 1957) through Vol. 3 # 2 (Nov.-Dec. 1959). 13 issues known; Vol. 2 # 3 may not exist.
Real West Romances # 1 (April-May 1949) through Vol. 2 # 1 (April-May 1950). 7 issues.
Western Love # 1 (July-Aug. 1949) through # 5 (March-April 1950). 5 issues.
Young Brides # 1 (Sept.-Oct. 1952) through Vol. 4 # 6 (# 30) (Nov.-Dec. 1956). 30 issues.
Young Love # 1 (Feb.-March 1949) through Vol. 8 # 1 (# 73) (Dec. 1956-Jan. 1957). 73 issues.
Young Love Vol. 3 # 5 (Feb.-March 1960) through Vol. 7 # 1 (June-July 1963). 21 issues. (Formerly *All for Love*.)
Young Romance # 1 (Sept.-Oct. 1947) through Vol. 16 # 4 (June-July 1963). 124 issues.
—Prize/Crestwood total: 295 issues

Quality (Aug. 1949 to Dec. 1956)

Bride's Romances # 1 (Nov. 1953) through # 23 (Dec. 1956). 23 issues.
Broadway Romances # 1 (Jan. 1950) through # 5 (Sept. 1950). 5 issues.
Campus Loves # 1 (Dec. 1949) through # 5 (Aug. 1950). 5 issues.
Diary Loves # 2 (Nov. 1949) through # 31 (April 1953). 30 issues. (Formerly *Love Diary*.)
Exotic Romances # 22 (Oct. 1955) through # 31 (Nov. 1956). 10 issues. (Formerly *True War Romances*.)
Flaming Love # 1 (Dec. 1949) through # 6 (Oct. 1950). 6 issues.
Forbidden Love # 1 (March 1950) through # 4 (Sept. 1950). 4 issues.
G.I. Sweethearts # 32 (June 1953) through # 45 (May 1955). 14 issues. (Formerly *Diary Loves*.)
Girls in Love # 46 (Sept. 1955) through # 57 (Dec. 1956). 12 issues. (Formerly *G.I. Sweethearts*.)
Heart Throbs # 1 (Aug. 1949) through # 8 (Oct. 1950); # 9 (March 1952) through # 46 (Dec. 1956). 46 issues.
Hollywood Diary # 1 (Dec. 1949) through # 5 (Aug. 1950). 5 issues.
Hollywood Secrets # 1 (Nov. 1949) through # 6 (Sept. 1950). 6 issues.
Love Confessions # 1 (Oct. 1949) through # 7 (Oct. 1950); # 8 (March 1951) through # 54 (Dec. 1956). 54 issues.
Love Diary # 1 (Sept. 1949). 1 issue. (Becomes *Diary Loves*.)
Love Letters # 1 (Nov. 1949) through # 6 (Sept. 1950); # 7 (March 1951) through # 31 (June 1953); # 32 (Feb. 1954) through # 51 (Dec. 1956). 51 issues.
Love Scandals # 1 (Feb. 1950) through # 5 (Oct. 1950). 5 issues.
Love Secrets # 32 (Aug. *1953*) through # 56 (Dec. 1956). 25 issues. (Formerly *Love Letters*, first series.)
Range Romances # 1 (Dec. 1949) through # 5 (Aug. 1950). 5 issues.
Secret Loves # 1 (Nov. 1949) through # 6 (Sept. 1950). 6 issues.
True War Romances # 1 (Sept. 1952) through # 21 (June 1955). 21 issues.
Untamed Love # 1 (Jan. 1950) through # 5 (Sept. 1950). 5 issues.
Wedding Bells # 1 (Feb. 1954) through # 19 (Nov. 1956). 19 issues.
—Quality total: 358 issues

Rebound Romance Giants (1949–52)

These were several comics sold together in "giant" format with new covers. Since many Fox comics started stories on the inside front cover, the first page of many stories is missing in the rebound giants.

Fawcett—*Big Book Romances* # 1 (Feb. 1950).
Fox (1949–50)—*Album of Love*; *All-Great Confessions*; *All Real Confession Magazine* # 3 (March 1949) and # 4 (April 1949); *Book of Love*; *Burning Romances*; *Daring Love Stories*; *Exciting Romance Stories*; *Intimate Confessions*; *Love Problems*; *Love Thrills*; *Revealing Love Stories*; *Romantic Thrills*; *Secret Love*; *Secret Love Stories*; *Strange Love*; *Sweetheart Scandals*; *Teen-Age Love*; *Throbbing Love*. Total of 19 known issues.
St. John—Romance issues in the *Giant Comics Edition* series: # 7, *Romance and Confession Stories* (Aug. 1949); # 9, *Romance and Confession Stories* (1949); # 12, *Diary Secrets* (1950); # 13, *Romance* (1950); # 15, *Romances* (1950).
Others: *Romance and Confession Stories* # 1

St. John (Jan. 1949 to Feb. 1958)

Adventures in Romance # 1 (Nov. 1949). 1 issue.
Blue Ribbon Comics (*Diary Secrets*) # 2 (April 1949), # 4 (June 1949), # 5 (Aug. 1949). 3 issues.
Cinderella Love # 12 (Oct. 1953) through # 15 (Aug. 1954). 4 issues. (Purchased from Ziff-Davis.)
Cinderella Love # 25 (Dec. 1954) through # 29 (Oct. 1955). 5 issues. (Formerly *Romantic Marriage*.)
Diary Secrets # 10 (Feb. 1952) through # 30 (Sept. 1955). 21 issues. (Formerly *Teen-Age Diary Secrets*.)
Going Steady # 10 (Dec. 1954) through # 14 (Oct. 1955). 5 issues. (Formerly *Teen-Age Temptations*.)
Hollywood Confessions # 1 (Oct. 1949) through # 2 (Dec. 1949). 2 issues.
Hollywood Pictorial # 3 (Jan. 1950). 1 issue. (Formerly *Hollywood Confessions*.)
It's Love, Love, Love # 1 (Nov. 1957) through # 2 (Jan. 1958). 2 issues.
Perfect Love # 9 (Oct. 1953) through # 10 (Dec. 1953). 2 issues. (Purchased from Ziff-Davis.)

Pictorial Confessions # 1 (Sept. 1949) through # 3 (Dec. 1949). 3 issues.
Pictorial Love Stories # 1 (Oct. 1952). 1 issue.
Pictorial Romances # 4 (Jan. 1950) (Formerly *Pictorial Confessions*); # 5 (Jan. 1951) through # 24 (Sept. 1954). 21 issues.
Romantic Marriage # 18 (Sept. 1953) through # 24 (Sept. 1954). 7 issues. (Purchased from Ziff-Davis.)
Secrets of True Love # 1 (Feb. 1958). 1 issue.
Teen-Age Diary Secrets # 4 (Sept. 1949) (picked up from Blue Ribbon); no number (# 5) (also Sept. 1949); # 6 (Oct. 1949) through # 8 (Feb. 1950); # 9 (Aug. 1950). 6 issues. (# 7 and # 9 are digests with same contents but different covers.)
Teen-Age Romances # 1 (Jan. 1949) through # 45 (Dec. 1955). 45 issues.
Teen-Age Temptations # 1 (Oct. 1952) through # 9 (Aug. 1954). 9 issues.
True Love Pictorial # 1 (Dec. 1952) through # 11 (Aug. 1954). 11 issues.
Wartime Romances # 1 (July 1951) through # 18 (Nov. 1953). 18 issues.
—St. John total: 168 issues (see rebound giants)

Skywald (Feb. 1971 to July 1971)

Tender Love Stories # 1 (Feb. 1971) through # 4 (July 1971). 4 issues.

Standard (Dec. 1949 to Aug. 1954)

Best Romance # 5 (March 1952) through # 7 (Aug. 1952). 3 issues.
Dear Beatrice Fairfax # 5 (Nov. 1950) through # 9 (Sept. 1951). 5 issues.
Intimate Love # 5 (Jan. 1950) through # 28 (Aug. 1954). 24 issues.
My Real Love # 5 (June 1952). 1 issue.
New Romances # 5 (May 1951) through # 21 (April 1954). 17 issues.
Popular Romance # 5 (Dec. 1949) through # 29 (July 1954). 25 issues.
Thrilling Romances # 5 (Dec. 1949) through # 26 (June 1954). 22 issues.
Today's Romance # 5 (March 1952) through # 8 (Sept. 1952). 4 issues.
Western Romance # 1 (Dec. 1952) through # 10 (March 1952). 10 issues.
—Standard total: 111 issues

Stanmor/Gilmor (Sept. 1953 to April 1956)

Daring Love # 1 (Sept.-Oct. 1953). 1 issue.
Diary Confessions # 9 (May 1955) through # 12 (Dec. 1955); # 14 (April 1956). 5 issues. (# 13 has never been seen.) (Formerly *Ideal Romance.*)
Ideal Romance # 3 (April 1954) through # 8 (Feb. 1955). 6 issues. (Formerly *Tender Romance.*)
Radiant Love # 2 (Dec. 1953) through # 6 (Aug. 1954). 5 issues. (Formerly *Daring Love.*)
Tender Romance # 1 (Dec. 1953) through # 2 (Feb. 1954). 2 issue.
—Stanmor/Gilmor total: 19 known issues

Star (Oct. 1949 to Nov. 1954)

Confessions of Love # 11 (July 1952) through # 14 (Feb. 1953); # 4 (April 1953) through # 6 (Aug. 1953). 7 issues.
Confessions of Romance # 7 (Nov. 1953) through # 11 (Nov. 1954). 5 issues. (Formerly *Confessions of Love.*)
Film Stars Romances # 1 (Jan.-Feb. 1950) through # 3 (May-June 1950). 3 issues.
Flaming Western Romances # 3 (March-April 1950). 1 issue. (Formerly *Target Western Romances.*)
Intimate Stories of Romance # 1 (Sept. 1953) through # 2 (April 1954). 2 issues.
Popular Teenager Secrets of Love # 9 (Oct. 1951) through 23 (Nov. 1954). 15 issues.
Target Western Romances # 106 (Oct.-Nov. 1949) through # 107 (Dec. 1949-Jan. 1950). 2 issues.
Top Love Stories # 3 (May 1951) through # 19 (Nov. 1954). 17 issues.
True-to-Life Romances # 8 (Nov.-Dec. 1949) through # 9 (Jan.-Feb. 1950); # 3 (April 1950) through # 23 (Oct. 1954). 23 issues.
—Star total: 75 issues

Sterling (Sept. 1955)

My Secret Confession # 1 (Sept. 1955). 1 issue.

Story/Premier (March 1951 to Jan. 1956)

Romantic Hearts # 1 (March 1951) through # 10 (Oct. 1952). 10 issues.

Romantic Hearts # 1 (July 1953) through # 12 (July 1955). 12 issues.
True Love Confessions # 1 (May 1954) through # 11 (Jan. 1956).
—Story/Premier total: 33 issues

Superior (Aug. 1949 to July 1956)

G.I. War Brides # 1 (April 1954) through # 8 (June 1955). 8 issues.
Love and Marriage # 1 (March 1952) through # 16 (Sept. 1954). 16 issues.
My Secret # 1 (Aug. 1949) through # 3 (Oct. 1949). 3 issues.
My Secret Marriage # 1 (May 1953) through # 24 (July 1956). 24 issues.
Our Secret # 4 (Dec. 1949) through # 8 (June 1950). 5 issues. (Formerly *My Secret.*)
Secret Romances # 1 (April 1951) through # 27 (July 1955). 27 issues.
—Superior total: 83 issues (printed in Canada)

Toby Press (1951 to 1955)

Great Lover Romances # 1 (March 1951) to # 3 (1952); # 6 (Oct. 1952) to # 22 (May 1955). 20 issues.
Doctor Anthony King # 1 (Jan. 1953) to # 4 (May 1954). 4 issues.
Sorority Secrets # 1 (July 1954). 1 issue.
Young Lover Romances # 4 (June 1952) to # 5 (Aug. 1952). 2 issues (formerly & becomes *Great Lover Romances.*)

Trojan/Ribage (Dec. 1952 to Aug. 1954)

Youthful Romances # 15 (Jan. 1953) through # 18 (July 1953); # 5 (Sept. 1953) through # 9 (Sept. 1954). 9 issues. (Purchased from Youthful.)

Youthful/Trojan (Sept. 1949-Oct. 1953)

Daring Confessions # 4 (Nov. 1952) through # 8 (Oct. 1953). 5 issues. (Formerly *Youthful Hearts.*)
Daring Love # 15 (Dec. 1952) through # 17 (April 1953). 3 issues. (Formerly *Youthful*

Romances, which also continued as a title under Trojan/Ribage.)

Truthful Love # 2 (July 1950). 1 issue. (Formerly *Youthful Love.*)

Youthful Hearts # 1 (May 1952) through # 3 (Sept. 1952). 3 issues.

Youthful Love # 1 (May 1950). 1 issue.

Youthful Romances # 1 (Aug.-Sept. 1949) through # 14 (Oct. 1952). 14 issues.

—Youthful total: 27 issues

Ziff-Davis (1950-Winter 1952)

Cinderella Love # 10 (1950) through # 12 (Sept. 1951); # 4 (Oct.-Nov. 1951) through # 11 (Fall 1952). 11 issues. (Two # 10 and # 11 issues.)

Dearly Beloved # 1 (Fall 1952). 1 issue.

Perfect Love # 10 (Aug.-Sept. 1951); # 2 (Oct. Nov. 1951) through # 8 (Fall 1952). 8 issues.

Romantic Marriage # 1 (1950) through # 3 (1950); # 4 (May-June 1951) through # 17 (Sept. 1952). 17 issues.

Strange Confessions # 1 (Jan.-March 1952) through # 4 (Fall 1952). 4 issues.

Women in Love, no number (Winter 1952 giant size). 1 issue.

—Ziff-Davis total: 42 issues

(1949); *All Picture All True Love Story* # 1 (Oct. 1952). Total of 7 issues.

Bibliography

Books

Benson, John. *Confessions, Romances, Secrets and Temptations: Archer St. John and the St. John Romance Comics*. Seattle: Fantagraphics Books, 2007.

_____, editor. *Romance Without Tears*. Seattle: Fantagraphics Books, 2003.

Coates, John, with Nick Cardy. *The Art of Nick Cardy*. Lebanon, N.J.: Vanguard Productions, 2001.

Cottrill, Tim. *Bookery's Guide to Pulps and Related Magazines*, second edition. Fairborn, OH: Bookery Press, 2005.

Daniels, Les. *DC Comics: Sixty Years of the World's Favorite Comic Book Heroes*. Boston and New York: Little, Brown, 1995.

_____. *Marvel: Five Fabulous Decades of the World's Greatest Comics*. New York: Harry N. Abrams, 1991.

Disbrow, Jay Edward. *The Iger Comics Kingdom*. El Cajon, CA: Blackthorne, 1985.

Duin, Steve, and Mike Richardson. *Comics: Between the Panels*. Milwaukie, OR: Dark Horse Comics, 1998.

Dunning, John. *Tune In Yesterday: The Ultimate Encyclopedia of Old-Time Radio, 1925–1976*. Englewood Cliffs, N.J.: Prentice-Hall, 1976.

Ellis, Doug. *Uncovered: The Hidden Art of the Girlie Pulps*. Silver Spring, MD: Adventure House, 2003.

_____, John Locke, and John Gunnison. *The Adventure House Guide to the Pulps*. Silver Spring, MD: Adventure House, 2000.

Esposito, Mike, and Dan Best. *Andru & Esposito: Partners for Life*. Neshannock, PA: Hermes Press, 2006.

Gerber, Ernst, and Mary Gerber. *The Photo Journal Guide to Comic Books*, two volumes. Minden, NV: Gerber, 1989–1990.

Goulart, Ron, editor. *The Encyclopedia of American Comics from 1897 to the Present*. New York: Facts on File, 1990.

Hamerlinck, P. C., editor. *The Fawcett Companion*. Raleigh, NC: TwoMorrows, 2001.

Mason, Tom, editor. *Teen Angst: A Treasury of '50s Romance*. Newbury Park, CA: Malibu Graphics, 1990.

McKnight-Trontz, Jennifer. *The Look of Love: The Art of the Romance Novel*. New York: Princeton Architectural Press, 2002.

Miller, John Jackson, Maggie Thompson, Peter Bickford, and Brent Frankenhoff. *Comics Buyer's Guide Standard Catalog of Comic Books*, fourth edition. Iola, WI: KP Books, 2005.

Nyberg, Amy Kiste. *Seal of Approval: The History of the Comics Code*. Jackson: University of Mississippi Press, 1998.

Overstreet, Robert. *The Official Overstreet Comic Book Price Guide*, 37th edition. New York: House of Collectibles and Timonium, MD: Gemstone, 2007.

Phillips, Charles. *Archie: His First 50 Years*. New York: Abbeville Press, 1991.

Plowright, Frank, editor. *The Slings & Arrows Comic Guide*, second edition. Great Britain: Slings & Arrows, 2003.

Robbins, Trina. *A Century of Women Cartoonists*. Northampton, MA: Kitchen Sink Press, 1993.

_____. *From Girls to Grrrlz: A History of Girls' Comics from Teens to Zines*. San Francisco: Chronicle Books, 1999.

_____, and Catherine Yronwode. *Women and the Comics*. Forestville, CA: Eclipse Books, 1985.

Scott, Naomi. *Heart Throbs: The Best of DC Romance Comics*. New York: Simon and Schuster, 1979.

Simon, Joe, with Jim Simon. *The Comic Book Makers*. New York: Crestwood II Publications, 1990.

Uslan, Michael, and Jeffrey Mendel. *The Best of Archie*. New York: Putnam, 1980.

Vadeboncoeur, Jim, Jr., and Everett Raymond Kinstler. *Everett Raymond Kinstler: The Artist's Journey through Popular Culture, 1942–1962*. Palo Alto, CA: JHV, 2005.

Voger, Mark. *Hero Gets Girl! The Life and Art of Kurt Schaffenberger*. Raleigh, NC: TwoMorrows, 2003.

Von Bernewitz, Fred, and Grant Geissman. *Tales of Terror! The EC Companion*. Seattle and Timonium, MD: Fantagraphics Books and Gemstone Publishing, 2000.

Weist, Jerry. *100 Greatest Comic Books*. Atlanta, GA: Whitman, 2004.

Wertham, Dr. Fredric. *Seduction of the Innocent*. New York: Rhinehart, 1954.

Wyman, Ray, Jr. *The Art of Jack Kirby*. Orange, CA: Blue Rose Press, 1992.

Zimet, Jaye. *Strange Sisters: The Art of Lesbian Pulp Fiction, 1949–69*. New York: Viking Studio, 1999.

Magazines

Amash, Jim. "Interview with Al Jaffee," *Alter Ego* # 35 (April 2004).

_____. "Interview with Mike Esposito," *Alter Ego* # 53 (Oct. 2005).

Becattini, Alberto. "Baker of Cheesecake (Matt Baker)," *Alter Ego* # 47 (April 2005).

Boyd, Jerry. "Bullpen Romances," *Back Issue* # 13 (Dec. 2005).

Burlington, David R. "EC Pre-Trend Romance Comics," *Comic Book Marketplace* # 80 (July-Aug. 2000).

Jenks, Bill. "Investing in Romance," *Comic Book Marketplace* # 61 (July 1998).

Lee, Andy. "Incredible Ink-Slinger," *Comic Book Marketplace* # 24 (June 1995).

Lustig, John. "Beyond Capes," *Back Issue* # 13 (Dec. 2005).

Nolan, Michelle. "1950s: The Love Glut," *Comic Book Marketplace* # 28 (Oct. 1995).

_____. "DC's Sensation Romance Comics," *Comic Book Marketplace* # 29 (Nov. 1995).

_____. "Writers of the Purple Sage," *Comic Book Marketplace* # 32 (Feb. 1996).

_____. "They Weren't All Archies!" *Comic Book Marketplace* # 34 (April 1996).

_____. "Venus Comics!" *Comic Book Marketplace* # 39 (Sept. 1996).

_____. "The Dim-Dame Sweepstakes!" *Comic Book Marketplace* # 40 (Oct. 1996).

_____. "The Bad, the Strange and the Sleazy!" *Comic Book Marketplace* # 52 (Oct. 1997).

_____. "Romance Mysteries!" *Comic Book Marketplace* # 55 (Jan. 1998).

_____. "Calling All Girls!" *Comic Book Marketplace* # 58 (April 1998).

_____. "A Timely Experiment in Female Fables!" *Comic Book Marketplace* # 62 (Aug. 1998).

_____. "Quality's Quality Romance!" *Comic Book Marketplace* # 76 (March 2000).

_____. "Adventures of the Lovelorn," *Comic Book Marketplace* # 77 (April 2000).

_____. "Osculations of Obscurity, Part I," *Comic Book Marketplace* # 80 (July-Aug. 2000).

_____. "Osculations of Obscurity, Part II." *Comic Book Marketplace* # 81 (Sept. 2000).

_____. "More Than 1950's Paperbacks," *Comic Book Marketplace* # 82 (Oct. 2000).

_____. "Setting the Standard for Prolific Production," *Comic Book Marketplace* # 96 (Nov. 2002).

_____. "All Those Marvel-ous Girls," *Comic Book Marketplace* # 99 (Feb. 2003).

_____. "There She Goes, Miss America," *Comic Book Marketplace* # 115 (Sept. 2004).

_____. "Dizzy Dames in Comics," *Comic Book Marketplace* # 117 (Nov. 2004).

_____. "The Mystery of Love Mystery," *Comic Book Marketplace* # 120 (March 2005).

Vance, Michael. "Forbidden Adventures," *Alter Ego* # 61 (Aug. 2006).

General Index

Title and Character Index

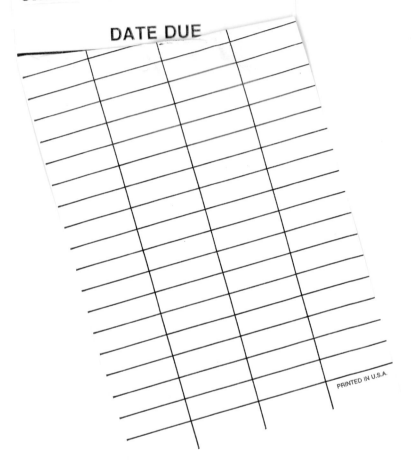

DATE DUE

PRINTED IN U.S.A.